Beacon Technologies

The Hitchhiker's Guide to the Beacosystem

■ ■ ■

Stephen Statler

With contributions by:

Anke Audenaert, John Coombs, Theresa Mary Gordon, Phil Hendrix, Kris Kolodziej, Patrick Leddy, Ben Parker, Mario Proietti, Ray Rotolo, Kjartan Slette, Jarno Vanto, and David Young

Apress®

Beacon Technologies: The Hitchhiker's Guide to the Beacosystem

Stephen Statler
San Diego
California, USA

ISBN-13 (pbk): 978-1-4842-1888-4   ISBN-13 (electronic): 978-1-4842-1889-1
DOI 10.1007/978-1-4842-1889-1

Library of Congress Control Number: 2016943844

Managing Director: Welmoed Spahr
Lead Editor: Robert Hutchinson
Technical Reviewer: Waqar Malik
Editorial Board: Steve Anglin, Pramila Balen, Louise Corrigan, Jim DeWolf, Jonathan Gennick, Robert Hutchinson, Celestin Suresh John, Michelle Lowman, James Markham, Susan McDermott, Matthew Moodie, Jeffrey Pepper, Douglas Pundick, Ben Renow-Clarke, Gwenan Spearing
Coordinating Editor: Melissa Maldonado
Copy Editor: Kezia Endsley
Compositor: SPi Global
Indexer: SPi Global
Artist: SPi Global

Distributed to the book trade worldwide by Springer Science+Business Media New York, 233 Spring Street, 6th Floor, New York, NY 10013. Phone 1-800-SPRINGER, fax (201) 348-4505, e-mail orders-ny@springer-sbm.com, or visit www.springer.com. Apress Media, LLC is a California LLC and the sole member (owner) is Springer Science + Business Media Finance Inc (SSBM Finance Inc). SSBM Finance Inc is a Delaware corporation.

For information on translations, please e-mail rights@apress.com, or visit www.apress.com.

Apress and friends of ED books may be purchased in bulk for academic, corporate, or promotional use. eBook versions and licenses are also available for most titles. For more information, reference our Special Bulk Sales–eBook Licensing web page at www.apress.com/bulk-sales.

Any source code or other supplementary material referenced by the author in this text is available to readers at www.apress.com. For detailed information about how to locate your book's source code, go to www.apress.com/source-code/.

Printed on acid-free paper

This book is dedicated to Tammie, Ben, and Sam Statler—my home team and source of support and encouragement.

Contents at a Glance

Contents

Foreword

You have in your hands a brilliant and informative resource written by a true thought leader in our industry. Having had a prime seat at the table as an early navigator in the space, I've watched Stephen lead the way, and I'm deeply honored to be able to provide an introduction to what I hope will help propel you into the bright and promising future of the beacosystem.

It used to be the retailers themselves were changing the way retail was done—with deals and promotions, coupons, and e-mail blasts. Now, it's the retail marketing and technology companies transforming how those retailers retail. Innovation, however, often comes in pockets, and you often have to throw a test against the wall to see what sticks. In the realm of location-based marketing, that can mean testing with beacons, sending targeted e-mail promotions, and engaging with customers both online and off.

Location-based marketing will be a $43.3 billion market by 2019, but the segment, which encompasses various channels to enable a brand to expand its reach, should not be confused with mobile advertising, which is only one part of a much larger marketing ecosystem that includes billboards, display advertising, and other channels.

So many retailers are bogged down with the bottom line and revenue that they forget about what drives the bottom line: customers and customer experience. Beacons are an important part of the wider location-based solution set available to aid in achieving these goals.

At the Location Based Marketing Association (LBMA), we believe that retailers need to invest in and develop a strategy for deploying these solutions. We call this strategy a three-layer location cake.

It's important to recognize that location-based marketing is really about recognizing location as a data set that spans many technologies, devices, and media types.

We all want to get to that top layer, the one with the icing and whip cream, the one that ultimately leads to transactions and revenue, but we can't get there unless we drive the right customers to the store and create an experience that is engaging and rewarding for them.

Layer One: Driving Location-Based Traffic

The first layer of the location cake is about getting customers into the store. This comprises a series of technologies that include social media, push messaging, geo-fencing, and more.

Geo-fencing and social location platforms are among the exciting new technologies available to digital marketers: it's a location-based service that sends content, messaging and promotions to smartphone or mobile device users who enter a certain geographic area. When smartphone users enter a geo-fence, they can potentially receive targeted ads on web sites or apps they visit on their mobile device.

You'll also see in this book how beacons are being deployed in stores and being used to track back to the e-commerce sites of those brands. Effectively bridging the bricks and clicks worlds together.

After all, a beacon sitting in a store by itself is useless if you don't have anybody there to talk to.

Layer Two: Driving Location-Based In-Store Engagement

Once you get the traffic into the building, you need to turn your attention to engagement. The second layer of the location cake is about increasing dwell time, basket size, and customer experience. It's at this layer that you should invest in technologies like Wi-Fi and beacons.

Beacons are about connecting the offline to online experience. Perhaps a customer walks by an item, looks at it, but doesn't buy. The store can later send them an e-mail about their shopping trip and remind them of items they passed over. Beacons also "listen" in on customer behavior, similar to how search engines are used to track browsing history and provide targeted online ads.

Beacons give retailers the ability to collect data—something they are missing out on with their brick-and-mortar customers but are able to gather online. By engaging customers digitally in store, they can later use that data to re-engage them online—where more and more shoppers' eyes and dollars are going these days.

It's about being able to deliver that message in real-time, based on the context of where you are. It's all about bringing that data into a single platform where you can act on it.

Beacons offer retailers a new way to connect with their customers, offering a more personalized, contextually based shopping experience. They not only deliver more value to the customers, but also empower your employees to consistently offer higher service levels.

Layer Three: Driving Location-Based Transactions

It's been called a lot of things in retail: the "till," the "cash box" or the "cash register." In today's digital age, the manual cash register has evolved into an electronic, scanning PoS (point-of-sale) system.

Whatever it's called, the retail checkout system is based on the decades-old store design concept that consumers come to stores to choose their goods from shelves, and then pass through checkout to pay for what they purchased. Perhaps the greatest single disruption to the retail store is the fact that consumers have literally become the "point of sale." They control where they shop, how they shop, how they pay, and where they receive their purchases. So, why do stores even need checkout lanes with "registers"?

The third layer of the location cake is focused on converting the great experience you've created with those customers into transactions and revenue. Here technologies like Apple Pay, near field communications (NFC), RFID, and loyalty platforms are key to winning the proximity-based transaction war.

Beacons play key role here too. Many of the early solutions work great as standalone mobile offer platforms, but without integration with the data you get from transactions and loyalty programs, those offers remain uninformed and often ineffective.

In *The Hitchhikers Guide to the Beacosystem,* you will hear all about each of these technologies, including who is developing them, where best to use them, and how they can be applied. Read on and you will find real-world examples of their application in scenarios from all three layers of "The Cake".

Having Your Cake and Eating It Too

It's about the integration of people, places, and media.

Retailers must move on from the one off pilots in location technology and instead embrace a full-fledged strategy that spans all three layers of the cake focused on driving traffic, creating engagement, and converting to revenue!

As a Canadian, I like to say we are still in the first half of the first period of the hockey game. There is much unexplored territory in the world of location-based marketing. This book goes a long way to helping the marketer, entrepreneur, and average consumer understand the value of location technology and data. The possibilities are endless and limited only by our imagination and ability to design and create.

—Asif Khan

Founder and President, The Location Based Marketing Association

About the Author

Stephen Statler is a writer, public speaker, and consultant working in the beacon ecosystem. He trains and advises retailers, venue owners, VCs, and makers of beacon software and hardware, and he is a thought leader in the beacosystem community. Previously he was the senior director for strategy and solutions management at Qualcomm's Retail Solutions division, helping to incubate Gimbal, one of the leading Bluetooth beacons in the market. He is also the CEO of Cause Based Solutions, creators of Give the Change, which is democratizing philanthropy and enabling non-profit supporters to donate the change from charity branded debit cards. They are also the developer of The Good Traveler program.

Stephen was born in the United States, grew up in England, and now lives with his wife, two sons, and a dog of uncertain origin in San Diego, California.

About the Contributors

Anke Audenaert is an adjunct professor at the Anderson School of Management at UCLA, where she teaches digital marketing and analytics. She is also CEO and co-founder of Favrit, a local bookmarking platform that will extend into a local native advertising. Previously Anke co-founded JumpTime, acquired in 2012 by OpenX, a global leader in digital and mobile ad technologies. Prior to that she worked at Yahoo!, building and leading its global market research and homepage network optimization teams.

John Coombs is the CEO and co-founder of Rover Labs. His company provides mobile app developers with a toolset to leverage beacon hardware with a UX that drops into apps to present relevant content.

Theresa Mary Gordon is a consultant in the corporate social, digital business, and RFID/NFC space for Near Field Connects. She is also a founding member of thinaire and tapGOconnect. Check out her presentations. tapGOconnect is a digital content management platform that connects people and "things" to communities, businesses, and events through real-time RFID/NFC m2m engagement.

Phil Hendrix is the founder and managing director of immr, where he splits his time as an industry analyst and consultant to leading companies and startups. As an advisor, Phil helps clients innovate and incorporate mobile, digital, and other disruptive technologies into their strategies. He has worked with clients in CPG, retail, consumer electronics, insurance, and numerous other verticals. Phil has prepared more than 20 analyst reports on mobile, location, proximity, data/analytics, and related topics. Before founding immr, Phil was a partner with leading consulting firms and a marketing professor at Emory University and the University of Michigan.

Kris Kolodziej is the founder and president of IndoorLBS, an advisory firm that published one of the first comprehensive reports on beacons. He was educated at MIT, was director of product management for cloud and location services at Verizon, VP of mobile at Aisle 411, and director of strategy at Toys-R-Us.

Patrick Leddy is the CEO and founder of Pulsate, an end-to-end marketing platform for real-world location. They provide a cloud platform and MicroBeacons™ that allow companies to turbocharge customer engagement. Previously, he founded Furious Tribe, a leader in mobile strategy, providing services to Citibank, Vodafone, RSA, O2, Danone, Nedbank, AXA, EMI, Investec, on their mobile strategies.

Ben Parker is a consultant working primarily with start-up and emerging growth companies with a focus on the mobile, wireless, and location services markets. He is currently advising several companies in the beacon. Previously he was a vice president at Procon (now Spireon) and was a senior manager at inCode Consulting, a business strategy and technology consulting firm specializing in the telecommunications and technology markets.

Mario Proietti is a co-founder and CEO of LocationSmart, the cross-carrier cloud platform for local, hyper-local, and context-aware application development, powering apps such as AAA's Find Me service for AT&T. Mario serves on the editorial advisory board of *GPS World Magazine* and was founding chairman of the Wireless Network Issues Committee of the E9-1-1 Institute.

Ray Rotolo is SVP of Out-of-Home Assets for Gimbal Inc. and is tasked with revolutionizing how brands, retailers, advertisers, and municipality services interact with displays that incorporate location and proximity-based services. Ray has held leadership roles at several agencies that focus on OoH, including as

COO of Posterscope, SVP, and MD for Chrysalis—the Havas OoH unit he helped to create. Ray serves on boards and committees at Traffic Audit Bureau and Digital Place Based Advertising Association, Consumer Engagement Technology World, and xAd. He holds an MSc in Finance from St. John's University in New York.

Kjartan Slette is the COO and co-founder of Unacast. Unacast powers the world's largest proximity network, enabling brands and retailers to retarget their customers based on offline behavior. Prior to that, Kjartan has held a number of senior positions in the Norwegian tech and music business, and his last company WiMP/Tidal was just acquired by Jay-Z.

Jarno Vanto is a lawyer specializing in international data privacy law. He has authored a number of books on the subject and has been editor-in-chief and co-author of the *International Privacy Guide*. Most recently, Jarno authored *The Data Protection Act in Practice*. Jarno is an adjunct professor of law at Pace University School of Law and teaches a class on international business transactions. Jarno is also a member of the board of directors of AMCHAM Finland NYC, Inc and an advisory board member of Unacast, advising them on their privacy strategy as they build their network of beacon networks. He heads the New York office of Borenius.

David Young is the lead software engineer and technical manager at Radius Networks, where he has overseen numerous beacon deployments, the development of one of the first beacon registries, the definition of the AltBeacon standard, and design of beacons that support both iBeacon and Google's Eddystone standard.

About the Technical Reviewer

Waqar Malik worked at Apple helping developers write Cocoa applications for the Mac during the early days of OS X. Now he develops applications for various Apple OS platforms. He is a co-author of *Learn Objective-C on the Mac* and the author of *Learn Swift on the Mac*.

Acknowledgments

First, let's acknowledge you, the reader. I'm more grateful than I can say that you are actually reading the acknowledgements (I bet you read the credits at the movies too, am I right?) We've been thinking of you throughout the writing process and hope you have found the subject as interesting as we have and that you have embraced the rather rambling style we have adopted for the guide. Hopefully this book has armed you with enough facts and folklore that you feel qualified to create something new yourselves and to grow this beacosystem into something even more interesting. So, if you have been, thanks for reading.

One of the things that has made this volume special is that we managed to convince so many leaders of companies that are helping to develop the beacosystem to contribute chapters and talk about their respective areas of expertise. It's not like you all have a shortage of things to do, and goodness knows you aren't doing it for the money. So—Asif Khan, David Young, Ben Parker, Jarno Vanto, John Coombs, Kjartan Slette, Anke Audenaert, Phil Hendrix, Ray Rotolo, Patrick Leddy, Theresa Gordon, Mario Proietti, and Kris Kolodziej—thank you.

What's in a name? Quite a lot, really. It set the whole tone and premise for this book as a survival guide for people who want to dive into this proximity tech space. We hope *The Hitchhiker's Guide to the Beacosystem* helps convey the magnitude of the subject and a sense of fun that is necessary for mental survival. Life is short, and you might as well enjoy learning. So thanks have to go to Douglas Adams, who first borrowed the Hitchhiker name from serious books about backpacking and provided hours of happy reading and listening to me as a kid. Thanks also to Sean O'Sullivan, who coined the "beacosystem" term, for letting us take it out for a spin and returning it with only a few bumps and scrapes, as well as for the pointers he has provided, both through his own writing and his suggestions on the book. Likewise, to Aisle Labs, who completely by coincidence adopted the Hitchhiker part of the name for their excellent report on beacons, which is available on their web site. Thanks for sharing.

This book originally started as a training course that we developed for our first-ever consulting client, Rick Belliotti, and his team at San Diego International Airport. SAN have gone on to create their own beacon-enabled app to help visitors navigate the terminals and track their baggage as they arrive at one of the world's best airports. We look forward to writing about their app in the future. Don't forget to buy a Good Traveler carbon offset as you are flying to or from San Diego. If it weren't for Paul Manasjan, who gave me the consulting task of developing that non-profit program, we wouldn't have been able to afford to pay the rent while taking the time to write this book.

Thanks to all of Statler Consulting's clients. We learn through doing. It's been a privilege to apply our knowledge to working on your challenges, be it talking with VCs and private equity firms about the best approach to investing in this space, working on business plans and patents for new ideas, or providing training to ramp up a team that is building new proximity services.

The experience that convinced me that there was an audience for our book was reprising the course that our friends at SAN airport had "piloted" and seeing it blossom up in Silicon Valley with beacon vendors, chip vendors, software experts, as well as venues in the audience. Thanks to Mario Tapia for the collaboration with Mobile Monday University to put that course on.

We learned a lot of the things that are in this book while working on wireless and retail technology issues at Qualcomm. Thanks to everyone there who was part of that journey. Thanks to Irwin and Paul Jacobs for creating a unique environment that valued creativity and engineering, to Brian Dunphy who hired me at QCOM, to Rocco Fabiano, who put me in a position to explore the intersection of wireless, payments, and retail as we created Qualcomm Retail, and to Mike Hess, who brought a huge amount of retail knowledge into our division and who introduced me to the fine beer made by his namesake. On leaving Qualcomm, I didn't expect ever to see another beacon at close quarters, but Issac Babbs persuaded me that it was worth staying with it. He was right.

I was reminded that writing could be fun thanks to David Kaplan and GeoMarketing, who have been a great publishing partner for the articles that preceded this book and who embraced the idea of mixing proximity marketing with Donald Trump, Arrogant Bastard beer, and arguments with your spouse. Thanks also to Ludovic Privat, the co-founder, editor, and managing director of *GPS Business News,* for first picking up and publishing my blog articles.

Staying in touch with the industry can be tough when you are working out of a home office. Fairbanks is a great therapy dog when a walk is called for to think things through, but he's really coasting when it comes to keeping up with the "phigital" news. Conversations at the water cooler tend to be about household chores rather than industry gossip. Untethered.tv has filled that gap, and thanks go to Rob Woodbridge and Asif Khan for providing some great food for thought and to Doug Thompson for his Beekn blog that raised the bar for writing about all things beacon.

Before Apress agreed to be our publisher, Katy Loffman's Rights Solutions helped give us a kick in the "right" direction and Kenny Waldron's input provided a model of how a smart solution designer might respond to *The Guide.*

Being born dyslexic (is that how you spell it?) may not be the best qualification for producing a tome like this. It's only thanks to Jocelyn Statler, my Mum, and Derrick Crowe that the text is as intelligible as it are. Jo is a role model and has a level of patience and dedication that I can only aspire to. Derrick has gone way beyond the expected in his generous and extensive, detailed, and creative reviews. It's great to find someone with a sense of humor, feel for narrative flow, and a pedantic insistence that we get the words and letters in the right order.

One of the best things about writing *The Hitchhiker's Guide to the Beacosystem* was talking to entrepreneurs and subject matter experts about the projects that they have been working on and hearing the lessons they learned. Thanks to Skype, we have spoken to people across the United States, China, Norway, Finland, Norwich, the rest of Great Britain, Germany, Poland, Australia, and Mexico. Thanks to all of the SMEs (subject matter experts) and case study subjects for their generosity and the free beacons!

Some special thanks has to go to Josh Marti and his team at Point Inside, the Gimbal team, Kevin Hunter and inMarket, Kontakt.io, HP Aruba, Sensoro, Estimote, Radius Networks, Steve Katz, Jon Azen, to Gustavo Litovsky from Argenox for a trove of great information on chipsets, and Shane Russell of ThoughtWorks for sharing his observations on signal propagation.

This book's expiry date has been significantly extended thanks to Proxbook.com, the database that is tracking the hundreds of companies working in the beacosystem, including case studies and ways of slicing and dicing the data that comes from those companies that share their data through the site. Thanks to Thomas Walle Jensen and Kjartan Slette, the founders of Unacast, for taking a clunky WordPress plugin and making it wonderful.

Thanks to Welmoed Spahr's team at Apress for giving us the latitude to do something out of the ordinary, subject-wise, with a crazy number of contributors, pictures, a quirky name, and an unorthodox mix of business and technical content. The Hitchhiker project wouldn't have been picked up (get it?) but for the advocacy of Steve Weiss, Jeffrey Pepper's stewardship, and the supportive massaging of the text by Melissa Maldonado, SPi Global, Waqar Malik, and James Markham.

Thank you to those of you who bought this book as a trophy for your book shelf but didn't read it. We appreciate the money, the shelf space, and don't consider you any the less for your lack of concentration or spare time. Chances are, dear non-reader, you bought our book because of the promotional video, which was created by our dear friend Don Rayner, whose rates are very reasonable, but are generally a lot more than what we paid in beer and hamburgers.

—Steve Statler

Preface

Computers are bursting out of the metal boxes and machine rooms where they were born and are becoming embedded throughout the world in which we live. The communication technologies that enable what is called *the Internet of Things* extends their reach to appliances in our homes and the meters and valves that regulate the flow in our heating, power, and water systems. The outputs have evolved way beyond the original paper printouts we used. Now these machines engage us through the voice of Siri, virtual reality headsets, and massive digital displays. The inputs are just as diverse, from finger-sensing layers on tablets, cameras that can guess our mood, and a wide variety of technologies that are designed to track the location of people and things. These are described variously as "presence," "proximity," and "real-time location systems". The ability for computer systems to know where objects are located is key to what is being described as "digital to physical convergence". This is where computers and the real world become melded together.

The Bluetooth beacon has taken center stage in this location technology revolution. These devices, which can be the size of a guitar pick, are being sprinkled around buildings, hidden away out of sight. They allow mobile phones to understand their location indoors, something that was very hard to do previously. They enable proximity triggers that can cause apps on our phones to start to interact with the world around us in new ways.

At one level they are very simple devices, but rather like the transistor, which helped to fuel another technology revolution, the possibilities are endless. Their successful use requires the understanding of a large array of related subjects.

Who This Book Is For

A lot of articles have been written about these Bluetooth beacons, but they tend to focus on fragments of the picture. This book is intended to be comprehensive. It's been written for anyone who wants to understand both the big picture and the details of what's required to create new products and services.

Hundreds of new companies are springing up to take advantage of the opportunities that beacons and other related technologies are creating. This book is written as a "survival guide" for anyone who has joined such a company or is thinking of starting one themselves.

Even for those of us who have spent a number of years working in this area, this guide to the beacosystem is proving to be useful. In the course of my consulting work for clients, I have found myself referring back to details of how the standards work and who some of the companies are in this space. In helping my clients get up to speed on beacon-enabled ad networks, it's been helpful to refer them to a chapter that explains this new area.

It's a big topic to understand thoroughly. In order to get the most out of the time you spend mastering this domain, we believe it's important to have fun, and to share and explore some of the stories behind the development of the technology. We can't promise as many laughs as Douglas Adams' masterpiece *The Hitchhiker's Guide to the Galaxy*, but if you are fond of understanding some of the events and people behind the technology, if you enjoy getting to know some of the details that make you feel like an insider, this book is for you.

What You'll Learn

We have divided the book into four sections. As computer scientists, we have adopted an approach of hierarchical decomposition (starting at the top and breaking the problem into smaller manageable chunks). The first one, Big Picture (Chapters 1-3), helps give readers a sense of the significance of the technologies and how they are being used. The second and largest section, Components (Chapters 4-15), breaks down into layers the products and technology in a beacon solution stack. This, along with the many real-world examples, will provide an understanding of how the pieces can work together. In the third chunk, Technologies that Complement Beacons (Chapters 16-19) and What They Do, we look at a large number of competing and complementary technologies, so that solution designers can figure out the right tool for the job. Lastly, in Section 4, Using the Building Blocks (Chapters 20-22), we review the applications of beacon technology and where it's making a difference. We drill down into payments in particular, because that's such a strategic area, and lastly we look at some of the issues and opportunities that face the industry in the area of the future of the standards for Bluetooth beacons.

CHAPTER 1

■ ■ ■

Introduction

Bluetooth beacons are changing the experience of using smartphones to travel, shop, work, and play. App developers can now link people's movements through the physical world to events in the digital world of mobile apps, the web, and cloud services. As we walk around, we can trigger actions on our phones, point-of-sale terminals, digital displays, door locks, lighting, or any appliance with an Internet connection. Typing, pointing, and clicking drove our interaction with digital devices before the advent of the Bluetooth beacon; now our movements, location, and physical proximity to objects can trigger digital actions.

A Great Leap Forward

It appears we are in the early stages of another leap forward in the way technology impacts our lives.

Every now and then, rapidly advancing technology changes the lives of consumers, who are often oblivious to the details of that technological breakthrough. The resulting changes can be even more profound in the lives of the people developing the technology. For example, the advent of the silicon chip created a new class of entrepreneur in the Bay Area. Those of us not involved on the inside of the semiconductor companies noticed that calculators were getting smaller and cheaper, watches became digital, and computers could now fit on top of our desks; then, gradually, our lives changed as a result of those products. Yet, for the founders and employees of Fairchild Semiconductor, Intel, Microsoft, and Apple Computer, their lives changed even more. They lived at work, their marriages were tested, and some of them became very rich and achieved celebrity status.

I have worked at the center of two such leaps forward and am convinced that what we are seeing is a third. This one is to do with proximity technology and, in particular, *beacons* that use a new Bluetooth standard that is resulting in a cascade of changes in solutions built on Bluetooth and other adjacent proximity technologies. Such leaps can make for a fun ride. This book has been written so that the readers can equip and ready themselves to join in and reap the rewards that come with such technological progression.

Servers, Smartphones, and Beacons

The first technology disruption I experienced was in the mid-80s, when the computer server was being born. Up until then, serious computing was done on expensive mainframes. Servers allowed low-cost hardware, open software, and relational databases to coalesce and allow computing to be much more flexible and cost-effective. As a result, computer technology became used much more broadly. It was a gold rush. New companies sprung up and raced to win a dominant position in their niche. Lots of money was made. Company jets were bought. Great parties were thrown.

© Stephen Statler 2016
S. Statler, *Beacon Technologies*, DOI 10.1007/978-1-4842-1889-1_1

The second big leap was the advent of mobile phones being used for computing tasks rather than phone calls. Through good fortune, I found myself working at Qualcomm, the largest provider of semiconductors for mobile devices. What would eventually become the smartphone revolution started with very basic, candy bar-shaped phones with small black-and-white screens. They were used for text messaging and browsing painfully crude (WAP[1]) mobile web sites. These applications then flourished with the introduction of devices with larger screens and powerful application processors, as well as fast wireless modems. This brought computing, video recording, and many other tools into the hands of those who might not have had access to them otherwise. Smartphones have been used to capture video of the Arab Spring, record views of crimes that would otherwise have gone unnoticed, and guide fishermen on the coast of India to where they can catch fish to feed their families.

Qualcomm owned essential patents for the deployment of smartphones and, as a result, received royalty payments whenever a smartphone was sold anywhere around the world. Qualcomm was making huge sums of money (over a billion dollars a month in gross profit), but it was also spending large portions of that money—as much as $5.5 billion dollars a year—on research and development in order to extend its lead and move the industry forward. These advancements were not limited to just faster CPUs and bigger screens, but incorporated a broad range of technologies and innovations. Qualcomm R&D developed computer vision technology, allowing phones to recognize objects in the real world. For instance, your phone could tell you if your car was getting too close to another vehicle. Another advancement augmented reality overlaid digital images onto views of the real world. This allowed Superman to jump from a poster in Walmart to entice shoppers into the toy department. Additionally, artificial brain technology started enabling phones to learn the significance of gestures that were personal to its owner. Then there came projects implementing some of the earliest Bluetooth beacon technology.

The first beacons were about the size of a guitar pick or a small key fob. These beacons were initially just going to be applied to help parents track their children. A child with a beacon laced to their shoes, for instance, could be automatically checked-in when they arrived at school, messaging a parent that all was well. Qualcomm's HQ is in San Diego, a beautiful Southern California technology hub, that in previous years had seen abductions of young women which had shocked the community. Qualcomm's President, Steve Altman, saw the opportunity for every smartphone to become beacon-aware and participate in an Amber alert network like no other. If a child were abducted, everyone's phone could start listening for the lost child's beacon and create a vast network, made up of the devices that we all carry, to help find the child and bring her home to safety.

The problem was that, in order to do this, the beacon technology needed to be added to everyone's phone. To achieve that degree of ubiquity, it would need to become useful for things other than just dealing with these occasional crises. After this realization, a team was assembled to develop the technology further, create a business plan, and sell beacons for a broader set of applications. Gimbal was born.

At the time, I was working as the head of strategy for Qualcomm's Retail Solutions division. Qualcomm Retail was given the opportunity to commercialize Gimbal and leverage our relationships with major retailers and retail technology suppliers. The process was a lot of fun. We borrowed a vending machine, sat it in my office, and tested what it would be like if beacons in a vending machine allowed selection and payment for the products with your phone. Armed with hardware purchased from Home Depot, we experimented with placing beacons in gas pumps and coffee machines. One of the biggest eye-openers was seeing what happened when we enabled customers at a cafe to pay by beacon: people loved it. No need to touch your wallet, just grab and go.

Then there was the work on business models. This required creativity with spreadsheets rather than computer code. We explored scenarios to understand how beacons could be sold, integrated, distributed, and supported. We searched the existing retail technology ecosystem to see whom the right partners to work with were and how those organizations could make enough money from this to sustain the ecosystem.

---

[1]Wireless Access Protocol

Then, with a change of CEO, Qualcomm Retail was no more. The Gimbal team carved out and became an independent company and I decided to start my own business, Give the Change, in the non-profit sector, unrelated to beacons. I thought I had seen the last of the beacon business, but a mentor, a venture capitalist, advised me to "keep my hand in," to ride the beacon wave. When it became clear that my start-up needed more funding, I took the opportunity to develop a one-day training course for our local airport authority. Having seen the beacon-enabled cafe, San Diego International Airport wanted to deploy beacons throughout their terminals and needed to get up to speed on what could be done and how to do it.

Business and Technical Readers

This book has been written for solutions architects, be they businessperson or technologist. Solutions architects have many titles: Venture Capitalist, Founder, CEO, Strategist, Product Manager, CTO, Business Development, or Developer. If you loved to play with Lego blocks (or still do), you're a solutions architect. This book is based on that training course, attended by the business and technical people required to make projects successful. It's written for a diverse audience—the retailer and venue owners who want to augment the experience of their guest, the technologists creating the hardware and software, and the business people who need to allocate the resources required for these projects.

Teaching the course has been great fun, with business and technical people mixing and working together across the many industry segments involved in making these solutions. People working at chip designers, beacon manufacturers, middleware companies, and application developers have attended our open enrollment class. Hearing these students talk about why they are attending has opened my eyes to the possibilities of what can be achieved with beacon technology. Misconceptions about how beacons work and what they can do abound, but it doesn't take much to build the type of solid framework where the chances of success for a project dramatically improve.

Understanding the technology at the root of this disruption is important if good decisions are to be made. This is a multidisciplinary revolution; marketing, finance, operations, business development and technology developers all need to work together for this to be successful. It is important that everyone understand enough of each other's worlds that their differences can be bridged. If a businessperson thinks a beacon in the ceiling of a store will drive the experiences described earlier, they are in for a rude awakening. These beacons are awesomely powerful, but also have major limitations. If those limits are not understood on at least some level, the both technical and business teams are going to waste so much time and money that their competitors are going to win out. In addition, the technology developer has to be thinking about business issues. Waterfall development (a highly structured linear planning process) won't work here. Unless the developers are customer facing and thinking about the operational and support issues, failure will be hard to avoid.

The purpose of this book is to establish a baseline of knowledge so that each of these disciplines understands enough about what Bluetooth beacons mean to their counterparts that they can move forward without wasting time on misunderstandings and conflict.

Part of breaking into a new ecosystem is learning the stories behind the technology. If these stories about how standards were named and the paths taken by the early pioneers seem superfluous to a strict understanding of how beacons work, they are. However, from my experience, assimilating into an ecosystem can be helped by knowledge of the folklore and the origin stories. Sometimes it helps to remember the more arcane facts. So a few such stories will be found peppered throughout the book, as well as an ample supply of metaphors that are characteristic of a high-tech industry that is always trying to bring excitement to what otherwise might seem quite dry.

Online Resources

The beacon landscape is changing very fast. In order to extend the life of the book, we decided to build a crowdsourced database of beacon technology providers and case studies that anyone can access. It has taken on a life of its own, becoming more popular than I ever anticipated thanks to some "adoptive parenting" by our friends at Unacast. At last count, there were 280 vendors of proximity hardware and software registered at www.proxbook.com. Check it out.

It Takes a Village

It has been an interesting learning experience to meet other beacon enthusiasts and entrepreneurs writing about our industry. My first response to these other writers was rather competitive. Then, inspired by a local brewery, it seemed like there was a better way.

Here in San Diego we enjoy the work of over 100 craft brewing companies. One of the most successful is Stone Brewing, creators of Arrogant Bastard beer. They have an unusual relationship with the other brewers competing in the micro-brewing space. Rather than knocking the competition, they collaborate with them on brewing projects. Every year on their anniversary they invite their fellow brewers to exhibit at a beer festival that is a celebration of good food and drink. Their mission is to convert people to drinking craft beer (rather than fizzy yellow beer). Market share isn't the issue; it is about building their category.

This seemed like a good strategy, so we have taken a similar approach with *The Hitchhiker's Guide to the Beacosystem*. If there was someone that we admired in this space who could help explore and explain it better, we have invited them to contribute. Everyone who has been asked has said yes. So we have chapters from experts whose time will be tough to get a few years from now. If the other leaps forward are anything to go by, a number of them will be too busy flying their executive jets around the world. Today the beacon ecosystem is small and early enough that it has been possible for them to collaborate, to write this book, and hopefully to grow the category by educating other enthusiasts to join in the beacon revolution.

We hope you have as much fun reading this as we have had learning about this space. Do join in and contribute to the crowdsourced information online. For interviews, updates and articles that supplement the contents of this book, visit www.hhgb.us. We want to read what you learn as the digital and physical worlds collide!

CHAPTER 2

■ ■ ■

Orientation

Who would have thought that the Bluetooth beacon story would turn out to be such a great soap opera? The cast of characters is made up of entrepreneurs and their companies who are fighting to find success. We wonder which of the characters will succeed and which will be killed off. You look at the players and speculate as to what they will do next, which alliances will hold, and which are really just for show. Whether you are a technologist, an entrepreneur, a retailer, or someone considering his or her next career move, this story has something for everyone. All the elements are here: power, conflict, the plucky, small guy battling giants, and fortunes that will be won and lost.

© Stephen Statler 2016
S. Statler, *Beacon Technologies*, DOI 10.1007/978-1-4842-1889-1_2

New Experiences Created with Bluetooth Beacons

The story feels like science fiction, with screenshots of Tom Cruise in *Minority Report*[1] being used to illustrate how beacons will change shopping, and scare stories about what will happen if this power is abused. Yet the technology to enable beacon experiences exists today. It is not a matter of being limited by technology, but by logistics and the evolution of an ecosystem. Deploying beacon enabled software takes a lot of time and effort. It is no small feat, and it means making changes to all the systems involved, upgrading hardware across thousands of stores in a chain, and all the staff training required for a roll out. Additionally, the user experiences we are creating are entirely new, so experimentation and rework is inevitable. We need to train the staff, and then we need to train customers, too.

Imagine beacons powering digital displays welcoming shoppers by name and promoting products based on their taste and demographics; payments being made invisibly without the aid of cash or plastic cards. Guests at a coffee bar approach a barista, are welcomed by name, offered their "usual," even though this is their first visit. They walk away having paid automatically, without having to touch their purse or phone. Television displays on gas pumps adapt the soundtrack being played so a patron's favorite song greets them as they get out of their car. Then their favorite infotainment starts to appear on the built-in TV display before they even reach for the pump. Restaurant concierges greet you, ushering you straight to your table, even though the place is new to you. They know what you like, your dietary preferences, and introduce the menu accordingly. Waiting in line becomes obsolete, or at least a lot quicker.

Whether it's a stall in the bathroom or a line for a beer, patrons are steered to where they will have their needs met fastest. Information about the world around you is fed to your phone and wristwatch automatically.

As in a presidential entourage, there will be an ever-present assistant providing the name of the person approaching you, the story behind the painting or statue that is nearby, and the details of a product that only a highly paid expert would know. Travelers at airports will be able to track the progress of their bags from the plane to the carousel. Waiting at the wrong gate for your flight? A helpful member of ground crew will know to steer you to the right location. Stuck in Home Depot trying to figure out which coupling to choose to fix your sink? Press a button on your phone and a helpful associate will find you, rather than the other way around.

Now realize that all of these experiences are being piloted and prototyped today.

Winners, Losers, and Unintended Consequences

Bluetooth beacon technology is disruptive. As a result, there will be winners and losers in this story. At this stage, there are some clues as to who those will be, but it will be interesting to see which players will come out on top.

This story started in stuffy meeting rooms and on boring conference calls when the Bluetooth 4.0 standard was first conceived. The architects of that standard did not design it to implement beacons specifically—you won't find a "Bluetooth beacon" specification referenced in the standard. The elements that enable beacons were created, but it took an ecosystem of onlookers to see the possibilities and put the new technology to work in this unanticipated way.

---

[1] http://www.imdb.com/title/tt0181689/

Apple

Then Apple ignited a firestorm of venture capital investment and innovation by a twist on that open standard with its own iBeacon offering, which formalized what had previously been created. Companies had been developing Bluetooth beacons prior to this, but when Apple briefly referenced its own standard (with a few words on a slide at their 2013 developer conference), the market took off. However, iBeacon did not define everything that was required to produce a beacon solution. In fact, that it had major gaps was a key reason for its success. Other companies felt that they could fill those gaps and create enough value that they could build their own business, and so an ecosystem was born almost overnight.

The full impact of this interest in beacons has yet to be fully understood. It certainly extends beyond the current bounds of Bluetooth players, and the ideas for new applications are rapidly streaming from software companies and advertisers that have been galvanized by the iBeacon opportunity. iBeacon is one way to implement a proximity trigger for the purpose of marketing or other automation. Proximity triggers can be implemented using other technologies, which in some ways have advantages over Bluetooth. For example, the use of LED lighting systems offers greater accuracy, magnetic resonance is more ubiquitous, and small cell and 5G bring new economic incentives for companies to invest. We will discuss these other technologies later, but our primary focus is on Bluetooth Smart technology because it is at the epicenter of the explosion. It is creating a structure upon which other things can then grow. One day those other technologies may become bigger than Bluetooth beacons. iBeacon is like Lewis and Clark[2], the first major expeditionary force from east to west, showing how the digital and physical worlds can be joined. Others technologies will follow, using their own approach to bridge these worlds.

Market Timing

The formation of successful technology ecosystems is like good comedy: it's all about timing. A lot of things need to happen at the same time. The technology must be mature enough. The hype needs to be strong enough to attract consumers and entrepreneurs. The ecosystem needs to show enough potential to inspire the many entrepreneurs needed to gamble on hundreds of variations of products using the technology. And investors need to have enough funds available to support all of this. This phenomenon is like achieving escape velocity in a rocket, in that, unless you have enough power to escape the gravitational forces of cynicism and inevitable setbacks, the rocket will be pulled back and crash, with much destruction of capital and few survivors.

The key to beacon technology flourishing is the mobile OS supplier. They can open up exciting opportunities for developers to fill, but they are also gatekeepers who can shut out whomever they want from the ecosystem. They can change or cut off services that developers have previously relied on and compete in areas where they previously partnered. They have a tough job, but an essential one. The OS provider needs to create a technical equilibrium, balancing battery life issues, accuracy, responsiveness, privacy issues, decisions on where to impose rules and standards, and where to leave the field open to a community to innovate. By defining a limited standard and putting enough of the necessary ingredients in iOS, Apple threw gas on the flames ignited by the Bluetooth Special Interest Group (SIG).

Enter Google

After two years of being largely absent from the party, with a Bluetooth stack that didn't provide the basics required for beacons to work well, Google has arrived. With its Eddystone offering, it "saw" Apple and raised the stakes significantly, with a beacon offering that delivered nearly everything that Apple had done with iBeacon and a lot more. Google appear to have made the most of analyzing the first movers and have entered

---

[2]The Lewis and Clark Corps of Discovery Expedition was commissioned by President Thomas Jefferson to make the first journey across the United States, from close to St. Louis to the Western Pacific coast of the United States.

the Beacon ecosystem with an offering that includes more in the way of functionality, security, management, and integration with the rest of the operating system. This was an important piece of the picture. Without Google and a native Android beacon offering, the largest part of the smartphone market (approximately 80% of the global handset market as of 2015) was unaccounted for.

Where Are We? Crossing the Chasm

Let's be clear, though, it's still in the early days. To use Geoffrey A. Moore's famous "crossing the chasm" model, we are in the "chasm" between the "early adopters" experimenting and the "early majority" buying in sufficient volumes to inject serious money into the ecosystem. This chasm is a long one. The walls are made steeper and the killing zone made longer because beacons are all about bringing the physical and digital worlds together. Software can be written and deployed faster than ever, but brick and mortar retailers and their armies of staff have to engage in these deployments as well. The human element has limits in terms of speed and resources that are more constrained than the world of cloud services. Amazon can update the way its catalog searching works overnight, but we are seeing that even the leaders in applying beacons are taking many months to go through the necessary pilot and proof of concepts required to figure out the best way to use them. The ecosystem to deploy, place, and adjust the placement of beacons is not fully established. Even Apple, who deployed iBeacon in their stores more rapidly than any other retailer, found its first efforts had major flaws that would take considerable time to address. Customers would get duplicate messages that became repetitive and unhelpful; the value was not clear to the customers in the store.

We should expect beacon companies to pivot[3] in order to survive. Some will supplement their beacon offerings with other technologies that can be deployed more quickly (such as GPS). Large numbers of them will exit this space because of the size of the "chasm," and there will probably be more than a few journalists writing stories about the demise of the Bluetooth beacon. Yet, the real value is being created, and the few survivors that make it through the journey will likely have a very robust future reaping the benefits of physical-to-digital convergence.

Summary

Fortunately, beacon technology is very simple at its roots—a lot simpler than the first Bluetooth headsets. Beacons are small devices. They typically range in size from half an inch wide for a USB plugin beacon to five and a half inches in diameter for a beacon with a heavy-duty battery designed to operate for two or three years without physical maintenance. They can be placed in rooms or outdoors and can trigger your phone to automatically do things when it gets close. Your phone senses the presence of the beacon, recognizes its identity, and can take action accordingly. The action could be to display something on your phone screen, or to make calls to a computer elsewhere that will unlock a door, turn on a light, or play music. The possible actions are limited only by our imaginations.

There is no complex pairing between beacon and phone. These beacons are like lighthouses that broadcast with a one-way signal that phones can choose to see or to ignore. The closer the phone is to the beacon, the stronger the signal. Proximity is inferred like in a child's game, where the seeker is guided by feedback that they are cold, getting warmer, warmer, and hot. If the signal is high, you are hot, and that means you are close to the beacon. If you know what the beacon is, knowing the proximity may be useful. Maybe it tells you that the keys that you desperately need to find, that have a Bluetooth beacon fob attached to them, are close at hand.

---

[3]A "structured course correction designed to test a new fundamental hypothesis about the product, strategy, and engine of growth." –*The Lean Startup* by Eric Ries

Like Lego blocks, which are simplicity themselves if looked at in isolation, beacons can be combined into amazing structures that have additional layers of sophistication. The creation of today's complex models surely wasn't envisioned when the first brick with eight knobs on it was originally designed. The inventor of Lego (Ole Kirk Christiansen) probably never dreamed that his bricks would be used to create replicas of amazing space ships or working digital printers. Likewise, what we see at the moment with simple Bluetooth beacons is surely only the start.

Our goal with this book is to guide you through the technology stack, use cases, operational considerations, standards and other pieces necessary to design new experiences. With this knowledge, you can build a strategy to take advantage of a disruptive technology that is bringing the digital and physical worlds together. When these worlds collide, great power can be released. Exploring the implications of that is the subject of our next chapter.

CHAPTER 3

■ ■ ■

Digital Physical Convergence

Digital and physical worlds collide

Digital to physical convergence is talked about in the same breath as The Internet of Things (IoT). How do they relate and what do beacons have to do with these concepts?

Inputting to the IoT

The Internet of Things (IoT) phenomenon describes the trend where more and more of the objects around us are becoming smart and connected. Low-cost processors and communications technologies such as Bluetooth enable this.

© Stephen Statler 2016
S. Statler, *Beacon Technologies*, DOI 10.1007/978-1-4842-1889-1_3

IoT forces us to consider a world where more and more appliances and devices are becoming intelligent and linked together with digital connections. Our TV, lighting, door lock, garage door opener, refrigerator, and water meter are all joined together in a digital mesh. Should we, say, leave the fridge door open, while we are pedaling away on our exercise machine in another room, our presence is detected and the alert from the fridge causes a warning to appear on an adjacent TV. Beacons have a role to play as an input to all this; beacon triggers can inform our house where we are in its structure, triggering devices to react to our presence, routing alerts like the one from the fridge to the right place and adjusting the heating and cooling to be more efficient. Outside of the home, digital displays in the street, in the aisles of a store, and at a point-of-sale, represent outputs where personalized information triggered by our movements can be displayed.

Phygital Marketing is a term coined to describe this idea of bridging audiences from the physical world to the digital world, for a deeper and more relevant engagement with a brand or product.

This interconnectedness opens up many possibilities for integrating new experiences where beacons are triggering inputs into the IoT. There are also a number of other potential inputs to the IoT alongside beacons that we should consider as we design user experiences and business models. One is the RFID tag.

Radio Frequency Identification (RFID) is sometimes seen as the older stepchild to the Bluetooth beacons. This technology has not enjoyed the meteoric rise and height of VC investment that beacons have received. However, RFID stickers have a number of strengths that have earned it a place in the palette of technologies that solutions architects can use. RFID stickers are lower in cost than beacons and they also transmit a wireless signal to identify the objects they are attached to. With RFID stickers attached to products in a store, an inventory check that might have taken days can be done in minutes.

Previously, the process would have involved laborious and error-prone manual counts. With RFID tags, a reader can be waved across the shelves and an accurate listing of each product, identified by its own serial number, can be entered into an inventory system. A heaped shopping basket full of tagged garments can be registered by a point-of-sale terminal in a second. The downside is that the hardware in our phones cannot read those signals, and so specialized readers are required, which is one of the limitations holding the technology back.

RFID is a great technology for tracking products, while beacons are great for tracking people (beacons are being used to track some high-value goods, but we will discuss this this later). Working together, with both a beacon and an RFID reader in a changing room at a clothing store, we can register what products a particular shopper is taking into the changing rooms to try on, and which of those products they then take to the point-of-sale to be purchased. This is a level of understanding of customer consideration and decision-making that was not possible before.

Outputs from the IoT

Smartwatches are an important output device from the IoT. Unlike displays anchored to walls, the smartwatch can be with us all the time. The importance of this becomes apparent when we start work on the spreadsheet to build a business model for a new beacon business. This can be a sobering process. We start off with the excitement of a new beacon-enabled user experience, and then try to figure out how a business can make enough money to make the dream come true.

Typically, these spreadsheets contain an estimated number of consumers that can be alerted by a beacon trigger compared with the value of that alert. If that alert is displayed on a phone in our purse or back pocket, the economic value is nil. However, if our user has a smartwatch on, the equation starts to look more promising. A smartwatch on someone's wrist can display an alert to an opted-in user at any time along with a "haptic"[1] buzz. Now there is a fighting chance that our customer, who went to the trouble of downloading

---

[1]Haptic output from a device stimulates our tactile senses with vibration, pressure, or movement. It's used by the Apple Watch to attract our attention to an alert and can be used in virtual reality systems to add feedback to controls such as joysticks to create an experience that is more immersive and realistic.

a beacon-enabled app, will see the advertisement our business is getting paid for. Rather than a one in ten chance of revenue being generated, maybe the odds go up to 50/50 and our business is worth five times more. Of course this depends on the level of smartwatch adoption among our customers base, which adds another variable to our spreadsheet.

Location as Context for Mobile Apps

As we start to get creative, the beacon-enabled user experiences we design can seem futuristic and complex. Yet, some of the first examples of beacon-enabled apps were easy to appreciate and beautiful in their simplicity. One such app is called *Blush*, which provides recommendations for shoppers at wine merchants. Using GPS, it determines which store you're at and presents product information and recommendations by identifying what bottles might be in the store. With a few beacons dotted in different regions, it can also determine whether you are standing in the white wine or the red wine section of the store and focus its recommendations on the kind of wines you are likely to be seeing.

A shopper considering red wine could open their Blush app and, without having to provide any input, see recommendations for the red wines in that store. No need to swipe and tap. This is so simple that it's likely that the users of the application may not even realize what is happening; they are just experiencing a more intuitive shopping experience. Like good industrial design, good user interface design becomes invisible and unremarkable.

The same kind of thing has been done with apps that are promoting items in a convenience store. When these apps are beacon-enabled, all of the same offers will be presented to the customer, but, as the user stands in front of the display of potato chips, the promotions are automatically sorted so that the product offers that are closest to the user are shown at the top of the limited display on the phone. In this instance, the ad for the potato chips would be featured at the very top. Having the right offer visible "above the fold" could make a big difference in the conversion rate and the happiness of both the shopper and the storeowner.

Of course, this contextual ordering based on proximity doesn't necessarily have to be about selling products. Mobile apps that show the times of trains arriving at a subway platform, for example, can now automatically present the times of trains arriving at the particular platform where the passenger is standing. Removing the need to do a scroll or search within the app can minimize the time it takes the users to get the information they require.

Art galleries and museums are one of the most popular venues for deploying beacons. Presenting information about the work of art that is in front of visitors—and saving them the trouble of having to key in dozens of codes as they wander around a gallery—makes for a much simpler, less frustrating experience. While many museums, such as the Los Angeles Contemporary Museum of Art, are creating their own apps, there is an app called Bubble that supports this use case and can be configured within a few minutes to operate in a new venue. A companion app is used to associate a beacon with some digital content, like a web site, text, image, or video. Seconds later, the user of the Bubble app can see the relevant content "bubble" up on their display, perhaps a video that describes how the art was created.

Automated Retail

The future of retail and the experiences enabled by beacons are intertwined. Beacons have many applications outside of retail, but this market has a special significance when it comes to the development of the beacon ecosystem. That is, retail is huge, with over 4.5 trillion dollars of spending each year in the United States alone[2].

---

[2]www.emarketer.com/Article/Total-US-Retail-Sales-Top-3645-Trillion-2013-Outpace-GDP-Growth/1010756

Most of us go shopping on a regular basis, so retail applications are a great way to get technology into lots of people's hands. Not just once, but frequently enough that their use can become habit forming and start to spread. It's no news that the retail industry is under intense pressure from ecommerce players like Amazon. As such, retailers are responding by attempts to capitalize on their greatest strength and their greatest liability: their brick and mortar stores and the staff who works in them.

High-end retail can be enhanced with beacon applications that allow the staff to be better informed about the needs of the customers in the store. Associates are being armed with tablets that display profiles of the customers as they arrive, in order to help provide a better experience. A customer's retail app can respond to a beacon trigger by sending information about the customer's history and preferences to the staff so that they might offer what has been called "clienteling" services.

These services were offered on a small scale in the old days when merchants knew all their customers personally, but that has become almost impossible in the modern world with multi-national retailers serving tens of thousands of customers at single locations. However, now beacon-enabled apps allow for the "mass customization" of retail, with experiences tailored to each customer. If a shop assistant at Home Depot knew more about us—such as the products we had previously bought and our level of expertise—shopping for hardware tools could be more like the experience high-end shoppers enjoy with a personal shopper at a Nordstrom or another premium merchant.

However, not every shopping experience can be improved with high-end clienteling. Sometimes a good shopping experience is about efficiently dispensing commodities and effectively using real estate and staff. This is where automated retailing has the potential to dramatically evolve away from the rusty vending machine that loses our small change. The kind of experience offered by Redbox when vending DVDs outside grocery stores and gas stations is expanding to include everything from high-end electronics to caviar and cup cakes.

Selling high-end watches may have large enough margins to support the hiring and training of a sales force that can deliver good service. Yet, more often than not, sales staff are paid poorly and, except for a few notable exceptions, you tend to get what you pay for. As a result, according to a survey commissioned by Trade Doubler[3], 72% of shoppers felt the information they got from their smartphones was better than what they got from the average shop assistant.

Spurred on by these statistics, the new generations of the 4.6 million vending machines[4] in the United States are becoming more intelligent. With the integration of the same mobile data modems we find in our phones, they are joining the Internet of Things. Vending machines are now downloading media to display on high-definition screens, calling back to base with orders for specific replenishment of their stock and accepting credit cards and mobile payments. This creates a great technology platform on which to add Bluetooth beacons.

Our Redbox machine could add a beacon that the Redox app would recognize and then inform us that the sequel to the movie we just watched is now available at the kiosk that we will pass on our way out of the store.

High-end coffee vending machines require us to tap through endless choices of beverage type, size, caffeine level, strength, and milkiness. Using beacons, these can now greet us by name and ask us to press a single button to confirm that we would like our usual. When customers get served faster and wait times go down, sales go up.

Beacons in airline kiosks at airports can trigger a conversation between the kiosk and our airline app, speeding us though the check-in process. Ordinarily, this is a frustrating task because we are often forced to reenter information that we previously entered online. With this beacon triggered machine-to-machine dialogue, our smartphone speeds us through check-in.

Even gas pumps are being enabled with the same high-end processors that are being put into our phones. Rather than getting the same short-form entertainment video that every other customer gets, why shouldn't a beacon trigger your petroleum app to personalize your experience? It could request news content to be displayed when one customer fills up, and fashion tips when another customer arrives. At the same time, we have the opportunity to eliminate the questions about payment method and the grade of gas our car needs by having our phone communicate directly with the fuel dispenser.

---

[3]www.mobilecommercedaily.com/retailers-lose-32pc-of-shoppers-to-in-store-mobile-use-tradedoubler
[4]www.statisticbrain.com/vending-machine-industry-statistics/

Ecommerce Meets Bricks and Mortar

From a retailer's perspective, digital to physical convergence means that nearly all of the marketing and analysis that Amazon can do in the digital world of its web store can be done in a brick and mortar store.

Amazon brought huge sophistication to retailing, analyzing the behavior of shoppers, what they looked at, and their click-path through the site. In the same way, beacons can enable an analysis of individual shoppers' footpath through the store, including how long they dwell at different locations.

This is something that was possible before beacons, but only in regard to shoppers in the aggregate, using video cameras and computer vision to track the flow of customers around the store. Computer vision can infer gender, age, and mood by applying algorithms to the video feed from security cameras, but beacons can monitor specific shopper's behavior in stores and then present that shopper with offers and promotions that relate to where he or she spent time when last in the store.

These promotions can appear in-store via digital displays and then again when they browse the web after leaving the store through a process called "retargeting". Retargeting is commonplace on the web today. Anyone who has browsed products on a retailer's site and has then seen ads for the same products when they move on to read the news on another site has experienced retargeting. With the use of beacons, the same analytics and recommendations that are seen as part of Amazon's strength can be determined and applied based on a customer's behavior in the physical world.

Amazon also offers advantages in terms of ease of payment (One Click Checkout). Beacons, though, can enable no-click checkout, certainly for small ticket items, at least. A beacon can be used to detect an individual's proximity to a point-of-sale (PoS) terminal, and that individual doesn't even have to touch their phone or wallet. A second authentication factor can be applied by using a photo of the shopper on the display of the PoS.

Amazon has created such an awesome shopping experience that they are able to provide those storefront experiences while seamlessly layering them onto other merchants' fulfillment/delivery services. In the same way, a beacon-enabled experience could allow inventory free storefronts to focus on the look, feel, multi-media, personalization, and clienteling. Apple's approach to selling the Apple Watch previews one retailer's strategy of removing inventory from the physical store, and instead focusing on the experience in the store to sell and take orders that are rapidly delivered from inventory stored elsewhere.

By abstracting the in-store shopping experience away from the inventory and fulfillment, the brick and mortar store can offer a much broader range of products. In some stores there may not even be a stock room. After all, the space used to stock inventory shrinks the space available to sell products. Now all of the store's space can be devoted to selling, with inventory cached in nearby warehouse facilities for same-day delivery.

Indoor Mapping

It's hard to remember a time when we couldn't use maps applications on our cell phones to find our way to new restaurants, businesses, and peoples' houses. I have a vague recollection of struggling to fold and unfold huge paper maps and a lot of arguments with colleagues and relatives about where we might be on these things as they flapped around the car.

Thanks to beacons, in the future we will probably take for granted the ability to find our way around any airport or shopping mall, and our ability to optimize our route through a warehouse store and go straight to the products we are interested in.

It's likely that providing self-sufficient navigation for the partially sighted may accelerate the infrastructure deployment. Currently, blind people can get help from sighted strangers to help find where they want to go, but they miss out on understanding the facilities that surround them. With beacons, they can be informed where restrooms, exits, stores, and kiosks that are especially equipped to help them are located. A voiceover commentary relayed to them via bone conducting headphones allows visually impaired people to listen to the ambient noise and this extra information at the same time. Ambient noise is important to the visually impaired in order to navigate around obstacles such as walls and people.

With beacon business models, one question that needs to be answered is "how do we get people to download the beacon-enabled app?". This can be the low point of the business modeling discussion. Smiles tend to disappear when the total available market (TAM) that a beacon app can address gets slashed by an order of magnitude.

The encouraging thing about indoor navigation is that our smartphones all have at least one maps application that we are very familiar with, so once they fully support beacons, that barrier to adoption will be removed. These maps applications are potentially going to be doing a lot more than telling us how to get from A to B. They will be surfacing relevant points of interest, businesses, and even products and services. As a consumer, my search isn't necessarily going to be for a hardware store; I could search for the product I'm interested in and could be guided from my sofa to the shelf the product is sitting on. What a great opportunity for any company that owns a maps application and also has an advertising business (Google?).

The Help Button and e911

Once the indoor mapping infrastructure is in place, there are additional opportunities. Customers that need help in a large department store will be able to press a "Help" button on their phone and an assistant will be able to find you, rather than the other way around. They may be coming to you with a lot of information about who you are. If you are a big spender, you may find that you get service faster than another shopper who is not so loyal to the store.

Government regulation can be a significant force in driving the adoption of technology. It was the U.S. Federal Communications Commission's e911 rules for phone carriers regarding their ability to locate 911 callers quickly that drove investment in the assisted GPS chipsets that help us to navigate to our appointments. In big cities and large buildings, e911 is quite ineffective, so carriers are being asked to solve that problem. One response is to build a GPS network that transmits from towers rather than satellites, an alternative is to use the low-cost beacons that have so many other commercial uses.

Location-Aware In-App Advertising

A large proportion of free applications are funded by in-app advertising revenue. Beacons have the potential to make those apps that sit at the bottom of our Angry Birds and Sudoku games a lot more targeted and so increase their value to the app developer. If you are sitting at a departure gate, avoiding thoughts of the pangs of hunger that are building by immersing yourself in the trajectory of small birds whizzing across your phone screen, you may be reminded that there is a McDonald's so close to you that you can probably smell the french fries. Early trials of location-based offers have shown they are significantly more effective the closer the item being promoted is to the viewer of the ad. This doesn't bode well for our waistlines.

Summary: What's Next?

These applications give you a sense that there are some engaging user experiences that can be enabled and add value for the stakeholders. Before we dive into how the technology works, in the next chapter, let's consider a framework to organize the kinds of components that will be required to deliver these experiences. From this framework, businesspeople and architects can get a sense of who they would need to engage with to build a solution. Developers can consider the components they will need to develop or build on. Investors can consider where the opportunities and the risks are greatest.

CHAPTER 4

Beacosystem Framework

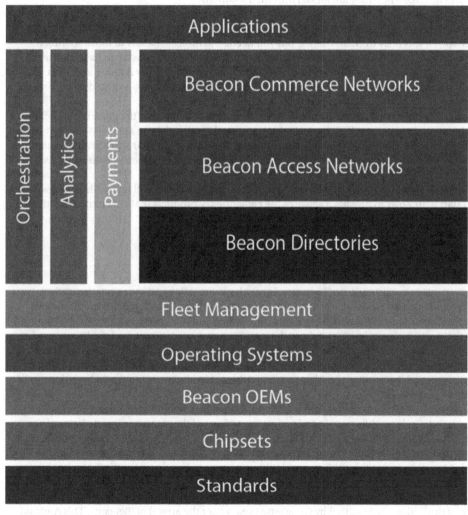

The contents of the stack, from top to bottom:

Applications

Orchestration | Analytics | Payments

Beacon Commerce Networks

Beacon Access Networks

Beacon Directories

Fleet Management

Operating Systems

Beacon OEMs

Chipsets

Standards

The Beacosystem Technology Stack

S. Statler, *Beacon Technologies*, DOI 10.1007/978-1-4842-1889-1_4

The framework we are about to explore is about more than Bluetooth beacons. The arrival of the beacon caused an explosion of entrepreneurial creativity and spawned an ecosystem that is enabling a whole range of proximity technologies. As we will discuss in the chapter on alternative technologies, each proximity technology has its own particular strengths and weaknesses, but they all benefit from the software and services that are coming together around Bluetooth beacons.

Our framework also forms the basis of a shopping list for the builders of solutions. They can look at vendors and decide which of the framework components they want to use from a given firm.

When evaluating the companies that you want to do business with, it's useful to refer to a framework such as this so you can evaluate the completeness of a vendor's offering. Ticking more boxes doesn't necessarily mean the offering is stronger; if a vendor is trying to cover the requirements of products in all the boxes, this may be cause for concern. It's hard to do all things well, and in terms of managing the risk associated with a solution, it's advisable to design in the ability to achieve a level of interoperability so that components can be switched out. Adopting monolithic proprietary solutions can leave a bad taste in the mouth of those held hostage when they are locked into such solutions.

When I was learning to drive, my instructor was very keen to instill a sense of "lane discipline". The idea being that you would stick to your lane on the highway, rather than weaving from one to the other in an unpredictable way. It was okay to change lanes, but you needed to indicate clearly to those sharing the road what you were about to do. This approach can work well in technology if you want to have partners to complement and extend your offering. If partners are not clear what your company is doing and what it is not doing, those partners will probably be suspicious and not commit the resources required to work well with your offering.

I can think of one beacon vendor who has enjoyed early success and has used the resulting cash flow to rapidly develop functionality in most of the boxes in this framework. Some of these are token elements that lack the depth of the core product, which brought them their initial success. They are now finding it hard to attract the partners that could complement their core product because those partners see them as having competitive offerings.

Since each of these elements is described in a chapter later in the book, we will review the framework at a high level to start with, so as to provide a sense of the categories of products that are coming together to create the Bluetooth beacon ecosystem or "Beacosystem" for short.

Standards

Bluetooth beacons came into existence, not because of some huge breakthrough in science, but rather because of the introduction of new standards that were widely adopted for other applications. Bluetooth 4.0 was built into low-cost chipsets that consumed very little power and provided a means to trigger actions in smartphones that came into proximity with these devices. The power consumption of the beacons using these standards was so low that they could be run on batteries lasting for years. Battery powered devices can be installed by anyone with a head for heights and the ability to follow directions, rather than requiring an experienced electrician and the routing of cables. So standards enabled huge economies in both the cost of manufacturing and operations.

iBeacon then provided a level of endorsement from Apple, which is unique in its role as a maker of phones owned by relatively wealthy people and an operator of one of the most successful chains of retail stores ever. These stores provided a great showcase for the technology. This endorsement boosted confidence among entrepreneurs. They saw momentum and opportunity, with VCs who were willing to fund them and a market to sell to, and with venue owners looking for ways to be relevant as digital technology became more important to shopping and entertainment.

These standards were not complete. They didn't address the world of Android phones (which came with the creation of the Eddystone standard by Google two years after the arrival of iBeacon). This Android market is larger than that of Apple's iPhone, especially when you look at it globally. The standards didn't address a number of important security and management issues, but these gaps have created opportunities for innovation. If anything, the gaps, rather than being seen as deficiencies, have drawn in more venture capital investment (to create products to fill them).

Chipsets and Beacons

The chipset vendors are largely invisible to the users of Bluetooth beacons, but their role is key. Beacon vendors have been able to build products around chipsets that support a large proportion of what a beacon is required to do. Purchasing a System on Chip (SoC) takes the beacon vendor a long way down the road to having a functioning product. A single chipset can include the components required to enable an API interface that responds to analog radio signals, temperature input, and motion sensing. This is not like the early days of computing, where the makers of computers had massive numbers of radically different internal components. A beacon vendor can expect the chipset vendor to provide a component that requires a few additions to be complete: a battery, an antenna, a circuit board, a case, system software, and a management system. To be sure, other components can be added, but the ease with which new beacons can be created helps to explain why there are so many startups that make their own beacons.

This is not to diminish the art of making a great beacon. It's all too easy to make a bad beacon—with poor reliability, inconsistent behavior, missing features, poor environmental characteristics, a short battery life, hard to manage, and doesn't keep up with the rapid evolution of the standards. As a beacon vendor, if you can avoid all those pitfalls, you are rare indeed. You then need to be able to master the same challenges that a good brewery does when producing beer in great volume. Producing a great product in small volume is just the start. You have to manage a supply chain, with sufficient inventory to respond to unpredictable peaks in demand. You also have to maintain quality and master sales and distribution. On top of that, you need to be good at strategically choosing markets that are maturing enough and large enough to feed the organization and provide the tools to cultivate a developer ecosystem to produce software that works well with your product in those markets. There are very few beacon vendors that have been able to do all of these things.

Operating Systems

The landscape of smartphone operating systems (OS) that worked well with beacons was easy to draw through 2014. There was a single box labeled Apple iOS. In 2015, Google's Android OS improved its Bluetooth stack to support the 4.0 standard. The beacon vendors filled some of the missing components required to create beacon-enabled Android apps. The role of Windows Mobile is insignificant as of 2015. Even though Bluetooth 4.0 is supported, few beacon manufacturers are acknowledging its existence. In a market as fast moving and competitive as the Beacosystem is, no sensible beacon OEM would divert the resources required elsewhere to support an operating system with less than 3% market share, absent a major deal sweetener from Microsoft.

The operating system suppliers are in an incredibly important position. What they do to balance performance, battery consumption, privacy, and ease of use is critical to the success of the beacosystem. Given the value in other areas of the beacosystem stack, it seems inevitable that they will gradually start to annex some of those more lucrative areas or commoditize them by growing the scope of the standards, cutting the lifeblood from some players and making the fortunes of the companies that they acquire. The beacosystem is such a fast moving market, it's hard even for Apple and Google to anticipate how the technology will evolve, so it makes sense to "outsource innovation," by seeing who has done a good job and acquiring those teams and their technology. Many a startup has created an exit strategy based on this scenario.

Fleet Management

Pilot projects and demos tend to require a small number of beacons, but a large venue can require many hundreds of the devices. If you multiply the number of venues by the thousands of outlets that a chain of big box stores might have across the United States, the management challenges of maintaining an inventory of these hundreds of thousands of devices is significant. Specialist software is essential to knowing where the beacons are. Tracking their health, making changes to their configuration, and updating the software becomes quite a challenge. It's the kind of challenge that causes CIOs to sweat and the CFOs at solutions providers who can solve this problem to smile. Using large numbers of people to solve these management problems is expensive and error prone, so the return on investment of effective management software is relatively easy to show.

This area is the natural refuge of beacon hardware vendors looking for a market to monetize their solutions. The solutions to applying software and adjusting parameters tend to be proprietary due to a lack of standards for the management interfaces for beacons (as of May 2016 Google have started to address this). For beacon vendors that have succeeded in having their products used in large-volume applications, they've had to solve these management problems to survive. The beacon vendors who may have sold one or two beacons to large volumes of consumers to track keys and other such items will not have had to develop such solutions.

Orchestration

The API calls that a beacon triggers are fairly low level and primitive. A beacon may be triggering a large number of events on the handset of a nearby user, which need to be filtered and interpreted in a broader context before it's sensible to send a message to a user of the device or report on something that would be interesting from an analytics perspective. Users don't want to receive a hundred alerts as they approach a beacon.

It may be that a welcome to a particular department in a big box store is appropriate only if the shopper has something on their shopping list that is available in that area. The application may want to check the signal from multiple beacons to be confident that the user is in the right place in order to record the presence of a shopper in that department. Converting lots of low-level proximity triggers and combining them with rules and other information is the key to unlocking the value in what can be achieved with beacons.

This is new uncharted territory, which makes it a great area for startups to carve out a niche. Unlike Bluetooth chipsets, there aren't a host of large incumbent firms that have been doing something very similar. This area is so new that we have struggled to decide what to call it. Today we are calling it *orchestration*. As with a large group of musicians, the role of the conductor here is key. The score that will be played is not fully defined in advance. It's likely to evolve based on the experiences accrued and develop in ways that are hard to predict. This makes it one of the most interesting spaces to watch. Companies like Rover Labs, Local Social, Pulsate, and indoo.rs are some of the players that are innovating in this space currently. Their focus is less on creating whole apps and more about creating middleware, which is software that other app developers can include in their apps so as to give them a leg up in building a proximity-aware app.

Analytics

Many of the early beacon hardware vendors described themselves as analytics companies. This is ironic as they often sold hardware with a minimum of software. There wasn't much in the way of tools that could take all the beacon data their hardware produced and turn it into actionable information. Customers were lucky if they got a bar graph. The slogan from the old Wendy's hamburger commercial comes to mind: "Where's the beef?".

There are a huge number of well-established analytics companies. They range from specialist statistical package vendors, providers of cool visualization tools, and companies that have focused on location-based analytics using technologies other than beacons that haven't included beacon event data into what they do.

A lot of very interesting insights can be gained with just the data from beacons, such as the dwell time in front of different paintings in an art gallery, or the different paths of people in a shopping mall based on the time of day. However, the most interesting insights normally come when integrating other external data. If we can integrate art museum membership data, we can segment that data and see where young men linger and where new members linger versus well-established members. We can analyze the impact of attending an educational event on what people do in a gallery. Do people who have watched the introductory video linger longer? Do they tend to look at a larger number of paintings? Our beacon insights get a lot more interesting.

Payments

Beacons can make the payment experience more convenient for customers and more lucrative for retailers and brands. They can create opportunities to buy more and to look at the effectiveness of those efforts.

We call payments out as a specific application because of the potential economic and strategic value. It's also a very challenging application and has been a dangerous siren for other technologies such as *near field communication* (NFC). The adoption of NFC technology was arguably close to being derailed because there was so much conflict between technology vendors, banks, and retailers on how it would be used. Payments is an important area and has such economic significance that people almost forgot that NFC could be used for other things that were quick and relatively easy to implement. Beacons have probably benefited because companies have applied the technology to other use cases.

Beacon Directories

Beacon networks are a hugely important and valuable phenomenon in the story of this technology. One beacon can be used by multiple applications. If retailers place beacons in their stores to enable their apps, but then allow other applications to access the same beacons, the value of the beacons increases considerably. These other apps could be developed by brands that are promoting specific products in the store, shopping list apps, or the maps app that can provide navigation around the store.

As Beacon networks have started to form, we have categorized them into three types. The most fundamental is the *beacon directory*, which tracks where beacons are and maintains metadata that describes the beacon and its location.

While there exists a range of beacon directories that do nothing more than track the location of beacons, the other types of beacon network, which do more than this, have this directory function as their foundation.

Beacon Access Networks

Enterprising builders of beacon networks often want to charge others for the privilege of accessing their beacons. In order to do that, they need to restrict access and make it conditional on a "pay-to-play" basis. This is referred to as a *beacon access network*.

Not all beacons are restricted in this way. In the case where there is no "conditional access" function, all you need is to discover the address of the beacon through a beacon directory and you are ready to access it for free.

Beacon Commerce Networks

Beacon networks can be used for all sorts of purposes, but advertising is probably one of the most lucrative areas. Beyond the functions we have just touched on, a proximity ad network operates at a much higher level, providing all of the functions of the online ad networks, with a lot more personal information that can be used to understand what kinds of people and what kind of circumstances might trigger an ad. Beacon-enabled ad networks then offer the possibility of new levels of personalization, interaction, and attribution that can measure the effectiveness of ad spending in ways that can't be achieved with web ads.

A beacon-enabled ad network could target people who had just come from cinemas at a certain time of day, present them with offers for certain kinds of restaurants, and then see how effective the ad was at influencing where that person goes to eat.

Beacon commerce networks may offer ad delivery features or they may allow the correlation between the presentation of an advertisement to an action such as a visit to an area within a store where the advertised product is sold.

The essence of a beacon commerce network is that there is additional business functionality built into the network service, beyond simply controlling the access to a beacon.

Applications

Having spent our time looking at the plumbing and the features that beacons can enable, we will look at some of the issues specific to creation of beacon-enabled applications.

It's easy to be overwhelmed by the possibilities of beacons, which can be debilitating. This is the paradox of choice. The more choices there are, the harder it is to find one that works.

Is there a structured way of looking at the use cases that beacons can implement so as to allow us to be more effective in applying the technology in creative ways? We think so. There are certain core patterns, such as "the check in" that are core to beacon apps. As we map those limited applications and organize the variations on those themes, it's possible to simplify the problem, while at the same time stimulating creativity and the boosting of new applications based on those core use cases.

Summary

Now we have looked at the beacosystem and its components at a high level, it's time to dig into the details of each of these components and build a solid understanding that we can use to design our solutions and business ideas.

CHAPTER 5

■ ■ ■

Standards

The International Space Station relies on standards for its components to integrate. Image courtesy of NASA

Standards Overview

Fundamental to the explosive growth of the beacon market is the role of a number of key standards. Imagine where we would be without technology standards. Life would be harder for both developers and consumers. Developers would have to work in isolation, building out almost every component of their systems by themselves. These monolithic systems would be expensive to produce and would require a huge amount of expertise across all of the components. Costs and risks would be prohibitively high. Fortunately, that is not the world in which we live.

© Stephen Statler 2016
S. Statler, *Beacon Technologies*, DOI 10.1007/978-1-4842-1889-1_5

These days we take for granted the ability to plug any DVD player into an amplifier. In days gone by, when standards in that area were less mature, systems tended to be monolithic. You had to buy your record player, amp, and speakers from the same manufacturer. Now consumers have choice in the components they choose. Building a solution from best of breed components is a given. The same principle that goes for the audiophile consumers and their HiFi systems goes for solutions architects building their solutions using Wi-Fi and Bluetooth standards.

With standards and interoperability, reuse becomes possible. With reuse, ecosystems grow faster and bigger. Growth in the volume of components produced for one application of a technology can bring down costs that make a second application of the technology viable in a way it wouldn't have been otherwise. The economics change, and the benefits of experimentation and innovation reach a whole new level as different companies, with no relationship other than their use of a common standard, can build on each other's work. Best of breed combinations add extra competition and increase quality.

The Bluetooth 4.0 standard provided the foundation for what inspired the beacon movement. When Apple added on their own iBeacon standard, they threw gasoline onto a fire that was already smoldering. Bluetooth beacons were being built prior to what Apple did, but Apple's endorsement was key. Beyond defining a standard, Apple enhanced their operating system to provide features that helped to make sure beacons could work, and work well. They developed privacy controls, optimized response time, tuned handset battery consumption and integrated beacon functionality into a pre-installed app, Passbook (now called Wallet). They also became early adopters of iBeacons within their own retail stores.

The Apple retail stores are seen as being leading edge by other retailers and boast the highest revenue per square foot of any major retail chain. Apple's Enterprise Sales teams (who focus on selling Apple products to businesses) open up their stores for other retailers to see, using them as a demonstration environment to illustrate how Apple devices and software can be used to build a compelling shopping experience.

The iBeacon standard also had impact on Google's Android mobile operating system, which can respond to the same iBeacon hardware that iOS apps see. Beacons operate the same way, no matter what device or OS is receiving the signal. While Google hasn't endorsed Apple's iBeacon standard, it has improved its Bluetooth stack so that beacon-aware Android apps can be triggered by a Bluetooth beacon, whether that is an iBeacon or a beacon using some other standard. Two years after iBeacon was introduced Google introduced a competing set of standards called Eddystone. One of the standards included in that portfolio (Eddystone URL) aims to go beyond the limitations of iBeacon by removing the need to install an app in order to act on a beacon broadcast. Also known as the Physical Web project, Google's vision is that we will use the browsers on our mobile devices to select from URLs broadcast to us by nearby beacons. This has the potential to make a profound difference in the way beacon technology permeates our lives.

While Google was planning their response to iBeacon, others attempted to fill that gap. Radius Networks created a standard called AltBeacon as an "ALTernative" to iBeacon. These are standards that are key to the beacosystem. Let's get to know each of them in more detail.

The Bluetooth Standard

The great thing about Bluetooth as a standard is that its market penetration is massive. It also has significant brand recognition (see Figure 5-1). It's hard to argue with any standard that has been responsible for tens of thousands of products and more than 10 billion Bluetooth devices[1]. For those of us who want to build solutions, this kind of momentum is great because it introduces a level of confidence in at least one component of the solution. Less argument about the technologies an architect uses implies a lower perceived risk and a greater willingness for stakeholders to move forward with confidence. The momentum behind Bluetooth is accelerating.

---

[1]ABI Research: Bluetooth: The Next 10 Billion Devices https://www.abiresearch.com/webinars/bluetooth-next-10-billion-devices/

Figure 5-1. *The Bluetooth standard logo[2]*

Bluetooth 4.0 is the original standard that inspired the beacon revolution. Shipments of Bluetooth 4.0 devices are forecast to grow to 2.9 billion by 2016. Big numbers are important as the input to any business development professional's planning spreadsheet. They also provide a great basis for economies of scale to reduce the cost of hardware.

The "not so good" thing about Bluetooth is that with familiarity, there also comes some baggage. When you say "Bluetooth," many people think of problems with connecting their headset to their phone and frustrating searches for setup instructions that have long been lost. The fact that Bluetooth has been synonymous with pairing devices is problematic because the Bluetooth Smart part of the 4.0 standard is what our beacons use, and for the most part there is no paring or connection between a beacon and a phone.

Bluetooth 4.0 consists of two separate protocols under one banner: the legacy or Classic connection-orientated protocol used for linking audio devices, and Bluetooth Smart, a quite different set of protocols that coexist with Classic but behave very differently.

Broadcast versus Connect

In order to understand how Bluetooth beacons work, think of another kind of beacon, the lighthouse on a rocky peninsula. Passing ships that see the beacon can judge the distance between their ship and the rocks, but do not have a connection with the lighthouse itself. The lighthouse keeper doesn't know how many ships are passing by in the fog, but the ships are hopefully seeing his signal. So it is with Bluetooth beacons. A single beacon can be broadcasting its signal from above the stage in a concert hall. Thousands of smartphones can register that signal, but the beacon won't know if there are ten or ten thousand phones listening to its broadcast, or maybe none at all.

The same is true of radio stations. I remember working at a radio station on a college campus, reading the news and playing records into the small hours of the morning. A skeptical student wandered in and asked us how many people were listening. We had no idea; we could have been playing music to ourselves. Embarrassed, we told our visitor that there was a meter we could look at to see if we had any listeners. Of course, it wasn't true. Such is the case with beacons: there is no indication on the beacon side of things as to how many mobile devices are picking up their signal.

Eliminating that connection simplifies the protocol and allows it to scale beyond the eight device limit that constrained the number of connections possible between Bluetooth 3.0 devices on a Bluetooth "piconet".

---

[2]The author is a member of the Bluetooth SIG and is licensed to use the Bluetooth trademark.

Origins

Early on in its history, the Bluetooth standard was managed through the Institute of Electrical and Electronics Engineers (IEEE). It was known as 802.15.1. The spectrum it used (2.4 - 2.485GHz) happens to be the same band of spectrum that is used by another IEEE 802 standard, the standard for Wi-Fi 802.11. Now, the IEEE no longer plays a role in the Bluetooth standards process; instead it's managed by the Bluetooth Special Interest Group or SIG. There are over 20,000 members of the SIG, and over 48,000 Bluetooth product models. You have to join the SIG if you want to make a device that uses Bluetooth. Fortunately, membership at the basic level is free. If you want to get access to the Bluetooth standards documents, go to their web site at `www.bluetooth.com` and sign up. It's a quick process.

The biggest category of devices that use Bluetooth is the Audio and Visual collection of devices (26,759). There are also over 11,000 other devices using the standard in a range of categories from mobile phone accessories to emerging categories such as medical devices[3].

The spectrum that Bluetooth and Wi-Fi share is called "unlicensed," because, unlike the cell phone spectrum, companies don't have to buy a license from the government to use it. We all share that piece of bandwidth. This has the benefit that consumers don't have to buy a Wi-Fi or Bluetooth plan from a telco to use a Bluetooth device. The downside is that there is no one managing the level of use of this shared part of the airwaves relative to the capacity available. As a result, it can get crowded with an unlimited number of devices competing to use the spectrum. This creates some uncertainty and the risk that if you get a lot of Wi-Fi and Bluetooth devices operating in the same vicinity, they will interfere with each other. The responsiveness of Bluetooth beacon apps and the timing of when an app sees a beacon can be unpredictable. The fact that the spectrum used by beacons can be crowded with Wi-Fi is one of the reasons for this unpredictability.

To deal with this, the Bluetooth protocol uses a rather clever technique called frequency hopping. Bluetooth divides the spectrum that it can use into 40 separate channels and sprays packets across those channels, hopping from one channel to the next 1,600 times a second (how cool is that?). So rather than having conflicting devices locked into using the same channel, shouting over each other, the packets will generally pass each other by. This technique dates back to World War I when it was used by the military to avoid malicious attempts to jam signals or listen in.

Some More Bluetooth History

The telecom vendor Ericsson invented the technology that became Bluetooth in 1994.

The Bluetooth name originates from the medieval (Figure 5-2) King of Denmark, Harald "Bluetooth" Gormsson. One of the explanations for his nickname is that, due to the poor dental care available in the 10th century, he had a severely discolored "gnasher". The king's name was used because he united Norway and Denmark, two countries that would otherwise have wasted their resources warring with each other. The idea of the new standard was to unite the different groups within Ericsson, IBM, Toshiba, Intel, and Nokia, which had previously been working on competing standards.

---

[3]See `https://www.bluetooth.com/what-is-bluetooth-technology/bluetooth-devices` for more details.

Figure 5-2. *Lewis Chessmen (of Harald "Bluetooth" Gormsson) in the British Museum were probably made in Norway, about AD 1150-1200*
Photo Courtesy of Rob Roy `www.flickr.com/photos/robroy/`

Bluetooth was the temporary working title for the standard, to be used while the marketing team came up with the proper name. That marketing project started in 1997. The main contenders for the proper name, "RadioWire" and "PAN" (Personal Area Network), never saw the light of day[4] and so the working title "Bluetooth" became the commercial name.

The Bluetooth logo is derived from a combination of the Nordic runes (ancient alphabet) for the king's initials. The H (ᚼ haglaz) and B (ᛒ berkanan)[5], when combined, become 🅱.

---

[4]For even more of the background story, read Jim Kardach's account `http://www.eetimes.com/document.asp?doc_id=1269737&page_number=2`
[5]`http://en.wikipedia.org/wiki/File:Runic_letter_ior.svg`
`http://en.wikipedia.org/wiki/File:Runic_letter_berkanan.svg`

The standard was conceived as an alternative to using wires to connect local devices. The different versions of Bluetooth, up to version 3.0, focused on improving quality, speed, and robustness.

By 2001, Nokia had identified some use-cases that were not supported by Bluetooth and developed a product called Wibree. It offered a new, low-energy protocol for rapid connection and transmission of simple messages.

The new protocol used the same spectrum as previous versions of Bluetooth, but was different from the Classic Bluetooth protocol in terms of its functionality, throughput, security, and latency.

The protocol was brought into the Bluetooth fold in 2007. Its working title was Bluetooth Low Energy (BLE), but was ultimately called Bluetooth Smart in 2010 because its capabilities went beyond simply using less power. "Smart" has application specific features organized into a large number of profiles that enable integration of new devices beyond those traditionally associated with the Classic standard, devices such as watches, heart monitors, bikes, and thermostats. Use of the BLE acronym is officially frowned upon by the SIG as they attempt to gain momentum around the use of a unified brand name (Bluetooth Smart) that encompasses more than the low-energy features within the standard.

So, how much lower is the energy consumption? Nominally the low-energy chipsets consume half the power, or less, of their Classic predecessors. This enables devices using the new technology to potentially last for over a year on a coin-sized battery (see Figure 5-3). Although exactly how long will vary wildly, depending on a number of factors that we will explain later.

Figure 5-3. *A coin-sized CR 2032 battery*

To recap, Bluetooth 4.0 is the version of the standard that encompasses both Classic and Smart stacks. In other words, Bluetooth Smart is a subset of Bluetooth 4.0.

Classic, Single Mode, Dual Mode, Smart, and Smart Ready

As you consider the applications you want to support, it's important to understand whether the chipset that you are using at the heart of your system is Bluetooth Classic, dual mode, or single mode.

Classic Bluetooth is the term used to refer to the version of Bluetooth (3.0 and earlier) that predates the support of the functions we are concerned with here. Dual-mode Bluetooth chipsets support the Classic functions, like streaming audio signals, as well as the new low-energy functions such as sending beacon packets or communicating with a heart monitor. A dual-mode chipset can drive a connection with an "old school" voice headset using the Classic stack, while also sensing the presence of a Bluetooth Smart beacon.

The Bluetooth Classic chipsets don't support the new 4.0 standard including the low-energy operations required. So if your PC doesn't have a dual-mode chipset, no software upgrade can enable it to talk to a Bluetooth Smart blood pressure monitor.

One real-life example where this limitation impacted a project was when we realized that a Bluetooth Smart device we had developed would not be able to detect the presence of the Classic Bluetooth devices embedded in many car radios. This became an issue when a business partner wanted to create a futuristic gas pump with our Bluetooth device looking for the Bluetooth signature from car radios. They wanted the pump to recognize the brand of the cars that approached the pump. If you could recognize the make of car, you could infer a lot about its driver. You could then have used the pump to sell all sorts of things to the car's driver based on that insight. Unfortunately, our chip was a Bluetooth Smart Single Mode device, so it couldn't detect the Bluetooth Classic signals coming from the radios in older cars.

A Bluetooth device such as a PC that can interface with both Bluetooth Smart devices, like beacons, and with Bluetooth Classic devices such as keyboards, will have a dual-mode chipset and is called *Bluetooth Smart Ready*. Smart Ready devices work with the classic devices but they are also "ready" for the new ones (see Figure 5-4).

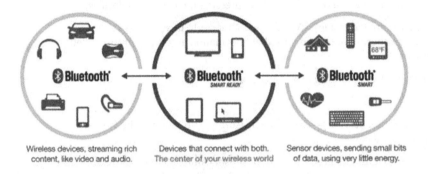

Figure 5-4. *The relationship among Bluetooth (Classic), Bluetooth Smart Ready, and Bluetooth Smart devices Graphic Copyright Bluetooth SIG*

Economics Favor Smart Devices

The new dual-mode chipsets are no more expensive than the old Classic chipsets, so device manufacturers have been using the new hardware and making devices that supported Smart even before having software that makes use of it. As a result, in 2014 there was a large number of Android phones that were Bluetooth Smart capable, but they lacked the version of Android that would expose the Smart functions. Users who upgraded to Android 4.3, which added Bluetooth Smart support, suddenly found they had access to Smart functions they never knew their phones possessed.

Conversely, single-mode chipsets are even smaller in size, cost, and power consumption and are what most beacon manufacturers use in their beacon devices.

The first device to ship that supported Bluetooth Smart was Apple's iPhone 4S in October 2011. Given that the typical replacement cycle of smartphones in the United States is two years, the majority of iPhone users in the United States should now have a Bluetooth Smart capable device.

Bluetooth Profiles

Who would have thought that we would have Bluetooth Smart enabled locks on our front doors? Beyond emitting a cool blue glow from the bezel, these devices are remarkably useful. Such doors can be unlocked with nothing more than the touch of your fingers, relying on a secure authentication by the phone in your pocket. Digital keys, which expire after a few hours, can be sent to visitors and contractors. Bluetooth functionality has come a long way since the days of simply replacing the cable on your keyboard.

Bluetooth Smart uses an architecture that enables a large and growing number of profiles, which can be used to support applications to connect devices in the Internet of Things. An example of a Bluetooth low-energy profile is the Find Me Profile (FMP). When a button is pressed on one device, this profile causes an alert signal on another associated device to activate. Using FMP, your phone could active a buzzer in your wireless headset to help you find it when it gets lost in the sofa.

These profiles are written using an underlying, lower-level profile specific to Bluetooth Smart called GATT (Generic ATTribute profile). GATT enables a set of lower-level operations, such as setting a value on a remote device that might be used to change its behavior. The higher level profiles built on GATT include general-purpose profiles like BAS (the battery service that exposes the state of a battery within a device), as well as collections of profiles applicable to vertical markets. Examples of these in health care and sports and fitness include:

Health Care

- **BLP** (Blood Pressure Profile)—For use with blood pressure measurement devices

- **HTP** (Health Thermometer Profile)—A nurse or doctor could take a patient's temperature using a thermometer and have that information automatically uploaded to the patient's file

- **GLP** (Glucose Profile)—For blood glucose monitors

Sports and Fitness

- **BCS** (Body Composition Service)—To enable measurement of body fat, body water, bone mass, and muscle mass

- **CSCP** (Cycling Speed and Cadence Profile)—For sensors attached to a bicycle or exercise bike in order to measure cadence and wheel speed

- **CPP** (Cycling Power Profile)—Measuring the cycle crank revolutions and torque

- **HRP** (Heart Rate Profile)—For devices that measure heart rate

- **LNP** (Location and Navigation Profile)—Shares location, speed, and estimated time of arrival characteristics

- **RSCP** (Running Speed and Cadence Profile)—Gathers information such as speed, stride length, and distance traveled

- **WSP** (Weight Scale Profile)—Can transmit the name of the person being weighed, how much they weigh, and the time of the measurement

Profile use isn't required in order to write applications that use Bluetooth beacons, but it does give you a sense for one of the dynamics influencing the broader adoption of a key standard at the heart of the Internet of Things. Quite surprisingly, there is no SIG-defined beacon profile.

Device manufacturers can develop their own profiles using GATT, and so Apple has developed its own iBeacon profile that is part of its proprietary standard. We will go into more detail on that in the next section.

iBeacon, You Beacon, We All Beacon

iBeacon is a standard defined by Apple and controlled with a license agreement that beacon manufacturers have to sign in order to use the logo and claim their product is iBeacon compatible. However, iBeacons are not Apple approved. Apple doesn't test the beacons. As a result, strict conformance to the iBeacon standard is patchy.

iBeacon defines the data packets that a beacon sends as well as the iOS APIs that software developers can use to access those beacons. That being said, entrepreneurs can create Bluetooth beacons that can be accessed on iPhones without signing the license agreement[6] or using the iBeacon brand. They can still broadcast packets that conform to the iBeacon structure or use their own proprietary format and write applications using the CoreBluetooth APIs instead. CoreBluetooth offers lower level, more general Bluetooth functionality. It doesn't offer the capabilities that Apple, as OS developer, has created for iBeacon that distinguish it from other proximity technologies.

When Apple defined iBeacon, manufacturers who had already been making beacons raced to embrace this new standard. Doing so meant changing the way their hardware worked and signing the iBeacon license agreement. So, why did so many go to that effort, just to earn the right to claim that they sold "iBeacons"?

This went beyond the mere desire for prestige and respectability that comes with claiming the rights to use what has become such a hot product name. As much as anything, it was the iBeacon-specific capabilities included in iOS that drove the stampede. These include:

- *Privacy controls*—The ability to integrate location privacy controls into iOS, managed under Settings ➤ Privacy ➤ Location Services (see Figure 5-5). Playing nice with privacy is an important element of keeping users happy and receiving Apple's approval to put your app into the App Store.

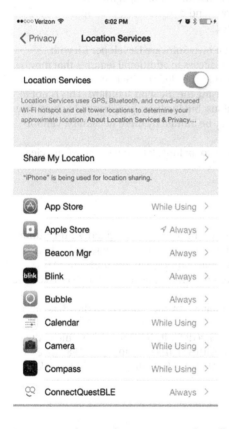

Figure 5-5. *The panel in iOS settings that allows users to control privacy and the ability for an app to be triggered by an iBeacon*

---

[6]The agreement is available within the Apple Developer beacon pages `developer.apple.com/ibeacon/` and `mfi.apple.com/enrollnew`

- *Alerts*—The ability to display alerts when a beacon is detected, even when your app is in background mode (i.e., another app is being viewed or the screen is locked).

- *Restart*—The ability for your app to be restarted when an associated iBeacon is detected. Even if the user quits the app, or if the phone is restarted, as long as your app has run once, it will be brought back from the dead when a relevant iBeacon is detected.

- *Regions*—The ability to efficiently act on triggers when entering a large number of geographic regions.

- *Ranging*—Use of the Ranging API that allows signal strength to be used to gauge proximity.

- *Apple Wallet*—Integration with Apple Wallet, which comes preloaded onto iOS and can't be removed. Apple Wallet is part of the foundation of Apple Pay and can display passes to the user when a geofence is crossed or a beacon is sighted. Passes can take the form of coupons, digital boarding passes, or tickets to the movie theater. They are easy for developers to create using XHTML and can be downloaded from ads, web pages, or by scanning a QR code. They represent a very useful way of engaging a user while they are carefully seduced into "going all the way" and downloading your app. We cover Apple Wallet in more detail in a later chapter.

Many beacon manufacturers that support iBeacon create their own Software Developer Kit with proprietary APIs that sit above the Apple iBeacon APIs. These offer access to additional features that may be important to the management and use of their beacons. By doing this, they lock in their customers in a way that may not be apparent, given those customers believe they are using the iBeacon standard. This is not to say there aren't good reasons to include these proprietary extensions, but business people need to be aware that their ability to switch from one iBeacon vendor to another may be limited by these necessary, vendor-specific APIs.

Before we go into the details of what these extensions are likely to include, let's make sure we are clear about the core components of the iBeacon Standard.

Universally Unique Identifier (UUID)

One of the most important things to understand about iBeacon is how beacons are identified. As the number of beacons around us explodes, applications need to establish which beacons they are interested in being alerted by. That selection is via the beacon's UUID. iPhone applications don't see all the iBeacons that surround the device; they only see beacons with the specific UUIDs that the application writer has asked iOS to look for.

Universally Unique Identifiers are 128-bit numbers that are assigned by the manager of the iBeacons to identify groups that will share functions.

iBeacons you receive from the factory may be programmed with a default UUID that is specific to the manufacturer. Estimote beacons, for example, come programmed with a UUID of B9407F30-F5F8-466E-AFF9-25556B57FE6D; Radius Beacons default to 2F234454-CF6D-4A0F-ADF2-F4911BA9FFA6, and Kontakt.io beacons default to F7826DA6-4FA2-4E98-8024-BC5B71E0893E.

THE NUMBER SYSTEM USED WITH UUIDS

UUIDs are represented as 32 hexadecimal (hex) numbers. Rather than decimal numbers (base-10 numbers) which range from 0 to 9, hex numbers are base-16 and range from 0-15, with 10-15 being represented by A through F. That is to say, A in hex equals 10 in decimal, B equals 11, and so on. Using hex allows a simpler translation to the binary (base-2) code that is used to store these UUIDs in the data packets that whiz from beacon to mobile device. Hex F can be represented in four bits as 1111. Unless you are going to be doing low-level programming, you don't need to remember the details. Suffice it to say, when it comes to UUIDs, think of the letters A-F as numbers (10-15).

UUIDs are not just used to name iBeacons. They have been in use for decades. First standardized by the Open Software Foundation, they are used across many databases, programming languages, and networks to identify objects.

While UUIDs are not guaranteed to be unique, you are statistically more likely to be hit by a meteorite than you are to create a duplicate UUID.

If you are going to be deploying your beacons for a serious application, you will probably want to choose a UUID to identify your beacons that is unique to your application. That way your app will only be alerted to the presence of beacons you own and care about. If you were to use the default UUID, your app would be alerted by the presence of beacons that had nothing to do with your intended use. In a world with iBeacons deployed in vast numbers everywhere we go, the battery life of handsets would be hammered if every beacon woke up every beacon-aware app that was resident on people's phones.

So how do you decide what your UUID should be and how do you make sure that number is unique? Unfortunately, there isn't a central registry of UUIDs to ensure your number is unique. And making a number up such as 11111111-1111-1111-1111-111111111111 or FFFFFFFF-FFFF-FFFF-FFFF-FFFFFFFFFFFF isn't a good idea; someone will already have used that one. Fortunately, you can use a utility to come up with a UUID that is fairly random. The theory is, given that between a series of 0s and all those Fs there are 340,282,366,920,938,463,463,374,607,431,768,211,456 possibilities, a random number is probably going to be unique.

Mac users can use the terminal command to get to a $ command prompt and type uuidgen to do this (as illustrated in Figure 5-6).

Figure 5-6. *Output of the uuidgen command from the Mac OS X terminal window*

Otherwise, you can go to https://www.uuidgenerator.net to generate your unique UUID (see Figure 5-7).

Online UUID Generator

Your Version 4 UUID:

99460c9c-2191-4694-803f-adba5049a1af

Refresh page to generate another.

Figure 5-7. *Output from the www.uuidgenerator.net UUID generator*

Major and Minor Device Numbers

The other two numbers used to identify an iBeacon are its major and minor device numbers.

Figure 5-8 shows a beacon configuration app (from Estimote) that is displaying the UUID and the major and minor device numbers of a beacon that has been sighted.

Figure 5-8. *Estimote beacons are managed via an app that displays their identifiers, the UUID, major and minor device numbers, and their MAC address*

The idea behind having these two numbers in addition to the UUID is that they can provide a hierarchy that can be used to organize an addressing scheme for multiple locations within an organization. This can be likened to our addressing scheme for traditional "snail mail" letters. Similar to the UUID, one's country is the root of the hierarchy, with town (comparable to the major device number) coming next, and then street (the minor device number). Combining them lets you identify a precise subset of beacons within a vast network.

Table 5-1. *iBeacon Identification*

Name	Size	Description
UUID	16 bytes	Identify owner's organization
Major device	2 bytes: 0 to 65,535	Top of the organization's hierarchy
Minor device number	2 bytes: 0 to 65,535	Index within the major number

As shown in Figure 5-9, if McDonald's were to deploy beacons, they might choose a random UUID, such as `34A5E9EF-7E09-4BCE-8D52-81357FA57AF3`, to identify all their iBeacons. Then the major device number might correspond to a specific location (36374 for Rancho Bernardo, CA) and the minor number might correspond to the logical location of the beacon within their stores.

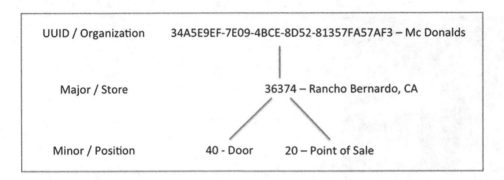

UUID / Organization	34A5E9EF-7E09-4BCE-8D52-81357FA57AF3 – Mc Donalds
Major / Store	36374 – Rancho Bernardo, CA
Minor / Position	40 - Door 20 – Point of Sale

Figure 5-9. *UUID, major, minor hierarchy example*

A minor device number of 10 could correspond to the first drive-through lane, 20 could correspond to the first point of sale terminal inside the store, 30 could correspond to the drink fountain, 40 could correspond to the front door, and 50 could correspond to a beacon placed in the seating area.

If this McDonald's app was triggered by a beacon at the door, identified by 34A5E9EF-7E09-4BCE-8D52-81357FA57AF3, 36374, 40 at 12:05 pm, and then was triggered by another beacon at the point of sale, identified by 34A5E9EF-7E09-4BCE-8D52-81357FA57AF3, 36374, 20 at 12:15pm, you could infer that it had taken a customer 10 minutes to be served by finding the difference between the times at which the customer was sighted by the door beacon and by the POS beacon.

Of course, while inside the store, the McDonald's app would probably detect all of the beacons. It would then need to use the relative signal strength of the uniquely identified beacons (using the major and minor device numbers) to infer the customer's position within the store.

Figure 5-10. *An example of identity masking*

Masking Your UUID

Having beacons broadcast three numbers (UUID and major and minor device number) to identify themselves is an elegant and simple idea. Knowing these numbers, multiple apps can use the same beacons to trigger actions when those beacons become visible. What could possibly go wrong?

As it turns out, quite a lot. These numbers are being broadcast "in the clear," unencrypted, so any application can read them, whether the owner of the beacon likes it or not. So in addition to the apps the beacon owner writes, these identifiers can be viewed by a myriad of Bluetooth scanning utilities using the CoreBluetooth libraries available on the Apple App Store, as well as apps that might choose to use this information against the beacon owner's interests.

Showrooming and Piggybacking

The nightmare example of this scenario is known as "showrooming," where ecommerce retailers make use of a brick and mortar competitor's store to influence the purchasing decisions of a prospective customer. And just when that customer is about to buy, they could steal the deal. Theoretically, an ecommerce retailer like Amazon could program their mobile app to look out for iBeacons that Best Buy, the electronics retailer, had deployed to work with their own mobile app. If Best Buy put iBeacons in their TV department to trigger the displays of specific offers and product information for customers looking at those products, the Amazon app could also wake up and engage Best Buy's customers with a lower priced offer to buy the same TV online. Best Buy gets to pay for the show room, the inventory and the staff, and in this example Amazon gets the deal without having to cover those costs.

Another example of unauthorized use of beacons where a third party is "piggybacking" their application onto the infrastructure funded by a retailer might be an app from a product manufacturer, such as Sony. If Sony provided you with a free app that could act as a remote control for your Sony TV, the app could also look out for the Best Buy beacon in the TV department and engage you if it looks like you are shopping for another TV. Best Buy would probably feel like they should get some compensation for providing that infrastructure to Sony, especially if they want to promote a competitive brand in situations where they are benefiting from better profit margins from that manufacturer.

Spoofing

Another potential problem with these UUIDs being in the clear is that, once the addresses are known, they can be reproduced by programing a duplicate set of beacons with the same numbers. If an app has been developed to offer prizes, coupons, or other value to a user as a reward for going to a specific location, the app can be tricked into thinking that the user has gone to the location when they have not.

An example of this is in the context of an exhibit hall, where visitors are being incentivized to visit certain booths. An app might see a beacon, recognize the UUID and the major and minor device numbers, and determine that the user is standing in an exhibition hall in the Las Vegas convention center, even if the user is sitting on his sofa at home.

This happened with a scavenger hunt at the Consumer Electronics Show (CES) in 2014. Visitors were being encouraged to visit a range of booths where they would check in and their app would register their presence and award a badge. After collecting a full set of badges, the visitor could collect a prize. Unfortunately for the booth owners, the minor numbers that distinguished the different booths were sequential from 65001 to 65009. Knowing this, programming a beacon to spoof these addresses was easy. A large number of apps on the app store allow you to turn your phone into an iBeacon, enabling you to set any UUID and major and minor device number to be broadcast in seconds. This method of completing the scavenger hunt would have been a lot less tiring for visitors than walking the halls of the exhibition center, but would have robbed the booth owners of the opportunity to make their pitch.

However, for this exact reason, the CES Scavenger Hunt used a secondary auditing system (collecting timestamps of when the beacon was sighted) to increase the confidence that contestants actually went to all the targets. The system could still be spoofed, but it would require quite a bit more conniving and manipulating, making it hardly worth the effort.

The risk of spoofing undermines the case for using what we will call "vanilla" iBeacons—plain beacons with nothing added—in environments where value is being exchanged for the simple knowledge that the customer showed up, and was in a given place at a given time. Most retailers would be unwilling to offer discounts, coupons, or loyalty points if they were unsure the data they were getting about the customer's presence was reliable.

As far as the showrooming risk is concerned, this is serious too. No executive at a retailer wants to announce a cutting edge proximity-marketing app, only to be seen to be helping their competitors. The leadership of retailers like Best Buy has already been purged as a result of not dealing with the most basic showrooming threat: customers using their Amazon app in stores to price compare. How much more damaging will the problem be when it's magnified by regular location-specific reminders to do this even more?

Showrooming is less of an issue if the retailer is vertically integrated. That is, they manufacture the products they are selling themselves, like American Apparel, whose stores sell the T-shirts that are made exclusively in American Apparel factories. Retailers like this don't mind so much where you buy your American Apparel T-shirt. Now, let's think, which other retailers are vertically integrated? Ah, yes. Apple.

This leaves the beacon manufacturers in a bit of a bind. On one hand, they want to have the marketing boost of claiming Apple iBeacon compatibility, and they want to get the benefit of the enhancements in iOS afforded to iBeacons. On the other hand, many want to solve the showrooming and spoofing issue. What to do?

Defeating the Spoofers

The solution that some beacon vendors have adopted is to blend a proprietary non-iBeacon packet piggybacked along with the standard iBeacon packet.

If the iBeacon UUID and major and minor device numbers are left to a default value, and are the same on all the beacons dotted around a venue, they no longer provide much useful information. The real information about the identity of the beacon can then be hidden in a proprietary packet that is broadcast separately.

Another approach to this obfuscation is to rotate the values of the UUID and the major and minor device numbers based on a predetermined sequence that uses a secret private key that resides on the beacon. The app that sees these values then calls up to a cloud service that resolves the ever-changing numbers and converts them to another ID that the app can use to figure out which beacon it is talking to. To any unauthorized app that doesn't have the benefit of this cloud service, the UUID just looks like a constant stream of changing numbers. Any map of UUIDs in a store becomes useless shortly after the UUID is recorded.

This approach to resolving a dynamic ID to a constant, static address is similar to the way the Internet works with Domain Name Servers (DNS). We expect www.google.com to be a consistent URL address, but the underlying IP address of the server we connect to can change. That mapping is done for us by the DNS.

Being Connected Becomes More Important

The downside of this approach is that the app relies on being able to make calls up to the cloud in order to make sense of the beacon UUID. With a vanilla iBeacon, connectivity is not required in order to read the UUID. The beacon can be identified in an underground bank vault, in the middle of the desert, or in a remote Walmart with no cell coverage or Wi-Fi. This downside isn't as significant as it might seem, given that most apps already require connectivity for other reasons that are central to their operation, e.g. the ability to pull down product information, offers, or payment authentication via the cloud. For situations where disconnected operation is essential, it is possible for the app to pre-cache the information required to resolve the identity of the beacon in advance of losing wireless contact.

The upside of requiring a cloud connection with your beacon is that you insert a point in its architecture to be able to record the app's location events. This can become the cornerstone of analytics services, pricing models based on number of location triggers and the ability to piggyback a whole range of other cloud-based services, from configuration management and over-the-air firmware updates to advertising.

Received Signal Strength Indication (RSSI)

The measurement of signal strength is central to the way Bluetooth beacons work. At a high level, it's simple. When your mobile device detects a beacon, if the signal is strong, then you know you are close to the beacon. If the signal is weak, you are farther away.

Figure 5-11. *A meter measuring signal strength in dB*

Let's double-click on that. There are some more complex factors that impose fundamental constraints that should be understood by business and technical people alike. Invest a bit of time understanding this and you can avoid misconceptions that impact the user experience, the business model, and operational considerations. Skim this section at your own peril. The simple view of measuring signal strength can be thought of like those hide-and-seek games most of us played as children. As you get closer to the thing you are looking for, your friend is shouting at you, "You're cold, you're getting warmer, warmer, you're hot, you're on fire!" In fact, that's about as accurate as you may be able to get in many situations when using beacons. See how Gimbal's app conveys the cold, warm, hot measures in Figure 5-12. Don't expect your beacon app to act like a tape measure with centimeter) accuracy at all times.

Figure 5-12. The Gimbal app displaying the signal strength of a beacon: one inch away from the phone, eight feet away, and 50 feet away

Even though they only have limited accuracy, don't despair. Beacons have a lot of strengths to make up for these limitations. There are techniques that can mitigate the issue and, if need be, there are alternative technologies that we can pull from our "proximity solution kit bag" to work in conjunction with beacons when needed. For most simple uses, though, high levels of accuracy aren't required. Which is good, because all those alternative tools have their own limitations and costs, making it important to understand which tool to use and when.

We will go into a number of these other tools later in this book in the chapter that covers alternative technologies.

Non-Linear

The first detail to understand is that there isn't a linear relationship between signal strength and distance. Rather, signal strength and distance have a logarithmic relationship. So the farther you are from a beacon, the less accuracy you will get; the closer you are, the more accuracy you will have. So when someone asks, "How accurate is a Bluetooth beacon at measuring distances?", the answer depends on how close you are to the beacon. There isn't a single answer that can be given in feet and inches. The farther away you are from the beacon, the less accuracy you will have. You can detect the difference between a phone being one inch versus twelve inches from a beacon, but you can't tell the difference between a phone that is 19 feet versus 20 feet away from a beacon.

The Medium Impacts the Message

Another factor that impacts the signal strength is the medium that the signal is traveling through. Lower frequencies of radio signal are better at penetrating through mass. Bluetooth operates at a 2.4GHz frequency, which is a high frequency with a lot of hertz, or cycles per second. Mobile phone carriers consider the lower frequency spectrum more valuable, but they have to pay more for it. The 2.4GHz bands, on the other hand, are free, but you get what you pay for. One of the consequences of using this high frequency spectrum is that, if you wrap your hand around a beacon or stand between a Bluetooth beacon and someone's phone, you will significantly decrease the strength of the signal that gets through. That drop in signal could be misinterpreted as meaning that the phone is farther away from the beacon.

Figure 5-13 provides an illustration of the last two topics we have been discussing. You can see that when the Bluetooth signal is traveling through air, the difference in signal strength between zero and ten feet is over 20dB, while the difference between 20 and 30 feet is about half that. When we get out to 60 versus 70 feet, there is no difference. We also see that when you stick a person in the way of the signal, at 10 feet we measure a similar signal strength to what we were getting at 15 feet when there was only air between the phone and beacon. So in our app, we don't know if we are 10 feet away or 15 feet away. The takeaway from this is that it becomes very important to be conscious of where we place the beacons in order to minimize the effects of interference from people's bodies, or to account for that in the way the app is designed. We will get back to this later.

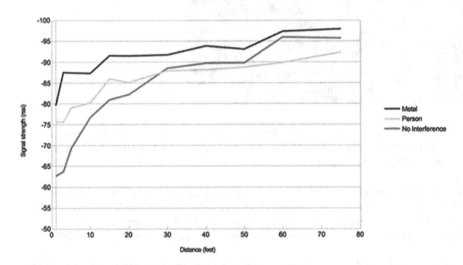

Figure 5-13. *Signal attenuation as distance increases differs depending on the interference from objects Courtesy of Shane Russell and ThoughtWorks* www.thoughtworks.com

Water is an effective signal shield. The fact that our bodies contain so much water explains why our presence attenuates the Bluetooth signals so much.

Notice also that the introduction of metal objects makes an even bigger impact on the attenuation (reduction) of signal strength. That metal could be in the shape of shelving, a milk shake machine, or even the metal in the walls of an office. Placing a metal plate in the path of the signal made the beacon appear to be another ten feet away.

It's important not to be discouraged by these factors, because, while they can create problems, they also create opportunities to control where the signal goes. For instance, if you want to stop the Bluetooth signal from spilling outside a store, using metal objects to shape the signal can be a helpful tool.

Decibels (dB)

Those of you who are more detail orientated will have noticed the vertical scale on our signal/distance graph is made up of negative numbers, which can be a bit off-putting.

Figure 5-14. *A drill sergeant transmits a signal at a high number of decibels with a minimum of signal attenuation due to the close proximity of the receiver* http://commons.wikimedia.org/wiki/File:Drill_ Sergeant_Shouting_Orders_MOD_45155579.jpg

Bluetooth signal strength is measured in decibels, or dB for short. This unit of measure was named in honor of Alexander Graham Bell, the Scotsman credited with inventing the first practically used telephone, and whose name the Bell Telephone Company, now AT&T, adopted. A decibel is one tenth of a Bel. In the context of Bluetooth beacons, dB should more precisely be expressed as dBm (sometimes dBmW) or decibel-milliwatts.

It's worth getting comfortable with this form of measurement and the strange negative numbers used to quantify signal strength, because a lot of the apps that measure Bluetooth beacon signals will quantify their measurements in dBm.

The key thing to remember is that more dBms mean more signal, which implies closer proximity. In the graph in Figure 5-13, the strongest signal we see is -63dBm and the weakest signal is -97.

So when you look at your beacon measurement app, remember that -63 is a bigger number than -97, despite the way graphs are often plotted.

The values are negative because the numbers are a tiny fraction of a milliwatt. Decibels use a logarithmic scale where the dBm value is a power of 10. With a log 10 scale, a value of -2dBm represents 10 to the -2 of the power we are measuring, put another way 10^{-2} or 0.01. A negative dBm means that you're applying a negative "exponent" or "power of" in your power calculations. -10dBm equals 0.1mW, -20dBm equals 0.01mW, and -30 equals, you guessed it, 0.001mW.

The other noteworthy implication of this is that if your signal went from -63dBm to -73dBm, the drop was a lot bigger than it may appear.

Calibrating Signal Strength

We are starting to see that there are more variables than simple proximity that affect the signal strength a mobile device receives from a beacon. An obvious factor to consider is the strength of the radio signal that is broadcast by the beacon in the first place. This can vary depending on the amount of electrical power that the beacon uses to broadcast via its tiny antenna.

Given that battery power needs to be conserved to extend the shelf life of the beacon, a beacon may be configured to transmit with lower power. Although this economy may not be necessary if the beacon is USB-powered rather than powered by a small battery.

The decision to reduce transmission power can be driven by factors other than battery conservation; factors such as the "use-case"[7] (i.e. the desired user experience) are also important considerations. Enabling detection of the beacon at long distances may not be necessary or desirable. For example, when a beacon is being used at a point of sale, where the phone will be waved over the beacon to indicate that the owner of the phone wants to pay with a digital wallet. Not only is the necessary range very small in this case, it may be that we also want to avoid the signal being detected by customers' phones that are next to other point of sale terminals.

Another factor is the efficiency of the antenna. Antenna design is an art and a science. The size, shape, composition, circuitry, and location of an antenna are all factors. All beacons are not created equal in this respect.

Given that the signal strength transmitted by the beacon can vary for any number of reasons, Apple included a Received Signal Strength Indicator (RSSI) parameter in the iBeacon packet that the beacon sends. The value of this field should be set when the beacon is deployed, based on the results of a calibration process that measures the strength of the signal received from one meter away. So if the beacon's signal strength is reduced to save battery, the new signal should be measured as part of a calibrating process and the RSSI number should be reduced accordingly. In this way, beacons with different characteristics and from different manufacturers can be used without the variations in the signal strength causing inconsistent behavior in the apps being triggered by them.

Different Phones for Different Folks

One more inconsistency to beware of is that different phones report different signal strengths from the same beacon. This can be a function of differences in antenna and other circuitry in the phone and of the different techniques implemented by the firmware and operating system software to measure the signal.

The graph in Figure 5-15 comparing Apple's iPhone versus the Google and Samsung Android devices shows different signal strengths measured from the same beacon. It also shows a difference in the consistency of the signal; with Google's Nexus 4 being the least consistent at the time this analysis was done.

---

[7]"A *use-case* is a written description of how users will perform tasks on your web site [or mobile app]. It outlines, from a user's point of view, a system's behavior as it responds to a request. Each use-case is represented as a sequence of simple steps, beginning with a user's goal and ending when that goal is fulfilled." www.usability.gov/how-to-and-tools/methods/use-cases.html

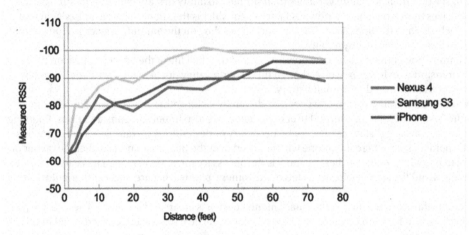

Figure 5-15. *Signal strength as measured by different phones*
Courtesy of Shane Russell and ThoughtWorks www.thoughtworks.com

There may be better alignment of the performance of these systems so the numbers become more similar in the future, or maybe some entrepreneur will publish information that helps software developers abstract the difference. In the short term the software developer can reduce the number of phones supported to those whose Bluetooth performance can be measured and calibrated using in-house methods, accept the variability in the design of their software, or be coarse-grained about the signal levels that they pay attention to.

Signal Fluctuation

A phenomenon that will test both the skill and sanity of the beacon software deployer is signal fluctuation. This is particularly vexing when the participants in the system—beacon and mobile phone—are stationary, but the signal is still fluctuating. This can be measured with the mobile app tools provided by beacon vendors, which will typically display a dynamic readout of the signal strength from the beacon. Figure 5-12 shows the Gimbal app's presentation of the signal strength both in terms of a color indicator and the dBm. The dBm number was rising and falling even when there was no movement between the beacon and the phone. Figure 5-16 indicates the magnitude of those fluctuations over time.

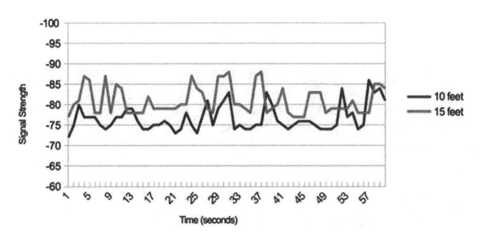

Figure 5-16. *Signal strength over time between a beacon at 10 feet and 15 feet away from a phone; with no smoothing, the signal fluctuates significantly*
Courtesy of Shane Russell and ThoughtWorks www.thoughtworks.com

The reason for this lack of stability is that the Bluetooth signal is subject to interference and phenomena like multi-pathing, where a signal from a single source can arrive via more than one path due to signals bouncing off other objects along the way. Occurrences of multi-pathing are not confined to Bluetooth signals, as it affects many other sorts of wireless signals such as LTE, where a subscriber making a call indoors can have the signal from the cell tower arrive via more then one route. One route might be through a doorway, while another might be through a window. Those two paths can actually be used to increase the throughput of LTE by sending additional data along the additional path. However in the case of Bluetooth beacons, it results in confusion, with signal strengths jumping up and down when they should be stable.

One way to address this issue, which is sometimes adopted by beacon manufacturers in their SDK, is to smooth the signal by taking samples over time and averaging the result reported to the application. Figure 5-17 shows the effect of such an approach using a three-second smoothing window.

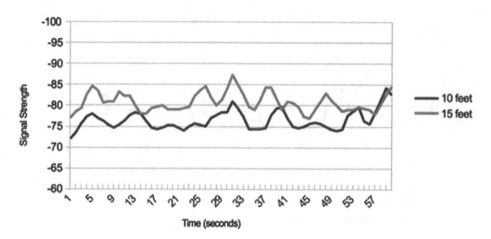

Figure 5-17. *Signal strength over time between a beacon at 10 feet and 15 feet away from a phone; with smoothing enabled, the signal fluctuation is reduced*
Courtesy of Shane Russell and ThoughtWorks www.thoughtworks.com

Of course, as they say, there is no such thing as a free lunch, so there is a tradeoff in doing this smoothing over time. The smoothing introduces a latency that is proportionate to the time intervals over which the smoothing takes place. If the smoothing is done over a relatively long period of time, say ten seconds, then we can expect a very smooth signal, but will also have introduced an up to ten second delay before the signal strength can be reported. Such a delay will lose valuable responsiveness to movements that may be required to trigger an event such as a tap with a phone to complete a payment.

If you are bringing your phone into close proximity with a beacon to indicate that you want to purchase an item, a 10 second delay is likely to be unacceptable. So, in many instances, the smoothing window will need to be performed over a shorter period of time.

Advertising Frequency

The data that a beacon broadcasts is referred to as an advertising packet, because there is very little content contained in the packet. By broadcasting their UUID and major and minor device numbers, they are simply sending alerts to mobile applications that might be listening for them, signaling that the beacon is present.

A key parameter for the developer to decide on is how often the beacon should transmit its advertisement packet, in other words, the frequency of transmission. Mind you, this frequency typically ranges between once a second and ten times a second. This is not to be confused with the frequency of the spectrum that Bluetooth uses. You don't have any control over that.

It's worth taking a few moments to get comfortable with how this advertising frequency is described and what the factors are that impact the settings you might choose. This parameter impacts the uses that the beacon can be put to and the life of the battery. The more rapidly the beacon is set to broadcast, the faster it will burn through the life of its battery.

The frequency is often measured is in terms of milliseconds. There are 1,000 milliseconds in a second. So if a beacon is broadcasting 10 times a second, it can be said to be broadcasting every 100 milliseconds. If you set it to broadcast five times a second, it can be said to be broadcasting every 200 milliseconds, or at 5 hertz. Figure 5-18 encapsulates a digression on the origins of that term.

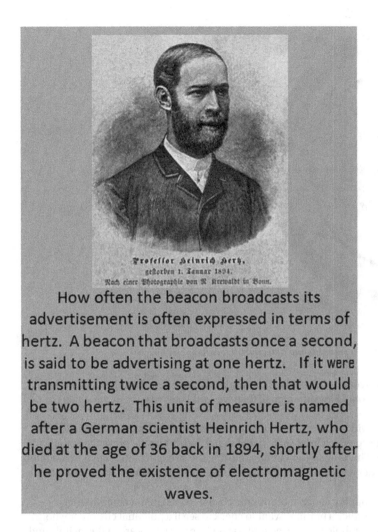

How often the beacon broadcasts its advertisement is often expressed in terms of hertz. A beacon that broadcasts once a second, is said to be advertising at one hertz. If it were transmitting twice a second, then that would be two hertz. This unit of measure is named after a German scientist Heinrich Hertz, who died at the age of 36 back in 1894, shortly after he proved the existence of electromagnetic waves.

Figure 5-18. *Heinrich Hertz*

So if increasing the frequency of broadcast depletes the life of the battery faster, why do it? There are a couple of good reasons. The most obvious one is that if the subject being measured is traveling at high speed, like kids entering a school—no, forget that, like kids *leaving* a school—then there is a chance that a beacon broadcasting infrequently might miss registering their presence altogether. How could this be? Imagine a scenario in which a beacon in a child's backpack transmits a signal to be registered by a hub near the entrance to the school. This hub will have a finite detection range. So if the kid happens to be running along the outer edges of that range, and if he is moving fast, it is entirely possible that he will pass through the detection area in the window between iterations of the beacon's broadcast. Such a case would let the child through without being registered by the hub.

Alternatively, imagine we are watching Robert Mitchum in "The Enemy Below," one of those old World War II movies where the destroyers are trying to hunt down the submarines using radar (similar to Figure 5-19). If the sub is far away and trying to slip past Robert Mitchum and his crew, Radarman Andrews has to really be paying attention, otherwise the sub may show up once on the edge of the radar screen and then disappear again. If the radar is scanning more frequently, Andrews is much more likely to see the sub.

Figure 5-19. *An iconic representation of a signal being detected on a radar screen*

Back to the beacons and real-life scenarios. If the kid is running and there are also other kids in the way, or there are walls and doors that could block the signal, then we could be in trouble if the signal isn't broadcast frequently enough.

Other factors can cause our brief window of exposure to a beacon signature to be missed. The signal smoothing, for instance, may cause us to miss a brief spike in the signal, indicating the presence of the beacon at the periphery of our range. This is an argument for adjusting the strength of the signal transmitted by the beacon to the maximum, in order to extend those fleeting moments to be sustained long enough to persist through the smoothing process.

Let's think about this issue in a shopping context. Brands may be interested in tracking whether a shopper has come into view of their product. They may want to check to see if a potential customer who can see their display is attracted by the graphic being used and walks closer, or if they are in the vicinity and then move away. This could provide clues about the effectiveness of the display in attracting different kinds of customers. We could combine demographics gathered elsewhere in the app with the proximity data, and might see that men are attracted by a certain display, but women of a certain age are not.

If the beacon isn't broadcasting frequently, by the time we have dumbed down the fidelity of the signal with frequency smoothing and factored in some other issues we will cover shortly, we might entirely miss the presence of the fast moving shopper who was near our display and then walked away.

Of course it isn't as simple as that. There is another factor: the mobile device that is scanning for the advertising packets doesn't necessarily scan all the time. Phones have batteries too and if the Bluetooth radio on the phone were constantly scanning, that battery would be depleted pretty fast.

With iOS, if the process that is looking for the beacon is running in the background, the scanning will become less frequent. Apple doesn't tell us how often iOS scans, but it recommends that the beacons broadcast 10 times a second in order for the signals to be detected reliably. If your app has control of the screen and is scanning for a beacon, it will generally be detected a lot more quickly than if the app is in the background while another app is active.

By meditating on Figure 5-20 you can see how the more frequently the beacon broadcasts, the shorter the window is that the handset operating system needs to scan for in order to be sure of sighting the beacon. In effect, we are trading the battery life of the beacon for the battery life of the phone. Frequent beacon broadcasts enable shorter background scans from iOS.

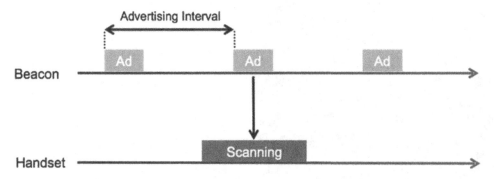

Figure 5-20. *Beacon advertising intervals coinciding with scans from a phone*

An app running in the background is like if Radarman Andrews keeps dozing off while on watch. He jolts awake with sudden awareness every so often, but immediately finds his eyelids growing heavy again, making him much less likely to detect the enemy sub on the radar screen as a result. What should we do to mitigate this problem? One thing would be to try to get users of the app into the foreground with functionality that is amusing or useful. Alternatively, we could broadcast our advertising packet more often (ten times a second rather than once a second) so that the beacon is more likely to be spotted when the operating system occasionally wakes the process up to check for beacons.

Lastly, if we increase the frequency of broadcast then this provides more data for the signal smoothing that we described earlier to operate on, so the accuracy and consistency of the signal can be increased.

Region Monitoring

By this point in the chapter it's probably become clear that, while Bluetooth beacons have some exciting properties, centimeter accuracy across all distances is not one of them. To accommodate that reality, Apple developed a model for alerting apps based on a much coarser grain measure of proximity. When an iOS app wants to be notified of the proximity of a beacon, it gets to monitor four regions: Immediate, Near, Far, and Unknown. If an app says, "Alert me if I'm in the immediate proximity of a beacon with the UUID x," this corresponds to a proximity of half a meter or less; Near corresponds to 2 meters, and Far corresponds to up to 30 meters away. Unknown is exactly that: we think a beacon with a desired UUID is there, but the errors from the packets don't give us a clear sense of how close the beacon is, so it's probably not very close.

In the Apple documentation, these regions are presented in a diagram that makes them seem comparable in size. Figure 5-21 is drawn to scale so you can see that this isn't the case.

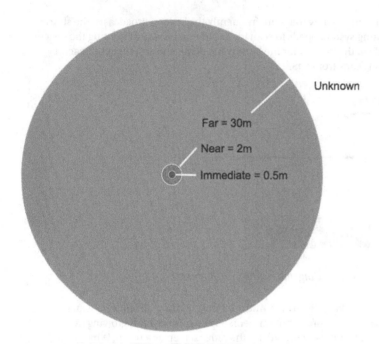

Figure 5-21. *Relative distance of the regions that iOS monitors*

When an app has iOS monitoring regions, a hollow blue arrow will be displayed in the status bar to indicate that some additional battery resources are being consumed, in order to be transparent to the user about what is going on. This is the right thing to do, given region monitoring has both privacy and battery life implications.

Ranging

Ranging is a much more energy-consuming operation, which is generally only allowed when an app is in the foreground, or for a few seconds when a background process has been alerted to entry into a new region. Ranging involves the ongoing monitoring of signal strength in decibels. This allows the app to go beyond the very coarse measure of Immediate, Near, and Far regions and apply logic to translate a given signal strength to a given distance. iOS displays a solid blue arrow in the status bar to indicate that this more battery hungry form of activity is taking place.

Applications that want to do ranging on an ongoing basis when running in the background will need to explicitly request that ability from Apple (in what's called a "plist" file) and will be regarded with some skepticism when going through the approval process in order to get into the App Store. Apple will want to see a compelling reason for consuming those resources before the app will be approved.

Trilateration

One of the approaches to measuring proximity more accurately, beyond applying an average over time, is to look for multiple beacon signals. For instance, there may be beacons in three or more corners of a room, and a mobile device can pick up signals from all of them. This is sometimes referred to as triangulation or, more correctly, trilateration.

Trilateration is the process of determining absolute or relative locations of points by measurement of distances, using the geometry of circles. By combining the signal strength from beacons A, B, and C, as shown in Figure 5-22, we can get a more accurate sense of the user's proximity to each beacon. We can also plot its position on an X and Y axis. In its description of the role of beacons, Apple has designated their use only for proximity (understanding how close a phone is to another object), whereas Wi-Fi would be used for positioning (understanding the longitude and latitude of the phone). This is an artificial distinction.

Figure 5-22. *The signal from beacons A, B, and C can be measured and, through geometry, the position of a mobile device receiving those signals can be estimated*

As of writing this, the Apple APIs are engineered around the proximity use-case, but through the use of ranging and additional software to do the trilateration geometry, beacons can be used for positioning as well. This allows phones to display the user's position relative to a floor plan.

This can be a useful way of guiding a shopper around the store. However, it adds significant complexity to the developer's app and the operational complexity, both of which will increase cost. The location of each beacon needs to be recorded relative to a floor plan, which in turn needs to be anchored to a latitude-longitude position, requiring a lot of extra effort. The deployment of beacons for exact location positioning requires an investment in staffing that will be significant when deciding if the approach is economically viable. It's probably not practical to just mail the beacon to employees in a given branch with instructions to place it behind a certain display. Trilateration will likely require a team familiar with the dynamics of the technology to be dispatched to obtain or create a floor plan, record X, Y, and Z coordinates (latitude, longitude, and height), place the beacons accordingly, and enter that information in an appropriate system. Not the kind of thing store managers across, for instance, a large chain of fast food restaurants can be relied on to do. At least, not without a lot of guidance, support, and training. If you as a solution architect who decides that you need to use multiple beacons, either to achieve greater accuracy in your proximity measurement, or because you want to do positioning, the system complexity can be outsourced to vendors such as indoo.rs and Point Inside, which provide the software tools to perform trilateration and management of the floor plans.

Other middleware vendors, such as the providers of the mobile app BlindSquare, have developed a rules engine that infers the location of the user by using the relative position of beacons. This approach may not yield an exact X/Y location, but the system is remarkably effective. It uses movement relative to the beacons to trigger audio directions to the user. The BlindSquare app provides information to blind people about the locations nearby from the database maintained by FourSquare.

OTHER WAYS OF CALCULATING INDOOR LOCATION

It would be possible for Bluetooth technology to evolve and enable more accurate calculation of where the blue dot should be displayed on a floor plan. It wouldn't be surprising to see these techniques, which have been used with other wireless technologies, to appear as new features in future versions of the Bluetooth standard.

Round trip time (RTT) substitutes a measurement of the time it takes for packets to be sent from transmitter and receiver for the current signal strength measurement we use with Bluetooth 4.0. This is more accurate but is likely to introduce additional cost to the beacon hardware.

Angle of arrival builds on this idea by comparing the timing of packets delivered from different nodes in an antenna array.

Rather than plotting the longitude and latitude of a user, some applications are focused on establishing the relationship between that user and a given product. This could be in order to guide them to it, to see if the packaging has attracted them to it, or to see if a coupon delivered earlier has resulted in a visit to the product on the shelf. To achieve this, other data sets are required, specifically *planograms*. Planograms and other inventory databases record the position of specific products on a shelf and are maintained by the merchandising teams of larger merchants trying to organize and optimize placement of products across their stores.

Use of UUIDs and the 20 Region Limit

iOS limits the number of regions that an application can monitor to 20. A *region* can be a latitude and longitude that is tracked primarily by GPS, or it can be a UUID that the operating system is looking out for. Given that thousands of beacons can share the same UUID, 20 isn't a major limitation, but it's important to understand in order to organize the identification of your beacons so that your system can scale.

If a shopping app, say, is going to work across a large number of different retailers, then those retailers either need to agree that they will use the same UUID, or the app needs to get more sophisticated about rotating UUIDs in and out of the set of 20 that it asks iOS to look out for. This could be done based on an algorithm that anticipates the stores that a shopper is likely to see based on their GPS coordinates.

For example, if there is a region that encompasses the west wing of a shopping mall that has 20 retailers, each with their own beacons, then the app will want to have iOS look for one set of UUIDs. As the shopper gets closer to the east wing of the mall, the set of UUIDs will need to be swapped out for a different set, ones that will correspond to what the shopper may see in the other half of the mall. Like trilateration, this kind of UUID management can be delegated to third-party software.

We have focused on Apple's iBeacon but despite its strength in the U.S. market, over half of the smartphone devices in the rest of the world run Google's Android operating system. Therefore, the next section will look at a beacon API standard that works on this alternative OS.

AltBeacon: An Open Source Standard

by David G. Young, Chief Engineer, Radius Networks, Inc.

The AltBeacon standard (Figure 5-23) is an open source variant that came in response to iBeacon technology. Because Apple's iBeacon is proprietary, the company can impose limits on how it is used by others. Apple sees iBeacon as something that only iOS devices (iPhones, iPads, and iPod touch devices) are allowed to use and enforces this through its iBeacon certification program. This leaves Android devices in the cold.

Figure 5-23. *The AltBeacon logo*

While many people use iBeacon technology on Android devices despite these restrictions, Apple's proprietary approach inspired Radius Networks to create the open AltBeacon standard.

Unlike iBeacon, AltBeacon comes with an open source license, open source code for using it on Android, Windows, and Linux platforms, and detailed open documentation so there is no mystery about how it works.

AltBeacon defines a Bluetooth transmission packet that is different from iBeacon but works the same way, creating interoperability. While supporting a variety of identifier formats, AltBeacon is typically used with a three-part identifier with the same byte lengths as those used on iBeacon. Whereas iBeacon defines a proximity UUIDs and major and minor numbers, with AltBeacon you use Id1, Id2, and Id3, which work exactly the same way.

This provides a way to build a system based on iBeacons and extend it to Android and other platforms besides iOS without violating Apple's intellectual property terms. Most usage is on Android with the open source Android Beacon Library, which provides Android apps with the equivalent beacon functionality that is built into iOS.

Because AltBeacon is a different transmission format from iBeacon, systems using iBeacon on iOS and AltBeacon on Android typically use what's called an interleaving beacon. This is a beacon that sends out two different formats in a single package. Radius Networks' RadBeacon product line puts out transmissions with both the iBeacon and AltBeacon format. Instead of just sending out an iBeacon packet ten times per second, these products alternate between sending out an iBeacon packet and an AltBeacon packet, sending 20 packets per second, one for each packet type. The end result is applications that work cross-platform without intellectual property concerns.

The Locate app shown in Figure 5-24 can identify beacons broadcasting iBeacon and AltBeacon protocol packet or frame types.

Figure 5-24. *Radius Networks Android Locate beacon app*

While its open nature is AltBeacon's primary draw, its toolset provides some significant advantages on the Android platform versus iBeacons on the iOS platform. Working with iBeacons can be frustrating, in part because the closed system documentation is vague. Developers often have to study and reverse-engineer the iBeacon APIs on iOS in order to figure out how they work in specific situations. How long does it take to detect an iBeacon transmission when an app is in the background? When ranging for beacons, what is the averaging interval for the distance estimates? Nobody knows the answer to these questions for sure, and Apple won't say.

With AltBeacon and the Android Beacon Library, there are no mysteries. The answers are fully documented, and the source code is there for everybody to see.

This open nature lends itself to great flexibility. The Android Beacon Library lets you decode a wide variety of beacons (even proprietary ones like iBeacon) if you provide it with the format. It then allows you to detect any beacon even if you don't know its proximity UUID up front. This is something that iOS won't let you do; it only lets you see your own beacons or those whose identifiers you know up front. The Locate Beacon app for Android is based on this technology and demonstrates this ability. Going further, it can even report the location of beacons it discovers to an online database called WikiBeacon.org, which maps known locations of beacons worldwide.

The Android platform lets you do other interesting things with beacons that iOS does not. On Android, an app can continuously range for beacons in the background, allowing an app to spring to life when the phone is a specific distance from a beacon. And unlike iOS, an app can launch itself to a full screen view on these events.

With the release of Android 5, apps can also transmit as beacons, even when in the background. This makes Android 5 tablets an alternative to physical beacons for retail and other applications where tablets are present anyway. Simply turn on a free transmitter app (such as Locate Beacon) in the background and go about your business.

While most of its use is on Android, AltBeacon is a cross-platform standard. Implementations exist on Linux, and small Raspberry Pi computers are sometimes used as beacon transmitters and detectors. A Windows Beacon Library is available in pre-release and will allow detection of beacons with the release of Windows 10, which is the first Windows version with full Bluetooth low-energy support.

Google's Eddystone

Two years after Apple launched iBeacon, Google was missing from the beacon battlefield. At a time when Android enjoyed a 78%[8] share of the smartphone market globally, the lack of any formal endorsement of the beacon paradigm from Google raised doubts as to whether beacons were here to stay. In the United States, Android's market share was more evenly balanced at 53.1% versus iOS at 41.6%[9]. This combined with the fact that iPhones tended to be adoption by more wealthy users and Apple's prestige among retailers allowed brands and agencies to ignore Google's absence and to adopt an Apple-only solution. To fill the void, beacon vendors provided their own Android APIs as a stopgap.

EDDYSTONE LIGHTHOUSE

The lighthouse is a great metaphor for the way Bluetooth beacons work. They broadcast their signal without any connection and offer a scalable way of alerting people to their proximity.

Eddystone Lighthouse is not to be confused with Edison Lighthouse, the one-hit wonder group that enjoyed Top 10 popularity in 1970 with "Love Grows (Where My Rosemary Goes)". The group were named after the lighthouse, but were a lot less durable.

The name is said to derive from "stone of the eddies" or turbulent water. Many (but not all) British people pronounce it as "ediston".

If Eddystone Lighthouse was a software project, it would be version 4.0.

Version 1.0 was built in 1698. When Louis XIV heard that one of his men had taken the builder prisoner, he is said to have ordered his release with the phrase, "France is at war with England, not with humanity". Alas, the tower and its builder were swept away in a storm five years after it was built.

Version 2.0 was made of wood and burnt down. Version 3.0 started to wobble and was moved to the main land preemptively. The stump remains, next to 4.0, which was constructed in 1880. It is now unmanned and has a helipad on its roof to enable maintenance.

What Was Google Up To?

There were rumors that Google was going to do something. Beacon manufacturers had been receiving orders for large numbers of beacons from different groups within the Googleplex, but there had been no beacon announcements during the two Google I/O developer conferences following Apple's announcement. Beacon manufacturers' own libraries allowed Android smartphones to respond to the same beacons used to

---

[8] http://www.idc.com/prodserv/smartphone-os-market-share.jsp
[9] https://www.comscore.com/Insights/Market-Rankings/comScore-Reports-March-2015-US-Smartphone-Subscriber-Market-Share

trigger apps on iOS. However, these lacked some of the core OS support that enabled more efficient scanning of beacons in the background. Google's Bluetooth stack improved in 5.0 of Android to fill this gap, but there was still no endorsement from Google or integration with other parts of the Android OS.

There was one interesting initiative that could be attributed to Google. Scott Jensen, a Google user experience expert, had left Google, worked at Frog Design, one of the Bay Areas' leading agencies, and returned to initiate an open source project called "The Physical Web". This defined a standard for UriBeacons that broadcast URLs to browser apps. It relied on users taking the initiative to browse these URLs when they wanted to interact with objects or appliances in the Physical Web. This was a very different approach to iBeacons that could trigger actions in a broad variety of apps with no user intervention. The fact that this wasn't an officially endorsed project by Google and there were no hooks into Android, or its apps such as Chrome, contributed to an air of uncertainty about the project.

On the other hand, when analyzing the opportunity, Google seemed, if anything, to be better placed to capitalize on the Bluetooth beacon trend. Surely the largest provider of web and mobile advertising services could monetize the ability to better target mobile ads and use beacons for attribution, in other words to measure the effectiveness of those ads. As the leader in maps, surely Google could benefit from being able to enhance the ability to map indoor locations. In retrospect, the obvious answer was that it could indeed.

On July 14 2015, the uncertainty ended. Google saw Apple's bet on Bluetooth beacons and raised the stakes with a mountain of chips that dwarfed the original iBeacon specification. Their beacon offering was named Eddystone, after the first offshore lighthouse in the world, situated in the English Channel, 13 miles south west of Plymouth. Their announcement included not just commitments to support from third-party beacon manufacturers, but shipping products from six major producers of hardware (Bkon, Bluevision, Estimote, Kontakt.io, Radius Networks, and Signal 360).

Apple's iBeacon approach had been minimalist, with just enough technology to provide the foundations for the ecosystem and convey the possibilities of beacon use-cases. Apple left lots of space for third parties to fill in the gaps. Google, on the other hand, studied the ecosystem created by Apple and identified interesting gaps that could be filled. As a result, Eddystone provides a more comprehensive foundation, while also cherry-picking some additional lucrative areas beyond that basic OS foundation that would benefit their business.

Google has tried to contrast its approach to beacons by positioning it as being more open than Apple's. Rather than secret specifications for Beacon OEMs secured by non-disclosure agreements, Google has made the protocol a GitHub open source project. The Eddystone protocol specification is there for all to see, but rather like Android, it maintains control of the open source project through proprietary apps and services.

Another major contrast is that Google provides support for its competitor's operating system (iOS) as well as its own (Android).

Eddystone Components

Eddystone consists of four layers of functionality:

- *The Eddystone Protocol*—The packet or frame types that Eddystone beacons send

- *OS Support, Widgets, and APIs*—The root of the power and control for the OS provider

- *Fleet Management and Registry*—The foundation of tracking the location, metadata, and health of beacons, a component absent from iBeacon that is a major source of value

- *Integration with Google Apps*—"Eating your own dog food," Google's iOS and Android apps that use these components

Let's examine these components in more detail.

The Eddystone Protocol

An Eddystone Bluetooth beacon can broadcast four beacon packet types. These are also referred to as "frames" in the Eddystone Protocol Specification[10].

- Eddystone-UID (Unique ID)
- Eddystone-TLM (Telemetry)
- Eddystone-URL (Uniform Resource Locator)
- Eddystone-EID (Ephemeral Identifiers)

Eddystone-UID

Of the three types of Eddystone frame, this is the one that directly corresponds to the functionality of Apple's iBeacon 1.0 packet. It's used to trigger actions in mobile apps that are running in the foreground or background.

While the format is similar to iBeacon, the details of its structure differ sufficiently that the two are not compatible. An iBeacon device can't trigger an Eddystone app and a beacon that is only broadcasting to the Eddystone specification can't trigger an iBeacon app. Beacons need to broadcast both iBeacon and Eddystone-UID frames if they are to trigger actions in both iBeacon and Eddystone apps.

Tx Power

As with iBeacon, Eddystone-UID frames contain a field to allow the calibration of the signal strength that the beacon is using to broadcast. This field contains the signal strength measured from the beacon at zero meters, whereas iBeacons are calibrated at distance of one meter. This value can range from -100dBm up to +20dBm.

UID

Eddystone-UID packets contain a 10-byte UUID that identifies a group of beacons. This corresponds to the iBeacon UUID only it's six bytes shorter.

Google recommend two ways of generating the UID. One is to take the UUID used for the corresponding iBeacon and remove bytes 5 through 10. Alternatively, Google suggests a transformation of the owner's alphanumeric domain name, using a hash algorithm, to create the hexadecimal UID.

Like iBeacon, Eddystone apps can filter the callbacks they receive to wake themselves up using this number, so that unrelated beacons do not trigger the app and waste CPU cycles and battery power on the phone.

Instance ID

The Instance ID identifies the beacon within the UID group. For example, the instance ID might identify the store where the particular beacon is located. iBeacons uses two numbers to do this, the major and minor device number. The six bytes available (two more than provided by Apple's major and minor numbers combined) allow for ample space to construct the kind of hierarchies required to map the beacons within an organization. For example, the first two bytes (ranging in value from 0 to 65,536) might map to the store number; the next two bytes could be used to represent the department in the store; and the last two could identify the logical position within the department, e.g., a point of sale position.

---

[10]https://github.com/google/eddystone/blob/master/protocol-specification.md.

Eddystone-EID

We will discuss the EID (Ephemeral ID) next as it is a variation of UID, in that it triggers actions in apps. The difference being that it does so in a way that supports more privacy and security safeguards than UID.

In our discussion of iBeacon, we explored the issues with piggybacking and spoofing. When a beacon broadcasts a static identifier, this opens up the possibility that others will record and map these and use them for their own purposes or even rebroadcast and forge the identity of the beacon.

Google changes the MAC address and the ID of an ephemeral frame on a regular basis[11] in ways that can only be deciphered by authorized entities, so that unauthorized third parties can't spoof or piggyback.

This capability to obfuscate the ID of a beacon used to be an unusual feature offered only by a handful of beacon vendors such as Gimbal, Swirl, Shopkick, and inMarket. Now it has become quite a common feature. The issue is that the approach to doing this differs between each vendor, thus making the hardware proprietary and eliminating the promise of interoperability, which is fundamental to iBeacon. The vendors advertise they support iBeacon but since iBeacon doesn't address this area, they are bound to make their beacons incompatible with the applications developed for the other vendor's product.

This isn't healthy for customers deploying such systems. They become locked into one vendor's protocol. This also fragments the application ecosystem, increasing porting costs and limiting choice.

For venue owners that invest in iBeacons, it also means that if they wanted iOS apps such as Passbook or Wallet to work with their beacons, they couldn't use rotation of the UUID if they want Passbook/Wallet to detect the beacons.

Eddystone-EID promises to eliminate this unpalatable choice between security and standardization.

The EID feature underpins the control of who can access a beacon and when, which is fundamental to a number of very significant approaches to monetizing beacons. We will explore this important topic further in the chapter that covers beacon networks.

Eddystone-TLM

Management of beacons is another area where beacon manufacturers have had to step in with proprietary methods to monitor the health of the beacons they produce. Eddystone-TLM (telemetry) offers a standardized way for beacons to report battery level, temperature, and the time since power-on or reboot.

Google leaves it up to the OEM to regulate how often the frames are broadcast. The TLM packets are supposed to be interleaved with the other packet types that identify the beacon (UID, EID and URL). Since TLM broadcasts consume power, the frames can be sent quite infrequently. If the beacon will be seen by apps frequently, these broadcasts can be sent less often. Conversely, if the beacon will not be sighted very often, the frequency of TLM broadcasts needs to be increased.

Apps may use an API to relay the telemetry reported in TLM frames to Google's beacon platform. The platform will then analyze the information and predict when the battery will expire, when the beacon has been moved from its registered location and unexpected changes in how often the beacon is being detected (that might indicate problems with the beacon). This analysis is reported via an API (`beacons.diagnostics`).

Eddystone-URL

Eddystone-URL frames include a field to calibrate the power at which the beacon transmits. This works the same way as with Eddystone-URI. The next field is a compressed URL up to 17 bytes in length, for example `https://goo.gl/Aq18zF`. Any URL compression service can be used, including Google's own URL shortener `https://goo.gl`.

---

[11]Typically, EIDs changes pseudo-randomly every 8.5 seconds, although this is configurable and varies slightly in order to enhance security.

Eddystone-URL beacons can be configured using a configuration service that allows beacon URLs to be modified, the frequency of broadcast to be adjusted, and a lock code that secures future changes to the beacon. The beacon enters the configuration mode when power is cycled or a physical configuration button is activated. This button can be physically secured within the case of the beacon.

We will explore the important strategic implications of Eddystone-URL more fully later in this chapter.

Management and Registry

While iBeacon 1.0 leaves the management of beacons to the developer, Eddystone provides important foundational elements to support the registration and monitoring of beacons.

- Proximity Beacon API—The Proximity Beacon API allows a beacon to be registered with Google's beacon cloud service, recording metadata about the beacon such as its location (indoor floor level, longitude, and latitude) and "attachments" that are stored in Google's cloud. Attachments can be arbitrary in their structure but are limited to 1024 bytes in length, so media objects such as images and video would need to be stored in a parallel structure. These attachments can be served only to those of the same Google Developer Console project.

- Place ID—When a beacon location is registered, a Google Place ID can be associated with the beacon and it improves the accuracy of the Google Place Picker widget, which is used by third-party apps and Google apps such as Google Maps to display map information about points of interest. Prior to the launch of Eddystone, Apple had not integrated iBeacons into its own Maps product but subsequent to Google's initiative, they appear to be doing so.

- Registry and Monitoring—In addition to registering Eddystone beacons, the Proximity Beacon API can be used to register and track AltBeacons and iBeacons. This is either very helpful, or cunning, depending on your perspective. Whereas Apple has avoided supporting competitive beacon technology, Google's approach is to encapsulate it into its own ecosystem. Venue owners such as retailers have expressed reservations about registering details of all of their beacons with Google.

Once a beacon is registered, another API (`beacons.diagnostics`) can be used to monitor when the beacon battery is likely to expire and whether the beacon may have been moved.

Nearby Messages API

The Nearby Messages API is Google's recommended method to receive notifications when a beacon is sighted. It works across Android and iOS operating systems. In addition to subscribing to notifications about nearby beacons, the API can be used to subscribe to proximity notifications based on audio signals and Wi-Fi. Filtering just on Bluetooth beacons increases the responsiveness of the notification.

Google Apps

In addition to using beacons to enable better indoor navigation in Google Maps, Google's personal assistant app, Google Now, will use Eddystone beacons to order the cards that it displays to provide contextually relevant information. These cards could correspond to exhibits in a museum, information on exercise machines at a gym, or a menu at a restaurant or a bar.

AltBeacon's Role in a Beacosystem with Eddystone

by David G. Young, Chief Engineer, Radius Networks, Inc.

Eddystone and AltBeacon perform two different roles on Android. A key feature of AltBeacon is that it is interoperable with iBeacon, specifically allowing developers to use the same beacon identifier scheme on Android as they are using on iOS. Because Eddystone does not use the same identifier size (the Eddystone-UID identifier is only a total of only 16 bytes versus 20 bytes for iBeacon and AltBeacon), the same identifiers cannot be used. For solution designers who want to use Eddystone on both iOS and Android this does not pose a problem. But for folks who want to use iBeacon with iOS and have the same solution work on Android, AltBeacon solves the problem.

While Eddystone can work on iOS in some use-cases, use-cases requiring fast background detection will need to use iBeacon. This is because Apple has optimized this with hardware-accelerated Bluetooth LE packet detection for iBeacon that is not available for other beacon types. For such use-cases, Radius expects solution designers to continue to choose an iBeacon/AltBeacon combination and not Eddystone.

Eddystone URL and the Physical Web

This section is based on an article originally published in *GPS Business News*.

The browser model of the Physical Web (Figure 5-25) and the Eddystone URL protocol that forms its foundation could prove to be bigger than the app-centric model of iBeacon in its disruptive role. Let's explore why that is, how Eddystone URL beacons work, and what to expect when you browse the Physical Web.

Figure 5-25. *A tube of three Blesh Physical Web beacons*

The Myth of the Long Tail

The target market for the Physical Web is any and all organizations that don't have the resources, skills, market position, and luck to develop a very successful app. That would be most organizations.

The success of iBeacon is predicated on the success of mobile apps. iBeacons require beacon-aware apps to receive their UUID and major and minor device numbers. With all those apps in the app stores, that seems like a fairly safe bet.

However, the painful truth is that the vast majority of apps are financial failures. Gartner calculated that less than 0.01 percent of consumer mobile apps would be considered a financial success by their developers[12]. Developing a successful major app is like making a major movie: very difficult and very expensive. Most of us only use a handful of apps regularly and with well over a million apps each on the Android and Apple stores, competition is fierce. That's not to say that you can't make money with apps. You can. Big money even. But truth be told, the chances are that it won't be you or me who hits the jackpot.

Is it un-American to talk like this? After all, our society is largely founded on the idea that anyone can be president, be a movie star, or sing to a billion people during the Super Bowl halftime show. Be that as it may, there's no denying that most of us don't get to put our feet up in the Oval office or win an Oscar, let alone fly from a wire around the University of Phoenix stadium with fireworks exploding around us. The most fortunate one percent isn't just a political issue, it's also the way it is in the world of mobile apps. Fortunately, as Americans, we don't let logic get in the way of ambition, so there is very little chance that people will give up innovating and publishing apps, or hitchhiking to Hollywood to start their movie careers. We will continue to have the best looking waiters and waitresses in LA for some time to come.

The exciting thing about Physical Web beacons is that you don't need to be able to write an app to use one. With Eddystone URL, you push a button to get a beacon into setup mode, copy and paste the URL that you want it to broadcast, and the job is done. This is a 10-minute task for a first time user, rather than the weeks and months that are required to write a mobile app.

The Physical Web Experience Is Different

Rather than triggering behavior in custom apps that may be running in the background, Eddystone URL broadcasts short web URIs (Uniform Resource Identifiers) that can be browsed by a general-purpose browser working in the foreground. Eddystone URL relies on more of a pull from the user, scanning their environment rather than the push of an alert from the beacon to user who is not seeing that interaction.

The idea is that this interaction will be enabled by ubiquitous apps like the browser. As part of Google's Eddystone, the Google Chrome browser is becoming Eddystone URL-aware. The first step to that browser integration has taken place not on Android, but in Google Chrome for iOS. As you can see in Figure 5-26, the Chrome "Today Widget" (which can be accessed by swiping down from the top of the screen) has a Physical Web component that displays the URLs broadcast from surrounding beacons. In this case the URLs being broadcast are www.thegoodtraveler.org/#2 and google.github.io/uribeacon. Subsequent to the iOS release, Chrome on Android added support for the Physical Web, as did Opera with the addition of a "Nearby" tab, which shows which beacons are close to you. Another alternative to Chrome is for users to download the Physical Web browser app from the app store or one of the many variants of that browser provided by beacon OEMs.

---

[12]http://www.gartner.com/newsroom/id/2648515

Figure 5-26. *The Chrome for iOS Today widget*

Eddystone URL is not about replacing iBeacon or Eddystone-UID; it's a complementary tool set. Preinstalled apps like Apple Pay/Wallet will leverage beacons more and more as we close the loop between promotions and purchases. For many very successful apps like Facebook, OpenTable, and Shazam and for games that don't translate to the browse environment, the iBeacon app-centric model makes sense. They have broad adoption and can benefit from being able to respond to beacon triggers in the background. It makes sense for Walmart and Target to invest in their own apps, but we know that it doesn't for the other 99% of retailers.

For enterprises that can afford a web site but can't afford a mobile app, Eddystone URL brings them the benefits of digital-to-physical convergence. We should expect tools like WordPress and Adobe Creative Suite to extend the web publishing system to cater to Eddystone URL. These offerings are in a position to tie Physical Web into the digital web publishing tools with which millions of content producers are already familiar.

The Physical Web is an open source project. Visit the GitHub site[13], where you can see who is working on it and see the specification of the Bluetooth packet structure. They have published Android and iOS Physical Web browsers that can also configure the beacons.

---

[13]https://github.com/google/physical-web

Deploying a Physical Web Beacon

One of the most exciting things is that there is so little to do in order to take the first steps. Copy and paste the URL from your existing mobile site into the Physical Web setup tool and you are good to go. From a business perspective, if a new technology can augment an existing ecosystem and make it better, its chances of success are clearly a lot better than one that requires extensive retooling.

Let's get to some specifics of how this works at the moment.

Step 1: Buy a Physical Web Beacon

While most of the major beacon vendors now support the Physical Web as an option, a Turkish vendor called Blesh was one of the first to ship a product. Its packaging consisted of a cardboard tube to ship the beacons (see Figure 5-27), which added to the novelty.

Figure 5-27. *Blesh beacons unboxed*

When you start up the Physical Web browser, you see the beacons as something that looks like a Google search listing, with the page title, URL, and the abstract (which a web page has encoded for search engine optimization). It appears that this metadata is pulled from the Google search catalog. When you update the description for a site in the HTML of the page, the change isn't immediately reflected in the listing that the app displays.

Step 2: Assign a URL

To change the URL that the beacon transmits, you press a reset button on the beacon. With the first Blesh beacons, a screwdriver was required to open the beacon and access that reset button (see Figure 5-28).

Figure 5-28. Inside a Blesh Physical Web beacon

The device is then enabled and the Physical Web browser can be used to update the URL the beacon broadcasts (see Figure 5-29).

Figure 5-29. The Blesh app's Physical Web configuration screen allows the beacon's URL to be set

In order to replicate what a venue such as an airport might want to do, you could simply copy and paste a URL to a YouTube video that explains the background to a piece of artwork on display (see Figure 5-30). To continue the "airport guide" use-case, include the URL to flight information to be broadcast near to the display flight boards. Then include a URL to a book that may be on sale at the airport bookstore.

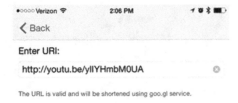

Enter URI:

http://youtu.be/yIIYHmbMOUA

The URL is valid and will be shortened using goo.gl service.

Figure 5-30. *The generic Physical Web app simply also allows the beacon's URL to be set*

Step 3: That's It

The procedure is that simple.

In the case of this example, there are additional parameters that allow you to adjust the standard advertising interval, the signal strength broadcast at various configuration levels (High, Medium, Low, and Lowest), and the ability to password-protect any changes to the configuration.

Links to Media and Devices

You can see how the search results shown in Figure 5-31 could provide a jumping off point to a wealth of information, media, and rich interactive content in the same way the Google results page does today.

Figure 5-31. *The GitHub Physical Web app displays the metadata from three Blesh Physical Web beacons*

However, these links can open up more than media; they can invoke interactive web-based services with devices such as thermostats, vending machines, gas pumps, microwaves, door locks, hot tubs, … the possibilities are enormous.

Critical Success Factors

For Google this makes complete sense. Not only will its ads be on the landing pages which will get viewed more often, but there are opportunities to increase the click-through rate and "Cost Per Click" that it charges because these ads are now potentially more relevant.

You can also imagine that the Physical Web could be used to extend the AdSense model. The current AdSense model allows site developers to get a revenue share from Google in return for making space on their pages for Google ads to be displayed. Why not apply the same revenue-sharing model to Physical Web Beacons? The landing pages the URLs point to could contain ads. In the case of a beacon in a vending machine, Google can keep track of the context of the beacons that are registered using its Proximity beacon API.

The context in this case is the fact it is in a vending machine that stocks snacks. Frito-Lay could pay to access all Physical Web Beacons in such vending machines and bid to promote their products right at the point of purchase. Hershey's, PepsiCo, and Frito-Lay could bid for their ad to show up as you approach the vending machine.

Strategically, Physical Web Beacon and the Proximity beacon API opens up the possibility for Google to build and apply their own content framework in this intersection of the digital and physical worlds, monetizing it with more effective advertising.

An "Opportunity" for Beacon Vendors?

What should all the Beacon vendors that jumped on the Apple iBeacon bandwagon do? Should they support the Eddystone URL Physical Web paradigm? They already have too much to do just keeping up with the changes pushed on them by the OS vendors as new point releases of their operating systems come out, plus they have to build out their management, analytics, and partner programs. Physical Web could be a major distraction, a resource sink, fragmenting the beacosystem.

No, Physical Web is more than likely going to be a plus for the major beacon manufacturers. Engaging users by browsing their physical environment is a sensible way to entice them to download a mobile app. Given that web pages are an order of magnitude lower in cost and quicker to develop, a lot more business owners are likely to move forward with projects. Physical Web means your TAM (Total Addressable Market) just grew by an order of magnitude. And if your TAM just got multiplied by 10, that means your valuation just got a lot bigger too. Exciting? Well, not if adding support requires more resources than you have. Then Physical Web just becomes another major risk in your business plan.

Fortunately the major beacon vendors have already gotten used to accommodating multiple beacon standards within a single unit. As we discussed earlier in this chapter, many of them are already sending out iBeacon packets, with their own proprietary packets piggybacked on the tail of iBeacon data. So if you are a beacon vendor already broadcasting two kinds of packets, why not add more?

One reason not to is that, when you broadcast more data you use up more power. So if you increase the packet broadcast by 50%, your battery life just got correspondingly shorter. Fortunately UriBeacon only broadcasts once a second. Remember the use-case is a pull model where the browser is in the foreground, so the issues of trying to catch the attention of the OS by broadcasting at the iBeacon prescribed rate of ten times a second don't apply. Therefore, the tax on the battery in order to support Physical Web is of the order of 10% more; probably worth it given the value to the beacon vendor.

What About Apple?

If this such a good idea for Google, it would seem that Apple's instinctive reaction would be to try to undermine the adoption of Physical Web. So far they have not done that. The Physical Web apps have even been allowed onto the iOS App Store. The iOS version of Chrome supports Physical Web. When you speak to the Physical Web team, they are very careful not to position this as an Eddystone URL versus iBeacon horse race. Positioning Eddystone as open source is smart, but it's still a Google-owned open source project.

Hopefully economics, the good of the users, and common sense will prevail. Enabling the same cool experiences on iPhone as will be available on Android makes sense for Apple. Google is not the only company with an ad business. Apple's iAd is focused on in-app advertising, but when you have a market as big as the Physical Web, it would make sense for Apple to see that "a rising tide lifts all boats."

Filtering, Ordering, Prioritizing, Personalizing, and Anticipating

Today, some beacon browser apps order the Physical Web listings based on the strength of the signals being received from the beacons. So the closer the beacon, the stronger the signal, and the higher in the ranking the beacon is likely to be. You can play a shell game experiment, reordering three Physical Web beacons that are lined up, two feet apart with a phone running the beacon browser app next to the third beacon. It takes about three seconds for the beacon browser to detect the changes, reordering the beacon information on the screen to correspond with the change in relative position of the beacons as you moved them around. There's a scam that could be designed around that if you were unscrupulously minded.

What is it that makes Amazon and Google so great to use, beyond the fact they have vast coverage of things you are interested in? The "paradox of choice" means that while we all want more, we can easily be overwhelmed. How often have we looked at the hundreds of TV channels on cable and thought "There is nothing on!"? Amazon and Google are great at surfacing relevant content in a sea of choices.

If the Physical Web reaches its potential, the sea of location-specific content could become a tsunami. If this is really about context, the winner of the next round of browser wars could be the Physical Web browser that blends the perfect recipe of preferences, past behavior/click-throughs, segmentation, artificial intelligence, and recommendation engines to present the Physical Web that is most relevant in the most compelling way.

Privacy and Security

UriBeacons are arguably even less of a threat to our privacy than iBeacons. Like iBeacons, they are just broadcasting to you, not monitoring you. iBeacons require an app to act on the trigger that an iBeacon can invoke. The danger of lots of different apps is that there is more chance for a rogue app to do something that it shouldn't do, by abusing the knowledge of where you are and who you are. If a small number of browser apps are the readers of all these URLs being broadcast at us, there is more of an opportunity to verify that the browser can be trusted, with a single set of permissions and policies on what we want to share with the web pages to which the URL is pointing.

If we look at security from the point of view of the beacon owner, then they have a number of options to control who gets to access the information and resources the URL is pointing to. The owner can constantly change the URL using a sequence that only trusted users can understand. They can require login to the pages being pointed to. The network that is hosting the resource could be locked down to specific devices or IP addresses. There are a lot of options.

The Bottom Line

The Physical Web is exciting. The barriers to entry are low for beacon makers, for software developers, and for individuals. The Physical Web opens up the world of proximity to anyone who can produce a web page, which is most organizations. The technology makes all those informational proximity use-cases a lot cheaper to implement, and has the scope and architecture to enable a single app to interface with all of the gadgets that are being wired into the Internet of Things. Let's hope Apple agrees.

One Beacon, Multiple Standards

They say that the great thing about standards is there are so many to choose from. We have seen that Eddystone encompasses not one but four frame types (UID, EID, TLM, and URL). iBeacon brings us a fifth, AltBeacon a sixth, and many beacon vendors add their own proprietary beacon packets for secure identification and management purposes.

When choosing a Bluetooth beacon, it's important to understand which of these frame types is supported. Just because a beacon supports Eddystone-UID, doesn't mean that it supports Eddystone URL.

There are a variety of reasons why a beacon vendor may not support certain frame types, from limited engineering bandwidth, through to more strategic reasons. Google's steps toward building a cloud-based registry of beacons may look predatory to beacon vendors who are trying to build their own advertising-based beacon networks. As the standards become more comprehensive, the ability to buy beacon hardware from one vendor and work with another vendor's software and services stack becomes more of a reality. This can challenge some of the business models of vendors selling beacons at low margins, or even at a loss.

When Google launched Eddystone, a number of beacon vendors (Estimote and Kontakt.io) allowed their beacons to be switched from iBeacon to Eddystone, but not to interleave them (although both vendors have since announced products that do support this). Why not support all frame types and broadcast them together? There are certainly advantages beyond the flexibility and openness. When iOS sees an iBeacon frame, the scheduler responds, and callbacks from APIs that are looking for non-iBeacon packets become more responsive. Shopkick does this. They boast tens of thousands of beacons deployed in retailers' stores, broadcasting an iBeacon packet with the same UUID and major and minor device numbers from every beacon, thus rendering the UUID information useless. In doing this they get to claim iBeacon compatibility and ensure their app is responsive to the proprietary packet they broadcast following the dummy iBeacon packet.

The main reason given for not broadcasting multiple frame types is that, with every frame broadcast, there is a draw on the battery. Many retail focused beacon vendors mitigate this by providing larger batteries—Gimbal, Shopkick, and Swirl being examples of this. With that there is a tradeoff on size and cost. It's clear there isn't a single right answer.

Summary

Congratulations, that was a lot! If you have made it this far, you should have a good sense of some of the capabilities that the Bluetooth standard opens up to us via the mobile operating system. Both the capabilities and constraints should stimulate your ideas for what can be achieved with beacons as well as give you a sense of some of the limitations.

Next we will look at the chipsets that sit inside the beacon hardware and then at the beacons themselves. These implement the standards we just reviewed and form the most tangible part of the beacosystem.

CHAPTER 6

■ ■ ■

Chipsets: Understanding the Main Building Block in a Beacon

A Dialog Bluetooth Smart SoC and a Nordic Bluetooth Smart Module

Who Cares About the Chip in a Beacon?

If you are a proximity solutions provider considering whether or not to create your own beacons, understanding the different chipsets you can use is essential. That being said, those wanting only to write an app that uses beacon APIs don't really need to understand anything about the chipset inside the Bluetooth beacon. Therefore, this chapter is targeted at people who are selecting which type of beacon to deploy, or who want to convey to their colleagues the sense that they understand the beacosystem. For them, it will be a good idea to learn about the chipsets that are the engines driving this ecosystem.

The choice of chipset in a beacon plays a role in determining important characteristics, such as power consumption and signal strength. Understanding whether the beacon vendor has used a generic module or if they have invested in adding value with enhanced features, such as a more robust antenna, can be critical. It is also often worth noting where the beacon vendor has chosen to invest their limited capital, to help you consider their viability as a long-term supplier.

© Stephen Statler 2016
S. Statler, *Beacon Technologies*, DOI 10.1007/978-1-4842-1889-1_6

Chips, Chipsets, SoCs, and Modules

Competitively priced, highly functional chipsets have enabled small startups to develop their own beacons at relatively low cost. These Bluetooth Smart System on Chips (SoCs) can cost around $2.50, if you buy them in volumes of 1,000 or more. If you've noticed how many companies have created their own brand of beacons, it's because the chipset vendors made it cheap and surprisingly easy to do so.

In the past, a beacon manufacturer had to assemble and integrate a range of chips that each performed discrete functions: a CPU, random access memory (RAM), read only memory (ROM), flash memory, a signal processor, interface controllers, and a radio transceiver. This is a costly, time-consuming process with an element of risk for each additional integration step. Now these components are integrated into a single SoC, which forms the main building block for most beacons.

The SoC is integrated onto a small printed circuit board (PCB) the size of a coin, with an antenna, additional sensors, and any buttons or LED lights required to create a Bluetooth beacon module. Some beacon manufacturers create their own modules when their volumes or their unique requirements justify the expense. As the beacon volumes scale from 10,000 to 20,000 units, it may become economical to produce your own module. Beacon manufacturers that create their own modules will incur overheads ranging from additional design complexity and risk, testing overhead, calibrating/adjusting the output of the signal baseband chip, certifications, and managing a more complex supply chain. Hence, only those that will be producing enough bulk should consider creating their own module, especially considering how inexpensive generic ones are.

Chip manufacturers, such as Nordic Semiconductor, provide either the SoC or a version of the SoC packaged in a module. Their nRF51822 module/kit retails for about $30 for quantities of one. Chinese manufacturers offer their own modules based on the same SoC for around $5. In other cases, such as with Broadcom, the SoC manufacturer will partner with a third-party company that will design, manufacture, and sell an approved module based on the SoC.

A basic beacon is likely to use a small (2 cm) antenna that is printed on the PCB of the module. Some beacons, such as the Gimbal S20, have two larger external antennae. One is directional and the other is omnidirectional. The quality of the antenna can enhance the range of the beacon as well as control the shape of the signal that is transmitted.

Once a module has been sourced, adding a battery and a case is required to produce a basic beacon.

Many of the beacon chipset vendors provide an example software stack that includes drivers that will enable the beacon to transmit iBeacon or Eddystone conformant radio packets or frames. The beacon OEM still needs to join Apple's MFi (Made for iPhone) program in order to be able to claim the beacon is iBeacon compliant.

Some History and Gossip

We won't enumerate the model number of every chip produced for the Bluetooth beacon market. (You're welcome.) These product names are typically made up of a concatenation of the initials of the manufacturer followed by digits that give a clue to the logical relationship of the product relative to its ancestors in that product family. Listing them all would render this book obsolete the week it was published and make its pages resemble a phone book. It is, however, useful to understand the lineage of a few of the dominant players and why they have been successful.

Nordic Semiconductor was the first of the Bluetooth chip manufacturers to focus on the beacon market. Their Bluetooth Smart nRF51822 offering was particularly attractive to the burgeoning market of small beacon OEMs. Nordic's approach was different than the larger chip vendors such as Broadcom, which focused on supporting a small number of customers who could commit to purchasing very large numbers of chips, like major PC or phone vendors. These bigger vendors provided their VIP clients with personal service and support via a limited number of systems engineers.

Nordic, on the other hand, provided their support via an online portal that could service the needs of an unlimited number of smaller developers. They also provided modules that could be easily leveraged with a minimum of additional work, as well as example apps and the software drivers required to support the iBeacon standard. Their low-cost developer kits included a module along with connectors and a power supply—a complete beacon—but it lacked a case and the cloud services to manage it. Nordic was enabling "the long tail". As a result, their nRF51822 product gained the largest market share in the early stages of the beacosystem. Among their customers were companies such as Estimote and Kontoct.io, small companies that rapidly grew to be among the leaders in this emerging market.

More recently, the other chip vendors, including Broadcom, have moved to adopt the same support strategy with its Wireless Internet Connectivity for Embedded Devices for Bluetooth SMART (WICED SMART). It's argued that they still have a legacy of restricted access to WICED and a way to go before addressing large numbers of smaller developers.

In this initial phase of the development of the market, Texas Instruments (TI) achieved second place in market share. Its product was used in Gimbal beacons such as the S10, which was produced in very large numbers and was one of the lowest priced products ($5) on the market. Gimbal's S20, a higher-end product, was used by Apple in its retail stores. This win by TI was not publicized but became generally known in the industry. Qualcomm, which owned Gimbal at the time, competed with TI and produced its own Bluetooth chips via its QCA (Atheros) subsidiary. These chips, however, were Bluetooth Classic and Dual mode chips, unsuited for use in beacons, and didn't require the Bluetooth Classic protocol stack. It would have been embarrassing for Qualcomm to have one of its subsidiaries selling beacons with a competitor's Bluetooth chip inside.

This is a great example of why beacon vendors are reluctant to disclose whose chip they may be using in their beacons. The chipset vendors themselves are typically bound by non-disclosure agreements and so are unable to confirm the details of who their customers are. This can be a convenient but legitimate excuse when they have very few wins in the market. The truth can typically be unearthed by speaking to competing chip vendors, who may not be keen to disclose where they lost a deal, but are not typically barred by an NDA from talking about business they didn't win.

Another source of information about which beacon vendor is using a particular chip are the "tear down" analyses published on blogs such as `www.aislelabs.com/reports/beacon-guide/`, where new beacon models are dismantled and the chipset is listed.

Third place went to Cambridge Scientific Research (CSR).

In a push to grow revenue and strengthen its position in the Internet of Things market, Qualcomm acquired CSR in 2015. Prior to the acquisition, CSR had been exploring a strategy of marketing their own beacons to pull through a cloud service offering and so had not been as aggressive in selling to the beacon vendors. With the acquisition by Qualcomm, that strategy has been dropped and they are competing for business as a provider of SoCs for beacon vendors.

Other vendors are now aiming to displace Nordic by focusing on value-added features such as lower power consumption (Dialog) and mesh networking (CSR), which provides an alternative approach to management of beacons.

Silicon Labs offerings to beacon manufacturers came from its acquisition of Bluegiga, a smaller Scandinavian company that brought its Blue Gecko BGM111 Bluetooth® Smart Module to CSR's portfolio. Bluegiga used TI silicon but with its own custom stack (which in several cases was reported to be more reliable than TI's). Power consumption of this product was higher than Nordic's product, but newer generations became competitive.

Dialog was the first Bluetooth Smart vendor to reduce their transistor size to 55 nanometers (55/1,000,000,000 meter). This has enabled them to reduce their power consumption, which in turn extends the battery life and makes power harvesting viable. When a beacon's appetite is modest, its power can be harvested from interior lighting and sunlight using photovoltaic cells, from heat, kinetic movement, and even from the magnetic radio signals of other sources.

Table 6-1 lists some of the more notable Bluetooth Beacon chip vendors.

Table 6-1. *Key Bluetooth Beacon Chip Vendors*

Vendor	Web Site
AMICCOM Electronics Corporation	amiccom.com
Broadcom	broadcom.com
Cypress Semiconductor	cypress.com
Dialog Semiconductor	dialog-semiconductor.com
Freescale	freescale.com
Qualcomm (Atheros & Cambridge Silicon Radio)	qualcomm.com
Silicon Laboratories (Bluegiga)	silabs.com
STMicroelectronics	st.com
Texas Instruments	ti.com
Nordic Semiconductor	nordicsemi.com

Attributes of Bluetooth Smart Chipsets

This section discusses a few attributes to consider as you evaluate the choice of chipset for a beacon.

Flash Memory

Flash memory is used to store the firmware code used by the beacon to operate. Unlike ROM (Read Only Memory), it enables over-the-air updates of beacon software. It represents an additional cost and consumes more power compared to ROM with code written at the factory, but, given the volatile state of standards and changes to best practice in management software, it's a valuable capability.

Software Stack

Chipset vendors typically provide a baseline implementation of the software that constructs the frames or packets in a way that enables the beacon to broadcast data that conforms with the iBeacon and Eddystone format.

Scripting

Some vendors offer higher-level scripting interfaces to make it easier for developers to program the functions of the chip.

Antenna

There are several antenna types, ceramic chip and Printed Circuit Board (PCB) trace antennae being the most common. Not all antennae are equal; they vary in efficiency and directional characteristics. A PCB antenna has the advantage of relatively low cost and compact size. It has the risk of interference from the other components on the PCB, lower performance if the size is too constrained, and a susceptibility to interference from environmental effects (people). Unless manufacturing is accurate and reliable, this type of antenna can be detuned by relatively small variations in production. A chip antenna requires more expertise to implement and increases the cost of the bill of materials, but tends to deliver more robust performance and is more easily tuned.

Signal Power

An additional low noise amplifier can increase signal strength and reduce the noise in a signal. The current 10dBm signal maximum that is set by the Bluetooth standard may be raised in the future, which will make this capability more important. Figure 6-1 shows that there is a significant variation in the maximum signal strength of chips from the leading providers.

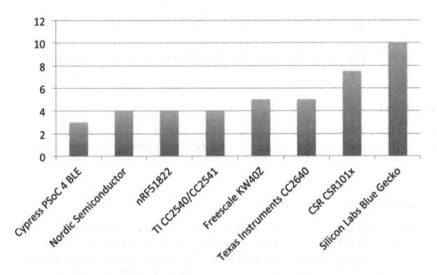

Figure 6-1. *Maximum Signal Transmission Power in dBm of Bluetooth Smart chipsets Data courtesy of Argenox Technologies at argenox.com*

Power Consumption

Power consumption needs to be evaluated when the radio is in sleep state and is at the peak when it is transmitting. Power consumption is directly influenced by the size of the circuits etched into the silicon chip. By reducing this size, power consumption can be reduced. While a lot more power is consumed when transmitting, the power consumed in sleep state is also important, as beacons spend most of their time sleeping.

In Figure 6-2, Dialog's DA14580 is shown to have the most frugal power consumption. However, the Cypress part needs only 60nA of power in full sleep mode, which is lower than almost all other devices. The amount of time spent transmitting versus sleeping becomes important in evaluating these characteristics.

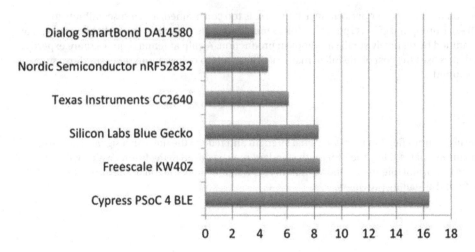

Figure 6-2. *Power consumption in milliamps (mA) while transmitting at 0dBm Data courtesy of Argenox Technologies at argenox.com*

Development Support

This is an important area to evaluate. How much access to support engineers can you expect and how good are the online resources, documentation, code samples, knowledge base, online Q&A, and developer communities?

Cost of Development Tools

Before committing to a vendor, it's important to understand any licensing costs for the software and any necessary development tools. Proprietary CPUs (sometimes referred to as an MCU—Micro Controller Unit—in these applications) can have proprietary development tools. These may require you to spend even more on licenses. The radios on a Bluetooth chip are often defined in software, which makes for a very flexible environment, but can put constraints on the development tools used to link this software with the applications that a beacon vendor may choose to create for the beacon. This may imply a cost that a startup may not want to incur.

ARM HOLDINGS

"Mighty oaks from little acorns grow."

ARM is an unusual designer of processors; they don't manufacture anything. Instead, they license their designs to chip OEMs. This business model has been very successful. As of 2015, over 60 billion ARM processors have been shipped, 95% of smartphones use ARM processors and their licensees include Apple, Samsung, Qualcomm, and TI. Their processors also power fridges, thermostats, and most Bluetooth beacons.

Originally known as Acorn RISC Machines, ARM got its start in the early 1980s making processors for the British Broadcasting Corporation's BBC Micro Computer.

The Acorn Reduced Instruction Set Computing (RISC) architecture was a revolutionary change from the Complex Instruction Set Computing (CISC) designs that were widespread before this.

The engineer who led this revolution was Sophie Wilson (born Roger Wilson), a heavily awarded Cambridge university graduate and Fellow of the Royal Society.

Mesh

With a mesh architecture, beacons could occasionally (daily) connect to their neighbors to transfer status information, such as battery life, and propagate configuration changes and firmware updates. The Bluetooth SIG is working on a standard in this area, but as of 2015, the offerings in the market are all proprietary.

Security

In addition to the standard Bluetooth encryption, some vendors offer additional levels of encryption and key exchange. One architectural feature, which is standard for an application processor, is the implementation of separate hardware-enforced segmentation between the data and code segments used by the chip vendor and those used by the beacon OEM. This can make spotting bugs easier as well as preventing rogue code from overwriting code in the beacon for malicious purposes.

Processor

The processor performance requirements for beacons to operate are modest. These devices aren't streaming media or doing complex analysis, so speed isn't a major priority. In fact, having an overpowered CPU is likely to consume more of the beacon's battery power, something that is in limited supply. Many of the chipset vendors license the generic ARM Cortex M0 design, which is the smallest and most energy-efficient of the processors that ARM offers for embedded applications.

Sensors

In addition to sensing temperature, which is very common, chipsets integrate other sensors for barometric pressure, acceleration, direction, magnetism, and light. This can be useful if the beacon is being used in shipping, industrial, or medical applications to measure the integrity of packages, other devices, or products.

Certification

One of the questions that needs to be answered is how to make sure your beacons are certified with the Bluetooth SIG and with the appropriate regulators in all the countries where you want to deploy beacons. Bluetooth chipset vendors can help with this, but they don't necessarily cover all regions that you may have designs on. And if you are manufacturing the beacons, there are still additional certification costs that have to be considered.

Bluetooth Certification

Most mainstream Bluetooth chipset vendors will provide software and radio frequency (RF) circuitry in their reference design that is qualified as compliant with the necessary parts of the Bluetooth standard they support. This requires them to go through a testing process with authorized testers and an approved test house, providing evidence of their conformance. This is an expensive process. But you can avoid that expense; so long as your design is "similar enough" to the original, your company won't have to go through a recertification process.

Using a qualified design, all a beacon OEM needs to do is join the Bluetooth SIG and pay the requisite fee (as of 2015 this is between $2,500 and $8,000, depending on your size and SIG membership status), do some paperwork, sign a Declaration of Compliance (DoC), and voila! Your beacon is Bluetooth qualified. You can then use the Bluetooth name and logo to describe it. Purchasers of beacons should be looking for these trademarks to be confident that the beacon will be interoperable.

In order to be able to sell products in major markets such as the United States, Europe, Canada, Japan, and Korea, companies must comply with different regional certification processes. These tests verify that the device is not causing harmful radiated emissions or interference on regulated frequencies. The IDs, marks, and logos associated with those certifications (see Figure 6-3) generally have to be permanently displayed on the products in a way that is visible to purchasers (see Figure 6-4). When deploying beacons in small pilot projects, verifying that beacons have been through this process may not be high on the priority list, but as deployments scale, this should be something that is confirmed. It's surprising to see how many Bluetooth beacons sold in the United States don't have the mandatory FCC ID 4-17 character identifier.

Figure 6-3. *The CE Mark and FCC logo indicates compliance with mandatory standards for products to ship in Europe and the United States, respectively*

Figure 6-4. *FCC and other regional certification marks on Gimbal, Swirl, and Shopkick beacons*

Regional Certification

The beacon OEM, under certain conditions, may use the FCC ID of the module vendor. In particular, the antenna needs to be of the same or similar type and equal or less gain to that used in the module manufacturer's testing.

Given that testing for a region can cost $25,000, it's important to understand the regions where your supplier has already gained certification.

Operational Temperature Range

Certain modules and chipsets may be designed to work in extended temperature ranges, up to 105 degrees Celsius. It's advisable to validate your temperature requirements. A beacon may be subjected to harsh environmental conditions if placed outside on signage, in a storage environment, gas pump, vending machine, or an industrial location.

Summary

The platform provided to the makers of beacons by manufacturers of Bluetooth semiconductors is impressive. As solution designers, we are standing on the shoulders of giants. These giants have spent years developing very functional building blocks for us to use at a remarkably low cost. But there are still tradeoffs and decisions to be made and they will drive the choices of silicon vendor and product. While the details may be technical, the decisions will be driven by business strategy and priorities—the geographies where the beacon will be sold, the features where differentiation will be required, and the performance that is expected.

Having studied what's inside the beacon, the next logical step is to look at the beacons themselves.

CHAPTER 7

Choosing the Right Beacon

© Stephen Statler 2016

S. Statler, *Beacon Technologies*, DOI 10.1007/978-1-4842-1889-1_7

What do cable TV and the line-up of Bluetooth beacon vendors have in common? The answer is "choice," or to be more precise, the paradox of choice. As of writing this chapter, there are over 300 beacon vendors listed in our sister[1] online database of Proximity Solution Providers (PSPs), Proxbook (see Figure 7-1). There are so many choices that it can feel like "there's nothing on".

Figure 7-1. The www.proxbook.com directory of PSPs

So Many Vendors, So Little Time

Why so many beacon vendors? As we saw in the prior chapters, the barrier to entry for aspiring beacon vendors is low. The silicon vendors make creating a beacon relatively easy and the huge flow of venture capital has enabled many to take that route.

Predictions are a dangerous game, but one that's a fairly safe bet is that most of the 300 beacon providers won't be able to survive as beacon hardware vendors for the long run. This means that for us as solution designers, there are plenty of opportunities to pick a dud.

---

[1]Proxbook is a crowdsourced listing of PSPs that grew out of a realization that any list of beacon providers we captured in these pages would be out of date before the publisher's CMS could send its pages to the print-on-demand service. Our clunky WordPress database was then adopted by the folks at Unacast, taking the crowdsourced database from 80 PSPs to over 300. So strictly speaking we are the birth parents of www.proxbook.com (which has since been adopted by wealthier parents), not the sibling.

A Platform Decision

Your choice of beacon has significant ramifications. Once you are into the production phase of your project, you face major switching costs because while beacons are built around a set of standards, there are major gaps where solutions are still proprietary. We will highlight these areas as we review the criteria you should consider to make your choice.

When choosing a beacon vendor you are making a platform decision. The beacon is a foundation of firmware, hardware, cloud software, and hopefully a range of third-party solutions built on top of the platform. Building on a platform saves time, reduces risk (if you choose wisely), and opens up an ecosystem of third-party products that can be easily integrated.

Choose the wrong platform and you could be impacting the viability of the app that's being developed, saddling yourself with costs and constraints that could kill your project.

So is there a single vendor that's clearly the best? We don't think so. We will provide a brief profile of a handful that we think deserve to be on any short list, but first we should run through the criteria to use when selecting a beacon vendor.

Some of these criteria will sound generic, or applicable to any product choice. Things like price, but in every case there is something specific to the beacosystem that should be considered.

There is one criterion that deserves its own special place in the sun, but will be the last to be discussed in detail, and that's volume. A quick preview: unless the number of development kits your chosen vendor has sold is in five figures, you need to look seriously at their ability to survive in the long term and at what the impact of their demise might be on your solution.

The Criteria

To make navigating the criteria manageable, we have grouped them into three clusters:

- Physical aspects of the hardware

- Firmware, software, and services

- Business aspects of your solution

Physical Aspects of the Hardware

When you start to apply this criteria, the number of viable vendors for any given requirement starts to get manageable pretty quickly.

The Case: Looks

Are looks important? They are if you are an American newscaster[2] or a Bluetooth beacon. It's amazing how many different designs have been created to package a Bluetooth beacon. One of the first questions to answer is, do you want your beacons to be noticed or to blend into the background? As you can see in Figure 7-2, Estimote's delicious industrial design creates an object that looks beautiful and attracts attention. Their design is arguably a major factor behind the success of the company.

---

[2]I personally prefer newscasters who have bad teeth and rumpled clothing; it shows they are focused on journalism rather than hairspray and were clearly promoted on that basis.

Figure 7-2. *Estimote beacons are conspicuous by design*

As beacons came to the notice of the press corps, no article on the subject was complete without a photograph of these colorful space-age devices. Estimote's web site has benefited from the highest web traffic of any of the major vendors, partially as a result of the eye candy they sell. For solution providers who want to make an impression, this can be a major plus.

However, the reverse is also true. Many larger retailers have a strong desire to control the look and feel of their stores. Distracting shoppers with colorful beacons can be problematic. Gimbal's S20 beacons were produced in a tasteful but discrete rectangular case, with a white finish and no brand name visible. The thinking being that this will not compete with the displays on which the retailer's professional merchandiser is trying to focus the customer's attention.

The Gimbal beacons that have been deployed by Apple in the Apple retail stores are the same metallic finish as much of the rest of the store. You have to look carefully to see them. Shopkick's shopBeacon achieves an appealing design aesthetic (Figure 7-3), with a white gloss finish and a curvaceous shape (to accommodate its D batteries) that can simultaneously blend in and look good.

Figure 7-3. *Shopkick beacons blend into the background despite their size*

Having a beacon that is visually appealing and distinctive can make it irresistible to children who want to take "toys" home, especially if the toys have flashing lights.

Chinese vendor Sensoro takes a similar approach with its most compact beacon, the Yunzi, shown in Figure 7-4. With its brushed steel edges, it would fit in well next to any display of high-end watches or phones. This is good because Sensoro beacons have been deployed in jewelry stores across China[3].

---

[3]The beacons enabled a campaign at 237 of Chow Tai Fook's 2,300+ jewelry stores in China. This drove the presentation of over 24,000 coupons and $16 million of sales revenue during the Chinese New Year. Check out the case study, full of specific metrics, at post.sensoro.com/case-study-for-monetized-beacon-deployment-in-china/.

Figure 7-4. *The Sensoro Yunzi beacon combines aesthetics with a more discrete package*

This has been observed in beacon deployments at schools. The fact that the beacons were useless to the kids didn't prevent them being "borrowed".

The Case: Protection

The next major factor to consider is, does the beacon need to be weatherproof. Many deployments will be inside and this won't be an issue, but there are quite a few applications where environmental conditions can be challenging: drive-throughs, parking lots, outdoor signage, statues, street furniture, car washes, and industrial facilities are all locations where beacons have been deployed and where they need a well-sealed outer shell.

If this is the case, there are standards to look for. One such standard is the International Electrotechnical Commission's (IEC) Ingress Protection (IP) Code, International Protection Marketing IEC Standard 60529[4]. Under this standard, a product's protection level is designated by three numbers, although generally only the first two are used. The first number designates the level of protection against solid objects, the second deals with protection against liquids, and the third deals with impact protection. For example, IP686 is the highest level of protection against all of those factors. Check out Figure 7-5, which illustrates the qualities of an IP67 beacon case.

---

[4]The British Standards Institute online store provides a copy of this 48-page standard `shop.bsigroup.com/ ProductDetail/?pid=000000000030214185`

Figure 7-5. *The Sensoro Pro beacon is designed to the IP67 standard, being waterproof and dustproof*

Figure 7-5. (*continued*)

IEC 60529: Ingress Protection Against Solid Objects

0	No protection
1	Protected against solid objects up to 50mm, e.g., accidental hand contact
2	Protected against solid objects up to 12mm, e.g., fingers
3	Protected against solid objects up to 2.5mm (tools and wires)
4	Protected against solid objects up to 1mm (small tools and wires)
5	Protected against dust, limited ingress (no harmful deposit)
6	Totally protected against dust

IEC 60529: Ingress Protection Against Liquid

0	No protection
1	Protection against vertically falling drops of water, e.g., condensation
2	Protection against direct sprays of water up to 15 degrees from vertical
3	Protection against direct sprays of water up to 60 degrees from vertical
4	Protection against water sprayed from all directions—limited ingress permitted
5	Protection against low-pressure jets of water from all directions—limited ingress permitted
6	Protection against low pressure jets of water (such as use on ship decks)—limited ingress permitted
7	Protection against the effect of immersion between 15cm and 1m
8	Protection against long periods of immersion under pressure

IEC 60529: Impact Protection

0	No protection
1	Protection against 150g falling from 15cm height (0.225 joules)
2	Protection against 250g falling from 15cm height (0.375 joules)
3	Protection against 250g falling from 20cm height (0.5 joules)
4	Protection against 500g falling from 40cm height (2.0 joules)
5	Protected against 1500g falling from 40cm height (6.0 joules)
6	Protected against 5kg falling from 40cm height (20.0 joules)

The United States National Electrical Manufacturers Association (NEMA) has a standard (250-2003[5]) for electrical enclosure types that provides an alternative benchmark. It goes beyond what might otherwise be vague assurances from a vendor. A NEMA Type 3 enclosure is designed to "provide a degree of protection with respect to harmful effects on the equipment due to the ingress of water (rain, sleet, or snow); and that will be undamaged by the external formation of ice on the enclosure". Type 4 enclosures provide "a degree of protection against ingress of water from a hose". Type 6 protects against "occasional temporary submersion," while 6P protects against occasional prolonged submersion.

There is a potential tradeoff in terms of cost and ease of access as the standards increase. Estimote's Proximity beacon can be completely submerged in water, but the case needs to be cut open with a knife if you want to change the batteries (as you can see in Figure 7-6).

---

[5]www.nema.org/Products/Documents/nema-enclosure-types.pdf

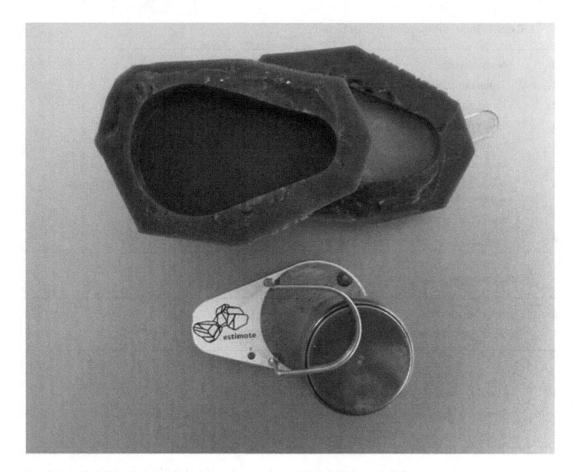

Figure 7-6. *Inside an Estimote beacon, cut open to reveal the motherboard and battery*

Fixing and Physical Security

Since most beacons are relatively light in terms of weight, the most popular method of fixing them to walls is with some kind of adhesive strip, which usually comes prefixed to the case. Some vendors produce an industrial case with screw holes (see Figure 7-7) and a very few have bayonet screw sockets, the kind used to attach cameras to tripods.

Figure 7-7. *Beacon casing with screw holes*

Maybe because the cost of beacons is relatively low and they have little value to individuals, there is generally a lack of physical security such as locks to protect access to the beacon case. This would significantly increase the cost of the "bill-of-materials" for a product.

Gimbal's S21 beacon case can be secured using a Torex tamper-resistant six point star screw head[6].

Often beacons are hidden behind products, out of reach or within other more secure casings, in order to avoid tampering.

When this is done, care needs to be taken that any additional casing doesn't interfere with the signal direction or strength. When metal sheets make up the casing of a vending machine with a beacon inside, this can create issues, whereas plastic covers shouldn't be a problem.

Signal Strength

As we saw in the previous chapter on the chipsets used in beacons, maximum signal strength and range can vary. Achieving a 50-meter range with a strong (0dBm) signal is generally possible, assuming there are no physical obstructions that might attenuate the signal.

Chip manufacturer Silicon Labs' Bluegiga has produced a long-range module, the BLE121LR. It transmits at +8dBm and claims to be able to achieve up to 450 meters of range. This module is used in BlueSense networks' BlueBar beacon long-range product.

---

[6]Patent for the Torex screw at www.google.com/patents/US3584667

Generally beacons powered from main or USB power supplies are designed with stronger signal output, as there is no need to reduce power consumption to conserve battery life. Most beacons allow for the signal strength and thus signal range to be modulated, in order to support specific use-cases and to preserve battery life.

There can be variations in signal strength between beacons from the same manufacturer of the same model. For this reason, it's a good idea to calibrate the signal strength of each individual beacon when deploying them for use-cases that require higher accuracy. Calibration involves measuring the received signal strength of the beacon at a specified distance (1 meter) and recording that in the setup parameters of the beacon. The RSSI number can then be broadcast by the beacon to receiving devices, so the receiver can factor this into the decision at to when to trigger actions.

Antenna

While many beacon vendors use the antennae built into the modules provided by the chipset vendors, some have external antenna, which may more efficiently extend the signal range of the chipset.

The antenna also affects the shape of the signal. Most Bluetooth beacons have an omnidirectional antenna, meaning that the signal generation radiates fairly evenly from the devices. However, the shape of the signal is not perfectly round; it's actually doughnut shaped (Figure 7-8).

Figure 7-8. *The omnidirectional antennae used on most Bluetooth beacons radiate a signal that is doughnut shaped (illustration selected for memorability)*

This is something to consider when positioning the beacon vertically (sideways) rather than horizontally, as the signal may not go as far as you expect if you are pointing the hole of the doughnut at the space where you want the signal to go.

There is no substitute for testing the signal with the beacon in place.

The signal from a directional antenna is cone shaped. Unfortunately, this cone lacks clear structural integrity. Its borders are not clear-cut and there is likely to be signal radiation that comes out of the bottom of the cone. Think of an ice cream melting and the contents spilling onto your shorts (Figure 7-9).

Figure 7-9. Directional antennas create signals that are more cone shaped

This impacts the applications in which we can use beacons in significant ways. Consider when you have beacons in gas pumps and you want to be sure that you can differentiate between the two sides of the pump island (pump #1 versus pump #2). The directionality of the beacon on its own may not be enough to shape the signal in order to avoid a false positive effect. A false positive is where a driver is thought to be on one side of the island when they are actually on the other side. These issues can be managed and will be discussed in the chapter on beacon placement.

The Gimbal S20 and S21 beacons have both an omnidirectional and a directional antenna. The selection of which one to use is made during the configuration process. Zebra Technologies (previously known as Motorola Solutions) offer an MB2000 beacon with directional antenna with a 120-degree beam width.

Sensors

The iBeacon specification doesn't incorporate any support for beacon sensors, yet from early on many Bluetooth beacons have integrated a battery sensor, a temperature sensor, and an accelerometer into their design. The sensors may be configured and read using a custom Bluetooth Generic ATTribute Profile (GATT) command. Beacon vendors provide a proprietary API that uses the profile to connect to their beacon. Google defined a more standard approach to reading the output from a basic set of sensors with the Eddystone TLM frame. This transmits just the temperature and battery level.

Sensors on beacons have proved valuable for use-cases such as measuring the weather for marketing campaigns for soft drinks, sales of which are influenced by how hot the weather is. Beacon sensors have been used to monitor the status of refrigeration units and the integrity of valuable packages shipped by logistics companies.

TI's SensorTag (shown in Figure 7-10) is probably one of the most "sensitive" beacons on the market. It's attracted a lot of interest and stimulated creative projects from the "maker"[7] community, due to its plethora of on-chip sensors (monitoring local temperature and battery) plus seven sensor peripheral chips integrated onto its motherboard:

- Infra Red temperature (measuring the temperature of objects at a distance when the beacon is pointed at them)

- Accelerometer for XYZ axis measurements

- Humidity

- Barometric pressure

- Magnetometer

- Gyroscope

- Light

Figure 7-10. *The Texas Instrument's CC2650 SensorTag*[8]

All this plus an LED and a buzzer make it an impressive package. It's priced competitively at $29 for a single beacon. It appears that TI's goal with SensorTag is to illustrate the capabilities of the underlying chipset, rather than competing aggressively with its own customers, the beacon manufacturers.

Cell Batteries and Power Beacons

The slim and economic CR2032 coin cell battery is the power source that captured the imagination of the Bluetooth low-energy ecosystem. In other cases, taking the beacon to the power and taking the power to the beacon is often not practical. But sometimes it works out. Let's review both these options now.

Long Live the CR2032

How could such a tiny battery sustain a beacon for months of operation? The low-energy consumption of Bluetooth Smart is remarkable, and it would be even more remarkable if a CR2032 battery could sustain beacons for more than a month when configured to meet most use-cases. Sadly, that's not the case.

---

[7]For an introduction to the maker movement, read http://www.wired.com/2013/04/makermovement/.
[8]Image courtesy of Texas Instruments. Image cropped and used under license creativecommons.org/licenses/by-sa/3.0/.

If a beacon is configured to broadcast at full power at the frequency required to conform to Apple's iBeacon specification (10 times a second), you will be lucky to get a month of life out of that tiny CR2032.

That's not to say that you can't throttle back the beacon's battery consumption to eke out a longer life. Vendors such as Estimote and Ubudu have been resourceful in making it easy to dial down the signal strength and frequency to extend battery life and to layer on other energy saving schemes, such as shutting down transmissions at times when the beacons are not likely to be needed—at night for instance.

Conversely demands on power are rising as beacons are asked to work harder by broadcasting multiple packet types to maintain compatibility with different standards. As beacons are accessed by multiple applications, supporting the lowest denominator in terms of signal strength and frequency is no longer possible. Adding management features where beacons are talking to each other in a mesh and broadcasting telematics and the CR2032 seems very limiting.

The labor cost of organizing battery changes far outweighs the savings on the battery. Vendors such as Swirl, Gimbal, Zebra, and Shopkick, with a focus on larger retail deployments, have produced devices that run off much larger batteries, to extend battery life to more than a year.

As discussed in the standards chapter, it's necessary to broadcast beacon packets frequently (10x a second) if the goal is to ensure an app in the background detects the beacon. However, if a beacon is broadcasting Eddystone URL packets that are meant to interact with a browser running in the foreground, we can safely reduce our broadcast frequency to once a second and our battery life extends proportionately.

Battery life is complex to predict. In addition to the chemistry of the battery itself, it's influenced by the current that is drawn, the temperature of the environment, temperature fluctuations (are your beacons going to be sitting outside in New York or San Diego), and how long the battery has been in storage[9]. The higher the current drawn, the more energy is lost in heat for example. We haven't been operating beacons for 20 years, so there has been a lack of history from which to extrapolate. All this, combined with the changes in the software that is running on beacons, helps explain why vendor predictions have not always been as accurate as we would all want.

A very rough rule of thumb is that a beacon will consume over 250 milliamps a month if broadcasting 10 times a second at full power[10]. Using that rule of thumb, we can look at the battery capacity in Figure 7-11 and get a sense for what kind of battery packs we should be looking for in our beacon. Your mileage will vary considerably, but if in doubt (and let's face it, we are in doubt), go for a bigger battery.

---

[9]Energizer's handbook on battery technologies provides a lot more detail http://data.energizer.com/PDFs/alkaline_appman.pdf

[10]We have already discussed the multitude of variables, including the chipset technology, but in this case let's throw caution to the wind in the interest of figuring out the battery requirements at a gross level.

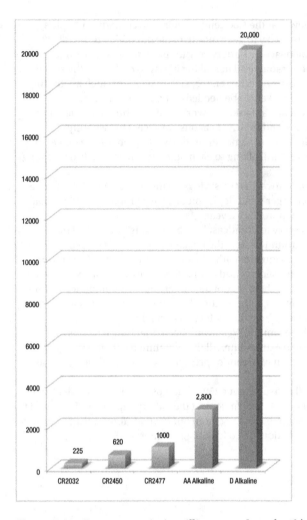

Figure 7-11. *Battery capacity in milliamps per hour (mAh)*

Powered Beacons

After wallowing in the challenges of using batteries in beacons, solution designers may start to contemplate eliminating the use of battery powered beacons altogether. Being able to plug beacons into a handy power socket is frequently not possible. If that's the case, we start to consider the feasibility in our plans of bringing the power to the places where beacons are required. Since beacons are still at an experimental phase, compelling proven ROIs are in short supply. In cases where beacons need to be placed in very specific locations in a store, laying in power cables to a new location is expensive in terms of people, capital, permits, and the union labor that is often required to deal with electrical systems. Beyond the cost, it also adds a level of complexity and disruption that makes projects a lot less likely to happen.

In cases where a single beacon is simply being used for a basic check-in use-case, placement may not be an issue. If the beacon needs to be near a point of sale terminal, a vending machine, a ticket kiosk, a gas pump, or a digital display, it's likely there will be power available, either from a power socket or a USB connector. Power can also be obtained from network cables, with additional power over Ethernet splitter hardware that provides power to a beacon via a USB connection.

Therefore, selecting a beacon vendor that can provide the option to deploy a USB version of your beacon of choice is highly desirable.

All of the major industrial lighting companies that sell LED lighting for retail, office and industrial applications are introducing beacon offerings. GE Lighting and Acuity has been public about this. One of the things that they bring to the market is the fact that their product is already wired into power.

Firmware, Software, and Services

With so much of the hardware value being provided by the chip vendors, the software and services required for an effective beacon are the most significant technology components that differentiate beacon vendors from each other.

Beacon vendors can be divided into two broad categories:

- General-purpose beacons (e.g. Estimote, Gimbal, Kontakt.io, and Radius Networks)
- Vertically-integrated solutions (e.g. Facebook, GasBuddy, Shopkick, and Tile)

The general-purpose beacon vendors offer a product that can be used for a very diverse set of applications. They have to provide a very broad set of features and functions to support thousands of use-cases.

The vertically-integrated solution vendors currently don't offer their product for developers to buy as a building block for their own solution, and because of that they can be a lot more focused in terms of the protocols they support and the tools they offer. The GasBuddy beacon isn't for sale on the GasBuddy web site; it comes as part of a package of advertising services for convenience stores that only come from GasBuddy. Tile doesn't have to worry about supporting the Eddystone URL standard because it's not necessary for the solution they provide, i.e., finding lost keys, wallets, and other items from their app.

Firmware and Configuration Updates

One thing we can be sure of is that the firmware on beacons will continue to change. Protocols will evolve, energy-saving schemes will improve, management techniques will evolve, and requirements in terms of signal strength and broadcast frequency may change as new use-cases are introduced.

There are a variety of approaches to performing these updates. Assuming the beacons you have selected have flash memory (not all do), they all involve sending the updates over the air (OTA). The differences are in the distribution source and the way the transfer is initiated. There are five main approaches:

- **Admin App to Device—Hard Reset.** This first approach requires an administrator to perform a physical reset of the device either by pressing a button inside or outside the beacon case or removing the batteries and re-inserting them. As the beacon reboots, the admin app can then be used to transfer the changes OTA. Blesh beacons have an internal switch to do this. The Physical Web reference beacons provide an external reset button.

  If the beacons are situated out of reach, then ladders are obviously required. Obtaining a ladder can be more difficult than it might seem, especially when heavy security or union rules are involved. So there is a penalty in terms of time. The argument in favor of these more physical methods is that they provide a level of physical security that mitigates the risk that beacons could be hijacked by armchair based hackers.

- *Admin App to Device—Software Reset.* The second approach is for the beacon vendors' administration app to be able to connect to a beacon and initiate a firmware update without any physical interaction with the beacon.

  BluVision, Estimote, Kontakt.io, Zebra MPact, and many other beacons support this approach.

- *Wi-Fi Hub Updates.* A less common approach is for the beacon vendor to use a Bluetooth to Wi-Fi gateway device. This connects to the beacons within range and then provides a cloud connection via Wi-Fi over which monitoring, configuration changes, and firmware updates can be performed. BluVision supports this approach using its BluFi Bluetooth-to-Wi-Fi sensor. Kontakt.io supports this using its Cloud Beacon. A main power socket powers the BluVision device. The Kontakt.io device is rechargeable, with 12,800mAh of capacity, or it can simply run off a USB connection. Neither device is a Wi-Fi access point; they simply provide a bridge to link to the outside world provided by a separate Wi-Fi access point.

  Vendors that offer Wi-Fi infrastructure (Aerohive, Aruba/HP, Cisco, Ruckus, and Zebra) are slowly integrating their management platforms so that they can monitor the presence of iBeacons. In the future it would make sense for them to be able to update the firmware and settings of beacons using that infrastructure. Given the lack of standards that apply to these update functions, this will require some strategic decisions to be made as to what beacon platforms will be supported. For Zebra, they already have a robust beacon offering MPact. As of Q4 2015, updates to beacons require an iOS device to be used, but that could change. Aerohive have partnered with Radius networks to promote plugging their powered RadBeacons into the USB port on an Aerohive router. Ruckus partnered with Gimbal to provide monitoring. Cisco, the master of corporate acquisitions, could well test the waters for its next purchase by partnering with one or two beacon providers. HP's Aruba appears to have gone the furthest in the integration of its own USB and battery-powered Bluetooth beacons with their Wi-Fi access points, enabling configuration updates to be pushed from the access points via Bluetooth to beacons that are in range.

- *Consumer App to Device.* An approach that can save on the cost of sending staff out to update beacons is to crowdsource updates using your customers' phones that are running your app. The Estimote SDK supports embedding this function in the customer's app. It downloads the updates over the cloud and then transfers them to beacons within range that require the update. Some customers may feel this is not a reasonable approach, so exercise great caution before adopting this strategy.

- *Mesh Updates.* Chipset vendors such as CSR and beacon vendors such as Ubudu are promoting using mesh networks to link Bluetooth beacons. There is potential in the future for monitoring, configuration, and firmware updates to be propagated across these networks, eliminating the need to have IT staff tour all the beacons in a venue to perform these tasks.

Management

We have devoted a whole chapter to this subject, but for now lets simply register the fact that evaluating the tools provided for management by your beacon hardware provider is key. With the exception of vendors implementing Google's Eddystone management interface, most of the management interfaces with beacons are proprietary, so management vendors can't easily address the task of managing third-party beacons, unless there is a strategic relationship in place between the suppliers. Solution providers currently look to their beacon hardware vendors to provide the tools here.

Security/Hijacking

The aspect of security we are discussing here is the protection against "hijacking," which is unauthorized configuration and firmware updates. This could be used to take down the proximity service and use it for unauthorized means.

This is another area where there is a lack of standards to support a cross-platform approach to authentication and prevention of such attacks. Unfortunately, there are enough standards in other areas to make hacks quite easy. Bluetooth's Secure Simple Paring enables a handset to connect to the beacon. Passkeys used by the beacons may be broadcast in the clear, so that someone in the vicinity of the wireless conversation could then monitor this and use the password. Once connected, standard Bluetooth GATT commands can make changes to the beacon setup. Ask your vendor what they have done to defend against this.

Some don't allow any configuration changes without physical access, others are implementing encrypted communication channels to prevent snooping on passkeys, and others are implementing industry standards such as OAuth as a way of controlling access to the beacon.

Power Consumption

The power consumption of a beacon is a function of both hardware and firmware. It's like the mileage of a car, a very significant factor that impacts cost and frequency of refueling which is a disruptive process. Despite the fact that there are a limited number of engines or chipsets in use and the chipset is a significant factor in the efficiency of the beacon, the chipsets is only the denominator in this equation. It's the way the beacon designer drives that engine that is the deciding factor in the mileage you will get. Do they have "a lead foot" pushing hard on the accelerator or are they judicious in the way they use the engine cycles?

Unfortunately, there is no federal standard on how this mileage is reported and so as a buyer you need to beware. Your mileage will vary. Consider the factors already discussed and you can decide whether you think this is going to be an SUV or a hybrid. How many frame types are being broadcast? What is the frequency of broadcast? Do we have the ability to throttle back the signal strength? What's the capacity of the batteries? There is no substitute for a test drive under the conditions that you expect to see for your application.

Operating Temperature

One other factor that will impact battery life will be the environmental temperatures (see example Figure 7-12). Low temperatures will tend to constrain the output efficiency of the battery.

Figure 7-12. *A gauge showing the current temperature in San Diego*

More fundamentally you will need to consider if there are extremes of temperature that will impact your beacon of choice and the ability for the beacon to survive at that temperature.

If you are deploying in a shopping mall or office, this is unlikely to be an issue, but if the beacon is going to be outdoors in Minnesota or Moscow, or in a gas pump or vending machine in Arizona, it's something to factor in. Machines like gas pumps will have been designed with extended temperature operating requirements in mind and anything that is included in those enclosures will need to operate within the same range.

Extended temperature ranges are a function of the core chipset or module, as well as the other components and circuit board that surrounds them. So just because the Bluetooth module is certified for hot temperatures, it doesn't necessarily mean that the other components can take it.

SDK

Although theoretically developers can use the standard iBeacon and Eddystone APIs offered on iOS and Android, most major beacon vendors provide their own SDK. Before the introduction of Eddystone, this was a necessity in order to support beacons on Android, because there was no native alternative. The beacon vendor SDK also enables the access control features that have been missing from the first release of iBeacon and Eddystone.

Surely you would want to avoid using these proprietary SDKs. In theory, yes, but usually there are features you will want to access that are only available by using the beacon vendor's SDK. These vary in the value add that they offer, but the features can include:

- Access to sensor data

- Conditional access

- Fleet management, tracking, monitoring, and configuration

- Analytics

- Location/mapping functions—trilateration/wayfinding

- Additional proximity and location features such as geofencing

- Orchestration features: content management and campaign management

These features may represent significant value for your solution requirements, or they may be a driver for increased pricing that makes the offering less attractive. So decide up-front where you want to source these functions before paying your beacon provider extra. For those of us who are averse to sports and have had to pay our cable providers every month for ESPN, why subject yourselves to the same annoyance of paying for features you never use with beacons?

Protocols

We discussed the iBeacon and Eddystone standards in Chapter 5, but it's worth emphasizing that using these native protocols offers significant benefit. There is no substitute for having access to the operating system hooks for both iOS and Android that enable control and integration with bundled apps and services that can't be achieved otherwise. Nearly all vendors support iBeacon, but there are vendors that don't support Eddystone, or only support a subset of Eddystone frame types. There are reasons for concern regarding Eddystone, specifically having to register the metadata about all your beacons in Google's cloud, but that choice should be yours, not your beacon vendor's. If the beacon vendor doesn't support Eddystone, this should be cause for concern.

The other area to clarify is the ability to have a single beacon interleaving all protocols simultaneously. Rather than having to choose one protocol or another, you should have the option to use both. Beacon vendors may claim that there are battery issues with doing this, but this raises the question as to whether they should be offering larger batteries. It should be you as a solution designer who makes that tradeoff, rather than having your hands tied by the beacon vendor.

In addition to the protocols discussed in other chapters, there are the beacon providers' proprietary protocols that were born prior to iBeacon (for example, Gimbal's native protocol and Swirl's SecureCast, which is supported along with iBeacon and Eddystone by Zebra). Zebra has done the best job of convincing other vendors to forsake their beacon offerings and use Zebra's, so that the vendor can focus on their value add further up the solutions stack, e.g., ad networking or analytics.

Conditional Access

Conditional access allows the beacon owner/manager to control what apps see a specific beacon. This can provide a guard against having your beacons used for showrooming, or it can be the cornerstone of the beacon networks and ad networks that we will explore later.

Not every application requires conditional access, but this has gone from an exotic differentiator to a commonplace feature. Selecting a beacon platform without this feature should be done with great care.

Now with Google releasing its Eddystone Ephemeral ID frame type, conditional access is even more broadly available. The question becomes, why would you use one of the current proprietary conditional access APIs rather than a standard that doesn't tie you to a specific beacon vendor?

Analytics

Beacons are often sold as analytics tools. The reality is they are one ingredient, a cookie, a data source for analytics tools.

Analytics is a huge technology domain. It's unlikely that a beacon hardware vendor will be able to create best-of-breed analytics tools to compete with the mutli-billion dollar corporations that already produce comprehensive suites in this area.

It's potentially dangerous for a beacon vendor to claim analytics as a core part of its beacon offering. It could end up producing a toolset that is so poor that it reflects badly on the rest of the package and drains resources from adding value in other areas that might be a more realistic focus.

Worse, by claiming to operate in this area, vendors could alienate the ecosystem partners that they should be integrating with, that do focus on analytics. This could have the effect of removing the alternatives to what may be a sub-par analytics offering.

Does that mean the vendor should offer nothing in the way of analytics? No. There is a good argument that a beacon vendor should provide some basic dashboard tools that provide a quick, simple, economic way of understanding the use of the beacons. This can be done without declaring war with the analytics software industry.

The analytics heavyweights are not as agile as some of the beacosystem players. There are beacon-specific features that an analytics giant like SAS may not address for some time. Being able to interpret what a number of low-level beacon triggers mean and express those low-level details in ways that can be understood by other tools offers opportunities. For instance, the ability to group a collection of beacons that cover a department in a store and to export the fact that there was dwell time in men's apparel, rather than a mass of entry and exit triggers from disparate beacons, could be very helpful.

As solution designers, we should look for evidence of integration between a given beacon vendor's middleware and the analytics providers' infrastructure. We can be sure that this integration will be painful the first few times it's done, so having "plugins" between a beacon vendor's tools and a broad selection of analytics tools is of significant value.

Integration Points

Analytics tools are just one example of where a beacon vendor can establish value with proven integrations with third-party tools. Other examples of integration points we may find interesting are with what we call *orchestration* tools (campaign management and content management), other beacon networks, advertising networks, and third-party apps. If a beacon vendor is providing a platform, they are likely to be a lot more successful if they can point to a large catalog of third-party applications and software. It's surprising that very few of the vendors in this space can provide a solution directory that lists those partnerships.

One proxy for assessing adoption of a beacon provider's platform by independent software vendors is to understand how many developer kits a beacon vendor has sold. Beacon vendors tend to directly equate the number of developer kits sold to the size of their ecosystem. This is optimistic. Often they don't know if the purchaser of the beacon is an adolescent hobbyist, or the architect from a Fortune 500 company working in stealth mode. The number of developers using the beacon vendor's development kits is important. If it's low, that's bad, but if it's high, it doesn't necessarily mean that software packages have been developed for the platform and that production systems are going to be rolled out on it. The platform that was originally used for the proof of concept is not necessarily the one used for the production system. It's not unusual to see customers buy beacons, learn, and then "jump ship" once they become smarter.

Company

If you are buying a commodity, the kind of company you source from is not that significant. If you are buying ball bearings or beef, so long as the quality is good, it doesn't matter so much who you buy from.

Despite the existence of standards, beacons are not a commodity, so the opposite is true. The moment you start building your solution, your source of beacons becomes really important.

Why? In the case of beacons, there are proprietary hooks that introduce unique ways of doing things. This introduces switching costs as soon as you start to invest your company's time into designing the use of those hooks by your solution. You aren't buying a static product. With software changes in the OS and firmware updates within the beacon, your platform will evolve. So, there are a number of factors about the company and its approach that you should consider.

Financial Viability

Most companies selling beacons are startups. Nearly all of them are burning more cash than they are making. So the one thing we can be confident of is that they will not be the same companies in two years' time. They will either have found a way to generate profits and be self-sufficient, or they will have been bought or merged with another company with a complementary business. We have to ask ourselves, is their current focus likely to be profitable or is it a stepping-stone to an adjacent market that will be profitable? There isn't a lot of money to be made from simply making beacons, so look at the beacosystem stack we reviewed earlier and ensure that you understand where they will extract value.

Is the answer to buy your beacons from a larger company? That may give you political cover, but the reality is that big companies can shut down underperforming divisions or sell them to companies that might not be organizations with which you want to do business. PayPal was one of the first major companies to produce a Bluetooth beacon. It was a beautiful looking product and the rationale for its existence made sense; it enhanced their payments system. They deployed it in trials, changed their leadership, and then decided the product wasn't viable. There are rumors of a warehouse filled with PayPal beacons that have never been unpacked.

At one extreme, we have visited beacon vendors with palatial offices situated on expensive real estate. Some vendors have big teams, including industry veterans, who are clearly being well paid. Both of these may be impressive to us as prospective customers, but are signs of a high burn rate. Other areas for concern are players that are trying to develop everything themselves. None of these factors is a disqualifier, but they raise questions about how the vendor pays for these overheads.

At the other end of the spectrum we see smaller teams with offshore developers. We see teams that have started their development with a consulting services strategy that has validated their focus and funded their growth. We see companies that have focused on a sub-segment, done well, generated either volume or even cash, and then started to grow into adjacent areas. Until the beacosystem matures, investors in beacon hardware need to think like venture capitalists and consider the fortunes of the company they are investing their own capital into, even if that capital is not money but their reputation, time, and opportunity to lead.

The key questions that need to be answered are, how does this business intend to make money, how fast do they appear to be burning through their capital (political capital or money), and how realistic are their plans?

From this perspective we would want our supplier to be commanding the kind of pricing premium that will allow them to make money. Our next criterion reverses this perspective.

Cost

When looking at costs of beacons, the equation is more complex than the unit price of the hardware.

An area to consider is one we have already touched on; whether a single beacon can accommodate all the required protocols or frame types. Some deployments have wanted to support both Eddystone URL and iBeacon protocols and have ended up deploying two beacons next to each other to achieve that. That's certainly a cost driver.

Consider both the capital cost and the recurring cost of any services that may be charged. These recurring costs could be for the monitoring, fleet management, or conditional access. Some beacon vendors will bundle geofencing and other value-added services such as analytics and orchestration services. This may reduce expenses elsewhere, or be redundant depending on the design of the rest of the solution.

Another component is the cost of replacing batteries, or the wiring required for powered beacons. Materials and labor can vary significantly.

A fundamental question to consider as a multiplier of cost is the density of beacons required. A few beacons are all that is required to indicate presence, but to deliver pinpoint accuracy and location in X, Y, and Z axes many more beacons are required. If navigation services are all that is required based on a rules engine, then the number of beacons may be at a mid-point between these extremes. If the requirement is for triggers near specific points-of-interest, then that will drive your calculations in a different way. The numbers will be driven by the use-cases that you want to support.

Supply Chain

Even Apple with a supply chain guru as CEO, mountains of cash, decades of experience, and huge clout with its suppliers has problems matching supply of its products with demand. Imagine the challenges for your beacon vendor. They have none of those advantages. They may have a ready supply of the processors and power supplies, but if the plastics they require have a lead time, or their contract manufacturing partner has other priorities, they may not be able to switch up supply from the trickle of developer kits to the thousands of beacons required for your project.

Maybe you don't need thousands of beacons. If you only need a hundred beacons, does that mean you don't need to worry? Unfortunately you still need to consider scenarios where your shipment is held hostage because a much larger customer is in short supply.

There is no magic solution to this challenge. The key is to be aware of the risk, get a sense of your beacon vendor's business and behavior in the market, communicate with your vendor, and don't leave it to the last moment to place your order.

Developer Community

While the current state of play continues and developers use the beacon vendor's SDK to integrate with their products, each beacon vendor needs to develop relationships with an ecosystem of software and services partners to build out the beacosystem software stacks into complete solutions. These stacks will provide the apps and all of the other layers of functionality we define in the beacosystem stack.

To the extent that your requirements are fully defined, you can make sure that all the pieces you need work with your beacon vendor's platform. Given that requirements change in unpredictable ways, you will want to have evidence of a broader set of solutions that are ported to your beacon platform.

Partners

Beacon vendors can't do everything themselves. In addition to their developer community, it's useful to understand the ecosystem of other partners that they can make available to you. Is there a choice of reputable systems integrators that have experience with their products?

Other types of partners include advertising agencies that can help bring advertisers that might be interested in your venue's beacon-enabled infrastructure.

Do they have partners that can help with the logistics of deploying and servicing beacons on a large scale?

Is your beacon vendor partner friendly, or are they trying to do everything themselves? Do they have competing products that might taint their ability to recruit partners to build out their ecosystem? Do they have people responsible for their partnerships? What do the partners say about the shortlisted vendors you are considering?

Relationship with OS Providers

One of the most important partnerships your vendor will have is with Apple and Google. In addition to the specifications that Google and Apple publish to describe iBeacon and Eddystone, there is information that is not public. The mobile OS behavior can change in unpredictable ways. A major beacon vendor will have relationships with insiders at Apple and Google to help them gain access to the unpublished information and respond to the unexpected changes to the mobile OS.

Beacon vendors should be able to demonstrate their participation in pilot projects working with the OS companies, early availability of support for their new standards, and even the names of the people with whom they have relationships. A strong relationship with the OS companies can help mitigate risk to your project and ensure that the best approach is being adopted with the services you require. Evidence of this kind of thing will help you to decide whether you are dealing with a tier one vendor or not.

Vertical

Beacons address a wide set of vertical markets from automotive, banking, retail, hospitality, real-estate, transportation, theme parks, advertising, logistics, education, museums, events, hotels, and tourism. On which verticals is your beacon vendor focused? If the answer is all of them, then the reality is they have no focus. Unless their resources are truly vast, in order to provide the necessary features, partners, and best practice, they must have a focus.

Quality

Quality of the beacon product has varied significantly between vendors. Some have a poor record of reliability. Their products are delivered with a significant percentage dead on arrival, with others failing after a short period. Other quality issues manifest themselves as inconsistency in signal stability and strength.

These issues often become visible in pilot projects. Word gets around. Some vendors may actually track their reliability and can quote Mean Time between Failure (MTBF) numbers. If they aren't measuring this, then that is a cause for concern.

Culture

The culture of companies in the beacosystem varies widely. Some are easy to do business with and are flexible, others are regimented sticklers for strong contractual agreements. Some companies are very guarded in discussing their results and plans, and others are transparent. It's up to you how you interpret these signs. Robust contracts show a sign of maturity and level of quality that will result in smooth acquisitions in the future. Your vendor should be busy. So there should be limits to what they are willing to do to accommodate one customer. In early markets like the beacosystem, you are likely to be spending more time with each other than if this market were really mature, so it might be well to put your lot in with a team that you like.

Geographic Coverage

Even though beacons should work anywhere in the world, they still need local certification, support, sales, and partner management. It quickly becomes obvious if your vendor is covering your current geography, but it's worth considering the ultimate scope of your deployment and making sure that your vendor of choice addresses all those markets.

Intellectual Property (IP) Position

There is a broad range of patent filings that read against beacons. Since very little money is being made in these early stages of the beacosystem, it doesn't make sense for anyone to waste time with patent litigation. Many entrepreneurs don't think it's good use of time to cross license each other's IP until they have a proven business model, but the time may come when it's worth considering this eventuality, once you have made your millions. It sounds bad, but in a sense patent litigation would be a good problem to have, since it indicates that players in the beacosystem are making money.

Your beacon vendor will have exposure to competitors who have patents that they probably have not licensed. It's useful to understand the patent filings that your vendor has made; this can help establish a balance of power, or a bargaining chip to settle disputes. Ideally the Bluetooth SIG and the OS venders will manage this issue as they have the lawyers and patent portfolios to best equip them to provide defensive cover for their developer community. In the case of the SIG, today beacons sit on top of the Bluetooth stack and so the "do not sue your fellow member" provision of the Bluetooth agreement doesn't apply. While the

OS vendors probably won't indemnify you (defend you in court if you get sued for using their product), there is some strength in numbers if you use their protocols. Make sure in your beacon supply agreement that your supplier is offering IP indemnification.

Volume

The manufacture of Bluetooth beacons is not a boutique or craft business. Unlike the makers of luxury automobiles, musical instruments, or fine chocolates, we are not talking about an artisanal process where dedicated craftspeople hone the delivery of a small number of beacons that have been polished and seasoned to perfection.

If a beacon vendor is not moving large volumes of product, it's unlikely they will have a close relationship with the OS vendors who control their destiny. Without volume, it's even more unlikely that software vendors will adopt their platform. In a low-margin business, you do need to make it up in volume in order to be viable as a business. The companies acquiring the best-of-breed beacon vendors will be looking for a high volume of sales too.

It's easy to produce a poor beacon. Buy the module from your silicon vendor, limit the value add software, the protocols, the management tools you provide and you can get a product out there. If, as a beacon vendor, you want to be able to do the hard work of filling all those gaps, it's going to require a significant cash flow to fund it. That flow of cash comes from sales volume.

Some Notable Providers

There is no one vendor who covers all the bases, supporting every feature that every solution designer would need. Solution designers who want a structured listing of capabilities should use our sister resource, the Proxbook.com database, to get the latest information about vendor capabilities. It would be an easy "cop out" to leave it there.

In order to avoid that, we have gathered a list of vendors that we think are notable, that we have had occasion to become familiar with. This is a sample out of the hundreds of companies competing with each other that we think you should consider.

With each we will discuss the things we like and the tradeoffs, or "development areas," that we see. Consider these criticisms as you would the barbed jokes in a comedy roast. We wouldn't be saying these things if the target weren't a significant player worthy of respect.

Just because a vendor isn't listed here, doesn't mean to say they are not worthy of consideration. Life is short, as is our attention span. So we have not enumerated every example of the distinctive types of vendor called out here. Enough of the disclaimers …

BluVision

BluVision are one of the contenders for the title of "beacon vendor that has sold the most product," with over one million beacons shipped in 2014. They have done this through a focus on two verticals, personal beacons for helping individuals finding lost items under their Stick'n'Find brand and their success in selling to a major logistics/shipping company. This was for an application where beacons were used to track the movement and care of valuable shipments. Unlike Tile, which sold even more beacons, tracking key rings and lost bicycles,

BlueVision provide beacons for venues too. They leverage the volume and cash flow from tracking assets to build a position in a market that is more about recurring services revenue.

Their expense burn rate appears to have been well matched to their revenue and they haven't had to raise significant venture capital in their first couple of years of operation. We first met their CEO when he was staffing a small booth at the Bluetooth SIG conference. He seems grounded, frugal, and in touch with the business, willing to do the marketing work that other chief executives might think is below them.

When Google launched Eddystone, BluVision were one of the first six to be selected to support the standard. That OS vendor relationship is key.

Their hardware product portfolio is comprehensive with powered beacons and battery powered beacons with a sizable capacity. They also provide a Wi-Fi to Bluetooth bridge for remote management of beacons.

BluVision has invested in its software stack. They have experience with fleet management of large numbers of beacons; they have the conditional access layer that is required to control who can see a beacon.

Their brand lacks the slick graphics and playful industrial design of Estimote. Perhaps it is their location in Florida or their down-to-earth culture that has kept them out of the media spotlight, as compared to Estimote and Gimbal. Our estimate is that their developer portfolio and number of customers is smaller than some of the tier one vendors they are competing with. That raises some risk to their ongoing revenue stream. Their acquisition of elements of a beacon orchestration module, the marketing layer that developers can build on to save themselves time and cost, may also be a turn-off to other software developers that they compete with in this space. BluVision's challenge is building the developer ecosystem on their platform that they need to succeed in the long term and breaking into verticals where their beacons are stationary and can form a network that can be monetized across multiple software vendors.

All of these challenges are manageable and fairly obvious, so we are excited to see their progress.

Estimote

Estimote has succeeded in capitalizing on having its development and management team based in Poland in order to manage costs, while projecting an image of the ultimate Silicon Valley startup. They have beautiful products that compete with major film starlets in their regular appearance in magazine, blogs, and journals. The visual appeal extends beyond their product and its packaging, through to the materials on their web site. The Estimote diagram of how iBeacon works in a retail environment should get its own YouTube channel, it has been spread across the Internet that much. As a result, their web site has been visited more often than any other beacon hardware company in the first two years of the iBeacon ecosystem.

This has been backed up with cultivation of probably the largest community of developers in the beacosystem using their SDK. We believe Estimote have sold more developer kits than any other beacon vendor.

Managing beacons using their iOS app is very straightforward, with simple access to the controls to change all beacon parameters.

They have added UUID rotation and support for Eddystone to compete with other tier one vendors. Given the huge volume of developers on their platform, they have a solid basis for relationships with the OS vendors. This was evidenced by their being in the first tranche of partners that Google announced as having Eddystone support.

Estimote adds value with an Indoor Location API that allows the simple mapping of a room with beacons placed on each of the walls and then offers near real-time user positioning within the mapped space.

Their product range addresses developer and personal applications with a sealed beacon using a CR2477 coin cell battery and an "Estimote Stickers" product, shown in Figure 7-13, where 10 very thin beacons are embossed with icons to indicate the objects they can be attached to (e.g. bike, dog, car, and laptop) in order to track them.

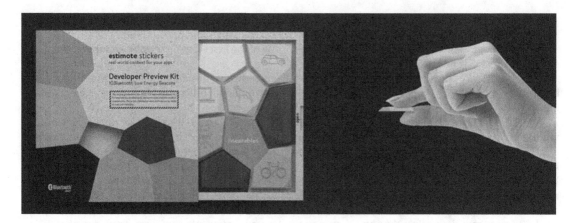

Figure 7-13. Estimote's Stickers product

While Estimote is arguably the leader in cultivating a developer ecosystem, the areas where Estimote has received criticism can be summed up as a product range lacking robust enterprise quality.

Their philosophy appears to center on the premise that the beacosystem is in the pilot stage and so if a beacon battery is exhausted, the device should be thrown out and replaced with the latest model.

They currently have no powered/plug-in beacons or Wi-Fi management hubs. Their maximum battery capacity is relatively small, topping out at the CR2477 coin cell level. As mentioned previously, when that battery is exhausted, the only way it can be replaced is if the beacon case is cut open with a knife. The plastic case is substantial, so that's no small task.

Historically their quality control has been poor, with a high failure rate on arrival and after a period of use. The calibration of their beacons has been inconsistent, so that one beacon may behave differently from another in the same batch. This may have been addressed as they have gained more experience.

Other beacon vendors such as Sensoro and Gimbal have positioned their antennas as being of a higher quality, yielding greater range, and a more stable signal, which results in more predictable proximity measurement.

All that said, none of these issues is insurmountable. Having the largest developer ecosystem is a very significant advantage. New products that address enterprise requirements can be deployed quickly. Creating the largest base of developers cannot. I have spoken to solution providers who have been delighted by their experiences working with Estimote's product.

Facebook

Facebook's launch of its Bluetooth beacon is one of the most exciting things that has happened in the beacosystem. This is not a quick-and-dirty market test. The industrial design and packaging are beautiful.

The strategic implications for the beacon market are significant, especially as we look at the rise of the beacon network phenomenon we will discuss later. The Facebook beacon has the potential to be a great success. However Facebook isn't likely to be selling its beacons for use by anything other than its own app any time soon. Solution designers looking for a short list of general-purpose beacons can cross Facebook off their list, for now at least.

We will revisit Facebook in the beacon network chapters.

Gimbal[11]

Beacon vendors can be split into two categories based on their genesis. Those born in the bedrooms, garages, incubators, the habitat of the start-up, and those that grew out of the lab, office cube, or meeting room within an established corporate player. Gimbal is in the latter category. It was incubated within Qualcomm, the largest producer of mobile semi-conductors in the world.

As a result, it has enjoyed a lot of the privileges that go with an aristocratic upbringing, having been cultivated by experts in their respective fields of hardware design, manufacturing, legal, cloud software, and business development. Gimbal had a lot of experiences in its youth that were denied to many less privileged beacon companies. It got to go to all the best sporting events (the Super Bowl and stadiums of all the major sports leagues) and parties (South by South West); it was exposed to culture (LACMA) and as a result of its parent's status it was introduced to business heavy weights (Google and Apple). It had a privileged place in clubs (the Bluetooth SIG). As a result of all this, it developed a sense of confidence that doubtless has helped it to gain further success, but may be off-putting for some. It's probably also true to say that as Gimbal was carved out of Qualcomm, it brought with it a lifestyle and a spending rate that was higher than a startup pulling itself up by its bootstraps. Like any offspring from a privileged background, the expectations are high too. It puts pressure on the team to drive revenue sooner, to scale larger, and to look for the big win.

What does this mean specifically? Gimbal can probably claim more high-profile pilot wins than any other vendor. Its beacons are in all the U.S. Apple stores, the first U.S. national retail deployment of a general-purpose beacon. They have deployed hundreds of beacons around New York City in partnership with Titan. Their partnerships with major app vendors, such as RetailMeNot and Shazam, have been significant. Their experience with deployments by major advertising agencies in Japan was formative.

Their hardware lineup is comprehensive, with personal tags (the $5 S10), enterprise grade beacons (the S21, shown in Figure 7-14) with robust battery capacity (four AAs), a powered USB device, and less well known Bluetooth to Wi-Fi hub, although that is not a formal part of the hardware lineup (think of it as being on the secret menu, like Animal Style Fries at In-n-Out).

---

[11]Full disclosure: As noted elsewhere, the author worked at Qualcomm as Senior Director of Strategy for Qualcomm Retail Solutions, the division that incubated Gimbal prior to its carve out from that company.

Figure 7-14. *The Gimbal S21 is powered by four AA batteries and has software selectable directional and omnidirectional antennae*

The Gimbal cloud software stack may be the broadest in the industry. The product is based on a marriage between a context platform (the original Gimbal product) that predates the introduction of beacons. So it includes robust geofencing, a messaging component to send alerts to users, as well as profiling of individuals based on their movements, tracking their most popular destinations. More recently, Gimbal acquired the Phigital platform, which added what we would describe as an orchestration layer to manage the experience that is delivered by apps using Gimbal beacons.

Gimbal's vision of building networks of beacons is exciting and ambitious.

The downsides of working with Gimbal can be inferred from their strengths and heritage. Major customers with money to spend will feel in good company. Smaller players may find it harder to get attention.

While most of Gimbal's peer group have a Fortune 500 company behind them, Qualcomm no longer has a majority equity share. So unlike beacon companies such as HP, SK Planet/Shopkick, Zebra, and Facebook, we don't know who will ultimately own Gimbal. It's unlikely it will disappear—there is too much value—but companies sensitive to the agenda of a potential acquirer may be concerned. The departure of a number of key executives (and to be fair, the arrival of a cast of well qualified replacements) suggests there is considerable pressure to achieve results that may not have been fully realized.

For a solution builder that simply wants to buy hardware and create their own cloud platform to support a network strategy or middleware offering, there may be some challenges in reconciling strategies.

Gimbal's hardware is very competitively priced because by default they charge a monthly active user fee. This isn't unfair, given the depth of cloud service functionality available. While the structure of the fee may change, this model may not be acceptable to solution builders that simply want high quality hardware.

Lastly, to satisfy their ambitious vision, Gimbal's market focus has been quite broad, which means a lot of the functionality is broad based, which makes it a good fit for developers building their own vertical solution. However, end users looking for a one-stop shop may find other beacon vendors have a more focused solution. Gimbal's success is therefore predicated on their ability to partner well with third parties.

Gimbal feels like the offspring of a very demanding parent. When most kids would be happy with an A-, the Gimbal team flinches, because they know that only an A+ is acceptable.

Kontakt.io

Kontakt.io represents a different model from Gimbal; one could say the opposite approach. It has established its strength in the European market, where it has a leadership position. Kontakt.io's presence is becoming more established in the United States.

They have focused on monetizing beacon hardware rather than charging for active users, or building out a beacon network. Like Estimote, Kontakt.io is headquartered in Poland. Their image is rooted in a focus on cause-based solutions, with a founding story that relates to providing assistance for blind people with beacon-enabled mobile apps.

The Kontakt.io hardware is distinguished by a Wi-Fi to Bluetooth gateway or cloud beacon (Figure 7-15) and a robust weather-resistant tough beacon.

Figure 7-15. *Kontakt.io cloud beacon provides a management gateway between its Bluetooth beacons and the ability to monitor and manage via Wi-Fi*

Kontakt.io was among the first vendors to support both Eddystone and iBeacon protocols. While their industrial design is not as conspicuous as Estimote, they have a well organized developer program with the most regular production of video content to guide entrants to the beacosystem.

There are limitations to their beacons' power options. Their beacon and tough beacon both rely on CR2477 thick coin cell batteries, which limits the battery life to six months when broadcasting at Apple's prescribed 100ms interval.

While their initial offerings have been free from monthly recurring charges and their pricing is reasonable, the question is how they will generate revenue beyond the small margins from hardware?

Sensoro

If Gimbal's geographic strength is the United States and Kontakt.io's is Europe, Sensoro's strength is Asia. Headquartered in China, they have capitalized on the size of that market to lay claim to having deployed more beacons in venues than any other vendor (110,000 as of Q4 2015). They have announced the following:

> *The network spans 25 movie theatres, 16 airports, 39 high-end retail stores, 40 major tourist destinations, 200 universities, 260 high-speed trains, 1,500 Pizza Hut restaurants, and 2,100 Chow Tai Fook (CTF) jewelry retail stores among other locations.*

These are significant volumes. The deployment in the Chow Tai Fook jewelry store leverages the communications app WeChat, which claims 600 million active users as of August 2015.

Sensoro claims that its beacons triggered proximity experiences that resulted in an amazing 63% coupon conversion rate during a campaign that prompted customers to shake their phones when they entered stores to reveal special offers.

We would argue that the "network" aspect of this announcement is more aspirational than a reality today. A third party can't yet programmatically gain access to all these beacons to launch a campaign, but no other vendor is as well positioned to achieve this in China as Sensoro is.

Sensoro's hardware has a reputation for quality antenna design, with a strong stable signal. They are unusual in having dual antennae, with a selectable short-range antenna that is designed to enable triggers when phones come within a few centimeters of the beacon.

As well as the aesthetically-pleasing Yunzi beacon (see Figure 7-16) that runs on a CR2477 coin cell battery, with a light sensor that can be used to trigger an energy saving mode, Sensoro offers more plainly packaged beacons that run off USB power, as well as the two 4xAA battery options.

Figure 7-16. *Sensoro's Yunzi beacons being used at a Real Madrid/Inter Milan match with more than 40,000 in attendance at the Guangzhou Tianhe Stadium*

Sensoro offers support for Eddystone and iBeacon protocols. It also offers an encryption technique to prevent unauthorized use of beacon UUID identifiers.

Currently beacon status, configuration, and software updates are achieved via an Inspection app. Going forward, they have announced a "station" that uses an additional radio technology to manage beacons within a much wider radius than can be reached through Bluetooth.

Sensoro has a small but significant staff presence in the United States and has a partnership with Microsoft, one of their original investors, which has helped raise their visibility and paved their expansion into the United States. They sold significant numbers of beacons to Google, which earns them a claim to have those all-important relationships with at least one of the key mobile OS vendors. They also have credible deployments at SeaTac airport, the Seahawks stadium, and a number of local museums.

U.S. customers must satisfy themselves that this satellite operation can support them adequately. With engineers in another time zone, and communications challenges when bridging the firewalls imposed by the Chinese government, this can raise issues if the kind of project being contemplated is pushing boundaries where collaboration across time zones is required. While the author has been impressed by Sensoro's responsiveness, we have had challenges getting communications to penetrate China's firewall. As they increase their presence in the United States, their challenge will be to replicate their success with WeChat in other apps with the same reach in the United States.

Sensoro beacons are competitively priced. As of writing this, however, the shipping costs to the United States are significant for small unit volumes. That said, the cost of beacons may not be relevant. Their executives understand the value of building a true beacon network, where they own the hardware and seem open to waiving charges for hardware in order to establish placement of their beacons in key venues. Venues with significant traffic may find Sensoro willing to invest in funding the cost of beacons in their location.

Shopkick, Swirl, and inMarket

All of these vendors have significant experience with offering beacons. While Shopkick, Swirl, and inMarket all provide beacons, they don't sell them as a commodity product to third-party developers. Their hardware is offered as an integral component of a retail services offering.

This recognition that the money is in the services, not the hardware, is smart but unfortunate. Shopkick's beacon is one of this author's favorite beacons. It is probably the largest beacon on the market, due to the sheer mass of the batteries that are packed into the device.

All three vendors have good experience with mass deployments in retail environments and were early to market with techniques to obfuscate the UUID of their beacons.

They have claimed support for iBeacon and benefit from those hooks into the OS to support the applications that use their networks, but because they don't service the general-purpose developer community as hardware vendors they haven't felt the need to be first in line to offer support for Eddystone.

We will explore their offers further in the beacon network chapters.

Quuppa

Quuppa is a very distinctive technology company based in Finland. Founded by ex-Nokia researchers, it offers what may be the most accurate Bluetooth beacon location technology on the market today.

Quuppa achieves extraordinary levels of precision, down to a small number of centimeters in some cases. They do this while tracking movements at high speed, plotting the location of their Bluetooth beacons in close to real time. Visualize ice hockey players skating at full pelt around a rink, with a beacon attached to the puck rocketing between them. The players and the puck can all be tracked in the digital world, with graphical displays that keep up with the real-world action.

Quuppa does this with proprietary receivers, or "locators," that use angle of arrival technology across an antenna array. Angle of arrival measures the difference in timing of the arrival of a signal across different elements of an antenna. If the signal arrives at the same time across all elements, it can be deduced to be perpendicular to the antenna array. As that angle changes, the timing and the phase of the arrival of the signal across the antenna differs. Based on computing that angle, the position of the signal source can be deduced (see Figure 7-17).

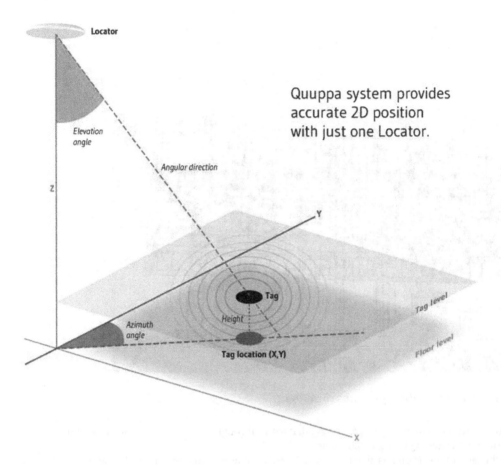

Quuppa system provides accurate 2D position with just one Locator.

Figure 7-17. Quuppa's locators calculate the angle of arrival of a signal to deduce the position of a Bluetooth beacon

These antenna arrays aren't like the sprawling antenna systems deployed by the Germans to plot the approach of enemy aircraft during World War II (Figure 7-18). They are housed in a sleek Frisbee shaped device. This device requires a power connection. A single antenna can track location in two dimensions; add a second one to track in 3D.

Figure 7-18. *German phased array antenna circa 1944*

Quuppa is a small company (seven key staff) that works through value-added resellers who build complete solutions around Quuppa's technology.

While the level of precision it is able to achieve is remarkable, it's important to understand the implications of this approach. In all the other cases we have discussed here, the beacon detection is being done by a consumer's phone, and uses signal strength to measure proximity to the beacon, whose position is fixed. With Quuppa, a stationary antenna array device (see Figure 7-19) is calculating the location of a beacon, which is the mobile component.

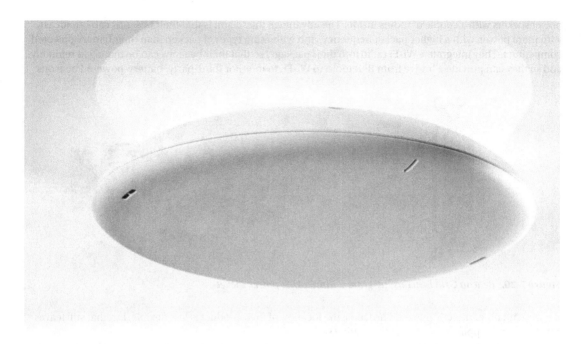

Figure 7-19. *The Quuppa receiver or locator device contains an antenna array used to pinpoint beacon location*

This means that you need beacons on the objects or people that are being tracked. Of course phones can be programmed to become beacons. In which case, they can be tracked too.

There are some potential issues with consumers who may not want their phones to be activated in this way. This may be due to a number of perceived issues, including privacy and an inability for iOS devices to listen for other Bluetooth devices while transmitting as a beacon, but these are probably manageable. Attaching dedicated beacons to shopping carts in a retail use-case mitigates these risks, and also has the benefit of eliminating the need for shoppers to have a smartphone, download an app, and grant it permission to use location services.

The key difference with the conventional beacon approach is that there are more upfront infrastructure costs with this approach. The Quuppa locators are more sophisticated than a simple beacon and cost about the same as a Wi-Fi access point to purchase. They also need the same power and networking connections as those devices, which involves greater installation costs. A 100,000-foot big box store might need of the order of 100 Quuppa receivers. So if all the venue needs is simple proximity alerts, the Quuppa solution is likely to be overkill. If there is an ROI on calculating accurate location, the upfront investment may be justifiable, especially as the maintenance costs of the fixed "locator" devices is lower than battery-powered beacon devices (no battery replacement or manual updating of firmware is necessary).

For tracking players on the field, "residents" in correctional facilities, people and assets in healthcare, along with retail heat mapping and wayfinding, the Quuppa solution has some exciting potential.

Beacon Grid

Beacon Grid's flagship beacon isn't battery powered and it doesn't plug-in, rather, it is the plug, or BeaconOutlet™ that other devices plug into (Figure 7-20). This infrastructure approach is similar in philosophy to that of Acuity, Philips, and GE Lighting, which believe that Bluetooth beacons should be a feature within the wiring of a building. Rather than being built into the lighting system, Beacon Grid provides power sockets with a couple of radios inside. The advantage they claim is that their beacons can broadcast with more power, with a higher packet frequency, and with more types of packet, than their battery powered competitors. They integrate a Wi-Fi radio into their package, so that their beacons can be managed remotely and so they can provide a bridge from Bluetooth to Wi-Fi, to monitor third-party, battery-powered beacons.

Figure 7-20. *Beacon Grid beacons integrate within a U.S. power socket*

As with other directly powered beacons, the location of their product is less flexible, but that still leaves a wide range of applications that can be addressed.

Although they are still a startup, Beacon Grid is seeing traction in a number of verticals. Their beacons have been integrated into systems for monitoring presence in offices and multi-dwelling units. They can provide information to better optimize heating and cooling, so that the HVAC (Heating, Ventilating, and Air Conditioning) systems only spend energy on conditioning the temperature in a room when there are people present. The physical security and ubiquity of sockets (people aren't likely to steal them) makes them a good fit for security applications, such as informing the e911 system where an emergency call is coming from, or fulfilling the same function for collage campus security, where students can summon help using an app in circumstances that might not warrant a call to 911.

Another interesting security application is to authenticate the presence of a person's phone as part of an electronic system. They can allow access to secure documents via a wireless device, but only if it's within the secure area of a government building.

Beacon Grid sees itself as a BaaS (Beacon as a Service) business where it charges a monthly fee for use of a BeaconOutlet, providing additional value with fleet management and asset tracking services, and integrations with the third parties that provide complete office, hotel, airport, and secure document applications. This is a prudent and exciting business model for them and for investors. For their customers they need a rock solid ROI to justify the $12-$40 a month that Beacon Grid charges as list prices (for small quantities).

Zebra

Zebra was one of the first "grown-up" companies to make and sell beacons and, among other things, offers a more stable source of supply than many other younger companies in this space. By "grown-up" we mean Zebra is over 40 years old, and is a relatively large, public company, with over 7,000 employees, global reach, and billions of dollars of revenue.

Zebra's name comes form its origins as a pioneer in barcode printing. Since then they have acquired capabilities in UWB, RFID, and Bluetooth beacons, through the acquisition of Motorola Solutions, the part of Motorola left after the company split and sold the handset business to Google. It has a broader base of retail technologies than most providers in this space.

Zebra is an example of an interesting class of beacon company, the Wi-Fi infrastructure provider (think Cisco, HP/Aruba, and Ruckus), using Wi-Fi access points as a means of managing a fleet of Bluetooth beacons.

Its beacon hardware range, MPact, encompasses USB-powered, CR 2450 coin cell and 2xAA batter units that can be controlled from a central Wi-Fi enabled server. They have succeeded in recruiting another major beacon vendor, Swirl, to use their beacon hardware by offering support for Swirl's proprietary SecureCast protocol. This protocol allows access to beacons to be regulated.

Their MB2000, AA-battery powered beacon is one of the few such devices that uses a directional antenna and uses "a next generation chipset" that should yield a two-year battery life even when broadcasting at 100ms intervals.

The platform includes location and analytics software. Zebra has done a good job of emphasizing its ecosystem partners (Coffee Bean, Phunware, Swirl, Aisle411, Localpoint by Digby, Codigo, and Retailigence) who have built on the Zebra platform in ways that other beacon vendors have struggled to do.

Zebra's strengths may also provide clues to its weaknesses. It is surprising that there is a lack of case studies and announcements of customer deployments using this comprehensive platform. One can only guess that with its size, the fog of war associated with the Motorola acquisition and the sheer breadth of its offering, that a lack of focus may be causing it to move more slowly in converting its existing customer base over to beacon technology. Having account managers with existing relationships based on purchases of other products is hugely valuable, but with it comes opportunities for internal politicking and change management issues that smaller companies don't experience to the same extent.

If Zebra's executives continue to believe in the opportunity and succeed in generating the profits to justify that patience, the company could be well placed to service accounts that appreciate its many strengths. These include breadth of product, size, focus on beacon management, and being a supplier with a more certain future.

Summary

Beacons are a fairly simple hardware component in a proximity solution with many layers. The vendors stand on the shoulders of silicon manufacturers who provide them with an impressive baseline platform to build on. There are hundreds of beacon vendors to choose from. However, if you consider the criteria we have described in this chapter, it's possible to select a small number that have the hardware, software, and business profile to deliver what is needed for your solution to be successful.

Along with selecting which beacon to use come questions about deploying, what could be, thousands of wireless devices. These devices have to support a set of applications that are new and will probably change over time. How do you prepare for that? This is the next question we consider in our *Hitchhiker's Guide to the Beacosystem*.

■ ■ ■

CHAPTER 8

Beacon Deployment Considerations: The 10 Ps

"Fasten your seatbelts; it's going to be a bumpy [ride]!"

Bette Davis, *All About Eve* (1950)

© Stephen Statler 2016
S. Statler, *Beacon Technologies*, DOI 10.1007/978-1-4842-1889-1_8

For technologists used to creating software and cloud services, the act of deploying beacons in the physical world, at scale, may be one of the most unfamiliar aspects of creating a beacon solution.

For our brethren (and sisteren) who deploy software-only technology solutions, life is relatively simple by comparison. Sure, they have to worry about staging their software and pushing it from development to production servers, but all this occurs in a fairly controlled datacenter environment, where the external factors are at a minimum. We, on the other hand, are bridging the digital to physical divide. This means that we still have to do all that software stuff and we also have to carefully situate these digital cookies (beacons) out into the physical world—very large numbers of them.

These beacons may be distributed across large swaths of unfamiliar territory, where lots of people believe they have control and we don't. What we are doing is more akin to what AT&T has to do when rolling out a new cell phone network. AT&T has to select sites, perform construction, and deal with the unpredictability of what happens to signals when the environment interferes with theoretical plans. Anyone who has suffered a dead zone in cell coverage knows how hard building a wireless network is.

In the future, when large multi-tenant networks of beacons have been deployed for us in advance, access to beacons will be achieved by selecting the beacons that interest us from a web console. Life will be a lot simpler. More on that in Chapter 13, "Understanding Beacon Networks."

Until then, welcome to the critical path, where lots of things can go wrong and there isn't much upside. How often do we expect a shopper to say, "Great job placing that beacon"? Will we get a call from the mayor's office to thank us for consulting with them on privacy issues when deploying beacons in the public space? Probably not.

So job one is to set your stakeholders' expectations on the size of the task and what could possibly go wrong when deploying thousands of beacons. Hopefully when the beacons are all in place and they trigger the app as expected, when small children don't steal them, and the bomb squad is not called out to defuse the beacon, you will get the praise you deserve[1].

How do you assess the magnitude of the task at hand when deploying the beacons? The goal with this chapter is to provide you a checklist of things to consider. Coincidentally, many of those factors can be grouped under headings that all begin with the letter "P" (see Table 8-1). Hopefully this makes it easier to remember them.

Table 8-1. *The Ten Ps of Beacon Deployment*

1.	Planning	Securing executive sponsorship, site surveys, maintenance cycles, training, deployment documentation, and sizing the number of beacons required
2.	Placement	Location, location, location—make sure you understand where beacons should be placed
3.	Propagation	Making sure the signal gets to where it should go and nowhere else
4.	Procurement	Making sure you have the beacons when you need them
5.	Permission	You probably need more people's permission than you might hope
6.	Privacy/Public Notices	Consider placing notices in public places letting people know that beacons are in use
7.	Process	Setting up beacons with the correct ID and tracking their placement
8.	Power	Consider carefully the implications of laying in power for beacons and maintaining batteries
9.	Presentation	Understand any branding or cosmetic issues
10.	People	Who will do the deployment and maintenance

---

[1]Both of these things have happened.

There is no substitute for experience, so we have included in this chapter direct quotes containing recommendations and lessons learned from the deployment engineers at Point Inside and Gimbal. These engineers have experience with beacon deployments at the top U.S. retailers, major sports venues, and events such as the Super Bowl and South by Southwest. We end the chapter with a case study from a deployment of over 1,000 beacons across a set of large shopping malls.

Planning

Let's start at the top. Having an executive sponsor whose authority spans all the organizations required for your project's success is important.

Sponsorship

You will need to communicate with and motivate people in lots of different functions, people who control the physical domain in which you will be placing the beacons, operations, facilities, marketing, and lawyers, to name a few. These people will feel their authority is being tested when this new technology attempts to "break on through to the other side," from the digital to the physical. Most organizations are built on inertia. When you start doing something different, some people will be excited, but many others will feel challenged. By breaking out of the pure software domain and placing beacons in places they haven't gone before, you are going to require cooperation and tolerance from many more functional stakeholders. The last thing you need is one of those stakeholders to feel their job is to hit the stop button on your project. Having a senior executive sponsor, someone who everyone wants to please, who is vested and reviewing progress, is the best way to mitigate these issues.

Cross-Functional Briefings

Having your executive support in place is not enough. Plan to confer with all the department heads and influencers whose cooperation you may need. If you can pick their brains, learn from them, and make this project theirs so it's a group win, all the better.

> *This is very critical. Often teams try to get beacons deployed in a few stores with minimal involvement from cross-functional teams. While that may work out, it almost always results in major hiccups when moving from a pilot stage of a handful of locations to a full-blown beacon rollout. Encourage your customers to involve all the right stakeholders and give them the right knowledge to get sign-off from different departments in their organization. (IT will need different info than Store Operations.)*
>
> Gimbal Deployment Engineering

Communications Plan

Point Inside is a specialist indoor location services provider to top-tier U.S. retailers such as Target and Walmart. Their StoreMode platform is beacon-independent and provides way-finding, analytics, and product-locator functionality to retailer apps. Their deployment team had this to say:

> *Don't underestimate the amount of communication needed to the stores. On a number of occasions, we have installed beacons and the next day come in to be told they were removed because they didn't know what the beacons were. It is hard for stores to communicate everything to ALL employees. Start early, share visuals, explain the value, and use creative methods.*
>
> - *Use internal company communication sites.*
> - *E-mail store managers and line managers directly.*
> - *Send a beacon care package in advance for the managers to see the product.*
>
> *All these activities will enable boots on the ground leadership to get the communication out.*
>
> Point Inside Deployment Engineering

Site Survey

Survey the site, or sites, where your beacons are going to be deployed. Do this as early as you can in the project cycle. Software, hardware, and processes may be impacted by what you find.

> *Deployments seem easy, especially when the tech team is familiar with the product, having used them for months before hitting the store. When you finally get to do your first test in the store, time yourself and your group through the installation. You may quickly realize 6-8 labor hours are needed per store to accomplish an installation—who pays for this cost across 1,000 stores?*
>
> Point Inside Deployment Engineering

The right beacon management tool can assist in streamlining the planning and deployment process.

> *Avoid hard coding locations, e.g. departments, into your beacon setup. Beacons represent a point on a sales floor—product will change underneath it—so should the messaging. Point Inside's StoreMode platform helps in this regard by digitizing your space (product and location) and removing any hardcode between the point and the products around it. Beacons can then be set once, and product can be set in many ways.*
>
> Point Inside Deployment Engineering

On the site visit, step through the use-cases from an app user's perspective, as well as from the deployment team's perspective. Talk to the people who work there, give them a preview of what's going to happen, and get their feedback.

Note where the beacons will go, recording each location, and consider the instructions that will be needed to enable that process. Make sure you understand the people whose cooperation will be needed. Consider the placement and propagation issues we will detail later.

Involve a local subject matter expert, for instance the store manager. They will have a good sense of what's gone wrong with deployments in the past. Being able to cite their input will be useful when you return to base and have to change plans that people may want to be left untouched.

A site survey serves three purposes:

- Find the best beacon placement for mobile apps triggering off a reliable beacon signal.

- Find the best placement location to fit the aesthetics of the physical location.

- Arrive at a process that can easily be replicated across as many locations as possible. Having a custom install per location is not feasible or scalable.

The third point is often overlooked. While you may have the right talent and tools to deploy across a handful of locations, you have to understand that a nationwide rollout usually means people unaware of what beacons are may be involved in the install process. So it is critical to arm them with very simple-to-follow instructions and pictures that allow them to easily install beacons correctly. The synonym I often use is, ask the store manager "What is the process you follow to install a new poster at every store in the country?" While that may seem like over-simplifying the process, it gives you a good sense of how the customer/ brand carries out similar operations across hundreds of thousands of locations.

Gimbal Deployment Engineering

Floor Plan

One of the key documents you will need to copy or create is a floor plan. Floor plans may come from a CAD system (Computer Aided Design), a corporate source, or they may be something that is held locally.

On one occasion we sourced such a document from the local store manager of a Staples we were surveying. We had no agreement with corporate HQ, but we did have our pocket protectors and laptops out and seemed to be official enough that he was happy to cooperate.

Some floor plans will be posted in public places simply to show the location of fire exits, for example, by the elevators in hotels.

Without digitizing the store space, beacons can and will move, get misplaced, or otherwise go missing. Digitization enables a clean placement plan, a digital record, and visualization of beacon locations for easy "findability" and further through mobile analytics, allowing retailers to understand the health of their network.

We create a digital index of each store for our retail customers. This is the digitized understanding of a store space, which is a crucial starting point for a beacon planning project.

Point Inside Deployment Engineering

The deployment of HP Aruba beacons at Levi's Stadium in San Jose was impacted when the hundreds of TVs in the club section of the stands were replaced. The beacons were plugged into the USB ports on the TVs in order to take advantage of the placement and power, but when the TVs were swapped out, hundreds of beacons went missing. The Aruba Meridian sitemap helped to track the holes in the deployment so they could be replaced.

Sizing the Number of Beacons

A very important aspect that should be part of planning your beacon rollout strategy is anticipating how mobile applications will trigger off the beacons. This is the single most important point that gets missed. Often a significant disconnect between teams deploying beacons and software engineers developing the mobile application leads to undesired user experiences.

Gimbal Deployment Engineering

Forecasting the number of beacons required to support your deployment is a highly visible and potentially critical element of your plan. Lots of people are going to be interested in this number. At the front of the line will be the finance person who has to budget for this and, of course, the salesperson selling you the hardware.

The numbers can get very big, depending on the number of venues, their size, and the use-case. This number can be very simple to forecast or quite the opposite, complex and the source of high anxiety. Let's consider some use-cases and their impact on these numbers.

The Check-In Use-Case

The number of beacons the Gas Buddy app needs per convenience store is simple, one per store. This is driven by their use-case, which is to see how many people who received an ad in their app go from the gas station forecourt into the convenience store. In other words, they are measuring *door swings*. For Shopkick, who measures the same thing—door swings driven by their app—the number of beacons is larger, because the venues they service (Macy's, Target, and Walmart) tend to have multiple entrances. When the Shopkick app measures how many American Eagle customers enter the changing rooms after being offered an incentive of "Kicks" points, they needed a second beacon in addition to the one by the store entrance to cover the changing rooms.

Considering use-cases where we are measuring traffic by a billboard or vending machine, then the numbers are simple, one per object where the app is "checking in". In the case of Apple's trailblazing deployment of beacons in the U.S. Apple Stores, the numbers were slightly bigger per store because there were numerous proximity check-ins, one at the entrance and one for each of the accessory displays.

In the case of a sports arena, you may have a beacon at the entrances, at each of the concessions, and by points of interest about which you want to provide information.

So the check-in use-case is simple. Right? Not always. Checking into meeting or conference rooms that are close to each other can be problematic. This is the case when the walls between the rooms don't block the propagation of the Bluetooth signals sufficiently to differentiate the location of two people sitting a few feet apart on either side of that wall. If the wall between the rooms is a wooden screen or a thin piece of plasterboard, this can be problematic, as the beacon signal can pass through these structures.

This issue can be mitigated with more beacons at a lower signal strength on either side of the permeable barrier, and/or enough beacons to do trilateration using extra logic in your orchestration or mapping layer. If you are sitting in a room with multiple beacons, there is a better chance of getting a less ambiguous fix on where you are seated.

The Wayfinding Use-Case

This solution brings us to "location," the use-case that makes forecasting the number of beacons more challenging because the variables are more complex. If our goal is to go beyond a simple check-in and to track movements to draw a heat map or to plot a green dot on a map, then the density of beacons goes up.

The variables include:

- Square footage of the location.

- Algorithms your location system uses. A rules-based guidance system like BlindSquare should require fewer beacons than a system that uses trilateration like Indoo.rs.

- Stability of signal. Different beacons vary in the stability of their signals.

- Signal strength. A lower signal strength will result in less overlap in signal, but will require more beacons to cover a given area.

- Accuracy required. Higher accuracy generally requires more beacons.

- Proximity of alternative locations that need to be differentiated. Consider, for example, corridors that run close to each other.

In challenging locations, an iterative process of testing, followed by adjustment of beacon locations, can resolve issues where location fixes are not consistent.

For benchmarking purposes, lets consider an example of a large location use-case deployment. Indoor.rs used over 300 beacons to implement wayfinding at San Francisco International Airport, Terminal 2, which is 640,000 square feet. That's one beacon per 2,000 square feet. The density of beacons most likely varied depending on what part of the terminal was being mapped. In a location near the TSA barrier, where proximity is key but no physical wall exists, more beacons are likely to be required. If the location is an empty/isolated corridor, fewer beacons would be required.

Looking for a rule of thumb? When reviewing journals you see rules of thumb that vary significantly. The CEO of ByteLight posited that a 102,000 square feet Walmart store (the average size) could need 32 beacons for coarse-grain estimates of the department a shopper was in, ranging up to 320 beacons for wayfinding. That's a range of one beacon per 3,187 square feet, to one per 319 square feet. At the top end, this could be an expensive proposition. Given 4,800 Walmart stores, that's over 1.5 million beacons, or $15m of capital expenditure, assuming the beacons cost $10.

Other vendors might argue that this is a pessimistic estimate, that fewer beacons would be required. ByteLight's perspective may be framed by their ability to deploy beacons as part of LED light fixtures, which helps resolve some of the cost and maintenance issues, since their beacons are powered by the light fixture. In addition to the up-front capital costs, think about the cost of replacing 6 million AA batteries every couple of years.

While it is possible to come up with rough estimates, as much as possible, never give out a number unless you have at least done one or two site surveys. Even after doing hundreds of beacon installs, you always get surprises when you walk into a new physical location. If the use-case is basic like described in the Gas Buddy use-case, you can easily say one beacon at the entrance will do the trick. But anything beyond that will require you to survey a location [and] run some signal tests to estimate what is the quantity of beacons required.

Note that most big customers actually will not cringe at the beacon quantity. Because it is a one-time cap-ex cost and the cost of beacons continues to go down, the hardware cost is not the biggest source of concern for the customer. However, if there aren't enough beacons or if there are too many beacons, which can cause challenges from determining proximity of user to the beacon, the software costs to make an application work can add up very fast and the risk of a poor user experience is more important to a brand. So always be prepared to back up your beacon quantity with very clear reasoning and map them to as many use-cases as possible.

Gimbal Deployment Engineering

Documentation

Depending on how big your deployment is and who is going to do what, you will need to create documentation for each of the players. Make it short and people might even read it.

> *Add photos as much as possible of how the beacons would look after they are installed in that location. Pictures speak a thousand words.*
>
> Gimbal Deployment Engineering

Training

If users of your app will have to do anything that is specific to using the functions triggered by the beacons, then plan to train the staff. When Apple deployed a beacon-enabled version of its Apple Store app, their training was very good. Most staff understood what the beacons were there for and the functionality it drove within their apps.

Training retail staff is challenging. The technical skill and motivation of retail employees varies widely. Some retailers invest extensively in staff selection and training, have strong store management, and low staff turnover. Others do the opposite. It can be extremely challenging to train retail staff to support a new mobile program if all these elements are not in place. It can be very exciting to close a deal with a retailer, but if you are relying on the local staff to do anything at all to support your app, be brutally honest in assessing the retailer's ability to execute its part of the program. Lastly, unless your application is going to be used very regularly (as the Starbucks app is and the ISIS/Softcard payment app was not), any knowledge from the training has a short half-life and will atrophy within a small number of weeks.

> *Another important part of training is to inform the staff of what the beacon does and any questions/concerns they may have around being in the presence of RF signals for a long period of time. Beacons themselves are extremely low-energy devices and the signals they transmit are several fractions to the tune of those emitted by mobile phones that users carry around all day. It is also good to clarify any misconceptions about beacons tracking people—beacons do NOT track people; they help detect the proximity of a user only if the user has opted into a specific mobile application.*
>
> Gimbal Deployment Engineering

Placement

There are some advantages that come with height. If you are thinking of running for president, you are more likely to win if you are the taller candidate[2]. Beacons benefit from lofty elevation, too.

A beacon placed high has the benefit of being out of reach of people who might want an electronic souvenir of their visit to a venue. Most importantly, height maximizes coverage of an area and minimizes the attenuation and signal fluctuations that come from signals being absorbed by people's bodies.

---

[2]"Between 1900 and 2011, 18 of the winning [presidential] candidates have been taller than their opponents, while 8 have been shorter, and 2 have been of the same height. On average, the winner was 1.0 inch (2.5cm) taller than the loser." en.wikipedia.org/wiki/Heights_of_presidents_and_presidential_candidates_of_the_United_States

You can have too much of a good thing. If the beacon is too high, geometry starts to work against you, especially if what you want is a very localized proximity trigger. As you can see in Figure 8-1, in a high ceilinged building, like a warehouse, with a beacon at 20 feet, it's unlikely that there will be sufficient change in signal strength to differentiate between distances that are within a five-foot radius under the beacon. If the goal is to detect a five-foot change in proximity to a particular product display, placing a beacon at a lower height is advisable.

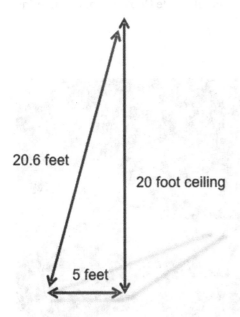

Figure 8-1. *A five foot movement from beneath a beacon elevated to 20 feet above the level of a phone will result in a 3% change in distance, a change so small that it is unlikely to register in terms of predictable change in signal strength*

A higher placement also has the inevitable consequence that should physical access be required for battery change or a reboot, ladders or elevated platforms need to be deployed. At this point, additional facilities staff may need to be involved.

> *Place beacons in a manner that will not cause additional operational overhead when the physical layout of the place changes (as an example, if a retailer has to change their store layout for different seasonal collections).*

> *Another factor that often gets overlooked, especially when installing beacons high on ceilings/walls, is to test for bleed between floors. In multi-level stores and even in some stadiums, we have seen bleed between floors. That can throw off your use-case completely. So it is important to include that in your test considerations when looking at beacon placements.*

> *In most cases, if you want to detect presence of users in a certain zone, installing it 7-8 feet from the ground level works out well. If you go higher, you run the risk of minimizing your beacon reach. Too low and you run the risk of people interfering with the beacon signals.*

> Gimbal Deployment Engineering

Be Prepared for Placement

Bring installation tools, extra tape, cleaning supplies, Velcro, scissors. Seems simple, but having a clean surface with a secure connection between the beacon and its surface pays off in the long run—otherwise, your beacons can quickly end up on your floor.

Point Inside Deployment Engineering

Propagation

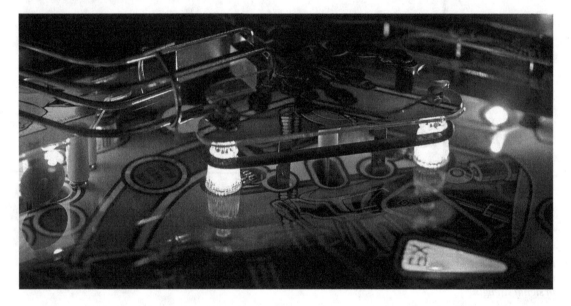

Test, Test, Test. Beacons are RF devices and RF behavior can different significantly based on physical environment. Behavior observed in a lab is very different from that seen in a retail store, which is different than that in a sports venue.

Gimbal Deployment Engineering

Signal Bounce and Multi-Pathing

Taming a Bluetooth signal is reminiscent of "Tommy" the "Pinball Wizard," blindly trying to direct a steel ball that is rocketing off hard surfaces in an unpredictable way.

Bluetooth signal paths don't always go in straight lines and can bounce off walls. When a signal bounces, it can be directed at angles that cause the signal to manifest its presence in places that are unexpected, resulting in a false positive, or a beacon triggering an event in a location that it should not. When the signal bounces and is detected along with the signal that has taken a direct path, this is known as *multi-pathing* and can result in signal fluctuations that make measurements less stable.

These effects can be mitigated with use of directional antenna (not a panacea), through adjusting the orientation of the beacon, and through reducing the signal transmission strength and metal shielding.

Shaping Signals

One of the most challenging signal-taming projects this author has experienced was placing beacons in gas pumps. These beacons were to be used for payments, so that a customer could stand in front of pump #1 and pay for their gas with a cloud payment app, without having to specify that location. Fuel dispensers have two sides that are very close to each other. We needed beacons on either side of the pump to register phones on one side but not the other. The two sides were not insulated from each other in a way that prevented a co-mingling of electromagnetic waves. The potential result of this was that someone standing in front of pump #1 could end up paying for the gas being pumped at #2, on the other side of the island.

Our temporary solution was to purchase two metal switch boxes from Home Depot (see Figure 8-2) and to place one beacon in each box, fixing the two boxes on the inside of the plastic fascia of the pump, so they were facing outward. The boxes cost pennies and proved to be excellent shields. Suddenly we had a clear separation of the signal from the two beacons going out of one side only.

Figure 8-2. *A metal switch box with no holes proved to be a great shield with which to direct and shape a Bluetooth signal*

Some appliances, like vending machines with metal cabinets, can form their own shielding for shaping a directional signal. This is useful if you have multiple vending machines next to each other that need to keep their signals separate. Unfortunately, more often than not existing cases have holes and vents, which provide opportunities for signals to escape and multi-path around the room. The metal switch box is a crude but effective solution in such cases.

> *In some cases, it is just not possible to control a beacon signal to your liking. This is where software comes to the rescue. Having the ability to "ignore" beacons seen beyond a certain signal strength can alleviate the need to achieving your use-case solely with perfect beacon deployments. Your beacon deployments can be "good enough" if you have software that allows you to control when your application can and cannot react to seeing beacons.*

> Gimbal Deployment Engineering

Procurement

You would be forgiven for assuming that, with a few weeks' notice, your beacon supplier will ship the beacons you order.

In the words of Felix Unger from the 70s TV show *The Odd Couple* (Figure 8-3), "You should never assume. You see, when you assume, you make an ass out of you and me."

Figure 8-3. *Felix (Tony Randall) and Oscar (Jack Klugman)—The Odd Couple*

Be extremely cautious and make sure that you are forecasting your needs and have clear expectations on lead times for exactly the kind of beacons you need. If you need large volumes, have clear confirmation from someone at an executive level in your supplier that your order can be delivered in the timescale on which you are depending.

> You will need to procure the tools and supplies for the install (ladders, tape, mounts, phone with a test application to test beacon signals).

> Also, in addition to achieving volume, you need to know if the supplier has the capability to ship individual orders of beacons to several different locations. In most cases, the beacons don't go to a single warehouse but end up being shipped to individual locations. This "packaging" can include a set number of beacons along with an instruction sheet for individual store managers, for example.

> Gimbal Deployment Engineering

Permission

You are the official responsible for the safety and security of a government building. Such buildings are vulnerable to terrorist attacks. A strange electronic device mysteriously appears, stuck on the wall. No one knows where it came from. It doesn't look like anything you have seen before. What do you do? a) Ignore it and take the risk that it's not an explosive device, or b) Follow procedure, evacuate the building, and call in the bomb squad. We know the answer.

Let's image the aftermath of this real-life situation. It happened in London. Do we think that, those executives in charge of the operation of the government facility a) Had a bit of a chuckle, appreciating that the evacuation and resulting disruption made for a nice break for everyone concerned, or b) Channeled the anger and frustration of the people whose day was disrupted and really let the people responsible "have it"?

It's worth conferring with someone in the know at the venue, as to who needs to give their permission for a beacon deployment. It always seems there are a lot more people who feel they should be in a position to say "No" than "Yes," but tempting as it may be, that shouldn't dissuade you from notifying them.

At an airport for instance, the list of people who need to buy in, or at least to be informed, may include:

- IT: They will probably be on the core team

- Marketing: Responsible for presentation of this service

- Public Relations: Ready to explain to the press what's happening

- Security: See above

- Terminal Operations: Responsible for the successful operations of the terminal

- Facilities: If you are going to be using ladders and installing things, they should be your friend

- Concession Management: Given retailers' interest in beacons, they should be aware of what your are doing

- Airline Management: Since airlines have a stake in beacon-enabled apps, arm the folks responsible for those relationships with what you are doing

- Legal: Chief counsel, privacy, contracts

- Contract Management/Procurement: As well as your contract, there may be agreements with other parties who have exclusive rights for certain wireless services, so these folks will need to be on board and confirm that no other agreements are impacted by what's being done

- Finance: They are holding your purse strings

- The Executive Team

- The Board: You don't want to surprise a board member with something that may generate public debate

This list will be different for each vertical market and organization. In retail, the merchandising team will be a key constituency. In petroleum retailing, the relationship among the oil companies, the convenience store franchise brand, and the franchisee can be complex and fragmented. This can make deploying systems in that vertical very challenging.

Stakeholder maps always seem to be more complex than outsiders would imagine. Whatever the vertical, mapping out those stakeholders and getting buy-in up-front will save you time.

Another thing that is helpful is to carry some extra beacons to leave behind with the appropriate authorities. Often it is helpful to give them the ability to show off the beacon to any additional people who need to approve and, plus, you have a much better chance of success when one of the customer employees can speak to the beacon and its functionality themselves!

Gimbal Deployment Engineering

Privacy/Public Notices

Look hard in a retail store and you will probably see public notices about the operation of surveillance cameras (along the lines of Figure 8-4).

Figure 8-4. *Generic security camera warning notice*

Despite the fact that beacons only broadcast and don't track people directly, the reality is that they enable apps to track people with a level of intimacy that is comparable with cookies in browsers. In certain regions, it's mandatory to declare your use of these cookies on web sites.

Given these two precedents, you would be wise to take the high road, do the right thing, and err on the side of full disclosure.

Consider placing signs that explain how the beacons are being used. These don't need to be billboards. It may save a lot of hassle down the road and increase the defensible position you have should a Congressperson challenge your program. The senior privacy lawyer at your venue will have as an objective keeping their CEO from having to testify in front of a Congressional Committee about their company's abuse of privacy. Respecting that goal and making them a friend will pay you dividends.

Process

Keeping track of which beacon was placed where will be key. If this is a process, it won't be a problem. Decide up front if you are going to:

- Place the beacon and then program it based on a preexisting addressing map.

- Program the beacon first and then place it at a predetermined location.

- Program the beacon, place it, then make a record of that location.

Or place the beacon, enable it in the application, and then look at incoming application data to reverse engineer where the beacon may have been placed. This can work only in certain scenarios like when there is a single beacon in a location. Otherwise, documentation is key. It is also helpful to label beacons with a ID or name allowing the person responsible for maintaining the beacon to easily identify the beacon.

Define a process for maintenance (replacement in case for failure, replacing batteries, firmware upgrades).

Gimbal Deployment Engineering

Power

If you have a single beacon that is being used for a check-in to your venue, having that beacon powered may be viable. This is what Gas Buddy does. Because their use-case is simple and convenience stores are generally quite small and separated from competing stores, it works. They don't have to worry about battery life and the replacement process for batteries, which is a huge benefit.

Shopkick's beacons can be in stores that are close to each other, so beacon placement becomes more critical. They moved from a powered audio check-in device to a battery-based Bluetooth beacon. Part of the rationale was to avoid the cost and complexity of having to run power to the beacon. As one of the first firms that has done national deployments of beacons across multiple retailers, that says a lot.

The vendors of LED lighting are in strong position to offer their services as a beacon provider for venues that need to be blanketed with beacons. They can offer a relatively low-cost way of powering beacons that are already fitting into a Bluetooth mesh network that's in place to control the lights. The complexity of coordinating a beacon deployment with a lighting refit works against them, but having a built-in power source is a compelling advantage. If your ROI is strong and the use-case is very well established, perhaps you can make the case that a powered beacon infrastructure is worth the up-front cost.

Given this is the exception rather than the rule, look for beacons with bulging battery packs and take advantage of the ease of deployment that you will have gained.

Presentation

When conferring with the stakeholders who control your venue, the way your device fits into the look and feel of the venue may be very important. Some categories of venue will be very relaxed; others will be manically controlling.

Gimbal beacons are generally white, but the ones in the Apple store are silver. One can infer that this customization of the color of their product for a single customer was not done lightly. Changing the appearance of your beacon can take time and planning. Be careful that efforts to conceal your beacon don't interfere with their operation. For instance, hiding beacons under metal shelving can create issues with unwanted signal absorption.

> *Beacons are not supposed to stand out in a physical location. Be it a retailer, a sports venue, or a museum, it is important that beacons just blend into the existing environment.*

Gimbal Deployment Engineering

People

Who will deploy your beacons? On a small scale the answers are relatively easy. If the there is a single beacon that needs to be deployed for a simple check-in use-case, mailing the beacon in a package with really clear instructions and a tested process that is as simple as pulling a tab, peeling off a label, and pressing the beacon on a wall could work. It's even more likely if the person receiving the beacon is highly motivated to make the program work. Facebook has done a good job with the instructions, packaging, and design to make that feasible for its beacon.

If there are strong unions in place, you may have no choice but to use their workers to deploy the beacons.

As soon as the number of beacons increases and the placement becomes more critical, the question requires some consideration. Relying on retail shop assistants to do this, or even on their managers, may not be the best course of action. Fortunately, deploying technology in venues is a common requirement and it's possible to piggyback on an established network of companies that service point-of-sale equipment, or perform merchandising (shelving displays) installation. Typically they have processes to track such deployments to make sure the work has been done.

Case Study

The following are edited responses to a questionnaire that we shared with a solution provider who deployed 1,400 beacons across six shopping centers in Switzerland.

Systems Integrator/Software Developer:

- Codeparc LLC; www.codeparc.com

- Michael Rava|CEO

Venues:

- Six shopping centers, each with 50 stores on average.

- Each center has its own app. The backend can aggregate all data into one consolidated picture.

Use-cases:

- News (based on users' interests), location information, promotions and games.

OS:

- iOS and Android

Beacon access controlling used (e.g., rotating UUIDs)?

- Yes. We protect the apps from spoofed beacons.

Number of beacons deployed:

- Between 150 and 250 per center, with another 100 per center due to be installed.

Beacon manufacturer:

- Kontakt.io, which was chosen for battery life, configuration options, hardware design, and service.

Frame types/protocols broadcast:

- Currently Kontakt.io/iBeacon. Eddystone maybe depending on market acceptance.

Planning

- Our client performed extensive surveys in advance to defining user preferences and requirements. They provided us with PDF floor plans.

- We calculated the number of beacons required based on testing at our headquarters and in-depth research on location, assessing the building structure and adjusting the plan based on local conditions.

- Center management, marketing planners, building technicians, engineers, and developers were all involved in the deployment.

- We provided plans and briefings for our customer in writing. Training is planned (on location).

Placement

- Beacon placement balanced cosmetics and access for maintenance, while keeping them out of reach, so they are not interfered with or stolen.

- Center technicians and center facility services performed the hardware deployment.

Propagation

- We had a few challenges with signal bouncing and interference. We made adjustments in beacon placement to deal with the effects of building materials and windows.

Procurement

- There were no issues in getting the number of beacons we wanted when we needed them. We ordered early.

- The key is to plan, order, test, implement, and have a contingency supply of spare beacons.

Permission

- We informed the customer's Property Management and Center Management about the project in great detail in advance.

Privacy

- Based on Swiss law, there were no privacy concerns that necessitated physical signage. For the beacons to be used, visitors must install the app on their smartphones and are presented with a privacy statement when they start using the app.

Process

- The beacons were programmed in advance of the deployment and then placed at a predetermined location.

Power

- We started with battery-powered beacons. Powered beacons will follow probably in 2016.

Presentation

- Depending on the color of the environment, we used white or black beacons.

People

- Roles:
    - Codeparc: Planning, programming, testing, ...
    - Client: On-location hardware installation by Center Facility Management
- People required to do the deployment: 6 people, 10 weeks
- At the moment, health monitoring is built into our consumer apps. However, we have plans to change that by 2016 where we will implement cloud-beacons to perform monitoring and updates.
- Center Facility Management will change batteries.
- Codeparc will do firmware updates manually or through cloud-beacons.

The acceptance of the new technology has been very positive. It's been important to provide customers meaningful benefit they couldn't get otherwise.

Summary

The 10 Ps provide a basis for preempting many of the issues that need to be navigated. A large-scale retail deployment is like whitewater rafting. We all have a general idea of what needs to be done—wear a life jacket and try not to hit any rocks—but having a guide who has done it before is advisable. That guide may be a consultant, it may be someone within the venue, or it may be a partner. So while Bette Davis was right—this can be a bumpy ride—with the right tools and some preparation, it can also be a fun one.

In the next chapter, we will look at some of the tools that can help manage your fleet of beacons as they are deployed.

CHAPTER 9

■ ■ ■

Designing with Management in Mind

Question: Lions gather in prides, geese group in gaggles, there's a murder of crows, and a leap of leopards. What's the collective noun for a group of beacons?

Answer: Planes, trucks, ships, and beacons all come in "fleets".

© Stephen Statler 2016
S. Statler, *Beacon Technologies*, DOI 10.1007/978-1-4842-1889-1_9

The Merriam-Webster dictionary defines "chaos" as:

"Complete confusion and disorder, a state in which behavior and events are not controlled by anything."

With thousands of beacons being deployed across chains of stores, cities, and entire countries, it's easy to see how chaos could ensue in the absence of a robust management system. Imagine what would happen if beacons were lost; if they started to fail; if their software needed to be updated or their configuration changed and there were no tools to manage this.

In the previous chapter, we discussed the process and planning required for a successful deployment. Now, let's look at some of the tools that can be used in that process. The goal here is to examine the state of the art of beacon fleet management, explore what can be achieved with it, and understand how four of the leading tools work.

In this chapter, we will describe:

- Functions that are offered by beacon fleet management solutions and the architectural approaches

- Standards

- A sample of some of the most popular products that are used for fleet management: Estimote, Gimbal, and Sensoro

This will arm you, as solution designers, with the knowledge to evaluate and select an approach that makes sense for your situation.

Fleet Management Functions

First, let's look at the functions performed by beacon fleet management tools in general terms.

Inventory

Beacons can be deployed in large numbers, with each of them performing a different function. Done carelessly, this immediately creates a logistical nightmare. Therefore, as we place our beacons on site, we need to be able to keep track of them. To do this, most fleet management systems track a device's unique serial number or MAC[1] address. This number is hardcoded and, unlike the UUID, is unrelated to where or how the device is used. Other attributes that need to be tracked include the logical addresses (UUID), firmware version, parameter settings, location, whether the location has changed, signal strength, broadcast packet frequency, battery level, and other contextual metadata.

With a growing number of beacon standards, the inventory database needs to track multiple address formats, be they the iBeacon UUID, major and minor device numbers (UMM), an Eddystone-UID, UUID and Instance ID, an Eddystone URL, the AltBeacon ID, or the beacon OEM's own proprietary ID.

The location information may be merely the latitude/longitude, but increasingly has started including a dispatchable street address, which will often include a floor level. Some systems even plot the beacon location against a floor plan of the building.

---

[1]A Media Access Control (MAC) address is a unique number defined and assigned in blocks by the IEEE to equipment manufacturers, who then use the addresses to identify each product they make. The MAC address uniquely identifies network elements and is used across different communication protocols such as Wi-Fi, Ethernet, and Bluetooth.

Many systems also enable contextual metadata tags to be associated with a beacon. These can be used to record that the beacon is in a certain part of a store, say, the men's shoes department, or the identity of a particular billboard, or an association with a certain painting in a museum.

For beacons with accelerometers, it's possible to track whether the beacon has been moved since it was placed. This can be useful to know, as unauthorized and unnoticed movements could cause serious issues.

Information about battery level and the metadata from sensors is also important to track online. Most beacons are not connected permanently to networks, and are thus not accessible at all times (unlike many other network elements). So this information is typically a snapshot of a measurement that was relayed when the beacon was last inspected. This status information can be gathered by passing apps designed to report that information back to the fleet management system, or, in more advanced cases, relayed by some kind of Wi-Fi or other network bridge that occasionally pings the beacon.

Configuration and Updating

Address and configuration parameters will need to be set as part of the deployment process. These changes are often performed with a mobile app, but the process that is used varies a lot. In some cases, the app will be a special management app. Sometimes the app will configure the beacons one at a time. Others will take a bulk approach to updating multiple beacons in a batch. Some beacons will need to be physically reset to change the parameters; others can be changed over the air with no physical intervention. Several vendors offer Bluetooth to Wi-Fi bridge products, so no app is required with them.

Some beacon vendors provide configuration and monitoring functionality in their SDK so that a consumer app can be used to perform these functions. For example, a Happy Hour app used to find bars with great deals could use beacons to trigger a check-in at the bar. Once checked-in, the Happy Hour app could initiate a beacon update. This might occur if the beacon was flagged as being in need of a configuration change. While this might go unnoticed by the users, should they find out their data charges have been increased by shipping software updates to a retailer's beacons, this has some potential satisfaction/legal issues associated with it.

Using Wi-Fi for Beacon Management

Most of the Wi-Fi infrastructure vendors (for example, Aruba, Cisco, Ruckus, and Zebra) are now adding Bluetooth radios to their Wi-Fi access points. With these in place, the vendors' management tools can monitor and in some cases manage the configuration of Bluetooth beacons, as well as fulfilling their main purpose of providing Wi-Fi connectivity for any device, including the smartphones running beacon-enabled apps.

Generally providing good wireless connectivity infrastructure and beacons go together. Very few beacon-enabled apps work well in communication black spots. So these Wi-Fi vendors have an advantage over the beacon startups entering this space, as they have well established sales and support channels. They are seen as a lower-risk supplier whose future is more certain, and they can consolidate the beacon-management function with that of managing the Wi-Fi network.

Some of these vendors make their own beacons and can configure them via their access points (see Figure 9-1). Unfortunately, due to a lack of standards, it's rare for a Wi-Fi access point vendor to be able to configure third-party beacons. Even so, the Wi-Fi access point vendors are in a position to grab a portion of the beacon market, annexing it into the market where they are already well established.

Figure 9-1. *HP's Aruba LS-BT1 Bluetooth beacons can be monitored, configured, and updated via either an Aruba Wi-Fi access point (AP), or for customers not using Aruba APs, via an Aruba AS-100 wireless sensor that bridges Bluetooth and Wi-Fi*

A prime example is Aruba Networks, which is owned by HP. Aruba manufactures Wi-Fi access points and Bluetooth beacons, and provides the Meridian cloud-based beacon management system (see Figure 9-2), which also includes app creation tools that enable the creation of wayfinding and "blue dot" functions within an app.

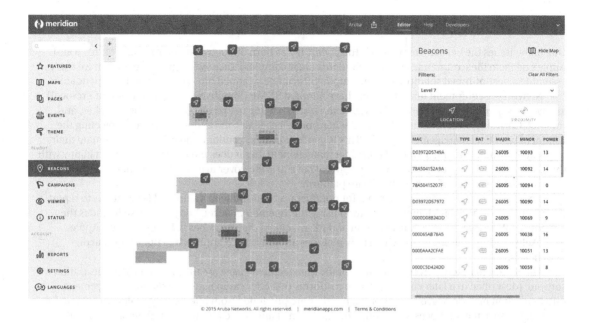

Figure 9-2. *Aruba's Meridian cloud-management platform can manage beacons via Aruba access points or via the Aruba AS-100*

Beyond Wi-Fi and Cellular

Beyond the use of Wi-Fi and the consumer's cellular connection, there are other approaches to establish connectivity for monitoring. There is the prospect that beacons may eventually be configured via peer-to-peer networks, where changes are propagated from one beacon to another.

One beacon vendor, Sensoro has included a second radio built into each beacon so that its beacons can be configured over a proprietary long distance radio protocol. With this approach, one venue's beacons could be managed by a single bridge node, rather than a larger number of Wi-Fi access points.

The work to perform these updates has the potential to impact the operational costs, service levels, and the ability to support new features. Therefore, it is one of the most important aspects to consider in a beacon management strategy.

Monitoring

Most beacon vendors offer a web-based fleet monitoring dashboard, with a linear list of the beacons, displaying the key configuration parameters and health status, such as battery life. This may change going forward, as it may make more sense for the listings to become hierarchical around certain regions or location brands. If the network of beacons has tens of thousand of devices, a linear list would just be cumbersome to navigate.

When monitoring beacons, it's possible that they may break or be removed, and so the status information reported could be out of date. The same issue may simply be caused because an app that is able to monitor the beacon hasn't been in range of the beacon recently. Having monitoring done via a Wi-Fi bridge eliminates this ambiguity.

That being said, just showing the status of a beacon that is detected is a necessary element, but is not sufficient by itself. Exception reporting is important. In the case of a beacon that has disappeared, for instance, one of the exceptions that should be reported is that the system hasn't received an update recently.

Fleet Management Standards

One of the issues the beacosystem faces is that, while it was born out of two standards, Bluetooth 4.0 and Apple's de facto iBeacon standard, these standards are incomplete. Incomplete in the sense that we can't assemble a best-of-breed solution, where components can be swapped out and upgraded independently.

Networking equipment manufacturers have adopted SNMP (Simple Network Management Protocol) as a way of separating management tools from the systems being managed (such as hubs, switches, and routers). Currently, with Bluetooth beacons, when you select a beacon vendor you are also selecting the vendor of your fleet management system. This is good for beacon vendors who want to differentiate their hardware solution with the quality of their fleet management, but it does mean that if you aren't happy with the antenna design of your beacon vendor, you will have to switch over to a new fleet management system in order to take advantage of another hardware platform.

Google's Eddystone offers some room for optimism, as it introduced a standard for beacons to report their battery level and any changes in position using the Telemetry packet. Eddystone also includes the proximity API to register a beacon's location and the metadata that describes it. Unfortunately, Apple is unlikely to adopt that standard, which now includes a standardized approach to updating beacon parameters.

The other ecosystem players vying to own the management space are the providers of orchestration software (described in a later chapter). These platforms that offer campaign and content management functions often include beacon monitoring, but they are precluded from offering a complete management solution because the interfaces to perform configuration changes and parameter updates are generally proprietary to the hardware manufacturer.

Fleet Management Products

Next, we will consider the fleet management offerings of three of the largest providers of beacons: Estimote, Sensoro, and Gimbal. This will give you a picture of how fleet management works in practice. You should get a sense of the similarities and differences in their approach, and can then apply these points of reference if you need to compare them with other vendors whose products you are interested in.

Estimote

As the beacon provider with probably the highest visibility of all the OEMs, Estimote is a good company to start with for our review of fleet management systems.

The design and user experience of their console and management app is in keeping with the high standard of industrial design of their beacons and their web site. The details of each beacon, including the address, broadcast interval, projected battery life, power, and firmware level are presented on the main Beacon dashboard (see Figure 9-3). Where the firmware version needs to be upgraded, or the battery is low, it is highlighted in red.

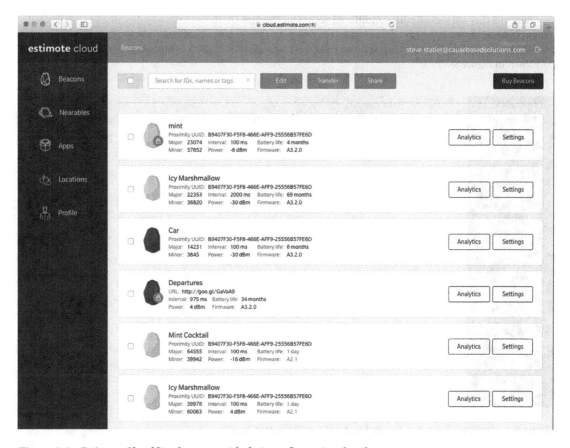

Figure 9-3. *Estimote Cloud lists beacons with their configuration details*

Beacons that are locked with conditional access, or "Secure UUID" as Estimote describes it, are flagged with a padlock.

The settings of these parameters can be edited on an individual basis via this web interface (as shown in Figure 9-4).

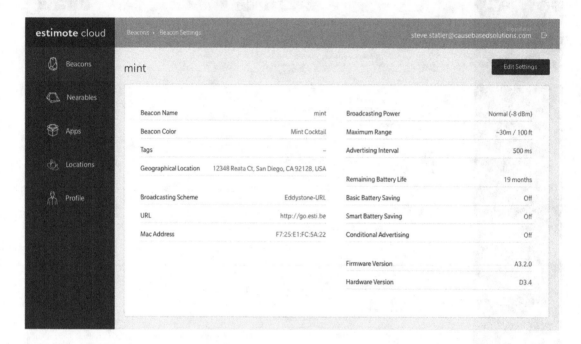

Figure 9-4. *Drilling down into the setting details in Estimate Cloud*

Data for the dashboard is collected via the Estimote app, which lists the known beacons and shows the ones in range (see Figure 9-5).

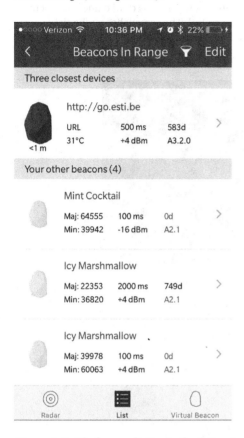

Figure 9-5. *The beacon listing in the Estimote app*

The app allows all of the parameters and metadata to be adjusted on site. These include the name, the dispatchable address of the beacon (geo location), and the indoor position, based on use of Estimote Indoor Location app. The fact that the beacon is owned by your organization is indicated by dotted lines connecting the beacon, the smartphone, and the Estimote Cloud icon (see Figure 9-6). The screenshot on the right shows what happens if you inspect a beacon that you don't own. The no-entry symbol indicates that access is denied, and none of the parameters is visible.

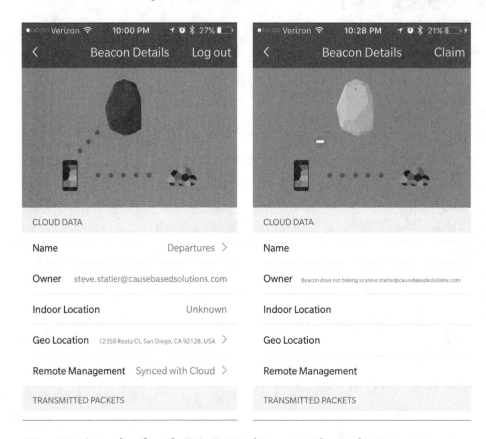

Figure 9-6. *Screenshots from the Estimote app: beacon metadata and settings*

In the Transmitted Packets section, the protocol/frame type that the beacon uses can be set to Estimote Default, Apple iBeacon, Eddystone-UID, or Eddystone-URL. The protocols offered are alternatives; you can't interleave these frame types (see Figure 9-7).

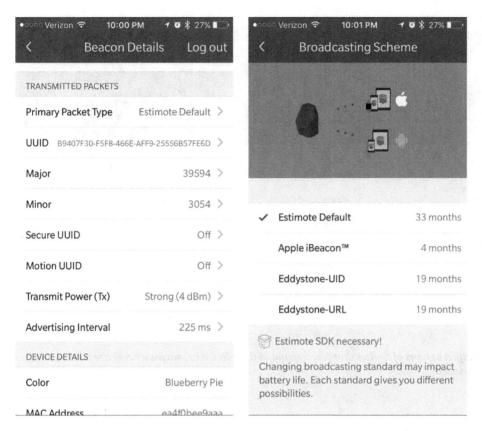

Figure 9-7. *The beacon's Primary Packet Type can be set in the Broadcast Scheme*

When selecting the alternative packet types, an estimate of the battery life is shown for each broadcast standard, as well as an indication of which types of devices will be able to respond to the broadcasts (see Figure 9-8).

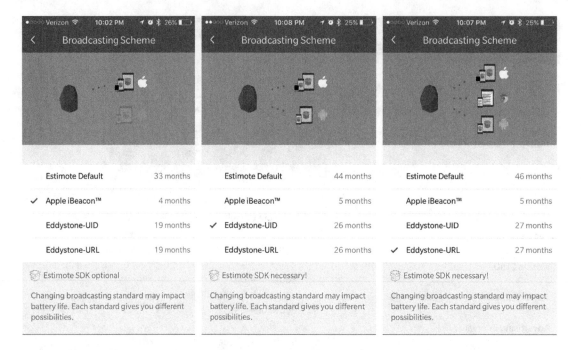

Figure 9-8. *The different types of devices that can respond to the selected broadcast scheme are rendered as the frame type is selected*

If you're selecting Estimote or Apple iBeacon, the UUID and major and minor (UMM) numbers can be set.

If the beacon is configured with Secure UUID, this initiates a random, slow roll of the UMM. The developer sees the "Real UUID," which remains consistent, while those with apps that don't have access to the beacon would see the "Visible UUID," which changes periodically so that any mapping and reuse of the UMM will not be possible (see Figure 9-9).

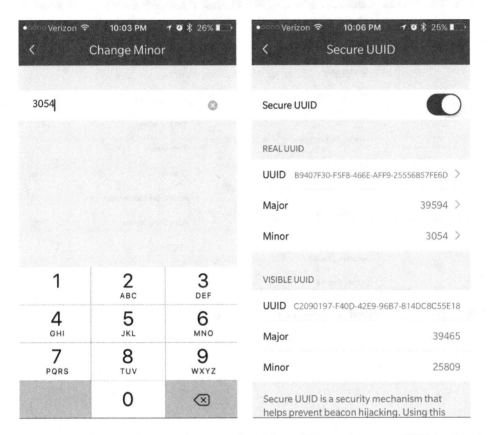

Figure 9-9. Changing the minor device number of the real UUID when secure UUID is selected

As you can see in Figure 9-10, when selecting Eddystone-URL as the broadcast scheme, the entry field switches from the UMM fields to include a URL, which is broadcast instead.

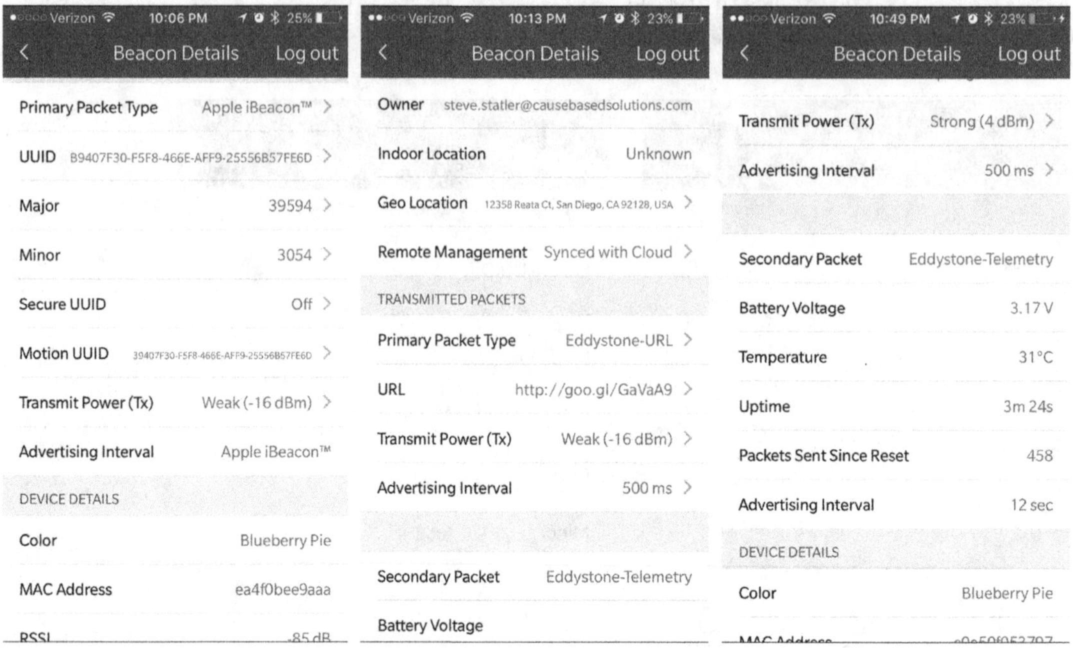

Figure 9-10. *With Eddystone URL selected, the data entry fields change*

When any Eddystone primary packet type is selected, a secondary packet, the Eddystone telemetry packet, is enabled. The data that is collected from those packets is then presented in the app, for instance, "Packets Sent Since Reset".

When motion UUID is set, the beacon will start to broadcast an alternative to the main UUID that indicates the beacon accelerometer is detecting movement. In Figure 9-11 you can see a still of what that screen looks like. In the actual app, there is animation to illustrate the movement of the motion UUID use-case.

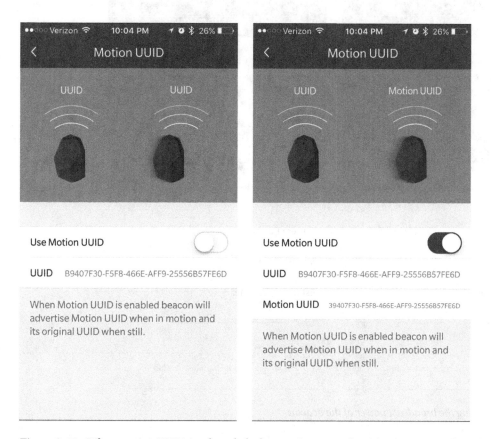

Figure 9-11. *When motion UUID is selected, the beacon image on the right starts to wiggle and an alternate motion UUID can be set*

If the beacon were attached to a shopping basket, for instance, this could be used to indicate it was in motion.

The broadcast power of a beacon can be set in the Estimote app with the slider at the bottom of the Broadcast Power screen (Figure 9-12). As the power goes from low to high, the estimated lifetime of the battery is dynamically reduced, while the maximum range estimate and broadcast field graphic grows. Making these adjustments is fun and feels like a game, which typifies the approach to user experience design of the Estimote solution.

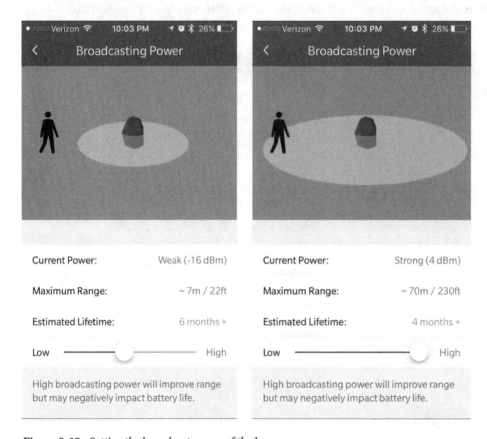

Figure 9-12. Setting the broadcast power of the beacon

The Broadcast Interval screen is designed in a similar way. When selecting a shorter broadcast interval, the beacon graphic pulsates faster and the battery life forecast is reduced dynamically.

Selecting Beacon In Motion allows selection of a feature that allows the beacon to be put to sleep, pausing broadcasts when it is flipped upside down (Figure 9-13). This can save battery, or be used for demos where you want to show events triggered by a newly sighted beacon.

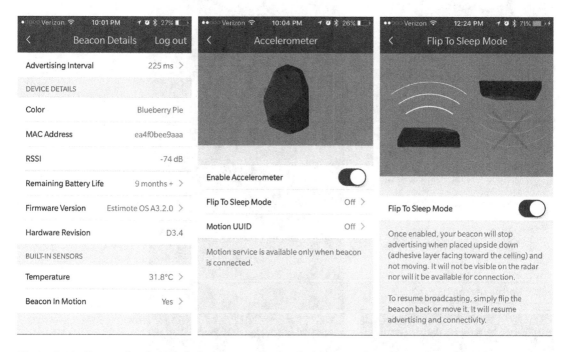

Figure 9-13. *Beacon details include firmware version and activation of accelerometer sensor*

The beacon details also include the firmware version. New firmware images can be downloaded and applied using the app (see Figure 9-14).

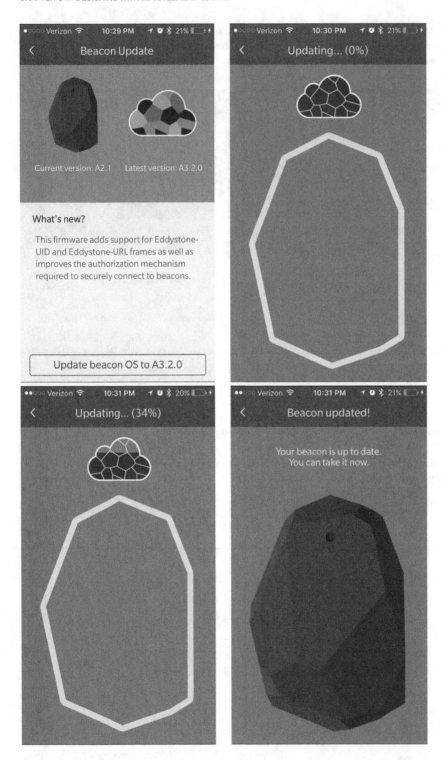

Figure 9-14. *When updating a beacon's firmware using the Estimote app, the progress is shown with an engaging graphic metaphor*

Figure 9-15 captures the setting change log, which tracks the application of the kind of changes we have been reviewing in this section.

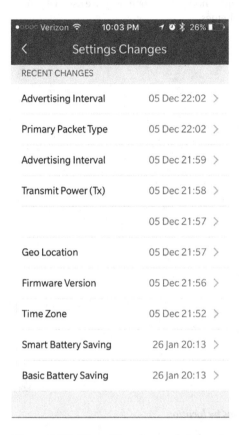

Figure 9-15. *The setting changes log showing recent alterations to the beacon's configuration*

It's hard to imagine a more interactive and engaging management system for beacons than Estimote's. True to its focus on pilot projects, the interface is a valuable asset in both selling the technology to stakeholders and learning about the technology.

Sensoro

Sensoro is an interesting player in the beacosystem. Their user experience design rivals that of Estimote, they have achieved a volume of beacon shipments for marquee customers that compares with that of Gimbal and, for deployments in China, they appear to be the undisputed leader. Their challenge is Anglicizing a product which has matured in Asia and bridging their go-to-market approach from China to the U.S. and European markets. The Sensoro fleet management system reflects all of these aspects of the company. It has clearly been used to deploy projects at large scale, with many features that earn Sensoro the right to claim the "fleet" in fleet management. However, there is still some work to be done to fully adapt it to Western markets.

All that said, the main dashboard screen in the Sensoro Cloud manager looks very familiar (see Figure 9-16), with the exception that it shows the output from the light sensors built into its Yunzi beacons. Cover up one of their beacons or turn out the lights, and you will see that status change. This light sensor may prove useful if you want to factor times when the lights are out in your energy saving schemes.

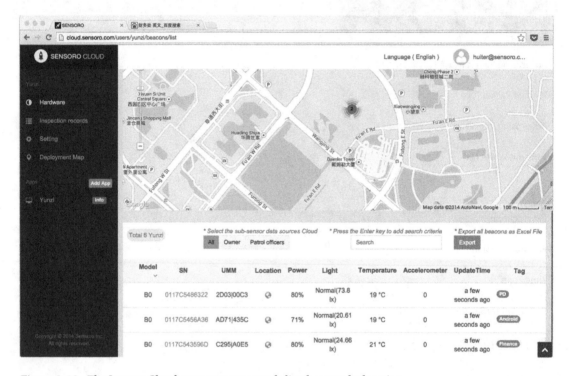

Figure 9-16. *The Sensoro Cloud management console lists beacons by location*

One of the concepts unique to Sensoro is that of the role of a "beacon inspector," which is a person who uses a purpose-built Sensoro Inspection app to "patrol" the beacons and relay their status back to the Sensoro Cloud. These inspection activities can be tracked from the management console shown in Figure 9-17.

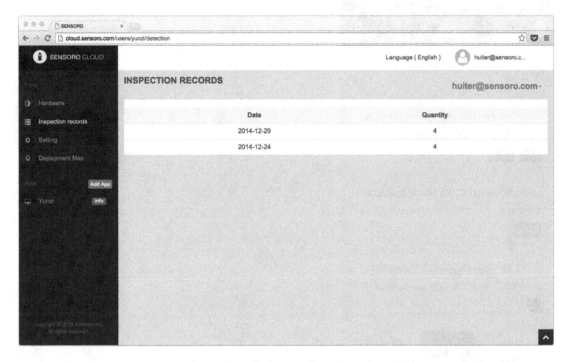

Figure 9-17. *The Inspection Records screen tracks the patrols performed to gather status of the beacons*

This app is simple and locked down (see Figure 9-18) so that someone with minimal training can be sent on patrols without the risk of configurations being interfered with.

Figure 9-18. *The main screen of the Sensoro Inspection app*

You won't find this app on the Apple App Store, either. It's an Enterprise app that is discovered via the Sensoro web site. Sensoro needs to be configured as a trusted developer using iOS in order to install the app on your phone.

Sensoro Cloud stores indoor maps to track the location of beacons in a venue (see Figure 9-19).

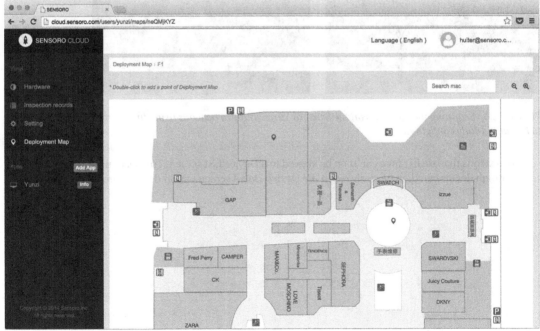

Figure 9-19. *Sensoro Cloud's indoor map management for tracking the location of beacons*

The Sensoro app enables individual beacons to be configured through a process that starts with scanning the barcodes that are printed on their case (Figure 9-20). This selects the beacon and avoids any confusion as to which device is being set up. Without this kind of tool, it can be quite confusing when dealing with multiple beacons that all look the same.

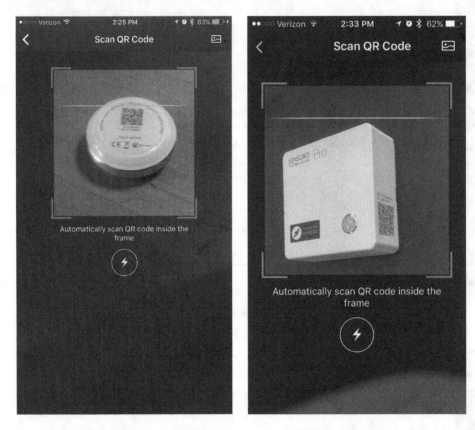

Figure 9-20. *Scanning the barcodes on the Sensoro Yunzi and Pro beacons using the Sensoro app allows them to be individually configured*

All beacons that are in range can then be viewed in a Device List screen. The beacon status and configuration details can then be reviewed in the Device Detail screen within the Sensoro app (Figure 9-21).

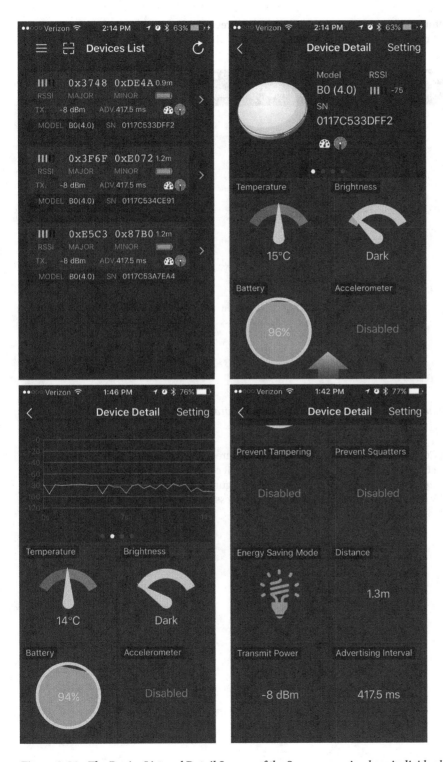

Figure 9-21. *The Device List and Detail Screens of the Sensoro app is where individual beacon parameters can be set interactively*

On selecting the Setting button, administrators can use the screen shown in Figure 9-22 to configure the various kinds of advertising packets that Sensoro can broadcast.

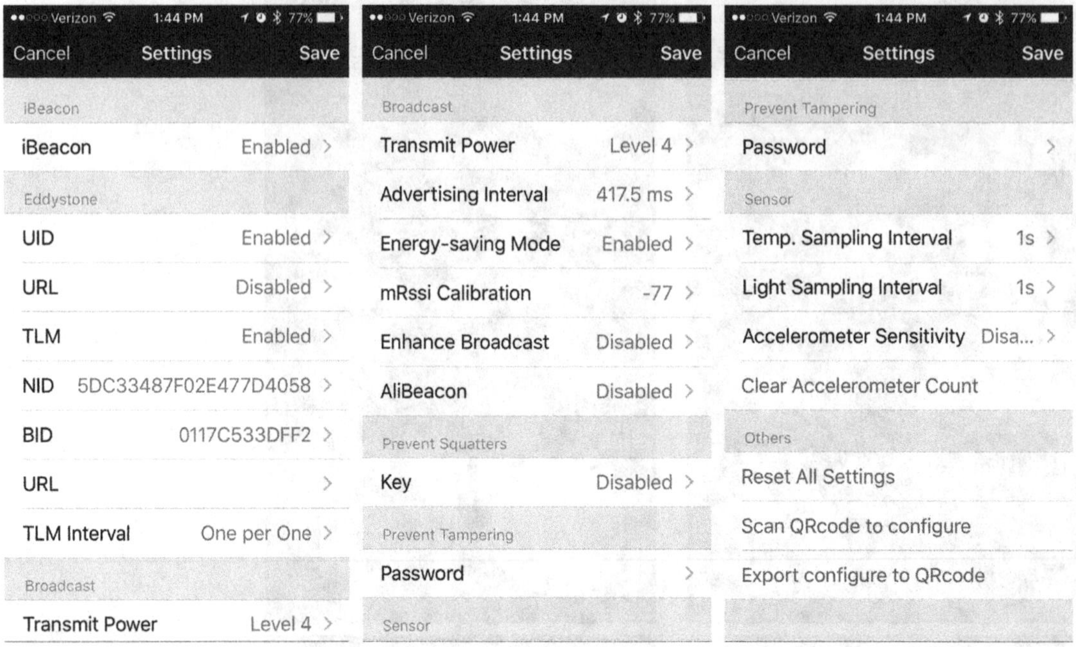

Figure 9-22. *Once in Settings mode, all of an individual beacon's parameters can be changed and immediately saved*

By selecting Export Configuration to QRcode, as shown in Figure 9-22, a selectable number of the settings can be saved in a template (shown in Figure 9-23). If the QR code is printed, it can be scanned again as part of a subsequent deployment process so that the same configuration parameters can be applied to the other beacons, one by one. This makes for a more reliable process for setting beacon parameters than manually adjusting each one in turn.

Figure 9-23. *Exporting configuration to QRcode*

Unlike some beacons where you have to choose between broadcasting iBeacon or Eddystone frames, Sensoro beacons can interleave a large number of packet or frame types: iBeacon, Eddystone-UID, URL, TLM, the (proprietary) Sensoro packet (that relays the sensor settings), and AliBeacon. The last of these is a protocol specific to China and the Alibaba commerce site.

The Deploy app offers another alternative to individually configuring beacons and is a distinctive feature of the Sensoro approach to fleet management. It enables changes to be made in more of a streamlined fashion. Multiple beacons that are in range can be selected, and a change to one or more attributes can be made in a batch process.

In Figure 9-24, the Eddystone URL frame is being added to the configuration.

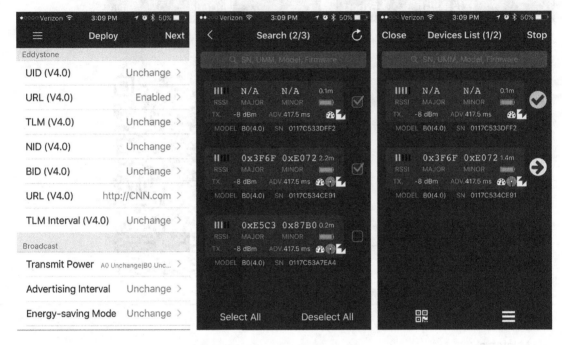

Figure 9-24. *The Deploy app applies a set of changes to a collection of beacons*

Gimbal

The Gimbal dashboard provides access to a broad set of functions that extend beyond mere beacon functionality, including geofencing, push communications (Communicate) and analytics, as well as the beacon-management facilities we are focusing on in this chapter. All these extras are a legacy of Gimbal's origins as a context platform, before beacons were added to the system. The Beacon element of the dashboard (shown in Figure 9-25) was designed with management of large numbers of beacons in mind, with features for controlling access, sharing, and interfacing with a public network.

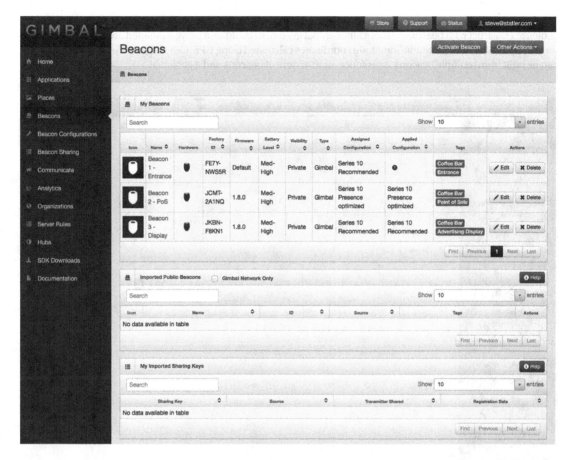

Figure 9-25. *The main beacon management and monitoring screen from Gimbal*

The beacons listed on the Gimbal management screen are identified by Factory ID, which is the fixed identifier for each beacon recorded inside its case. As with the other dashboards, firmware levels, battery status, and metadata tags can be viewed on this screen. Battery status is reported to the Gimbal cloud by any app with the Gimbal SDK integrated, no matter whether the app is known to the developer.

Beacons can be set to Public (the default is Private) on a settings screen. Private beacons may be viewed only by the developer's apps, or specific apps where the beacon key is being shared. Public beacons are equivalent to a generic iBeacon, viewable by any developer.

As shown in Figure 9-26, the beacon can be associated with *places*. A Gimbal place is a merging of their geofence construct with beacons. Historically, Gimbal geofences could be a polygon shaped area (versus round), formed by a collection of latitude/longitude coordinates calculated using GPS, Cell-ID, and Wi-Fi. Today, a place can be built from multiple beacons, a geofence, or a mixture of beacons and a geofence.

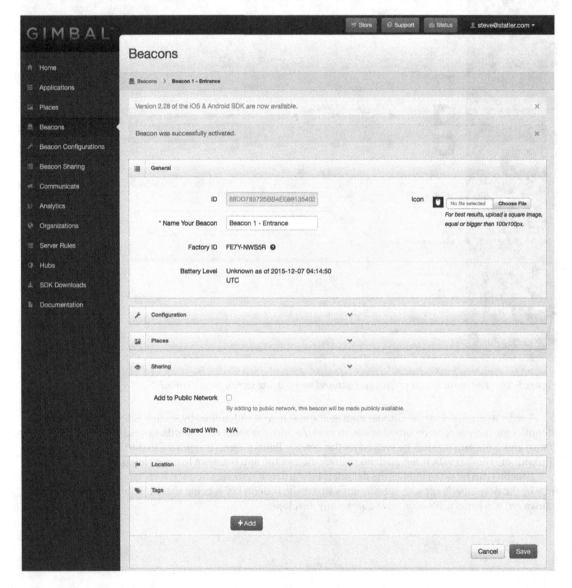

Figure 9-26. *The Beacon settings screen in the Gimbal management console*

Beacon configurations are templated in predefined configurations that have specific parameters preset, such as broadcast frequency, signal strength, and selection of directional or omnidirectional antenna (see Figure 9-27). These parameters are not selected on a beacon-by-beacon basis, or tweaked in the configuration app as the Estimote app allows. If you want to change these parameters, you need to create a new configuration template and associate the relevant beacons with that template using the dashboard.

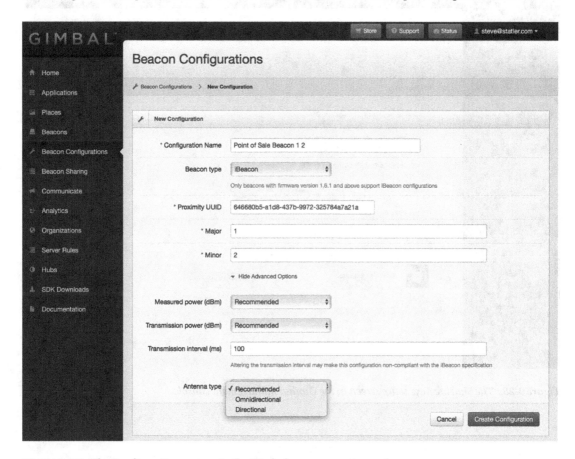

Figure 9-27. *The Configurations screen in the Gimbal management console*

When you configure a beacon as an iBeacon, each UMM setting requires its own template. This could result in a lot of templates needing to be created if the iBeacon frame type is used across a large network. Fortunately, the reality is that most Gimbal beacons are likely to use its native protocol, in which case this is not an issue.

For those experimenting with beacons, this may seem cumbersome, but this approach to enforcing uniformity is born out of organizing large deployments where consistency is key.

If a beacon is private, it can still be shared with a third-party developer's app by creating a sharing key (as depicted in Figure 9-28). This key can be associated with a subset of beacons. Access to the associated beacons is bound by a start and end time.

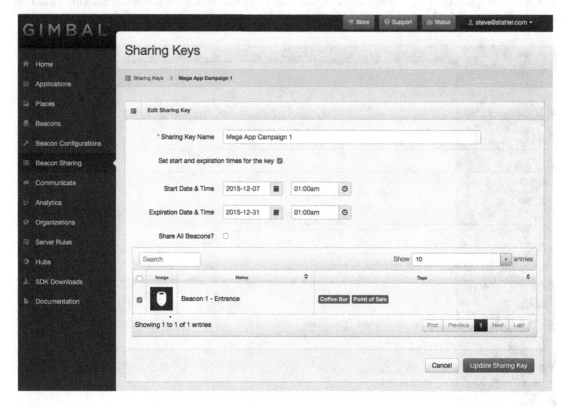

Figure 9-28. The Sharing Keys setup screen in the Gimbal management console

Once a beacon has been associated with a configuration in the Gimbal management console, it can be initialized by the Gimbal configuration app (Figure 9-29).

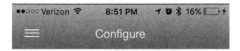

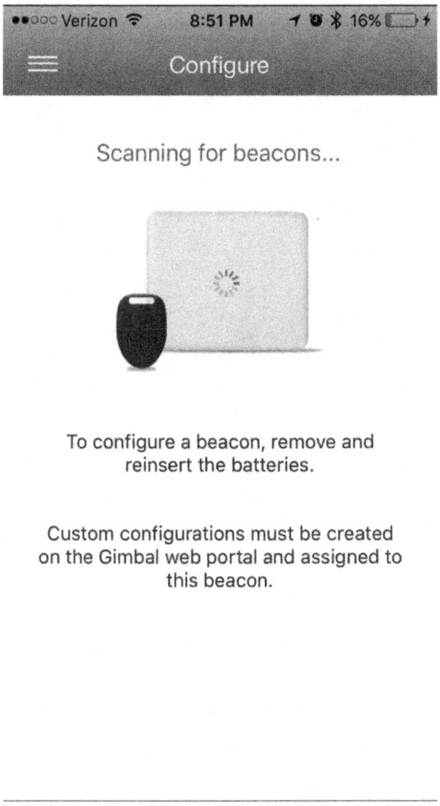

Verizon
8:51 PM
16%
Configure
Scanning for beacons...
To configure a beacon, remove and reinsert the batteries.
Custom configurations must be created on the Gimbal web portal and assigned to this beacon.

Figure 9-29. *The Gimbal configuration app scans looking for beacons to set up*

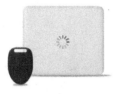

When a beacon is reset by reseating the battery, (or pressing the reset button on the S21), the Gimbal app will detect if any updates in firmware are available (Figure 9-30) or if configuration changes have been made in the management console and apply those over the air via a Bluetooth connection (Figure 9-31).

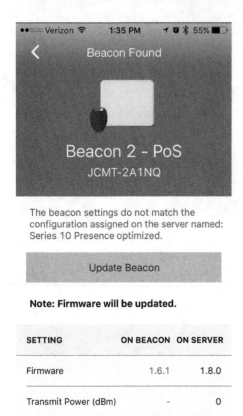

Figure 9-30. *The Gimbal app detects a beacon that requires an update*

The current beacon settings match the
configuration assigned on the server named:
Series 10 Presence optimized.

SETTING	ON BEACON	ON SERVER
Firmware	1.8.0	1.8.0
Transmit Power (dBm)	0	0
Antenna Type	Omni	Omni

Figure 9-31. *The app shows the beacon configuration is up to date*

The Gimbal configuration app can then be used to inspect the status of beacons that are owned by the developer, showing the name, ID, signal strength, battery level, and temperature (Figure 9-32).

Figure 9-32. *The app detects beacons owned by the developer*

These readings are also relayed to the Gimbal cloud. From there, they can be displayed on the management console and accessed by API.

Summary

After this chapter, you should have a good sense of how fleet management is performed by three of the largest beacon manufacturers.

There are similarities in their dashboards that track metadata and report status, but their approaches to configuring the hardware, managing those configurations across a fleet of beacons, monitoring the beacons status, and controlling the protocols broadcast are quite different. Estimote's starting point is creating a magical experience for the developer and demonstrator of pilot projects. Sensoro's collection of deployment apps and dashboards speaks to a focus on controlling large-scale deployments in an Asian context. Gimbal enforces a centralized approach to the discipline of fleet management and a vision for using beacons as part of a network of shared devices with a variety of other context serves included in the bundle.

Once we have decided how to deploy and manage beacons, our next task is to consider our approach to one of the biggest opportunities with these sensors: the insights from analytics.

■ ■ ■

CHAPTER 10

Designing an Analytics Architecture to Leverage Proximity Data

By Ben Parker and Steve Statler

Analytics is an important aspect of any beacon solution. If beacons are cookies that join the digital and physical worlds, then a key part of what analytics can bring is the ability to gain insights into what is happening in the physical domain.

This chapter looks at some background to what's happening in analytics, what big data is and its link with beacons, and how smartphones are changing this area. It then looks at the types of analytics software that can be applied to our solutions. We review some key providers of tools and then consider how beacon data can be structured so that we can best drill into those data sets. Lastly, we will consider a case study that illustrates what can be achieved with the data from beacons.

Big Data

Before we get into the beacon specifics, let's take a moment to consider the magnitude of big data to help understand just how significant the analytics market is.

Prior to the advent of the Digital Age, the Library of Congress was the U.S. benchmark for an attempt to inventory our collective knowledge. The Library's collection has grown from 740 books and three maps shortly after being established in 1800 to its current collection of more than 61 million manuscripts and 32 million books, as well as millions of prints, photographic images, sheet music, maps, and sound recordings. Facebook, just seven years after its founding, estimated in 2011 it had 3,000 times more data stored than the Library of Congress[1]. While no one would rationally compare the type of information being stored by Facebook to the Library of Congress' collection, it is still an amazing example of the scale of today's data collection activities.

This surge in information-gathering will only continue to escalate well beyond the 2.5 quintillion bytes of data already being collected every day[2]. Adding further fuel to this data collection fire is the emergence of the Internet of Things (IoT), with tens of millions of sensors now being embedded in cell phones, vehicles, industrial machines, smart meters, vending machines, retail stores, and public venues. One example of this proliferation is the average number of sensors in a car, which is expected to double over the next several years to over 200 per vehicle.

The amount of data being collected by leading U.S. companies—Google, Microsoft, Amazon, and Facebook—is simply staggering. In 2010, Facebook boasted that they had the world's largest Hadoop cluster with 21 petabytes (PB; see Figure 10-1 to appreciate just how big that is) of storage. By mid-2012, their stored data had increased to 100PB and the company was processing 2.5 billion pieces of content and over 500 terabytes of data each day. In early 2014, Facebook reached 600PB.

---

[1]"Moving an Elephant: Large-Scale Hadoop Data Migration at Facebook," Paul Yang, Facebook blog, July 27, 2011.
[2]According to an IBM estimate; www-01.ibm.com/software/data/bigdata/what-is-big-data.html

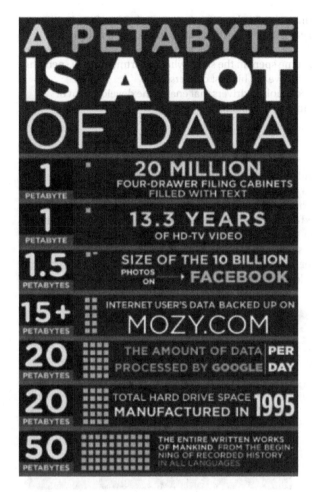

Figure 10-1. *A petabyte is a lot of data*
Source: Cisco

Many companies are attempting to capitalize on this huge influx of data, and so are building enormous data-center infrastructures to store all of it. As a result, this type of analytics, often referred to simply as Big Data, has become a "must have" core competence of any organization planning to stay relevant in today's business world. Additionally, the information gathered creates opportunities to disrupt the status quo in a market.

Web site click-stream data contributed to the need for Big Data tools and techniques. Now beacons are generating more sensor events that correlate to "foot-stream" data, further increasing the challenges and the opportunities.

Smartphones Changing Analytics

The prevalence of smartphones has created the ability for analytic platforms to combine online and offline data to offer new insights and a more comprehensive view of consumers. In one example, a retailer can now determine whether a customer, after viewing an online ad, went on to purchase the product online or visit the store to make the purchase.

The emergence of beacons further enhances this capability by collecting proximity data from locations that were previously problematic due to cell coverage issues. Using the retail example, the retailer can present a virtual coupon to the consumer while they are in the store to increase purchase intent. The retailer can then monitor, with the consumer's consent, the time spent in the store, what departments they spent the most time in during the visit, and what types of offers drive the highest conversions.

With this in mind, let's examine one of the key technology drivers that enable the development of sensors that can generate the data being crunched in analytics platforms.

MEMS Sensors

MEMS (Microelectromechanical Systems) is the underlying technology that enables sensors such as gyroscopes and accelerometers to be fabricated as a part of a silicon chip at very low cost.

The proliferation of MEMS sensors in smartphones, as illustrated in Figure 10-2, enables smartphones to automatically adjust settings and functions based in a variety of contexts. For instance, they can brighten or dim based on available light, detect the proximity of another lost phone, and enhance mobile gaming with gyroscopic controls. Going forward, the newer sensors being added to phones will create a wave of innovative solutions, like understanding which floor in a store has the most foot traffic and real-time tracking of pollution levels in a city. With each new sensor added, Big Data is becoming bigger.

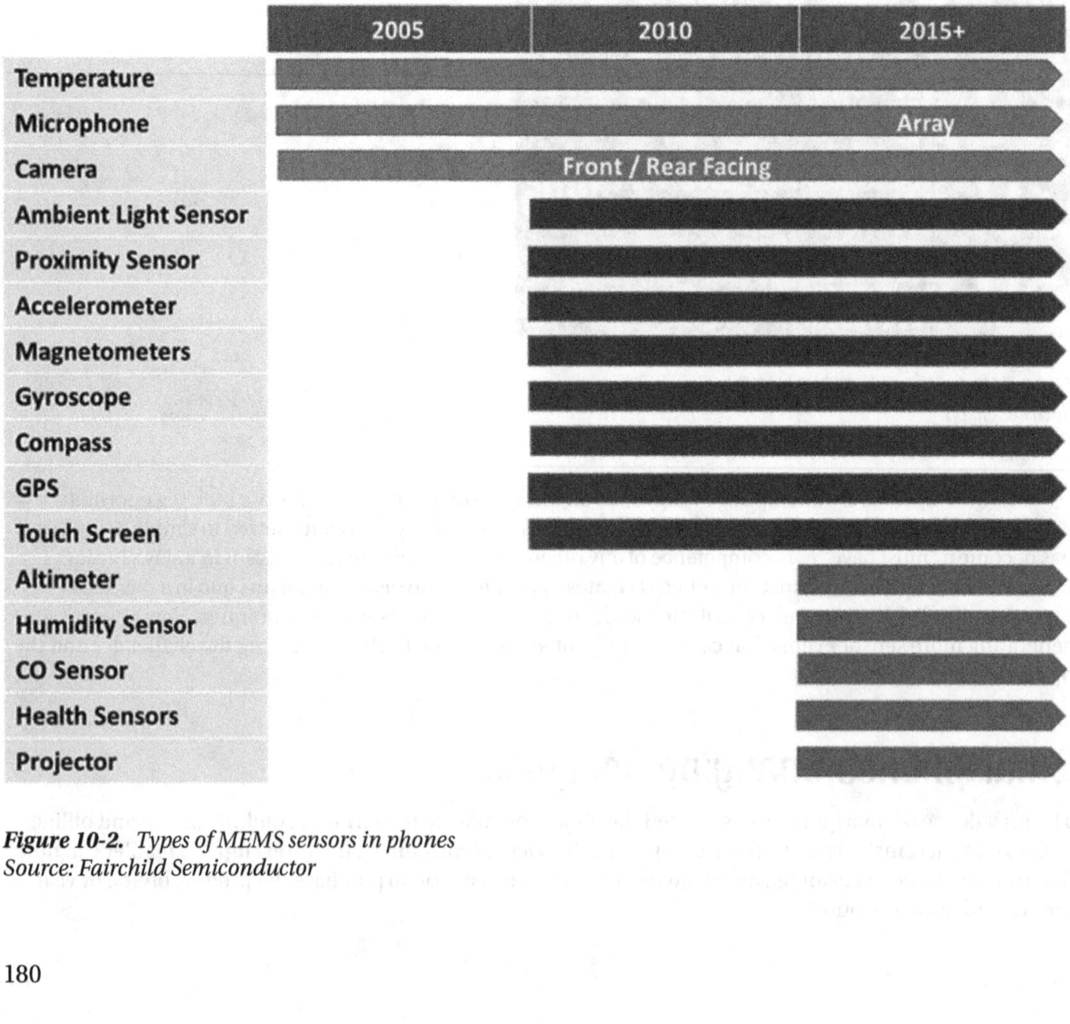

Figure 10-2. Types of MEMS sensors in phones
Source: Fairchild Semiconductor

Beyond leveraging device sensors to create indoor maps, companies are also developing novel approaches to address indoor coverage opportunities. Examples of these companies, with select profiles to follow, include Indoo.rs, Navisens, SPREO, and Trusted Positioning.

Types of Analytics Software

There are a wide variety of analytics frameworks available, ranging from general-purpose analytics tools and statistics packages to specific location technologies designed to work with beacons.

For our purposes, as designers of proximity and location-aware solutions, we need to understand where to go in order to best source the functions needed to achieve our business goals. If we are to choose the right tool for the right job, it's important to be able to classify the different types of analytics software that we might use to build our solutions (see Table 10-1).

Table 10-1. Analytics Frameworks Examples

Type	Description	Examples
General-Purpose Analytics	OLAP, data warehouse, and data mining tools. Proximity will be a plugin to these platforms.	SAS, SAP/Business Objects, MicroStrategy, EMC, Oracle, and IBM (Cognos, SPSS)
Vertical Market Analytics (i.e., Retail)	Typically leverage multiple technologies, including cell phones, Wi-Fi, POS, etc.	RetailNext, BrickTrends, Scopix, Prism Skylabs, and LocationSmart
Ad Network Analytics	Dashboards that show advertising metrics.	iAD, AdWords
Location Analytics	Leverages data collected from smartphones to enable brands and ad agencies to engage mobile audiences.	Factual, Placed, PlaceIQ, PathIntelligence, and Ninth Decimal
Specialist Beacon Analytics	Tools used to report on beacon activity. Works with third-party hardware.	Lighthouse, Phunware

General-Purpose Analytics

The first principle, which seems self-evident, is that we shouldn't waste time and money trying to reinvent the wheel, and we shouldn't bet the success of our project on tools providers that are doing that either. Therefore, the first and largest category of tools we should get to know is "general-purpose analytics" tools. These include Online Analytical Processing (OLAP), data warehouse, and data mining tools. These tools, such as SAS, Teradata, and Business Objects make up a mature, multi-billion dollar market. Though many of the thousands of players in this space are not beacon-aware, they frequently have hooks for location in their frameworks that may be adapted to our purposes. The key point is we should try to avoid rewriting tools such as databases, visualization, and reporting, and instead leverage the existing products in this segment.

We have found that large players in this space, who may not have an emphasis on proximity, location, or beacons on their web sites, actually have customers who are starting to use these tools, which are installed throughout their enterprise in beacon projects.

It's likely that engineers and developers in these companies will be experimenting with beacons and will welcome the opportunity to partner with a specialist technology provider or a customer who is an early adaptor. So the second key point is: look for opportunities to partner with the giants in this space.

Vertical Market Analytics

For the same reasons that we need to be mindful of the general-purpose analytics tools providers, we need to be aware of the vertical analytics providers who have focused their offerings on a specific industry. These providers may already be building their offerings on top of the general-purpose tools providers. Retail is one of the key verticals where analytics is being applied and beacons add significant value. Aligning with and extending the capabilities of the existing players here is a good strategy, as we can build on the technical infrastructure they have, and on their customer relationships too. We may have some exciting beacon technology, but if it is to be absorbed into an end user's environment, the best way to do that is to integrate with a solution they already have. These vertical partners also add value in being able to translate the language and needs of a given vertical into the language of our specialist area.

Ad Networks

Advertising is a key horizontal application for beacons. While serving ads is a key part of what those networks do, the segmentation, targeting, and measurement components are just as important. We can look at the tools provided by the players in this space and imagine how proximity and location can be used. More on this in later chapters.

Specialist Beacon Analytics

At the opposite end of the specialization spectrum is the specialist's tools, born to work specifically with beacons. These come in two forms, the more common of which are the dashboards and tools provided by the beacon vendors themselves. These can be tightly integrated into the sensors built into the beacon hardware. Less common are cross-platform tools developed for beacons. Examples of this are Lighthouse and Phunware. See Figure 10-3 for an example of a third-party beacon analytics dashboard.

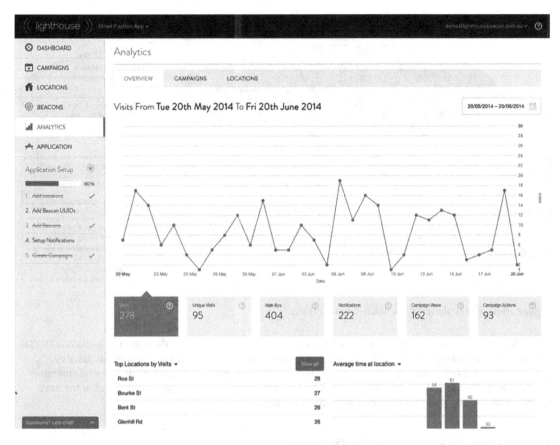

Figure 10-3. *The Lighthouse analytics dashboard for beacon campaigns*

Location Analytics

Sitting as a midpoint between general-purpose and the specialist tools, location analytics were conceived with location in mind, but predate the advent of beacons. These tools may actually be best placed to capitalize on the beacon revolution, in that they are already established and mature, and well suited to benefit from what beacons bring.

The analytics market is rapidly evolving from simple, location-aware or proximity analytics (such as a heat map of foot traffic in a retail store) to behaviorally-aware or predictive analytics that will enable retailers to anticipate when you'll return, what you're likely to buy, and at what price point.

As illustrated in Figure 10-4, we are in the early stages of phase 3.0, Behaviorally Aware, and this phase is being led by a new wave of interesting predictive analytics players, such as Opera Solutions, Fractal Analytics, and Revolution Analytics. The transition is supported by several key enablers, including the rapid proliferation of smartphones throughout the world, the emergence of wearables, and an increased number of device sensors and MEMS in devices.

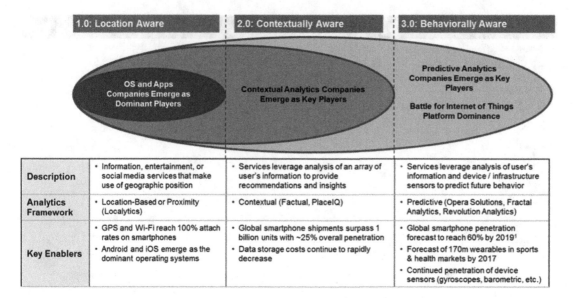

	1.0: Location Aware	**2.0: Contextually Aware**	**3.0: Behaviorally Aware**
Description	• Information, entertainment, or social media services that make use of geographic position	• Services leverage analysis of an array of user's information to provide recommendations and insights	• Services leverage analysis of user's information and device / infrastructure sensors to predict future behavior
Analytics Framework	• Location-Based or Proximity (Localytics)	• Contextual (Factual, PlaceIQ)	• Predictive (Opera Solutions, Fractal Analytics, Revolution Analytics)
Key Enablers	• GPS and Wi-Fi reach 100% attach rates on smartphones • Android and iOS emerge as the dominant operating systems	• Global smartphone shipments surpass 1 billion units with ~25% overall penetration • Data storage costs continue to rapidly decrease	• Global smartphone penetration forecast to reach 60% by 2019[1] • Forecast of 170m wearables in sports & health markets by 2017 • Continued penetration of device sensors (gyroscopes, barometric, etc.)

Figure 10-4. *The evolution of location-aware services*

While numerous companies or organizations have already developed outdoor maps—including Digital Globe, Open Street Map, INTERMAP, Google, and Apple—the race is on to map indoor locations. Key players in the indoor location space include established companies like Google, but also several emerging companies such Indoor Atlas, Micello, and WiFiSLAM. Some of these companies are profiled in the next section, and each is taking a different approach to creating indoor maps.

Key Location Analytics Players

While there are hundreds of Big Data or analytics companies, there are a smaller number of emerging players focused primarily on location analytics. These include Factual, Placed, Euclid, PlaceIQ, PathIntelligence, Walkbase, Ninth Decimal, Nomi, AreaMetrics, and RetailNext. This section looks at a selection of these key players.

Google

Google announced its Cartographer project in 2014, which uses a technology called "Simultaneous Localization and Mapping" (SLAM) in which a backpack-wearer generates floor plans, accurate within five centimeters, in real time as they walk through a building. The backpack includes a small computer connected to an Android tablet that enables the wearer to add points of interest along the way.

Indoor Atlas

Indoor Atlas, headquarted in Helsinki, offers a solution that utilizes compass sensors in smartphones to detect the unique magnetic signatures of buildings to create indoor maps. Indoor Atlas hopes to crowdsource its indoor maps by engaging a community of users similar to the way Waze has approached creating outdoor mapping.

Micello

Micello, founded in 2007, is an early pioneer in this market and now offers over 15,000 indoor venue maps in over 30 countries. Micello builds its indoor maps by using a team based in India to create a digital version of a map supplied by the venue. The digital version is then integrated into Google Maps.

WiFiSLAM

WiFiSLAM uses pattern recognition and machine learning to draw correlations between data gathered by device sensors (accelerometers, gyroscopes, and magnetometers) and then uses Wi-Fi trilateration to create accurate indoor maps. WiFiSLAM was acquired by Apple in 2013.

Navisens

Navisens uses its proprietary motionDNA™ technology to process data from inertial sensors (accelerometers and gyroscopes) to provide a 3D navigation solution without an underlying technology infrastructure such as Wi-Fi, GPS, or beacons. The technology was originally developed to locate firefighters and first-responders.

SPREO

SPREO uses beacon and Wi-Fi signal fingerprinting, inertial sensor fusion, map constraints, and other data inputs to provide indoor location coverage, step-by-step indoor navigation, location-based marketing and analytics. Taubman Centers launched a shopping app, powered by SPREO, to provide indoor navigation and positioning in 18 malls in the United States.

Factual

Factual was founded by Gil Elbaz who previously co-founded Applied Semantics. Applied Semantics was sold to Google for over $100 million in 2003. By Q1 2014, Applied Semantics' main product AdSense comprised $3.4 billion or 22% of Google's total revenue. So Gil has a track record of developing valuable companies. It's significant that he has focused on a building company that collects metadata for maps.

Factual has now built a data set of over 75 million local businesses and points of interest in 50 countries and analyzes billions of data points every day. For example, their Global Places service provides the name, address, phone number, web site, latitude, longitude, and hours of operation of the places in their database. Customers—including Yelp, Foursquare, Bing, The Weather Channel, and Groupon—are both suppliers and users of Factual's data.

PlaceIQ

PlaceIQ, founded in 2010, sources data on the location, movements, and behavior of over 100 million people from third-party apps that it integrates with. The company's platform layers this data over a map of the physical world via tiles. It uses nearly one billion of these tiles, each measuring 100 by 100 meters, to create an understanding of each space, including the types of locations, types, and number people and their behaviors. They can use this data to target certain types of people based on their movements, look at the behavior of people before and after a mobile or TV ad campaign, and then look at their visits to certain locations, such as a particular brand of car dealership, in order to measure the effectiveness of the campaign.

Ninth Decimal

Ninth Decimal, previously known as JiWire, was launched in 2006 to help businesses monetize Wi-Fi access by serving ads to users when they connected. In 2012 they pivoted, focusing on the audience targeting capability that they had developed to sell ads on their Wi-Fi network, but extending it to a broader mobile phone network enabled by mobile app publishers. By understanding the venues that people frequent with their phones, they can target based on profiles such as:

- Business traveler who regularly travels away from home

- Pet owner who goes to pet shops regularly

- Healthy living folks who go to gyms a lot

- Auto intenders who are visiting car dealerships

Having targeted an audience for a mobile advertising campaign, their LCI™ attribution analytics can measure "lift," which is the effectiveness of an advertising campaign at driving visits to a physical store, by comparing the behavior of a control group of consumers that don't receive the ads. Conversions can be reported against asset of dimensions such as:

- Cost per incremental visit

- Profile of visitors (see the previous examples, plus demographics such as age and income)

- Region/state/city

- Visitor's proximity to store when they received the ad

- Average time to first visit

- When the visits took place (day/time of day)

- Locations visited prior to the store visit (competitors)

RetailNext

RetailNext, founded in 2007, has emerged as a leading provider of in-store analytics for retailers, shopping centers, and manufacturers. They use a variety of data sources—including video cameras, Wi-Fi and Bluetooth devices, guest Wi-Fi, POS systems, promotional calendars, payment cards, and weather reports—to provide in-store analytics.

RetailNext tracks more than one billion shoppers per year by collecting data from more than 65,000 sensors in retail stores and analyzing trillions of data points annually.

They use Bluetooth beacons in conjunction with their heatmap product that uses the output from security cameras to track the areas of the store that are most frequently visited. Staff members carry beacons so that their presence can be factored out of the heatmaps. RetailNext places hubs at points that allow the location of the beacons to be calculated using trilateration.

Their customers include retailers such as Bloomingdale's, American Apparel, Brookstone, and Verizon Wireless, and manufacturers such as PepsiCo and P&G.

A Dimensional Data Model for Beacon Analytics

DIMENSIONAL DATA MODELING

Up until the late 1980s, most data warehouse schemas were based on complex entity-relationship diagrams that made querying these huge repositories a job only a programmer could perform. By the end of that decade, this bottleneck around the central warehouse had inspired a change in best practice that begat the data mart, which is a subset of the enterprise's warehouse data, designed for more rapid access to quickly answer specific needs. One of the strategies for accomplishing this was called *dimensional data modeling*, which is a technique that gained broad adoption as a way of structuring those data marts so that queries could be written simply and rapidly. A whole industry of On-Line Analytical Processing (OLAP) tools coalesced to enable business teams to query the data mart using this dimensional design.

A dimensional data model consists of a central table of facts or numbers that are "sliced and diced" along dimensions that help us to aggregate the facts in meaningful ways. Examples of facts might be sales data records, which can be summarized by dimensions such as time, region, and product. The schemas were represented as "star schemas" with dimension tables surrounding the fact table in the middle. When an OLAP tool was used to report on the star schema, it resembled a spreadsheet, where the dimensions were the column and row headings, and the facts were the numbers in the middle. Excel supports this model with pivot tables.

This way of organizing data allows business and IT users to quickly design systems that are efficient and informative.

In order to help explore the kinds of queries that a beacon-enabled analytics system can allow, we will construct a simple dimensional data model that represents the kinds of *facts* that beacons can collect and the *dimensions* that can be used to "slice and dice" that data.

Figure 10-5 shows an example. The facts in our dimensional data model relate to a campaign flow for a restaurant app that is beacon-enabled. The flow of the campaign starts within the app, with a count of app registrations, the number of those users who then go on to use the app, the number of messages sent to the user (messages that could be triggered by or filtered by location or proximity figures, like the presence of a user near a restaurant), the number of those messages that were clicked on, and the rate at which people opened the app.

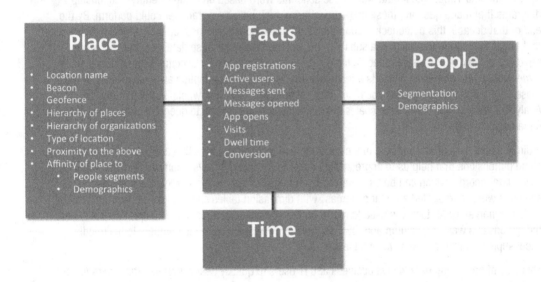

Figure 10-5. *A dimensional data model for analyzing beacon events*

We then count the visits to the property, which the app will detect, on seeing a beacon. Dwell time within the restaurant is calculated using entry and exit events from a beacon and conversion could be measured by the duration of the dwell time in the eating area of the restaurant.

These facts could be used to populate a funnel such as the one in Figure 10-6 showing the conversion from one stage to the next.

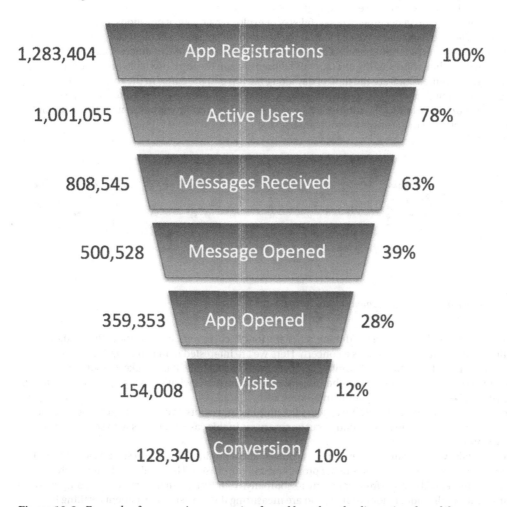

Figure 10-6. *Example of a campaign conversion funnel based on the dimensional model*

The "drill down" (as analysts call it) into those numbers can be done using any of the dimensions. The time dimension is, by its nature, hierarchical. You can look at the conversion from messages to visits over the year, by month week and day, and then by comparing time periods. For instance, is our conversion rate up this week versus last week?

We may have a variety of attributes to describe our customers that can be used to drill down into conversion rate. At the most basic level, we can compare conversion rate of first-time users of the app to regular users of the app. If the conversion rate of our regular users suddenly goes down, maybe it's time to check the menu to see if a favorite item has changed.

We can then use the place dimension to drill down into those numbers further, by comparing conversion rate down a hierarchy of places. At the top we look at the conversion rate by country, then by state, region, town, and then a particular restaurant. In this way we can see outliers, such as the conversion rate was up in California and was down in Oregon this week. Other attributes in the place dimension might be the type of restaurant; maybe different kinds of format or size of restaurants in a given chain. We may tag the restaurants by the affinity of a type of person to the restaurant. If we have demographic data on the visitors, we may be able to tag the locations with those demographics so that we can look at the performance of restaurants that have a customer base that is higher or lower income.

So our simple star schema becomes a powerful way of exploring a range of questions. Our fact table is enriched by the beacon data because we can look at the behavior of our guests in the restaurant.

Let us now refine our restaurant business analysis and focus on dwell time in different zones of the restaurant. We will do that by presenting our facts and dimensions in the form of a table presented in Figure 10-7. Here our dimensions are the time of day along the top and the zones in the restaurant on the side. By slicing the dwell time of guests in the reception area waiting for the maître d' to seat them, we can see that our early birds have to wait 10 minutes as the staff gets ready, and wait times remain short up until noon, when the lunch time rush causes a significant backlog.

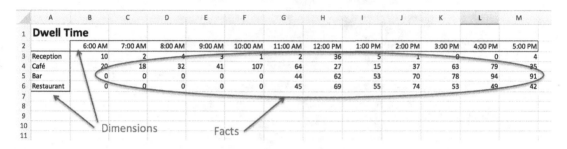

Figure 10-7. *Dimensional data presented in table format*

High dwell times in the bar are a good thing, since the longer customers stay, the more drinks they buy, but dwell time in the restaurant section is a concern. Here we are interested in maximizing "table turns" in order to get a better yield from the fixed number of tables we have available. It looks like at noon our dwell time is over an hour, a lot higher than any other time of day. Maybe this is what's driving up the dwell time in reception. This is likely to be a staffing problem of some kind.

Without beacons, all we would be able to see is the number of receipts. We wouldn't get a clear sense of whether low numbers are due to not enough customers or, as in this case, problems with servicing the customers we have waiting.

Your data model will, of course, differ. Perhaps you will add a product dimension so you can slice and dice the campaign based on the products being promoted and purchased. The details of the hierarchies for place and customer will change from company to company. Your facts even may relate to a completely different proximity application. If, for instance, you are measuring the time spent by patients waiting in a waiting room rather than customers in the bar, the goal will be to drive dwell times down rather than up.

The star schema provides a common way for business people and the IT staff to think about the information that can be collected and the kinds of questions that can be explored. Beacons don't change the techniques for organizing the data, but they increase the volume of the data and open up new sets of questions and answers to explore. They also make designing the way analytics are done even more important than it was before.

Case Study: AreaMetrics

AreaMetrics, originally known as Happy Hour Hawaii, was founded in 2011 by Carey and Brandon Bennett in Honolulu, Hawaii after a fortuitous decision by Carey to write a weekly Happy Hours column.

"We only knew of a few happy hours on the island, and we were becoming quite bored with our options. We looked for resources that would tell us the details of other happy hours in the area, but nothing existed. So, we created a web site and mobile apps for people just like us. It turns out, there were thousands of people who wanted access to detailed happy hour information so they could save money while dining out," said Carey.

Carey contacted a local periodical, the Star Advertiser, to write about interesting Happy Hour spots and was hired to write a weekly column. While writing the column, Carey and Brandon came up with the idea to develop an app to enable users to find nearby happy hour specials and provide restaurant owners with an opportunity to engage directly with customers.

Brandon developed the app in seven months despite having no prior programming experience. The solution offered to the restaurants included the app as well as beacons placed in each venue.

"YouTube was one of my best friends for several months. I'd spend about 12 hours a day watching tutorials on how to program in PHP. Eventually, I built up the skillset needed to create the web site. The site grew in popularity, and we quickly realized that we'd need apps for both iOS and Android. So, back to YouTube I went," explained Brandon in describing how he used YouTube to develop his programming skills.

After gaining some initial market traction, but needing additional capital to grow, the company applied and was selected to be part of the Blue Startups accelerator. The accelerator was launched by Henk Rogers, founder of Blue Planet Software (sole agent of Tetris).

Beacons

Carey and Brandon decided to use Estimote beacons due to an advisory member's introduction to the company's CEO. The Estimote beacons, with their unusual industrial design, were a key differentiator for the app, particularly when pitching to restaurant owners and managers. The beacon design is unique in the industry as they look like small rocks and are available in a variety of pastel colors, including blue, purple, and green.

The colorful appearance of the beacons, however, brought with it an issue. Children were drawn to them, so it quickly became apparent the beacons had to be placed high up, above the door, out of the reach of prying hands.

The beacons enabled venue owners to determine how many customers the app had driven into their happy hour. If a customer viewed the details of a restaurant in the app and then visited the same restaurant within 12 hours, the company could claim credit for that visit. The app would sight the beacon and, after about 30 seconds of being in range of the beacon, a visit could be verified.

Market Launch

The app was launched in Hawaii and immediately experienced rapid growth, reaching 50,000 downloads in the first six months. Based on this initial success, the company decided to expand beyond Hawaii and rebranded the app from Happy Hour Hawaii to Happy Hour Pal. They completed a market trial in the Hamptons during the summer and then launched in Portland, Oregon. Portland was chosen based on research that it has the highest per capita number of happy hours in the United States. The service was initially marketed door-to-door to restaurants and monetized via a monthly recurring fee.

Company Evolution

While the app experienced rapid growth in downloads, the restaurant owners wanted to use the service to gain greater insight into their own businesses, hoping to answer questions such as:

- How long are customers staying at the restaurant?
- What are the age and gender of my customers?
- How often do my customers return?
- Which customers are visiting my other restaurants?

- What is the "bounce" rate? (i.e., how many users walk by without entering? How many arrive and then leave right away?)

- What neighborhoods are my customers coming from?

To get restaurant owners to sign up for the app, the Bennetts found that emphasizing the analytics capabilities available to the restaurant owners was the key to closing deals. Soon, the pitch evolved to focus on the insights driven by the analytics before even mentioning the app. Based on this experience, as well as the challenge of competing in a crowded app market, the company decided to evolve from its proximity marketing services via its app to offering an analytics platform, the dashboard for which is shown in Figure 10-8. As part of this transition, the company also rebranded from Happy Hour Pal to AreaMetrics. They expanded beyond their core Happy Hour Pal users to secure strategic partnerships with leading location-enabled app players focused on the food and beverage, travel, and dating markets.

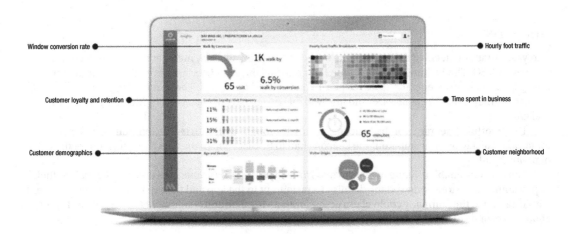

Figure 10-8. *An example of the AreaMetrics dashboard*

AreaMetrics Go-To-Market Strategy has evolved from direct door-to-door sales to an indirect strategy of partnering with companies that already service the restaurant and hospitality market.

Technology and Architecture

AreaMetrics is built in Ruby using the Rails framework. The database is Postgres, and the company uses an API to manage and access all data. The Software Development Kit (SDK) that interacts with their Bluetooth beacons is written in Objective C.

The platform leverages a network of millions of app users to gather its key analytics such as customer demographics, walk by conversions, visit duration, and bounce rates.

Business Results

AreaMetrics, via its partnerships with leading app companies, reached 15 million users in July 2015 and is adding 50,000 users per day. The company has thousands of beacons installed in restaurants and is expanding into other markets including retail, travel, financial services, sports venues, and gaming with plans for a full-scale national launch by mid-to-late 2016. AreaMetrics continues to charge a recurring monthly fee for access to its analytics platform.

Lessons Learned

AreaMetrics success to date is attributed to the team's ability to recognize the evolving needs in their market and then quickly respond to capitalize on the opportunity.

The company used a "dominate a niche" strategy by building tens of thousands of active users and installing thousands of beacons in the hospitality market before extending into other markets.

The use of beacons allowed them to differentiate their service to merchants, unlocking the real value of their offering, which was the analytics capabilities. Beacons acted as cookies in the physical world to link customers and venues in order to establish "attribution," and then to derive a dwell time that will provide additional understanding of the behavior of the visitors they had driven to the venue.

Their free app enabled the business to bootstrap the offering, building a base of users. They established the value in the offering was the analytics, which could be sold to the venue owners.

Beacons need apps. App adoption can be a major constraint. Carey and Brandon understood that their market penetration was limited by the adoption of their app, and they were able to parlay the value of their analytics sub-system to engage other app owners and scale using their success in adjacent markets.

Implications

As the astronomer and author Cliff Stoll stated, "Data is not information, information is not knowledge, knowledge is not understanding, understanding is not wisdom."

While we are now the beneficiaries of endless streams of data, companies are scrambling to make sense of it all in order to convert data into actionable insights. Companies must also navigate a delicate balance of the desire for additional data on consumer behavior against the privacy concerns of those same consumers. One of the companies mentioned earlier, Euclid, had two well-publicized incidents due to consumer backlash toward its tracking of shoppers. In 2013, Nordstrom cancelled an 8-month, 17-store pilot of Euclid's technology after the public found out about the pilots from news outlets. The following year, Philz Coffee in San Francisco also stopped using Euclid after the *San Francisco Appeal* ran an article about the coffee shop tracking its customers.

As a result of these concerns, leading analytics companies agreed to a self-policed Mobile Location Analytics Code of Conduct that allows consumers to opt out of tracking done through smartphones at retail locations. The Code of Conduct was drawn up through collaboration with U.S. Senator Chuck Schumer and the Future of Privacy Forum.

Yet despite these privacy concerns, location-centric analytics are already driving tangible consumer benefits. Examples include fans finding the shortest concession line at a sports stadium, shoppers being sent personalized coupons or discounts at the point of purchase, and finding your way through a hospital or airport. As additional sensors are added to smartphones and wearables see further adoption, other benefits may come to include environmental agencies understanding real-time pollution conditions in various cities, or consumers saving on medical insurance costs by opting in to provide their health and fitness information. Euclid now has a healthy business with large numbers of retailers using their services again.

Summary

Analytic platforms that develop insights from existing and emerging location technologies have the potential to transform the way organizations interact with their customers, employees, supply chain partners, and other key stakeholders. Sustainable success, however, will be created by the organizations that balance innovation with privacy concerns.

The next chapter looks at privacy from the perspective a lawyer who has focused on this subject and applied that knowledge specifically to the deployment of beacons.

CHAPTER 11

■ ■ ■

Designing with Privacy in Mind

Jarno Vanto, Partner, Borenius Attorneys, LLP

It is clear that beacon technology fundamentally changes the way retailers and advertisers communicate with customers. However, what is also clear is that the location-based technologies have attracted very polarized attention from the media. For example, in the fall of 2014 beacons were placed in NYC phone booths for testing purposes. City Hall ordered the beacons to be removed within hours as some were

© Stephen Statler 2016

S. Statler, *Beacon Technologies*, DOI 10.1007/978-1-4842-1889-1_11

concerned that the beacons would track the movement of users.[1] The fact that beacons can be used to collect consumer geolocation data has arguably turned out to be the greatest concern of many consumer groups. A recent Pew study found that location data has become even more precious and valued by consumers in the smartphone era. On the one hand, even though the majority of consumers will share their personal information in exchange for something of value, many feel unhappy about what happens to the information collected about them, especially if the data collected is used for other purposes than what they were originally collected for.[2] On the other hand, even though consumers claim to deeply care about privacy, studies show that consumers are in most cases ready to give up some privacy if they perceive that they are receiving some benefit in return, for example in the form of discounts or loyalty programs.[3]

The constantly evolving technology and consumer privacy scares have forced lawmakers and regulators around the globe to consider how, and if, the collection of geolocation information should be regulated. Given that legal instruments often lag behind technological developments, often outdated laws and regulations are applied to facts that they were not designed for in the first place. This can lead to mediocre results at best.

The Current Legal Landscape

Beacons have not yet been under much regulatory scrutiny, but this is likely to change in the near future. The main legal question thus far has involved the issue of choice or consent—people should have the right to choose whether information about them can be collected, and whether it can be shared with third parties. In essence, this is a right to control one's own information or informational self-determination. Are organizations using beacon technology thus required to obtain consent from the consumer? Or more fundamentally, should consent even be the way to solve the privacy questions surrounding beacon technology?

Although it often seems that technology erases the meaning of state lines, turning us into one big international community, laws continue to be inherently local. This forces organizations to be able to navigate a challenging jurisdictional jungle. Arguably two of the most globally influential privacy jurisdictions are the United States (US) and the European Union (EU). As we shall see, even though these two jurisdictions view privacy quite differently, their views on consent are not all that different.

The Legal Framework in the United States

Perhaps contrary to popular belief, the United States regulates privacy quite extensively. However, instead of comprehensive privacy laws governing all personal data processing such as in the EU, the United States has multiple sectoral laws and regulations that govern different commercial communication situations. This privacy scheme has rightly often been referred to as a "patchwork quilt."[4]

A number of parties are instrumental in shaping the U.S. legal framework in the privacy field. These parties include groups dedicated to promoting privacy and the regulation of privacy, private litigants who have sued companies for violations of privacy laws, the Congress, and the Federal Trade Commission (FTC), which focuses on encouraging a self-regulatory framework and promotes notice, choice, and transparency, as well as the advertising industry.[5] The FTC has become especially active since 2010, and it has put great

---

[1]See iapp.org/news/a/public-beacons-make-appearance-in-nyc-quickly-taken-down
[2]See Pew research at www.pewinternet.org/2016/01/14/privacy-and-information-sharing.
[3]See iapp.org/news/a/should-you-really-be-that-scared-of-your-in-store-retail-analytics.
[4]See, for example, Natasha Singer, *The New York Times*, "An American Quilt of Privacy Laws, Incomplete." March 30, 2013. www.nytimes.com/2013/03/31/technology/in-privacy-laws-an-incomplete-american-quilt.html?_r=0
[5]See 20-SPG Media L. & Pol'y 143, "Intellectual Property Legal Developments 2011-2012: The Year in Review," Peter Brown and Richard Raysman.

effort into promoting privacy, greater transparency, and consumer control over information gathering. The U.S. Department of Commerce also issued a green paper in 2010 about data privacy in which it, inter alia[6], promoted the significance of consent.[7] At the state level, California has definitely been the most active in regulating privacy.

The legislative branches, both at the federal and state levels, have been persistent in their efforts to protect privacy. During the past few years, multiple bills have been proposed in Congress, albeit without much success, with the intent to protect individuals' geolocation information. For example, the Commercial Privacy Bill of Rights Act of 2011 would have required an affirmative opt-in consent for the collection of sensitive information.[8] The Geolocation Privacy and Surveillance Act (GPS Act) would have set forth a clear legal framework for the usage of, and access to, geolocation information. The bill was introduced in the Senate and in the House in March 2013. Most recently, the Location Privacy Protection Act of 2015 (LPPA) was reintroduced by Minnesota Senator Al Franken. The LPPA would have prohibited companies from collecting or disclosing individuals' geolocation information from electronic devices without the user's affirmative express consent.[9] State legislatures have also considered regulating geolocation information, however, more so with regards to law enforcement access.[10]

Thus, federal law in itself does not currently require businesses to obtain consent for the collection of geolocation data, or to disclose whether or not they collect geolocation data. They are only prohibited from misrepresenting their data collection practices. However, note that if the Location Privacy Protection Act of 2015 were to pass, consent would be required before the collection of geolocation data.

The FTC has played a major role in enforcing consumer privacy, also on the issue of geolocation privacy. Even though location-based advertising is not currently subject to any specific federal regulations, FTC guidelines and industry standards do require that location information not be collected or used without consumer consent. The FTC has been involved in multiple cases where the collection of geolocation information was an issue. For instance, FTC v. Goldenshores Technologies was the first case in which the collection and sharing of geolocation data was the primary focus of the FTC. Here, a flashlight app collected its users' location information without disclosing it in its privacy policy. This decision is also quite unique in how it contains detailed instructions regarding the collection of geolocation information. The settlement agreement required, inter alia, the application to obtain an affirmative express consent from users before collecting such data.[11] FTC formally characterized geolocation information as "sensitive" in its privacy report from March 2012, in which it also strongly encouraged organizations to acquire consent before the collection or sharing of such data.[12] Moreover, in February 2015, the FTC published guidelines that further expand its advice with regards to the collection of user location data.[13]

---

[6]Among other things

[7]www.ntia.doc.gov/files/ntia/publications/iptf_privacy_greenpaper_12162010.pdf

[8]Commercial Privacy Bill of Rights Act of 2011, S. 799, 112th Cong. § 202 (2011)

[9]The Location Privacy Protection Act of 2015, s. 2270

[10]For example, Montana was the first state that passed a geolocation privacy bill in 2013, focusing on governmental inquiries.

[11]Goldenshores Technologies, LLC, and Erik M. Geidl, In the Matter of www.ftc.gov/enforcement/cases-proceedings/132-3087/goldenshores-technologies-llc-erik-m-geidl-matter

[12]FTC March 2012 privacy report, "Protecting Consumer Privacy in an Era of Rapid Change: Recommendations for Businesses and Policymakers." www.ftc.gov/sites/default/files/documents/reports/federal-trade-commission-report-protecting-consumer-privacy-era-rapid-change-recommendations/120326privacyreport.pdf. See also FTC 2013 report, "Mobile Privacy Disclosures: Building Trust Through Transparency," in which FTC further emphasized the requirement of notice and affirmative express consent. www.ftc.gov/sites/default/files/documents/reports/mobile-privacy-disclosures-building-trust-through-transparency-federal-trade-commission-staff-report/130201mobileprivacyreport.pdf

[13]The FTC published guidelines on the collection of location information when the app is not in use. The FTC recommends that mobile apps should clearly disclose their data collection when the app in question is not in active use. www.ftc.gov/news-events/blogs/business-blog/2015/02/location-location-location?utm_source=govdelivery

A couple of months later, the FTC had its first case against a retail tracking company, which eventually led to a settlement.[14] The FTC claimed that Nomi Technologies' privacy statement was inconsistent with the company's actual practices. Nomi provides technology that allows its clients to track customers by, for example, providing data on how much time customers spend in different sections of the store, and so on. Nomi's privacy policy provided that consumers have the possibility of opting out of the retail tracking. Even though Nomi's web site offered a possibility to opt-out, all of its clients' retail locations did not. In addition, Nomi did not require its clients to provide notice to their customers. FTC indicated that these factors rendered Nomi's privacy policy deceptive. Even though the case focused on the company's deceptive privacy statement, it can also be viewed as the FTC's first step in implementing the online world's notice-and-choice regime to retail tracking.

Even though the order did not per se impose an affirmative requirement, it does look like the FTC is moving to the direction of imposing an affirmative requirement for companies to disclose their tracking practices and acquire consumers' consent. In the light of Nomi, it is particularly important that all the participants in the beacon data value chain—including advertising networks, data aggregators, beacon service providers, retailers, and brands—must ensure contractually that proper notices are provided to customers and that each participant in the value chain uphold its privacy obligations.

The Legal Framework in the EU

Europe is the home of some of the oldest, most comprehensive, ambitious, and bureaucratic data privacy laws. The Directive on Privacy and Electronic Communications ("E-Privacy Directive")[15] forms a part of this comprehensive regulatory framework. The E-Privacy Directive deals specifically with data protection/privacy in the sector of electronic communications networks and services. Article 9 of the E-Privacy Directive sets forth that organizations may process location data only if it has been made anonymous, or with the consent of users and only for the duration necessary.[16] Given that EU directives have to be implemented into EU Member State law, the Member States have some leeway in implementing them into national law. For example, Finland has implemented the E-Privacy Directive into national law by enacting the Information Society Code.[17] Chapter 20, Section 160 of this code implements the respective "requirement for consent" provision of the directive, in addition to which it provides that location data can only be processed to the extent required for the purpose of the processing and in such a manner that does not unnecessarily invade a user's privacy. Moreover, following the processing of location data, the location data must be deleted or anonymized.

The Problem with Consent

Typically, most beacons themselves do not actually collect data as such. Rather, beacons transmit a signal to an application or a URL that is broadcasted directly to the mobile device of the individual. It is the application between the beacon and the device that receives the data. Beacon signals are not received unless a consumer has installed an application that is connected with the beacons in question. By themselves, beacons only detect the entering of a Bluetooth-enabled device into a particular zone or a "geofence." From this point of view, the individual is in charge of interacting with the beacon.

---

[14]In re Nomi Technologies, Inc. www.ftc.gov/enforcement/cases-proceedings/132-3251/nomi-technologies-inc-matter
[15]Directive (EC) 2002/58 of the European Parliament and of the Council of 12 July 2002 concerning the processing of personal data and the protection of privacy in the electronic communications sector [2002] OJ L201/37.
[16]Article 9 of Directive 2002/58/EC. See also Christopher Kuner, European Data Protection Law, Second Edition, Oxford 2007
[17]917/2014

However, the individual's control over the choice of interacting with the beacon can seem a little blurry. Beacons are often designed to be discreet and retail stores often decide to hide them, which makes it nearly impossible for consumers to notice them. When beacons are hidden, and the consumers do not know of their existence in a particular location, are consumers really in charge of interacting with the beacon? As we later suggest, instead of hiding the beacons and "tricking" consumers to provide their data, it is worth considering placing beacons in a visible location.

With respect to consent, placing consent language in long and convoluted privacy policies and terms of use does not provide customers with a meaningful notice or choice. Many consumers agree to terms and conditions as well as privacy policies without reading them. One study showed that it would take on an average 244 hours per year to read and skim privacy policies.[18] Most users are likely to miss the fine print that states that they agree to the collection of their geolocation data and allow it to be passed to third parties. As the comedian John Oliver has stated, you could put the entire text of *Mein Kampf* in the midst of the terms of service and users would still probably click "Agree." Even though, from a purely legal perspective, these consents most often are valid, best practices in the field suggest a different approach.

Suggestions for Best Practice

As discussed previously, the current laws and regulations are often unable to keep up with the rapid technological development. Therefore, governments often have encouraged "policing oneself" instead of relying solely on the current legal rules. For example, the FTC and the White House have published reports in which they promote the need for industry codes of conduct and processes that include multiple stakeholders. The Asia-Pacific region has also built a privacy framework around the concept of co-regulation.

For example, the Network Advertising Initiative has some of the strongest standards for self-regulation in the United States. Their Code of Conduct (updated in 2015) was strongly influenced by FTC's Staff Report on Self-Regulatory Principles for Online Behavioral Advertising.[19] The Future of Privacy Forum has also provided a self-regulatory framework, "Mobile Location Analytics Code of Conduct."[20] Another useful guide is the American Institute of CPAs' Generally Accepted Privacy Principles (GAPP), which provides a framework intended to assist in creating an effective privacy program that helps prevent and manage privacy risks.[21] Most recently in February 2016, the ACLU of Southern California issued a privacy guide for technology companies.[22]

We have identified some of the most important principles that together form the best practices for privacy and beacon technology. These principles include notice, choice, limited collection, transparency and consumer education, disclosure to third parties, and security.

Notice

Notice is one of the most fundamental privacy principles. It should be clearly linked with choice. Consumers cannot make a meaningful choice about their data collection if they have not been given notice, or if the notice has been hidden in the privacy policy or terms of use only. Moreover, since beacons are often camouflaged to match their surroundings, consumers need to be able to know that beacons exist in the store. As an alternative

---

[18]Aleecia M. McDonald and Lorrie Faith Cranor, "The Cost of Reading Privacy Policies." lorrie.cranor.org/pubs/readingPolicyCost-authorDraft.pdf
[19]www.networkadvertising.org/sites/default/files/NAI_Code15encr.pdf
[20]fpf.org/wp-content/uploads/10.22.13-FINAL-MLA-Code.pdf
[21]www.aicpa.org/interestareas/informationtechnology/resources/privacy/generallyacceptedprivacyprinciples/downloadabledocuments/gapp_bus_%200909.pdf
[22]www.itsgoodfor.biz/sites/default/files/Privacy%20and%20Free%20Speech%20Primer%20-%20Volume%203.pdf

to camouflaging beacons, for example, GameStop has embraced a strategy that puts beacons in the spotlight and encourages customers to engage with them.[23] A more discreet way to provide notice would be to place a sign inside the beacon zone or provide a push notification to the device in question.

In addition to getting notice that beacons exist and are used in the store, consumers should also be provided a clear notice of what information is collected from their mobile device. It is also important that the user be notified of whether the application continues to collect information despite being closed by the user. Many users do not necessarily understand this collection practice, which makes disclosure even more important.

Choice

Companies using beacon technology should provide consumers with the choice of whether they want data about them collected. FTC's settlement with the mobile location tracking company Nomi Technologies demonstrates that companies using cutting-edge technology need to be clear about what choices they provide to their users.

Users want to control how information about them is used or shared. Companies have the possibility of providing either an "opt-out" or "opt-in" mechanism for consumer choice. Opt-out by default tracks consumers but gives them the possibility to opt out from tracking, for example on the company web site. Following Nomi, consumers should also be made aware of their choice in retail stores. The consumer has to take an active role in removing him or herself from participation of the tracking or data sharing. The strongest argument against opt-out is that consumers are not always aware that their behavior is being tracked, and opting out may be a cumbersome exercise in itself.

Opt-in is a way to give consumers more control over how information about them is being collected as it provides them with the ability to actively choose to participate in mobile location analytics. Opt-in also tends to be more transparent than opt-out. Generally best practice favors opt-in over opt-out as opt-in provides consumers with a truly meaningful choice.

Disclosure to Third Parties

Many users are especially concerned about whether data about them is being shared with third parties. Therefore, the notice requirement should also include information about the company's data-sharing practices. The notice should explain whether information is shared in individual or aggregate form, who can access the information about them, and for what purposes.

Limited Collection

Collecting more information than the purpose requires may lead consumers to mistrust the company, and this can sometimes even violate the company's own privacy policy and/or terms of use. A good way to avoid these problems is to collect and retain only as much data as is needed. However, if a mobile application developer wants to collect more information than the purpose allows, the developer should obtain clear consent from the consumers.

Transparency and Consumer Education

Even though businesses invest great effort in developing applications for beacon data collection, many businesses do not inform customers about them. The more consumers learn about how beacon technology works and understand that they themselves are in control, the more likely it is that consumers will find the

---

[23]www.geomarketing.com/display-beacons-dont-hide-them-says-gamestop

benefits persuasive enough to opt-in to beacon-enabled applications. Multiple industry codes of conduct have put transparency in the center of their framework. Companies should be as transparent as possible about their data collection practices. For the benefit of both consumers and the market, it is important that consumers have a clear understanding of the operation of beacons and the applications that utilize beacons. Consumers should understand how their data is being collected and used. Transparency can also build loyalty and trust among users.

Security

Companies should protect the data they collect with strict security practices. The FTC requires companies to secure their user data, and it has the authority to, among other things, impose fines if it finds the company's security practices to be too lax. All methods of data collection and storage should be properly secured, and data encryption should be used when potentially sensitive information is involved. "Privacy by design" is a concept that suggests that instead of securing privacy by following regulations, privacy should become the default mode of operation. This means that applications and other products are designed with privacy in mind.

Summary: What the Future Will Look Like

Law has always been notoriously slow to adapt to new innovations. This is especially true when it comes to new technological innovations. Even though the legal framework for privacy is different in the EU and the United States, both jurisdictions seem to require consent for processing geolocation information. Notice and choice are often instrumental in keeping consumers comfortable with having their geolocation data collected and processed.[24] Acquiring consent before the collection of such data will also ensure compliance with legal requirements. However, considering the inherent shortcomings of the current legal landscape, it is likely that the self-regulatory frameworks of the industry will in the future have an even greater role in policing the use of new and emerging technologies.

What about data ownership? Many have suggested that digital contracting and data ownership would be the way of the future in the development of user privacy. This is not a novel idea. In fact, Hal R. Varian proposed assigning property rights in information 20 years ago.[25] Individuals could sell information about them, but this information could not be resold to third parties without an explicit agreement. Eli Noam also suggested that individuals should have the ability to sell information about themselves.[26] The concept of data ownership has, however, not been widely celebrated. The current framework has been successful, as consumers often choose to "agree" to the terms of service when the only alternative is to not use the service at all.

Moreover, the idea of owning data is much more complex than it seems, and it has been debated in the legal field for a long time. Information is quite different from tangible things in that many different people can "own" the same information at the same time. It is easily shared, leaky, and hard to control, which makes it difficult to be regarded as property in the traditional sense of the word. Even though the idea of data ownership is not completely vain, it is very likely not the road data privacy will be traveling on in the near future.

---

[24]See, for example, Turow – Hennessey – Draper, "The Tradeoff Fallacy: How Marketers Are Misrepresenting American Consumers And Opening Them Up to Exploitation," June 2015 www.ftc.gov/system/files/documents/public_comments/2015/09/00012-97594.pdf

[25]Hal R. Varian, "Economic Aspects of Personal Privacy." December 6, 1996, people.ischool.berkeley.edu/~hal/Papers/privacy

[26]Eli Noam, "Privacy and Self-Regulation: Markets for Electronic Privacy." [Date?] 1997, www.citi.columbia.edu/elinoam/articles/priv_self.htm

A more likely approach for the foreseeable future is a service such as www.locationcontrol.org,[27] which allows you to see the data that has been registered to certain beacons about your mobile device. The amount of beacons and retailers that use proximity marketing platforms is likely to grow exponentially in the coming years, which would make it nearly impossible to keep track of all parties tracking your data. A service such as that of locationcontrol.org allows the user to easily opt-out, which will ensure that no proximity data will be collected against a consumer's will. The Future of Privacy Forum has also provided a way for consumers to effortlessly opt-out of mobile location analytics by using the web site www.smart-places.org. All consumers need to enter is their Wi-Fi and/or Bluetooth address, and their devices will not be used for the mobile location analytics of the participating companies.

---

[27]Jarno Vanto and Steve Statler have advised Unacast, the developer of this service.

CHAPTER 12

■ ■ ■

Orchestration: Making Beacons Behave More Intelligently

John Coombs, Co-founder and CEO, Rover

The opportunity to better understand the physical context of our customers and communicate with them in a hyper-local and relevant fashion has beacon solution designers eager to execute and realize the great "promise" of beacons.

A simple scan through marketing industry publications might have us believe that with the purchase of some beacon hardware and a few sessions with our mobile agency, we can be in market, delivering the often-touted "customer experience of the future". However, the reality is that there is a significant gap between a simple Bluetooth-emitting piece of hardware (a beacon) and the type of scalable, end-user experience that drives the ROI we can really get excited about. As we have discussed in the previous chapters, there are indeed a number of components of the beacon "stack" that we must consider when looking to get real value out of a beacon strategy and have a deployment that behaves more intelligently.

The aim of this chapter is to make sense of the components of the stack beyond the hardware itself. This includes the creation, management, and design of your campaigns and content strategy—referred to here as *beacon orchestration*. Just as the symphony conductor ensures harmony through careful attention to his orchestra's component parts, so too should the beacon solution designer. A successful beacon orchestration requires thoughtful evaluation of the pieces that will make up your deployment and a data-driven approach with careful attention to the end-user experience.

Intelligent orchestration will create value for the app owner and the end user. Crafting the right content strategy for your brand is crucial to successful outcomes. There is no silver bullet use-case in proximity marketing and a content strategy that works for one brand won't necessarily work for another. Solution designers need to embrace this reality, recognizing that beacons and proximity marketing are new and determining your winning content strategy will require metric-driven iteration to ensure your approach is resonating with customers and driving the desired ROI for your business. A well architected orchestration layer can ensure that content iterations can be developed and deployed faster while consuming fewer resources.

What to look For

One of the most important factors in a successful beacon orchestration, whether in the early or later stages of your proximity marketing efforts, is the selection of your campaign or content management system (CMS). Whether you decide to build your own solution, or use a third-party proximity orchestration system, you'll want to evaluate the following areas when making a decision on the right solution for your business.

Features

At the most basic level of evaluation are the features and functionality that exist within the orchestration platform you choose to leverage. Some platforms will be loaded with glitzy features you'll pay for but never end up using, while others will lack function that might be core to your success. For example. a scannable barcode feature for mobile couponing might be crucial to evaluating the ROI of a retail deployment, but might matter little in a museum use-case. Take a long-term view of the types of features that might come up in your environment.

While we will dive deeper into some important orchestration features, at a high-level, some you should consider are:

- Content: Supported media types, native vs. web view, design customization
- Analytics: Content data as well as dwell time and customer pathing
- Segmentation: Ability to personalize and target content
- Frequency capping or content "limiters"
- Beacon mapping and fleet management
- Other proximity technologies supported

Usability and Support

When we think about beacons and mobile, a lot of attention is paid to end-user experience (UX) and user experience testing. Attention should also be paid to the UX and usability of your CMS itself. As you work through use-cases and build your proximity strategy, you and your team will likely spend more time than you might expect designing, authoring, and evaluating your beacon campaigns. Ease of use and usability can mean the difference between an extremely frustrating or positive experience that allows you to get the most out of the platform. In addition to the usability of the CMS, it's important to understand what support is provided in terms of online resources and dedicated account and developer support as you work through integration and launch.

Third-Party Integrations

No CMS will "do it all". While many platforms might claim to be a super platform that will solve all of your needs, the solution you go with will likely not excel at all of the components of the beacon stack that are important to your business. You'll want to know if the platform provider you work with supports any third-party integrations that enhance the core offering.

Beacon hardware—One of the first integrations you will likely consider will be on the hardware side. A number of beacon hardware providers have APIs that can connect with your CMS, displaying relevant data about your beacon fleet such as battery life or your beacon configurations. Having one login to craft your content and manage your beacon hardware will be important for scalable success.

Ad networks—As you look longer term, you might want to consider more advanced integrations such as platforms that pool or share proximity data or provide content feeds from ad networks or other sources.

Analytics—While your CMS might provide analytics out of the box, there are vendors that offer dedicated proximity analytics solutions that will likely outperform what a CMS provider will be able to provide on their own. If proximity analytics is important to you, you'll want to assess this type of option.

CRM—Working with beacons will open the doors to a sizeable and extremely valuable data set. Like any data, it will only be as valuable as your ability to derive insights from it and, equally as important, have it complement your existing customer data. Integration with your CRM will expedite your ability to have a more holistic view of your customer and drive smarter content.

Push—While our focus is on proximity-triggered content, content derived from other behavioral triggers will continue to play an important role in driving app engagement. Your beacon-based content should complement your other forms of notifications such as push, not compete with it.

Indoor navigation—Indoor mapping and navigation based on beacons and other technology is continuing to emerge as a highly specialized offering. Some newer vendors as well as large incumbents have compelling in-store navigation offerings that, if integrated properly, can complement your beacon content strategy.

Mobile SDK/UI

If you don't take a custom approach to building beacon content into your app, the CMS you choose to go with will likely have a corresponding mobile SDK, which will take care of beacon handling logic as well as the mobile user interface. Because the end-user experience is the pillar of successful beacon orchestration, this is an especially important consideration. At the heart of getting content right is the way in which beacon-triggered content is presented to your app users. You'll want to make sure you have a good understanding of the type of content you can deliver, as well as the way in which it is delivered. Some important things to consider here are:

- Is the content on the user's mobile device presented as a web view or native content?

- In what form is the content presented and how can it be customized in the CMS?

- How flexible are the design elements? Are they standardized or highly flexible to fit the look and feel of your brand?

- For more advanced use-cases, is the SDK open source allowing agency or internal developers to further customize?

- What media types are supported?

- Is deeplinking proximity content to native app functionality supported?

- Does the UI support scannable mobile coupons or other methods to track content conversion?

Segmentation and CRM Integration

While segmentation and content personalization might not be a priority in the first iteration of your beacon strategy, they will eventually play an important role. Proximity is a key pillar of relevance and engagement on mobile, but marrying proximity with personalization is a standard all proximity marketers should strive for. Some of the best engagement and ROI comes from content that considers both the user's location and relevant attributes.

In many ways, beacons act as cookies for the physical world, providing a host of data points that can paint a more holistic view of a customer and complementing digital data with a physical world understanding. A real-world example of this can be understood by comparing an e-commerce shopper's "clicks" to view bicycles online with a shopper's presence in the bicycle aisle of a brick and mortar retail store. Just as the online retailer can retarget and cater content based on their shoppers' potential purchase interests (as demonstrated by clicks), so too can the brick and mortar retailer turn physical world data (dwell time) into a more informed content strategy going forward.

Of course, this sort of data is useful only if it is actionable. On one hand, you may have a fairly robust CRM you have built over the years that could inform proximity content. In this case, the CMS you choose should have the APIs and integration capabilities to drive smarter proximity content based on the view of the customer you have already started to build. This "pipe" should go both ways. As offline brick and mortar data is gathered, it should complement your existing CRM, helping you round out the view of the customers.

The actionable step coming out of these integrations is to then tie this more holistic customer view into personalization of your content strategy. Whether through variable text features that make content highly personal, or offers and messaging specific to your customers' preferences, turning data into highly relevant and personal content is key to getting the most out of your proximity strategy.

Support for Complementary Location and Proximity Technologies

While the focus of this book is on beacons, a number of other technologies can be powerful elements of a proximity strategy. The most prominent example of these technologies is *geofencing*. Does the platform you are looking at consider other technologies in order to deliver a superior end-user experience? If done right, geofencing can be a very complementary and scalable addition to your solution. Geofences allow you to transition from "macro" proximity regions such as a city block or mall property down to the more micro proximity regions associated with beacons.

iBeacon and Eddystone—In addition to other proximity technologies, there are protocols that have been built on top of Bluetooth tech. Perhaps the most exciting and impactful is Google's Eddystone. As outlined in Chapter 5, the Eddystone protocol opens the door for different types of data and ways of communicating with mobile devices. This protocol is too big of a force to be ignored and you will want to feel confident that the CMS provider you choose to go with supports this other beacon "language".

The Vision Driving Your CMS Vendor

In addition to all the tech, features, and integrations a CMS vendor may provide, it's valuable to understand the underlying vision and direction of the CMS vendor itself. As the other chapters have articulated, the emerging beacon ecosystem is a "wild west" of opportunity and views around how the ecosystem should mature and take shape vary significantly.

For example, some teams view beacon infrastructure as a foundation upon which an ad network can be built. Others might simply view a beacon installation as the foundation for a more utilitarian mobile experience, guiding the user from point a to point b with a heavy focus on navigation. These are very different views of the beacon world and will result in different feature priorities and product development as their platform matures over time.

Additionally, some beacon platform providers are born out of predecessor technologies and might view beacons as simply another "feature" that can be added to an existing platform. I would argue that proximity content is not an afterthought that can be easily layered into any existing platform, but rather a pillar around which a platform should be built. Many push, and other mobile marketing automation businesses, were born out of industries such as gaming, with products crafted and shaped to reflect the sheer volume-based nature of that industry. Does a team who built a product around this type of engagement view proximity the same way? Do they have in place the user experience and design talent to help you execute the type of engaging and content rich campaigns that you desire?

Scalability

Another important question that would apply to the selection of most technical vendors is how they view scale and the underlying technology that supports your deployment at scale. This is particularly important in a space where scalability is one of the primary challenges facing beacon solution designers. In addition to the ability to monitor and manage large-scale hardware deployments, it is important to assess what provisions are in place on the content management side. For example, does your CMS provide user roles and permission to allow for content management by region? Your Manhattan content strategy may look vastly different from your efforts in Bismarck, North Dakota. What role does your content platform provider play in this configuration and set up, both in your physical venues and in the cloud? How do they view the challenges associated with deployment at scale? Can your beacons be configured in the cloud or do they require on the ground set up? It's important to ask these types of questions to better understand how your efforts can scale.

Looking to Smarter Content: Turning Hardware Into Engagement

The best campaign management solution can only be as effective as the content strategy it drives. The right content strategy will engage and drive frequency in mobile usage, while a poor content strategy will likely result in your users turning off notifications, or worse, uninstalling your app.

Frequency Capping or Limiters—Smart content strategy starts with some basics and progresses to more advanced considerations as the proximity strategy matures. At the most basic level should be content rules baked into your app or CMS vendor's SDK. This should include logic ensuring users don't see the same content twice if they happen to exit and re-enter a beacon region within a short period of time. The ability to limit the volume of content and frequency of how it is delivered (i.e., push notification versus passive presentation of content) should also be within your control as a beacon solution architect.

Context Triggers for Content—All marketers understand the importance of mobile, and most are aware of the fact that relevance and context are emerging as the most important elements of a successful mobile strategy. A user's proximity or location (whether micro or macro) is one of the fundamental building blocks of relevance, but it isn't nearly as effective without an additional context layer, often referred to as one-to-one or personalization. Marrying proximity data with CRM data can have a significant impact on the quality and relevance of your content strategy. While platforms and campaign management software can help with this type of execution, thought needs to go into the factors and objectives driving your strategy. Let's look at a grocery store use-case to further flush this out. From a CRM integration perspective, we may know that our shopper prefers healthy and organic options. In this case, we can drive smart content by choosing to present her with relevant content (the launch of our new private label organics line) at the right time (her "digital flyer" as she enters the store). Looking to the in-store experience itself, we could leverage a "pairing" or "purchase-path" driven approach, such as by directing our shopper to our rich selection of red wine after her dwell time in the meat section.

User-First Design—In general, the best content strategy is one that is user-first, marketing second. Beacons and proximity are emerging as the most powerful and engaging channels available to marketers but that power comes with obvious risk. There is no better way to get your app uninstalled than to push spammy or purely coupon-centric content multiple times as a customer navigates your store. Taking a user-first content approach builds a relationship foundation with your users that demonstrates your appreciation for their business, and the right to communicate with them using location. A proximity strategy built on this user-first foundation will give you more "rope" as you work through the inevitable mistakes and challenges of getting your strategy perfect.

Furthermore, your users will begin to associate your app as a utilitarian tool, or exclusive channel where they can get more out their engagement with your brand. The ability to use the channel to drive sales will come naturally from an audience who has already bought into their mobile experience with you. Your ability to influence on mobile is only as strong as the size of the user base you want to influence. Many mobile marketers fall into the trap of trying to get the marketing part right before they even have a base to market to. Surprise, delight, engage, and reward your users with utilitarian tools before you take a "coupon-first" content approach and you will be rewarded. With hundreds of retail deployments under our belts, we have seen a clear lift in campaigns that I would suggest were "user-first" in nature, with content open rates of 45-65%.

Three key focuses that can drive this user-first content are:

- Utility—Does the proximity feature or content improve the customer experience? Does it make purchasing faster? Does it make finding a product easier?

- Incentive or Reward—Is your mobile app, specifically the proximity content on it, a rewarding channel? Do you marry your loyalty program with your proximity content?

- Exclusivity or "surprise and delight"—Do you offer exclusive in-store only offers?

Summary

As architects work through how beacons can be applied to a business, one of the most important factors in a successful outcome will be uncovering the content strategy that engages the customers and the tools used to get there. Beacon or proximity content is still very new to most and it will take some trial and error to get to winning use-cases.

The emerging proximity opportunity is distinct from traditional push and opens the doors to completely new ways of connecting with mobile users. It's an opportunity to create value for users as they navigate their way through your physical space. You need to connect with partners, agencies, or proximity marketing teams that understand the nuances of proximity and have the long-term view to help you build that dialogue with your users.

Strategies should recognize the value of a user-first approach with careful attention to the specific journey of your customer and the nuances of your brand. Having utility, incentive, and exclusive offers driving your content strategy is one of the best ways to be user-first in your approach.

CHAPTER 13

■ ■ ■

Understanding Beacon Networks

By Steve Statler and Kjartan Slette, COO and co-founder, Unacast

"It's hard to break into a network once it's formed."

— *Elon Musk*

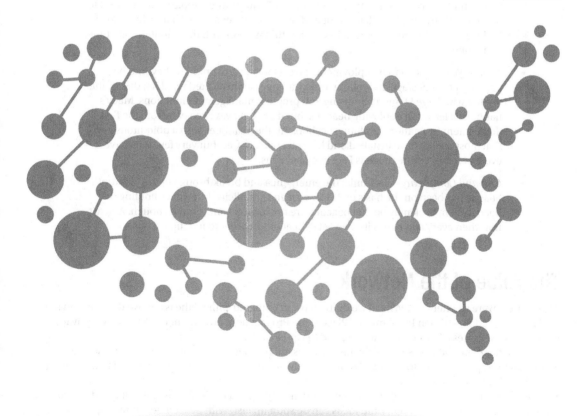

S. Statler, *Beacon Technologies*, DOI 10.1007/978-1-4842-1889-1_13

The emergence of beacon networks may be the most significant factor in the success of businesses fighting to succeed in the beacosystem.

Beacons have some remarkable properties. They are low in cost, easy to install, have increasingly sophisticated sensors, and can be used to create some really cool user experiences. We have grounds for optimism about the future of the beacosystem. The Proxbook report[1], which surveys the number of beacons deployed as reported by the vendors in its database, is seeing major growth. As of Q4 2015, approximately four million beacons had been registered as deployed worldwide. These numbers align with ABI's growth projections of 400 million beacons to be deployed by 2020.

However, with two years having passed since the deployment of the first Bluetooth beacon, it would be hard to argue that beacons have achieved the full potential that many of us see. Why aren't there more beacon-enabled apps? Why aren't beacons in every major retail, entertainment, and hospitality venue? What's missing? Do we need longer battery life, better range, improved accuracy, or more sensors? While all of those things would be great and will almost certainty happen, we don't think those are the critical success factors.

We believe that the success of the beacon ecosystem depends on the growth of beacon networks. In order to appreciate that dynamic, it's worth revisiting the following:

- *Physical effort*—Unlike regular software deployments, beacon-enabled apps require a lot of physical coordination: the investment of many more people on the ground to purchase, distribute, install, monitor and maintain the beacons. That's a lot of work for businesses, like retailers, that have other things to do with their limited staff, time, and money.

- *Time*—We have seen that deployments take a long time to graduate beyond the proof-of-concept stage and rollout, even for large, sophisticated retailers; that is, the top tier with large IT, merchandising and program management functions. Macy's has been a leader in deploying beacons, but it's taken over two years from the first deployment to a national rollout. Facebook hit the headlines with a ubiquitous app that most people have installed and beacons that are free, but very few of us have ever been into a store that has Facebook beacons.

- *Cost and Complexity*—It's ironic; the emergence and breakthrough of the Bluetooth beacon has been on the basis of its low cost and simplicity, but what's holding the beacosystem back may be that beacons are not low cost and simple enough. At least, not when every app needs its own set of beacons in order to function.

The Value of the Network

What if there were a better way? What if we didn't have to bothered with all the issues we discussed in the deployment chapter—the ten Ps: Planning, Placement, Propagation, Procurement, Permission, Privacy/Public Notices, Process, Power, Presentation, and (gasp!) People.

Well, it turns out there is. Some of the most successful businesses are using beacons that service more than one app. This one-to-many relationship between beacons and third-party apps is the defining characteristic of a beacon network.

These beacons are infrastructure. The hard work has already been done. Someone decided to make an investment upfront so that new apps and ideas can be spun up fast. With beacon networks, app developers, rather than waiting for beacons to be put in place, can use beacons that are already out there.

---

[1]www.proxbook.com/reports/

Infrastructure is hard, expensive, and requires vision to build. But thanks to infrastructure, when we plan a road trip to a major city, we don't have to worry about whether there are highways in place. We have the infrastructure of an Interstate Highway System that was built following Franklin D. Roosevelt's Federal-Aid Highway Act in 1938[2]. We find our way around those roads thanks to the standards for signage and numbering that date back to infrastructure decisions made in 1925[3].

What we see emerging in the world of beacons has parallels to these developments in road infrastructure that led to an explosion of road transport and growth in economic prosperity. Like America's first road systems, beacon projects are being deployed by a multitude of largely independent entrepreneurs. They are providing ease of access to the beacosystem, but they are operating in fragments. The maps of where they are located are often incomplete and disconnected, but the potential that comes with joining up these resources is clear.

Of course, all networks are not the same. We see them falling into three categories, each one building on the services of the former:

- *Beacon Directories*—These form a road map of beacons owned by other organizations. They don't grant access to the beacons, but finding where the beacons are is a start. The beacon owners, not the operators of the directories, control access to these beacons.

- *Beacon Access Networks*—These are more tightly integrated collections of beacons, whose access is controlled via the network, where you have to pay to play.

- *Beacon Commerce Networks*—These are a class of beacon network where the APIs and services offered are at a higher level than typical beacon APIs. A commerce network supports use-cases that are specific to certain commerce applications such as advertising, coupons, promotions, or payments.

Let's look in more detail at each of these, with a set of specific examples that we can learn from.

Beacon Directories

As beacons proliferate, inquiring minds want to know how many beacons have been deployed and where they are. Manufacturers self-report to industry analysts (like ABI) how many beacons they have produced and will allude to some of the projects where they are being deployed. They can also record this information on Proxbook.com, but it would be nice to have more precise information about what has actually been deployed and exactly where the devices are.

With iBeacon providing a standard way of identifying beacons across manufacturers and the proliferation of mobile apps capable of watching out for beacons as their owners travel around the world, sites have appeared that crowdsource the search of these beacons in the wild and record their details in directories that can be accessed online.

---

[2]President Dwight D. Eisenhower received credit for his key part in the building of the U.S. Interstate Highway system, as he presided over much of its construction and grew the scope of the project. His insight into the military applications of an Interstate Highway System allowed the scope of FDR's original vision to be greatly expanded. FDR proposed the Federal-Aid Highway Act, which was a study to investigate its construction. This was a works project that had to wait until after World War II before it started in earnest.

[3]A Federal Joint Board on Interstate Highways was formed to standardize the naming of highways and the signage, which, prior to 1925, were named by individual associations trying to attract drivers to use the roads they had built. Names and signs varied to the extent that even professional drivers would frequently get lost and confused.

WikiBeacon

One of the first, if not the first, company to do this was Radius Networks with their `WikiBeacon.org` project. See Figure 13-1.

Figure 13-1. The WikiBeacon.org home page shows the three ways to access its directory

WikiBeacon uses the tens of thousands of downloads of Radius' Locate App to look for beacons that are broadcasting nearby (Figure 13-2). The Locate App is free, available on both iOS and Android, and detects AltBeacon, iBeacon, and Eddystone beacons. The app can also be used as a beacon itself. While performing these tasks for users around the world, it reports back the details of each beacon it detects to the WikiBeacon database. Given that Locate is only installed on a fairly small subset of phones (and likely a self-selecting one, at that), the results it reports back are not a complete picture of every beacon installed. What it does provide is a small but indicative sample of where beacons have been deployed.

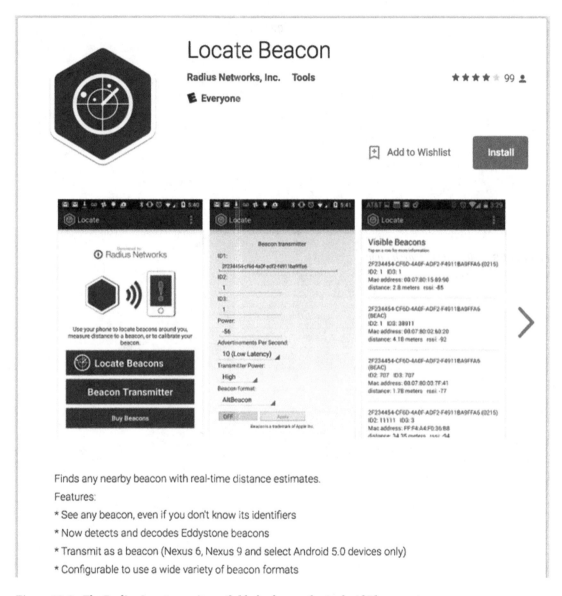

Figure 13-2. *The Radius Locate app is available for free on the Android Play app store*

WikiBeacon offers three ways to view the sightings in its database.

First, users of the registry can search for beacons using a given UUID, which will return how many beacons with that address have been found in a given time period (see Figure 13-3).

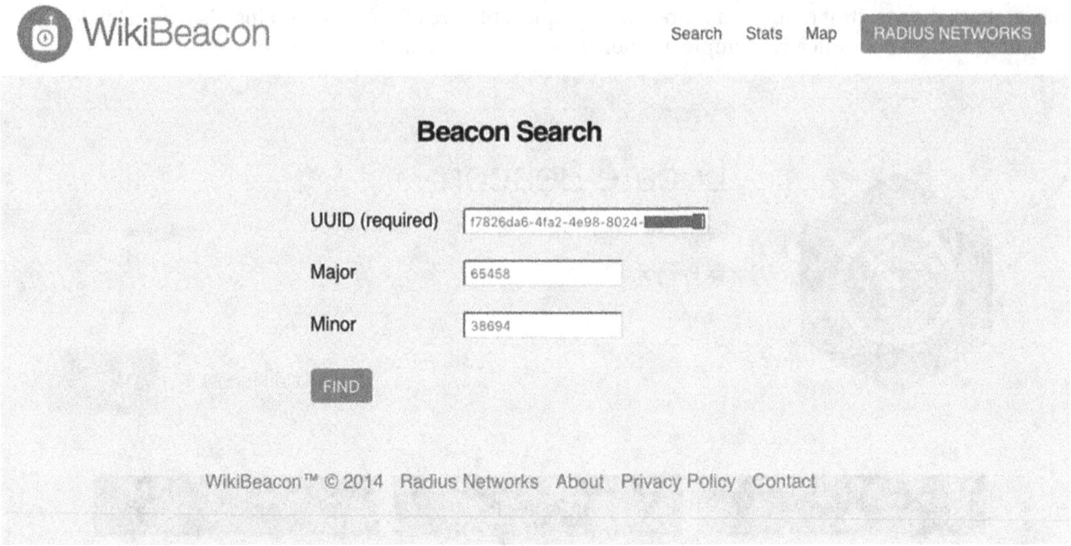

Figure 13-3. *WikiBeacon search page*

If the major and minor device numbers are added, a specific beacon can be located, in which case the location of the beacon is reported back (see Figure 13-4).

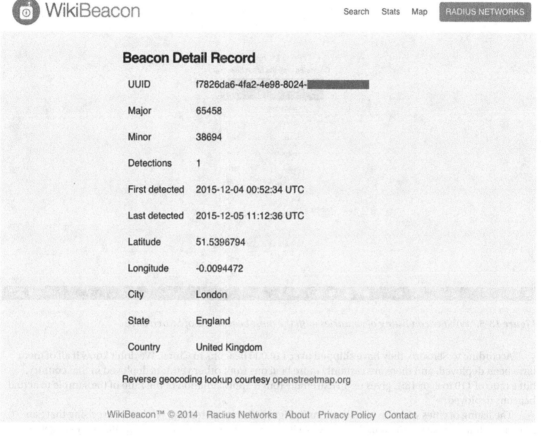

Figure 13-4. The WikiBeacon search results page

The second way to view the WikiBeacon database is with aggregated statistics. Figure 13-5 shows the top 12 countries by number of beacons sighted by Locate.

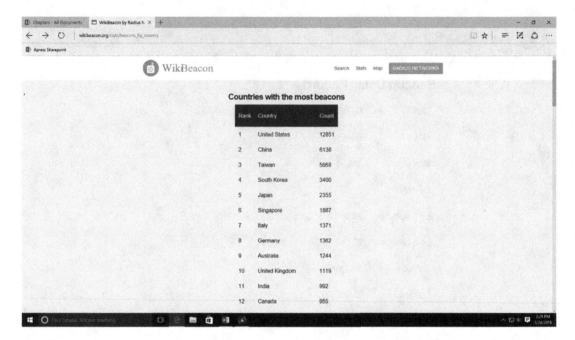

Figure 13-5. *WikiBeacon listing of countries with the most beacons as of March 2016*

According to Sensoro, they have shipped over 110,000 beacons in China. We don't know if all of them have been deployed, and there are certainly more beacons from other vendors deployed in that country, but a ratio of 110 to 6, or 18:1, gives us an extremely rough approximation of the ratio of the sample to actual beacons deployed.

The listing of cities with the most beacons in Figure 13-6 is interesting. While it's surprising that San Francisco didn't make the top ten, the Bay Area cities are well represented in the top 40. Interestingly, Mecca features at 23, versus San Francisco at 44.

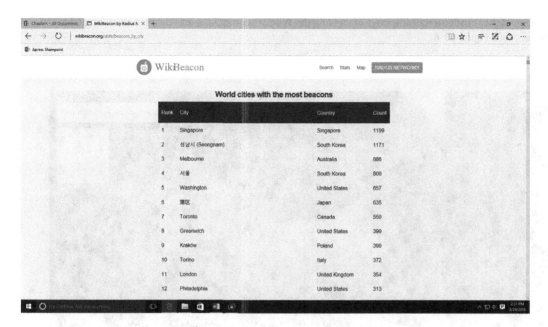

Figure 13-6. *WikiBeacon ranking of cities around the world with the most beacons as of March 2016*

The listing of U.S. states with the most beacons detailed in Figure 13-7 seems to be in line with what one might expect, given all of the high-tech innovation centered in California and Massachusetts. And one can imagine, given all of the theme park venues and hospitality applications, that Florida earns its honorable ranking in third place.

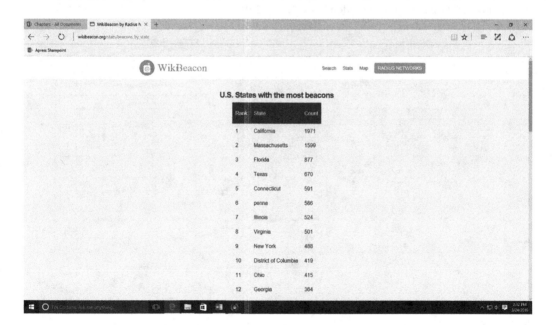

Figure 13-7. *WikiBeacon ranking of U.S. states with the most beacons as of March 2016*

One of the most entertaining ways of viewing the WikiBeacon database is through the Google Maps interface (see Figure 13-8).

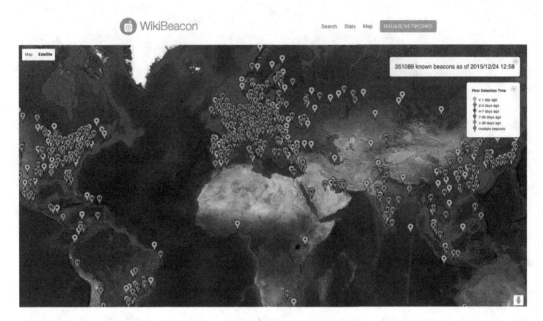

Figure 13-8. *The WikiBeacon map of beacons around the world*

From the world view, you can zoom down to the street level to see where beacons have been sighted around the world. From here, we can see the deployment of beacons all along Regent Street, one of the busiest shopping streets in the United Kingdom (see Figure 13-9).

Figure 13-9. *WikiBeacon's rendering of beacons along London's Regent Street*

Reveal's TheBeaconMap

A similar but more recently launched beacon directory service comes from Reveal Mobile (see Figure 13-10).

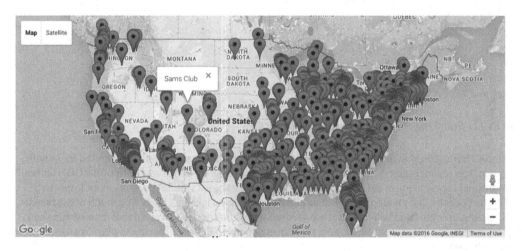

Figure 13-10. *Reveal Mobile's directory of over 100,000 beacons in the United States*

They also search for beacons from mobile apps that contain their SDK. Their main business is to provide a mobile analytics platform that can infer purchase intent and attribute the effectiveness of promotions by measuring visits to locations that have been promoted. Their SDK has been used in hundreds of news and weather apps. With this number of apps and the resulting increase in coverage, they have an opportunity to spot more of the beacons that are distributed in the United States.

Currently, most of the beacons listed in their directory come from lists that are sent by partners. According to their CEO, the dynamic addition of beacons that are spotted by the apps that contain their API is throttled back so that a beacon is registered only if it's seen very frequently (200 times). Apparently, this is done to avoid false positives from mobile devices that are broadcasting beacon packets.

One feature that distinguishes TheBeaconMap from WikiBeacon is its ability to search for beacons based on metadata. In Figure 13-11, that metadata is the name of the retailer hosting the beacons, but one can imagine other information, like the type of store or even the type of people that have visited the beacon, as useful additions.

Figure 13-11. *Searching TheBeaconMap for beacons at CVS*

For the TheBeaconMap to identify unaffiliated[4] beacons via the apps Reveal is integrated in, as with WikiBeacon, it is reliant on the beacons offering open access using iBeacon (and Eddystone-UID) without any conditional access features such as UMM rotation. We see these "vanilla" beacons as an important subset of the beacons that are deployed, but a subset nonetheless. It seems likely that much of the beacon growth is going to come from beacons that are secured with conditional access, so that their owners can charge for access. For investment to happen, there needs to be an ROI and "paying to play" is an obvious way to achieve that return.

The use (or future use) of conditional access is one of the attributes that distinguishes the next category of beacon networks that we will discuss.

Beacon Access Networks

Beacon directories are a great resource and have been provided as a free service. In contrast, beacon access networks are usually all about the money. Their construction is a very deliberate attempt to enable control and monetization of large numbers of beacons. They include the same functions as the beacon registries, but add features, such as more detailed metadata management, analytics, and conditional access control. Rather than surveying other peoples' beacons that are broadcasting in the clear, these beacons have been actively registered as a result of a deal between the venue owner and the network operator. The beacon access network operator either owns the beacons or there is some kind of business relationship that may involve revenue sharing between the beacon owner and the operator. With beacon registries, however, there may be no relationship between the registry operator and the beacon owner.

---

[4]Beacons owned by firms that they doesn't already have a data sharing agreement with.

We are going to drill down into several examples of different kinds of beacon access networks in this chapter: SITA's Common Use Beacon Registry, which is focused on airports; the Gimbal network, being deployed in partnership with out of home (OOH) advertisers; the Proxama network in UK high streets (or "main streets" in the United States) and London taxis; and, lastly, Unacast's Prox network, which is focused on retargeting.

Beacon Access Network Functions

Before we get into those examples, though, let's first think about the functions that need to be in place if beacons are going to be aggregated and access to them is to be sold.

Creating a beacon network is a non-trivial engineering and business development task, so the companies working on this are developing the pieces incrementally. What we are going to outline is a conceptual view of what we think will emerge based on experience so far (see Figure 13-12). There will, no doubt, be variations on this structure.

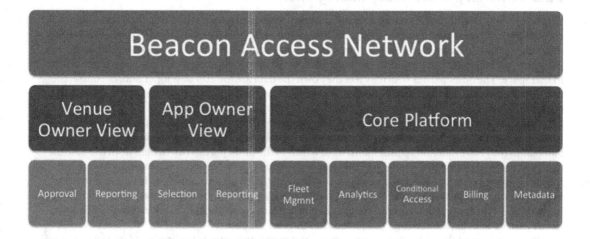

Figure 13-12. Components of a beacon access network

Venue Owner Approval and Reporting

If beacons are going to be situated in a venue, both the owner of the beacons and the venue owner will want a say in who is going to be granted access to those beacons. In some cases, the venue owner and the beacon owner will be one and the same, but that's not necessarily the case.

If the venue is a store, for instance, the retailer will not be happy if direct competitors are being sold access to beacons in their store. Each store may have views on which brands can use their beacons, depending on whether they stock the brand's product and any other deals they may have in place with the brand or its competitors. This is important, in part, because if a product doesn't reflect the values of the retail venue, (if it's a budget product in a luxury store, or an escort service targeting hotel bars), this could create issues for both the retailer and customers. For retailers in particular, control over their venue is a "hot button" issue. If they feel you are taking control from them, then your proposal to place beacons in their store is unlikely to be welcomed. This is a challenge for vendors like Google who were blocked from retailers' stores when they tried to implement their first mobile payments system.

Venues may also want control over how much should be charged for access to their beacons. Depending on how access to the beacons is being charged, they will want to know they are getting a fair rate. Remember, a core competency of most retailers is merciless negotiation with their suppliers (not to be forgotten when brainstorming ideas for beacon startups). Retailers also may want to limit the number of apps that are being triggered by their beacons in order to avoid a beacon trigger overload as people step into their store.

A console that allows them to approve which apps are going to be using their beacons is, therefore, a desirable function. It may be that, in some cases, this control is done via a phone call between staff working for the network operator and the retailer, or there may be a listing of access requests that the venue owner can use to approve requests.

Once the request has been granted, then the venue owner will want to know what the traffic has been like and, ideally, who was accessing the beacon. As such, a reporting function needs to be available so they can review that activity and leverage the intelligence that the activities will yield.

Data Ownership and Privacy Management

This brings us to one of the central issues with running a beacon network: who owns the data? All the stakeholders will raise their hands at this point. The venue owner will feel they own the data. The network operator will feel the same way. After all, they need to pay for the development of the beacon system somehow, and there is clearly value in understanding who has been visiting a venue and their movements in that space. The other parties who may feel they own the data are the app developer and, of course, the app user themselves. The platform, therefore, should track who has rights to the slices of the data each stakeholder has a claim to, and should manage the user's privacy accordingly.

And then, if a user opts out, their detailed data should be purged from this complex system that is building a picture of them with inputs from what could be a large number of companies. Each of those companies may have different requirements as to which of the other parties can benefit from the data they are collecting. For example, a retailer will not want to find that their competitor is benefiting from their insights into the behavior of a shared customer. Additionally, if a user opts out, there is the issue of how far back in history their records should be purged, and how that will affect the aggregated picture of what's been happening. For example, if a user opts out and their visits have contributed to a department's ranking as "most visited," should that ranking be adjusted after the user's data is removed?

But even beyond the technology, these privacy rights and agreements to share need to be considered in the contractual framework that all parties use to access the system. These considerations will also impact the design of the user experience. There need to be notices that make it clear to the user what is happening, but without making the sign up process scary or cumbersome. There also need to be opt-out mechanisms that are simple enough to be understood, but don't undermine the adoption of the system. Hopefully your lawyers, UE designers, and business development team get on well, because there is likely to be a lot of debate about this.

It should also be clear what happens to the data about the user if they opt-out and who has visibility of it if they opt-in. The beacon network needs to have this baked into all their contracts and contain a way to make sure the policies in those agreements are enforced by all the network participants. Otherwise, the network can quickly unravel in the event of a complaint or negative press or social media coverage.

App Owner View

App developers need their own portal into the network access management system that will allow them to select the beacons that they want to use. For many solutions, this could be based on selecting beacons on a map. A more scalable approach for bigger projects might be to select beacons based on metadata. For example, a developer might want a trigger based on three metadata filters: all entry beacons, in grocery stores, and in the Northeast United States.

In order to unlock the conditional access control of the beacons, the developer will need to use a proprietary API that allows beacons to be seen by those who are authorized to do so based on a period of time or number of times, depending on what they have paid for.

The app owners, because they also have the opportunity to enrich the metadata associated with each beacon beyond what the beacon owner has recorded, will also need their own view of the analytics offered by the system. It's the app owner, after all, that understands what the user is using the beacon for. They will know if a beacon trigger is a redemption of a coupon by a loyal customer or a visit from someone who is just browsing. The beacon owner won't know, but the app owner will. Therefore, there should be mechanisms to enable this capture and sharing of information.

The Core Beacon Access Network Platform

The beacon network will need a very capable fleet management system. Beacons, as infrastructure to third-party developers, are likely to have more stringent service level agreements than an internal deployment might require, so the ability to detect issues and resolve them in a timely manner becomes even more important.

At the center of this platform, there will be an increasing need for a very sophisticated billing system. The downside is these systems can be expensive to develop, and their limitations end up impacting the kind of business models that can be offered to close deals. Yet, having a flexible and efficient billing system is critical to reconcile the desire of the venue owners to maximize the monetization of the beacons on their site and the desire of developers to minimize their costs. As a result, the systems will need the ability to change billing rules for different customers. Further, they need to act as settlement systems by both administering different ways to charge for access to the beacons and sharing the revenue with the beacon and venue owner. If the billing system can't support the deals needed for adoption to grow, either the deals won't get done or they will get done and chaos will ensue, with legions of finance people trying to use spreadsheets to make up for the fact that what was sold is not what can be delivered.

Early in the life of these systems, the deals made are likely to be more simplistic, and so the need for this kind of sophisticated engine will be less. Indeed, for pilot projects, the beacon access may even be offered for free as the ROI is being proven. A simple system where developers are paying by active user is a sensible first step. Ultimately, though, developers may be asked to pay based on the number of beacons they want to use and how often they are used. It's possible to imagine that some beacons in premium locations might be charged for at a higher rate than others. For the highly coveted locations, bidding for access to beacons may become a requirement. On top of that, frequency limits on how often beacons can be used to prompt a given user could make these systems extremely complex.

Mind you, this shopping list of functions is a look far down the road. So, instead, let us consider some examples of beacon access networks that are live now and discuss the approaches that have been adopted.

Beacon Access Network Examples

SITA Common Use Beacon Registry

Airports: The Ultimate Target for Beacons

Airports have become early adaptors of beacon technology. The reason for this is, hopefully, clear. Most airports are like malls, but with a captive audience of affluent and tech savvy shoppers. And if that wasn't reason enough, once travelers have stocked up on food, drink and gadgets, they get on a plane. They then suffer long enough to develop more wants and needs, with exhaustion that erodes their will power enough to become an "easy mark" when they land at another airport. There, they can continue the retail therapy. Bear in mind, even a second tier airport can host 20 million passengers a year, and the top ten airports have twice as many visitors as the top 10 shopping malls.

Business travelers, in particular, are the surely the best marketing targets. They are away from the moderating influence of spouses, and so are prone to making purchases to comfort themselves or endear them to absent loved ones. They also tend to travel regularly, so the cost of customer acquisition can be amortized over years of repeated travel.

A significant portion of the funding for airports comes from a share of the revenue from passengers shopping and parking. At the same time, airlines are trying to optimize efficiency and differentiate the experience they offer in a scalable way, so all the big airlines and a number of airports have their own apps (see Figure 13-13). It's hard to imagine a better market segment for beacon technology to be deployed.

Figure 13-13. *Airport apps can benefit passengers and the merchants whose sales help fund their airport's operations*

Given that airports serve multiple airlines, and airlines fly into multiple airports, it makes sense to have consistency in the way beacons are used across those organizations. While this is a mouthwatering opportunity for entrepreneurs, there is already a non-profit organization that is probably best placed to meet the need: SITA.

SITA Who?

The Société Internationale de Télécommunications Aéronautiques, or SITA, is the number one provider of the information technologies that airports and airlines use to run their operations. SITA was founded by 11 airlines in 1949, and now has over 400 air industry members and over 4,000 employees. Their membership and governance boards are made up of a "Who's Who" of airlines and airports.

Common Use

In years gone by, every airline had their own IT infrastructure at airports; signage, computer terminals, networks, kiosks and phone systems were incompatible across the airlines. And why not? They were competitors, after all. The problem with this was that, when one airline grew and another shrank, the reallocation of the gate space from one to the other was expensive and slow. Think, if you can, of the airlines that existed 20 years ago. The names are different now. Since these changes are likely to continue, airport operators decided to adopt a strategy of building common use infrastructure, networks, displays, and terminals that were consistent and shared across all airlines. That way, when the next merger happens, all that is required is a few configuration changes and the displays, phones, and computers at one gate can be switched from one airline to another.

SITA Goals

In order for beacon-enabled apps from airlines, airports, and travel app developers to work across airlines and airports, it made sense for SITA to invest in building beacon management infrastructure that would help their customers adopt beacons in a way that is consistent across different locations. This aligns with the common use strategy that they have for management of other technologies.

The functionality of the SITA registry centers on the ability to search for beacons at a given airport, using a standard metadata structure that is specific to airport use-cases, to implement apps that can use location and proximity with the help of the SITA APIs.

SITA was early to market in identifying fleet management and monitoring of beacon health as a key requirement, and so this is also addressed in the services SITA provides.

Free is a pretty good price, too. SITA doesn't charge its members for the registry, which puts it in a strong position versus competing offerings.

SITA Beacon Use-Cases

There's no shortage of use-cases to be supported to make the life of passengers at airports more convenient. The selected use-cases will impact the number of beacons that need to be deployed; wayfinding will require more beacons than simple check-in use-cases, for instance. The number of beacons at a terminal can range between 500 and 2,000 for a larger airport with applications that require denser coverage. These are the use-cases that SITA has focused on (this is a restructured version courtesy of the SITA web site):

SITA BEACON REGISTRY USE-CASES

- Welcome
  - To the airport
    - Bag drop for your flight is at Desk 50.
    - The wait time at security is 20 minutes. Would you like to purchase fast track?
    - Your flight does not depart for three hours. Would you like to purchase lounge access for $20?
    - Your flight is on-time to depart at X.XX hours from such and such gate and terminal.
  - Home
    - Your bags will be on carousel 7 in 18 minutes.
  - To the Lounge
    - The Wi-Fi password is "Hello!"
- Beacon Assisted Kiosk Check-in
  - The passenger app detects that the passenger is standing immediately in front of a kiosk and either prompts the kiosk to pre-populate with passenger information for transaction completion and/or offers mobile check-in.
- Closing Gate Agency Tool
  - Enterprise app automatically monitors and polls for passengers who have check-in but not yet arrived at gate to determine their location within airport. This will help agents determine if a seat should be forfeited or other actions (e.g., paging) are best.
- Lounge Agent Assist
  - A network of beacons densely placed within an airline lounge guides agent to zone where passenger of interest can be addressed with a personal message.
- Airport Trains
  - Beacons at stations trigger an app to display time to next train.
- Airport Art or General Exhibits
  - Beacons at airport exhibits trigger an app to display additional information about the subject from a CMS web service.
- Zonal Context (Includes Where Is My Passenger)
  - If passenger is supposed to be in beacon zone X @ YY:YY am/pm and they are in another zone, then trigger a message with instructions for where they need to be.

- Walk Times

  - Connecting passenger deplanes at Gate X in Terminal X and whose connecting flight is at Gate Y in Terminal Y, surface current walk time to departing gate.

- Asset Tracking

  - Place beacons on airport infrastructure and track its location within the building.

- Crowdsource Wait Times

  - Use data from staff/passenger apps to crowdsource wait/dwell times to further refine how to guide passengers (e.g., if Security A is very busy, prompt passenger to go to Security B).

Metadata

The kinds of metadata associated with each beacon are airport specific. See Figure 13-14 for an example of that data. Beacons at departure gates are tagged with the airport code, terminal identifier, gate identifier, latitude/longitude, and the details of the next flight leaving from the gate.

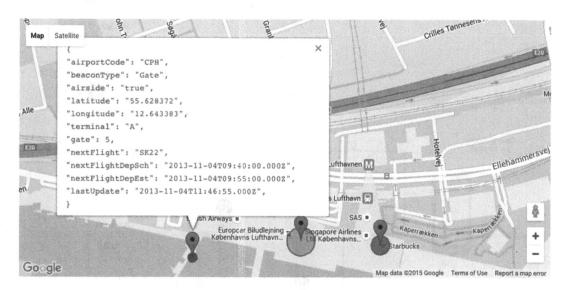

Figure 13-14. SITA dashboard showing the metadata captured for beacon sited at a gate
Courtesy of SITA

Part of the value added by SITA is that the metadata can be integrated with flight management and baggage management systems that are handled by other SITA systems, so that the context provided goes beyond simple proximity information and can include information like the flight that delivered the baggage at a given carrousel. In this way, SITA is making it easier for app developers to create useful apps as well as creating a barrier to entry for other competing systems, as those competitors might find such systems integration work quite costly.

Architecture

The SITA architecture uses a set of open sourced APIs published on GitHub to expose its services via the cloud. See Figure 13-15 for an overview of that architecture. A web console is provided to update the beacon information and monitor the system.

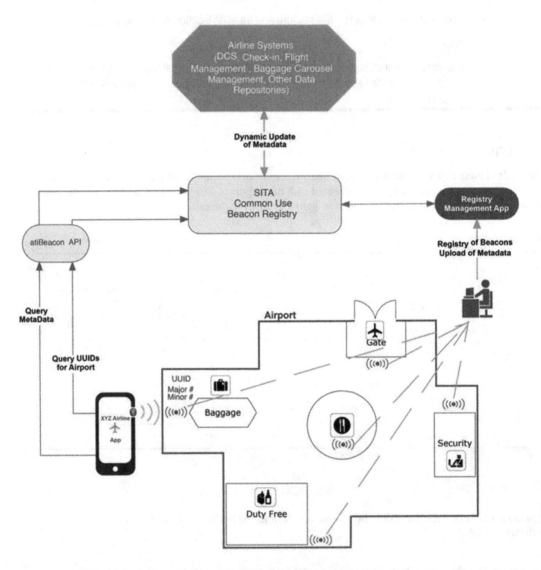

Figure 13-15. *The SITA common use beacon registry architecture*
Courtesy of SITA

For airports that have embraced the rest of SITA's applications infrastructure, this system (see Figure 13-16) is a very appealing way to ensure that beacon deployments can be well managed and will integrate with the apps being developed by airlines and third-party developers.

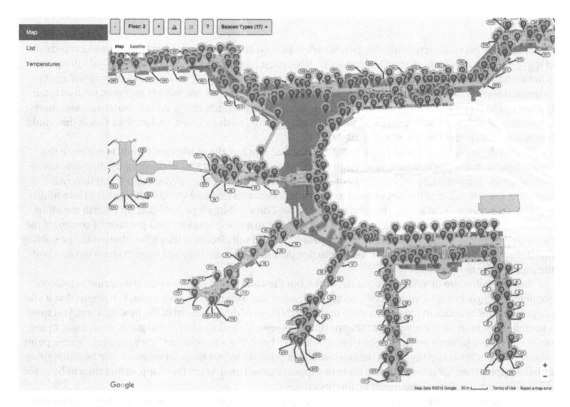

Figure 13-16. *The SITA common use beacon registry tracking beacons at American Airlines gates at Miami International Airport*
Courtesy of SITA

The Future

Currently, SITA only supports Apple's iBeacon protocol, but their product team has expressed a desire to support the Eddystone standard and to offer a conditional access layer so that airports can control which apps can see their beacons.

Eighteen months from its launch in 2014, 15 airports are using the registry, including Miami International Airport and an American Airlines hub. SITA is working with the other industry associations, IATA (airlines) and ACI (airports), who are reviewing the registry for their members with a view to recommending its use across the global industry.

While airports are just one vertical, we would argue that it's one of the most important in terms of volumes of affluent and influential users. SITA's progress in this focused offering provides a glimpse of how beacon networks could evolve in other market segments.

Gimbal

Gimbal represents what may be the biggest, broadest beacon access network play. Having been carved out of the semiconductor giant that is Qualcomm, its DNA must have "go big or go home" encoded into it. This is not a small bootstrap[5] approach to building a beacon business. Some of the networks that we will cover in the next section on beacon commerce networks have focused on a single market segment, such as retail. Gimbal's product play includes outdoors, indoors, retail, sports venues, cities, events, museums, and more. Its product includes beacons, geofencing, contextual targeting, push facilities, and analytics tools that could be applied to an incredibly broad set of markets.

Part of the challenge with taking this approach is that much of the market isn't ready to embrace the idea of beacon access on demand. Many venue owners are either suspicious of opening up their beacons to third-party companies, or they find it hard to comprehend a model where "you build it and they will come". As a result, many of the larger retailers are caught between fear and greed with respect to investing in a beacon network. That is, fear that this technology will be a "white elephant[6]" that isn't worth the effort, and fear that putting beacons in their store for CPG brands to use will weaken their position of control of the customer relationship (because brands may bypass them and sell directly online). Yet, there is the possibility that if they let a third-party beacon provider into this position of power, they will have to share too much of the profits if the network does well.

Some retailers are installing beacon networks, but they tend to be what we would describe as beacon commerce networks with a very specific retail application and a complete solution stack. It seems that if you are going to put beacons in a retailer's store in this early stage of development of the beacosystem, you need a complete solution with a specific set of apps that align with a retailer's short-term goals. As a result, many of the early retail projects we have seen Gimbal win have been like a beachhead. They support a single point application, but the company hasn't broken out of that position to join them all together. The beacons going into the Apple Store, for instance, were there to support Apple's own Apple Store app, rather than to be made available to any developer who might be interested.

Many of Gimbal's early employees came out of Qualcomm's app store business, a division that powered the app stores for over 60 wireless carriers long before Apple and Google's app businesses cannibalized the highly lucrative trade of selling Solitaire and other simple games for feature phones. The BREW[7] business resembled closely what the beacon access network business could be when it comes of age. Qualcomm's BREW platform offered app developers a dashboard of carriers covering territories around the world, whose app stores they could use to distribute their apps. The carriers could look at the catalog of apps and select those that were compatible with their service. Functionally, this resembled a Match.com dating service

---

[5]Pulling yourself up by your bootstraps, or improving your situation by your own efforts, is a figure of speech used as early as the 1922 when James Joyce referenced it obliquely in his book *Ulysses*. It was then adopted as a metaphor when describing the way that computers start up, with a sequence of small programs that invoke larger executables and higher-level functions, until the whole operating system is initialized, running and ready to do work. Since then, it has entered the business vernacular, with association to lean startups that build their businesses without borrowing large amounts of capital from venture capitalists.

[6]"White Elephant: Something that requires a lot of care and money and that gives little profit or enjoyment." – Merriam Webster Dictionary. White (Albino) elephants were said to be a status symbol for the kings of Siam (Thailand); they were rare and expensive. P.T. Barnham was said to have been very disappointed after spending lots of time and money to acquire a real white elephant for his circus. It turned out to be far from a crowd pleaser (maybe because it was actually grey and spotty). The resulting financial burden he suffered may account for the origin of the expression.

[7]BREW stands for Binary Runtime Environment for Wireless. It included a set of cross-platform APIs that ran on phones as well as the app store platform that merchandised, sold, and delivered the apps over the air. An entire division (Qualcomm Internet Solutions) grew up to manage a huge ecosystem of BREW developers, wireless service providers, and the handset providers that were mandated to support the BREW APIs. If the parties at the BREW Developer Conference were anything to go by, it was a profitable business. One year, entertainment was provided by the Goo Goo Dolls on the deck of the USS Midway Aircraft Carrier moored in San Diego. The point being, these kinds of ecosystems can be lucrative.

between cellular networks and app vendors, a marketplace that could presage what the beacon access networks could become. In this future vision, the venue owners, rather than wireless carriers, make their beacons available to a market of app developers picking and choosing the locations they are interested in using to trigger their apps.

Gimbal doesn't have a branded signature app like Shopkick or Piper (two beacon commerce networks). It has taken the route of partnering with app publishers such as major league baseball and OOH advertising via partners such as Titan, which sells billboard advertising space to brands[8].

This broader focus has yielded an incredible set of wins, including the beacons at the South by Southwest festival, the Staples Center, every major sports league, *Elle* magazine, and 500 double-decker buses conducting tours in New York, Chicago, Los Angeles, San Francisco, Las Vegas, and Miami. The challenge has been converting one-off deals, where beacons are serving a single app, to achieving the full vision of an on demand, multi-tenant beacon infrastructure. That challenge may have been met in New York City, which we will look at next.

LinkNYC

An example of the Gimbal partnering to deploy a citywide beacon network is LinkNYC, an ambitious deployment of free community high-speed Wi-Fi and cell phone charging stations rolling out across New York City. Link stations are taking the place of obsolete phone booths and are funded by the advertising displayed on the high-definition screens that are built into the futuristic stations (see Figure 13-17).

Figure 13-17. *One the first LinkNYC stations that are appearing around New York with beacons inside*

---

[8]The company is now part of Intersection, a merger of Titan and Control Group.

While Gimbal's beacons aren't mentioned on the LinkNYC web site, they are part of the means to underwrite this resource.

Their beacons are being used in two ways. First, as an aid to contextualizing the out of home (OOH) advertising on the large displays built into the LinkNYC kiosks (as described in the chapter on OOH). Second, quite separate from the LinkNYC displays, the beacons can simply provide a more accurate location fix on New York street locations. This is particularly valuable, given they are situated in some of the most expensive real estate in the world that is blighted by the urban canyon effect, where the very skyscrapers that it is famous for render GPS ineffective.

Gimbal is then open to partner with makers of apps that have broad appeal, such as Shazam and RetailMeNot, and can then add value to those services by making those apps' coupon offers relevant to the stores in the vicinity of the app, or their in-app advertising relevant to the cross street. Unlike a GPS fix, these more accurate location fixes can also come with metadata that describes the context around the beacon. For instance, the Gimbal Manager can include tags that list the shops nearby and the actual address of the cross street, rather than just a latitude/longitude coordinate.

Public Involvement

Titan and Gimbal's previous attempt to deploy beacons was mired in controversy when the media jumped on the objections of privacy "hawks" who felt there wasn't adequate disclosure of the presence of beacons. By comparison, the LinkNYC offering represents a much more equitable trade of valuable, free to use services, such as Internet browsing, phone charging, unlimited U.S. phone calls, and emergency services requests that are underwritten by the advertising and proximity services that beacons enable (see Figure 13-18). This initiative has been led by the mayor's office, rather than having local government as a bystander, which provides a much more robust coalition to deal with objections from those who feel the presence of beacons is intrusive in the public thoroughfare.

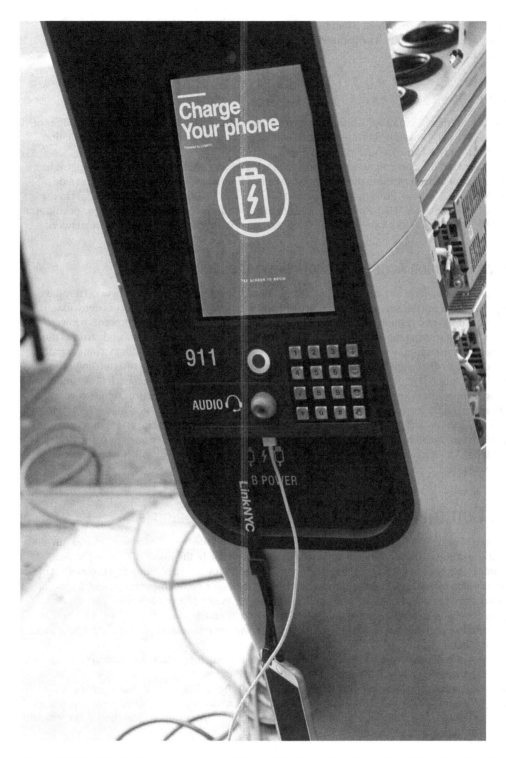

Figure 13-18. Link station being set up; the kiosks offer phone charging, Internet browsing, free phone calls, and emergency services calling

Since that first ill-fated experiment, Titan has been merged into a larger company, Interscape, which is funded by Google, among others. The contract was awarded to CityBridge, which is a consortium that includes Interscape and Qualcomm.

The Rollout

The deal is a 12-year franchise that will ultimately deploy 7,500 LinkNYC kiosks across the five boroughs of the city. The kiosks will be linked by hundreds of miles of fiber optic cables and start with the installation of 510 gigabit links targeted for completion in mid-2016.

Other cities are building beacon networks, too. Piper, another San Diego based beacon company, has deployed hundreds of beacons around the stores and streets of Columbus, Georgia. On "the other side of the pond," in Norwich, England, Proxama has deployed beacons in a UK government funded effort to use beacons to revitalize England's "High Street" shops. Both of these efforts center on supporting a specific app that can then incorporate services for multiple advertisers, rather than a more general-purpose network.

Summarizing Beacon Access Networks and the LinkNYC Project

Many of the early beacon networks are more specialized than a typical beacon access network. They have a specific use-case, or a smaller set of applications that the network supports. Beacon access networks, in contrast, are more open and support any use-case or application. In some ways, this represents a lower bar in terms of the engineering that is required. In other ways, this is a more challenging endeavor, as more beacons are required to support a broader set of use-cases. This broader focus can result in a longer path to revenue and a bigger challenge in terms of building momentum, since sustainable revenue only comes when a complete solution is in place. If all the vendor has to offer is a network of beacons, it is incumbent upon the network operator to find solution providers who can fill the gaps. Other, more complete, solutions can exercise control and offer a one-stop shop.

Gimbal's LinkNYC project is distinctive because of the scale and value of the real estate they are covering, and because the APIs can be used in any beacon-enabled app, implementing any use-case. It's a big bet with high risks, high rewards and a longer time to revenue than some of the other beacon networks that we will discuss next.

Beacon Commerce Networks

The last segment of beacon networks that we want to look at builds on the basic facilities of the beacon access network, and adds a more complete and focused solution stack. In the words of Geoffrey Moore, these companies have chosen a lead "pin" to focus on, rather than providing a solution to a broader set of applications. In some ways, this focused approach is a riskier bet. These companies need to build out more of the solution to meet a client's requirements. And, as they do so, their addressable market gets smaller. What happens if they are focusing on the wrong pin? On the other hand, it allows them to sell a complete package to a business, and then push in a much more intense way to acquire a set of customers and partners relevant to that focus.

Rather than talking about beacons to a retailer, the sales teams can focus the conversation on "targeting," "intent," and "conversion," speaking the language of the retailer.

We will look at some more examples to bring these abstract ideas to life. inMarket has focused on retail shopping apps and a beacon network to support them. Proxama, over in the United Kingdom, has an approach that ranges across a comprehensive set of OOH segments, transportation, and shopping apps. And lastly, Unacast has focused on ad retargeting.

inMarket

inMarket appears to have done something quite unusual: they have established what appears to be a financially sustainable beacon business, one that is supporting organic growth. This is a refreshing story to hear in a segment where many startups are highly leveraged with debt. By all accounts, their tight focus on retail and, in particular, grocery, has enabled them to avoid raising significant external capital, "bootstrapping" their way to a 50-person organization in five years, with APIs that are linked into 38 million installed apps, including app brands such as Epicurious, Zip List, Key Rings, ShopSavvy, List Ease, and CheckPoints, their own gamified[9] shopping app that predated the development of their beacon network.

See Figure 13-19 for examples of how different apps use beacons to engage users in a contextually relevant manner.

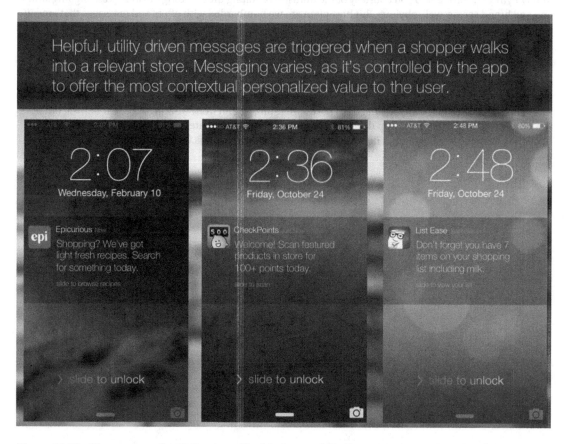

Figure 13-19. *The messages that Epicurious, CheckPoints, and List Ease can trigger using inMarket beacons when a shopper enters a store*

---

[9]*Gamification* is the introduction of game mechanics into applications that are not ordinarily considered to be games. Techniques include awarding points to encourage desired behaviors, awarding badges to associate status with certain desired actions, leader boards to instill a sense of competition, and progress bars to nudge people to complete a set of tasks.

By integrating with inMarket, these apps benefit from beacon triggers that present alerts to consumers upon entry to stores and during the shopping process. These alerts support the functionality that motivated the consumer to download the app in the first place; for instance, searching for Epicurious recipes that may drive product choices in the store, collecting CheckPoints (points) in stores that support the program, and not forgetting shopping list items that have been stored away in List Ease.

This interplay between app, brand, and store is the driving force behind a successful beacon commerce network. This group of three, this triumvirate, all need to be present if any of them hope to succeed.

But not only do all three need to be present, they need to be aligned in their focus. For example, WebMD would be the perfect app for shoppers in a pharmacy with advertising coming from brands like Band-Aid. The Viggle entertainment app, on the other hand, would be a better choice for a movie studio to promote a new Blu-Ray disk in the DVD department of a Target store. To quote what sounds like a line from Monty Python[10], "brought to you courtesy of the ministry of stating the bleeding obvious". Yes, aligning store, app and brand seems, well, obvious. But how often are we bombarded with offers and messages that are out of context and irrelevant? If your experience matches mine, then more often than you would expect.

So the question stands, how do we integrate and motivate all three players to work toward the same goal?

The Motivation of the Triumvirate

The simple answer is that everyone needs to have something to gain from working together. Barring out of the kindness of their hearts, the app developer has no reason to cooperate if only the store and brand are benefiting from the arrangement. The same could be said if the positions were switched.

---

[10]No survival guide would be complete without a quote from Monty Python, so we borrowed this turn of phrase. However, despite numerous quotes in newspapers attributing the phrase "bleeding obvious" to that esteemed comedy troupe, during our routine fact check we searched the Python scripts and couldn't find that expletive being paired with the word "obvious" anywhere. As it turns out, the phrase comes from John Cleese's *Fawlty Towers,* from the episode Basil the Rat "Can't we get you on Mastermind, Sybil? Next contestant: Mrs. Sybil Fawlty from Torquay. Specialist subject: the bleeding obvious."

Looking at each role, we will see that, when the interdependent nature of the relationship is understood, each member of the triumvirate will benefit most when they are all in accord (Figure 13-20).

Figure 13-20. *The retail-focused beacon commerce network requires alignment of store, app, and brand*

Looking first at the app developer, they get to share in the revenue from the brands that pay for in-app promotions triggered by proximity alerts within the store. Accordingly, the best way for the app developer to come out ahead is for the app to maximize visitors to the store, and to make it worth it for brands to pay for app-based promotions. In other words, they benefit most when the other members are also benefiting. This promise of a direct correlation between the enhanced functionality for the user and incremental revenue makes for a strong value proposition to app developers.

If inMarket's network (and those like it) is a good deal for the app developer, what about the retailer? For them, the value proposition is strong, too. In Figure 13-21, we get a sense of some useful insights into the engagements occurring in their stores that are being driven by inMarket's network of apps. The patterns can easily be seen in the engagements being generated by state, day of the week and time of day. This should help reassure the retailer that they are not being disintermediated, which is one potential fear. In fact,

239

the retailers approve each brand campaign before they are launched, as they would with a new endcap[11] promotion. It also shows measurable results from the program. The campaigns may be driven by the brands whose products are being promoted, but the retailer is benefiting from the potential lift in sales of additional higher margin products, and benefiting from the loyalty of customers who are buying deeper into a broader range of products stocked by the merchant.

Figure 13-21. *inMarket's Retailer facing dashboard*

But what is the cost to the retailer of these insights, additional sales and loyalty? When the brand (Coca-Cola, Levi's, Nestle, and P&G, for example) is paying for the campaign, then there is no cost. Quite the opposite; there is a share of the revenue the brand is paying which flows through inMarket to the retailer.

---

[11]An endcap is a display at the end of the aisle in the store. This is some of the most valuable space in the store. Traditionally, brands would pay in some way for access to this space. This payment may be in the form of cash payments, up to tens or hundreds of dollars per day per store, exclusive access to the product, or a lower wholesale price that yields larger profit margins.

What the retailer does pay for are the beacons themselves. In the same way that they pay for shelves or lighting, this makes sense. It also gives them ownership of the infrastructure to which they want to control access, and ownership for the success of the partnership. By buying the beacons, they "have some skin in the game". inMarket takes care of the actual deployment of the beacons, which may be more expensive than the cost of the capital equipment.

As with the app developers, the retailer has a vested interest in the success of the other two partners, since all of their revenues are linked to at least some degree.

All that's left is to ask why a product brand would be funding promotions that benefit the retailer, app developer, and inMarket. Their motive is clearly to sell more "product" and gain more market share from their competitors, but it goes beyond that. With this investment, they are getting a lot more insight into the effect of their promotional dollars than they normally would with investments in signage or coupons. Traditionally, the brand has no visibility as to who is responding to their promotions in the retailer's store. As you can see from Figure 13-22, now they get a precise readout of the demographics of the customer, including age and gender.

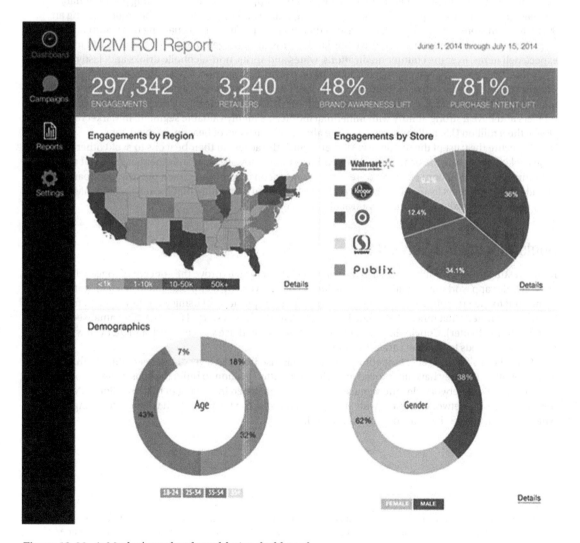

Figure 13-22. inMarket's product brand facing dashboard

It's the brands, after all, that have the budget to invest in promotion. Where the retailer is operating on razor-thin margins, the manufacturer traditionally has a lot more margin to use to drive the promotion of their product. Their challenge is knowing how best to use those promotional dollars. As John Wanamaker, the 19[12]-century inventor of the price tag,[12] said, "Half the money I spend on advertising is wasted; the trouble is I don't know which half."

The Secret of Great Timing

Presenting promotional messages isn't just about choosing the right place, it's also about choosing the right time. Getting a promotion as you are leaving the store is more than a wasted opportunity, it degrades the credibility of the platform. By tracking the timing of visits to specific locations and understanding the nature of those locations (a delicatessen, for example), it's possible to build a predictive model that can forecast when purchasing may happen. To this end, inMarket has introduced a function that it calls Quantum Receptivity that aims to predict and preempt patterns of shopping behavior, presenting promotional messaging just prior to the point of decision, at the right time and the right place. They report seeing an 8% increase in store visits and a 14% increase in dollars spent per trip when enabling this feature.

The top product categories that drive this kind of proximity-triggered promotion are, as you might expect, deli items, over the counter medications, wines and sprits, non-alcoholic drinks and, lastly, snacks.

inMarket's go-to-market approach is to focus on the brands and the creative agencies they use to create their campaigns. When selling to merchants, they can point out the reality of how tough it is for retailers to make their apps successful, whereas the apps that inMarket focuses on are already successful, work across retailers and have a strong affinity with millennial mothers, a highly valuable segment. inMarket reports that 38% of the 9 million U.S. millennial mothers are already active users of beacon-enabled apps.

To secure the trust of the retailers, inMarket secures the access to their beacons to avoid other apps piggybacking and using the beacons without authorization. They also scan for other beacons that are not authorized by the retailer to be in the store. Given that beacons can be integrated into the cardboard displays provided with products by brands, this is a real possibility, and something that the retailer and inMarket will need to prevent in order to maintain control of their stores.

Bootstrapping the Network

It's interesting to see how inMarket used its own CheckPoints app to prove the concept of triggers for a cross-retailer app working in retail stores. The idea of having your own app that can be used to "get the party going," but to then recruit what might be seen as competing apps to start using your network on an equal footing, is a strategy that others are also using to get their businesses started (see the "Proxama" section that follows in this chapter). Convincing competitors that they should use your network and that you will be even-handed needs to be done carefully, though.

CheckPoints' most direct competitor, Shopkick, has also built out a very large set of Bluetooth beacons across retailers, but they have not moved in such a committed fashion to build the ecosystem of competing apps that use their network, despite signals that they are interested in moving in that direction. inMarket has decided that it is a network business with an app, and it is reaping the rewards. It will be interesting to see what Shopkick decides it wants to be going forward.

---

[12]As a pioneer of the department store, Wanamaker's price tags were part of a movement to setting fixed prices for products and helped curtail the practice of haggling over price. `www.pbs.org/wgbh/theymadeamerica/whomade/wanamaker_hi.html`

Proxama

While Gimbal, inMarket, Swirl, and others have been blazing their own trails toward beacon network Nirvana in the United States, parallel paths have been pursued in other countries. One of these is Proxama, which has made very credible progress across the United Kingdom.

Similar to Gimbal, they have partnered with OOH advertisers, are developing their own app, Loca, serve proximity triggered promotions for retailers, and targeting a range of locations from airports, taxis, and buses (see Figure 13-23) to convenience stores, shopping centers, stadia, and city centers. Unlike their American compatriots, however, they have chosen to partner with beacon OEMs rather than make their own hardware. Kontakt.io is their partner for this. Beneath their Loca app is a platform, called TapPoint®, which provides APIs for third-party apps to use in order to make sense of beacons and perform orchestration functions.

Figure 13-23. *Promotion for Proxama's Loca app on the back of bus seats; a QR code and passive NFC tag enable downloads of the app for iOS and Android*

Doing This in Public

Unlike Gimbal and inMarket, Proxama is public, listed on the Alternative Investment Market (AIM), owned by the London Stock Exchange, and set up to allow smaller companies to float shares. As a result, we have more visibility into their fortunes. The view of the beacon business it affords isn't totally clear, though. Proxama actually has what is probably a larger business focused on next generation payments systems— moving merchants from older magnetic stripe systems to the new wave of EMV (a chip-based payment card system) as well as a mobile payments system. The payment versus proximity marketing numbers are not broken out, but, as reading goes, it is more of a thriller than a soothing bedtime story. Proxama's revenues have been growing, but their losses are still substantial.

Proxama are another "go big" play. Their modern offices on the edge of London impress visitors with Proxama's confidence—confidence in their ability to pay what must be significant rent and a determination to be taken seriously in their sales efforts.

This "go big" approach has enabled them to win a one million pound grant from Innovate UK (a government agency) to use their proximity technology to pilot an approach to "reinvigorate the UK high street".

Norwich

The first streets to be reinvigorated under this program were in Norwich, a city of 140,000 citizens and the largest in the county of Norfolk in the East of England (see Figure 13-24 to see an example of region-specific content in Proxama's app).

Figure 13-24. *Proxama's Loca app does more than push retailer offers; it promotes local events such as The Royal Norfolk Show and the Sandown horse races*

Norwich may not be the best-known English town, but it has enjoyed its share of notoriety thanks to British playwright Alan Bennett and British comedian Steve Coogan. One of Bennett's characters uses NORWICH as an acronym to signal to this wife his amorous intentions (look it up). Steve Coogan's Alan Partridge alter ego is the most un-hip DJ in the UK, a big ABBA fan, and proudly claims Norwich as his home. The citizens of Norwich, rather than succumbing to embarrassment, have owned this uncomfortable affiliation and have erected a statue of Alan Partridge in their city center.

Norwich may seem a strange choice to target as a potential "smart city," but the presence of the University of East Anglia means there is a good source of young smartphone users, along with the other folk, gathering in a contained area of manageable proportions that is the urban center in a beautiful agricultural landscape.

The Platform Beneath the Loca App

TapPoint, Proxama's orchestration or mobile campaign management platform, originally used geofencing, QR codes, and passive NFC tags as triggers. Merchants like Harrods, Ladbrokes (betting shops), and Argos (catalog sales) and brands like Ralph Lauren all use it. The platform now supports both iBeacon and, for those who don't have supported iBeacon apps on their phones, Eddystone URL protocols to enable consumers to access promoted content on the web. Within that, it performs frequency capping to regulate how many times a consumer receives a notification over a period of time.

Back to Norwich, beacons in shops trigger offers in the Loca app (see Figure 13-25).

Figure 13-25. *The Loca app serves up offers relevant to the user's location; dummy bar codes are added to provide a redemption click that can then be measured within the app as a conversion indicator for analytics purposes; the PoS systems are not actually integrated with the system*

For a starting price of 35 pounds a month (roughly $50 U.S.), business owners can see a count of customers in the vicinity of the beacons (Figure 13-26), the number of notifications triggered, and the percentage of click-throughs from those notifications. Proxama reports a 25% conversion rate.

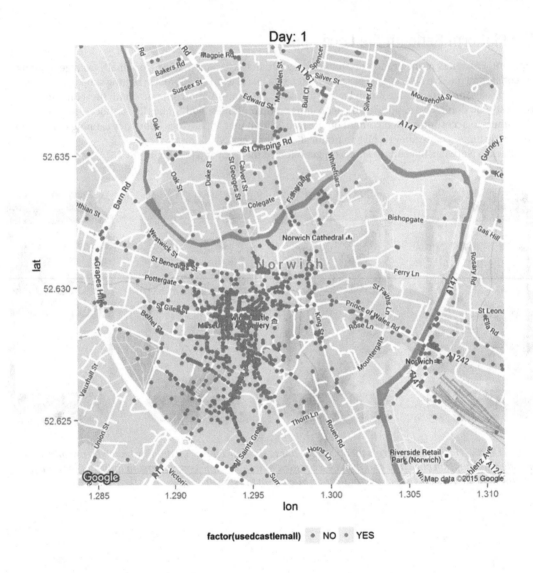

Figure 13-26. *Analytics plotting a day's footfall from Loca's users in Norwich*

Merchants control campaigns from a self-service web portal.

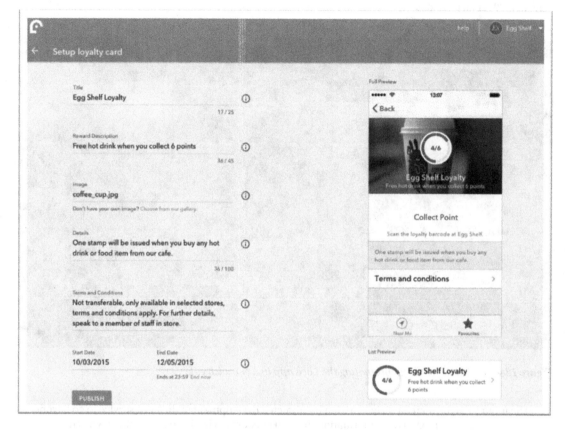

Figure 13-27. *Screen for a merchant to set up a loyalty offer to be shown in Loca*

Merchants use a variety of techniques to encourage their customers to use the Loca app, including "table tents," which are cardboard displays that engage people when they are "dwelling" at tables; see Figure 13-28 for an example.

Figure 13-28. *A "table tent" sign promoting the Loca app in a Norwich cafe*

The input from the merchants in Norwich has directed development of the Loca service to go beyond promotions, to provide more useful information that will encourage visitors to stay in the town center.

Simple analytics—measuring redemption rates, dwell time, and return visits—were added to a retailer dashboard, along with loyalty features in the roadmap. Retailers were keen to support a campaign aimed at workers commuting into the city to "Head out, not home!" by promoting bars, restaurants, and free cultural events such as poetry readings and films that could help to keep shoppers in the town center.

Beyond Norwich

As well as operating in Norwich shops, Proxama has placed beacons on 110 buses that carry shoppers into the city center, driving a 30% click-through ratio within Loca. For this, they partner with OOH advertising sales partner Exterion to sell the "inventory" of ads, and potentially coordinate the in-app ads with traditional poster ads on the buses. This partnership was extended to London, where 500 beacons have been installed, with a potential reach of 300,000 passengers every day. Public transport represents a captive audience of people with a high penetration of smartphones (94%) and time on their hands, with between 17 and 19 minutes for the average London journey. Another transportation option that is being targeted by Proama, and other entrepreneurs in other locations, is the taxi which has the same possibility of reaching someone with intent to spend, but likely with a greater disposable income (see Figure 13-29).

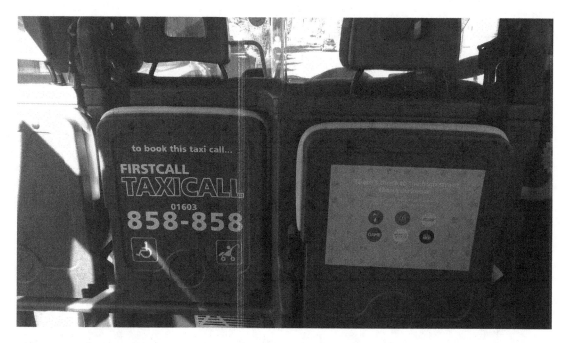

Figure 13-29. *Promotion of the Loca app on the seat in a Norwich taxi*

Proxama has partnered with Eye Airports, the largest owner of UK airport advertising space, to deploy 200 beacons across eight UK airports that handle 38 million passengers a year, including London Gatwick and Manchester International Airport. Eye Airport sells to advertisers such as duty-free concessions, brands, and airlines.

Other partnerships include Red Kiosk, a company converting London's iconic red phone boxes into tiny coffee stands and sandwich concessions, and Surrey County Cricket Club, which installed Proxama's beacons at the Oval, Britain's answer to Major League Baseball's venues. Additionally, its push into the taxi market is forecast to scale up to 4,000 cabs. If someone can afford to pay for a cab, they have self-selected as being a potential shopper, bar, or restaurant patron with money to spend, a valuable advertising target.

Proxama Summary

Proxama has been comprehensive in covering a breadth of different types of locations with its network and a broad set of OOH partners. Going forward, it needs to expand across more cities and more applications, using the positive metrics it has established in its pilot projects to scale the size of its network and achieve the volumes that will make the business achieve its potential.

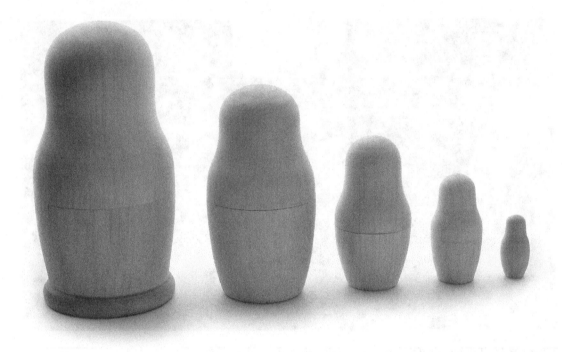

Unacast

Question: What could be bigger than a beacon network? Answer: A network built on other beacon networks. If the beacosystem were a series of Russian dolls, each a layer in the solution stack, then Unacast appears to aspire to be the last one wrapping up all the others. It's an ambitious project with some exciting rewards.

Their approach to building a beacon network is to partner with multiple beacon manufacturers and other proximity solution providers, and in doing so build a network on top of their platforms. These partners include beacon OEMs, both large ones such as Estimote, Sensoro, and Signal 360, and more specialist providers such as Bubbly[13]. These partnerships extend beyond the hardware world and include vendors of pure software and service or orchestration layer products, such as Urban Airship, Smart Fission, and Pointr. All of these in the Unacast vernacular are called proximity solution providers (PSPs).

The Value of the Network

Unacast's value proposition is to provide additional functionality to what PSPs can offer their customers, and additional opportunities to monetize the solutions that the PSP are selling. They do this by brokering the proximity triggers that a PSP can drive, and the insights they unlock, to third parties. One of the main areas where these insights are used is in retargeting.

An example of a retargeting use-case is, when a shopper dwells for a few minutes in the TV department of an electronics store, that shopper might receive a promotion for televisions when they read *The New York Times* on their laptop the following day.

---

[13]Bubbly provides a self-service kiosk with a space-age design, plus beacon-enabled point of sale and vending. See www.bubblygroup.com.

The process and data flow within Unacast's Prox platform is illustrated in Figure 13-30. Unacast can bring demand for a PSP's beacons from ad platforms that the PSP otherwise might not have access to. On its own, a PSP is unlikely to have the scale needed to be a standalone ad platform in their own right. For advertisers, "size is important".

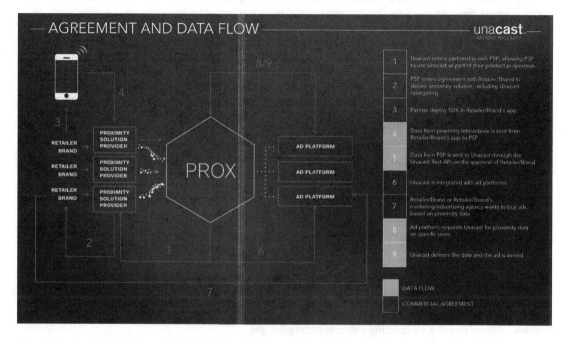

Figure 13-30. Unacast's Prox data flow

While there are a number of companies using proximity triggers in third-party apps to measure intent[14] and enable attribution[15], Unacast has succeeded in convincing them that it's better to collaborate than compete. A parallel is in the cell phone network business, where carriers that compete for subscriber business, interconnect their networks in order to enhance the services that they can deliver to consumers (the ability to receive service when out of range of their network, for example) and to better use the capacity of their network as callers from other networks roam onto their system.

Challenges

One challenge when building a beacon network is that, in order for the interactions with the beacons to be useful, the beacons need to be tagged with metadata that describes the context of the beacon location, and the tagging used across those beacon networks needs to be reconciled. This metadata tagging includes the latitude

---

[14]Intent to purchase can be measured with beacons by measuring dwell time at a certain kind of merchant or a department within a merchant's store. Similar to our intent to buy a TV example, a particularly valuable example is intent to buy a car, which can be detected by beacons at a car show room. If an app user is seen spending time at car show rooms, they probably have intent to buy a car. Given the cost of cars, this is a lucrative use-case to focus on.

[15]Attribution can be measured if an offer for a product at a store is presented to an app user and they then visit the store as measured by the beacon within an agreed period of time—36 hours, for example.

and longitude of the beacon, the street address, the business at that address (Best Buy), what the business does (electronics retailer), the area within the building that the beacon is in (Television Department), the product the beacon is associated with and its brand (Panasonic TV) and, lastly (and optionally), a model number for items of larger value.

If you consider the range of the types of venues where a beacon might be located (cinemas, sports stadia, airports, restaurants, trade shows, theme parks, etc.), this metadata hierarchy can be quite intricate, and there is a subjective element as to how the hierarchy should be organized. Venues may have one opinion, and PSPs may have another. The brands that are advertising may see things differently, too. Then there is the reality that there may be missing data, misspelled terms and with different names used for the same thing. You say sweater, I say jumper, she says jersey, and he spells it jersie. This problem of making sure these tags all equate to the same thing, spelling mistakes and all, is challenging but solvable. Data warehousing consultants and librarians have been working on it for years, albeit in a different context.

To help with this, Unacast provides the PSP, which is a Sensor API, to integrate with their middleware to implement the tagging, and then a series of functions to clean and organize it. Their Data Expander fills in gaps where tags are missing, using a contextual matching process that translates between synonyms. For example, their Relation Expander adjusts tags that are at the wrong level in a hierarchy, putting "yoga pants" under "sportswear" rather than beside it. Then these transformations are approved by the PSP with a workflow managed by the Tag Feedback tool.

With a robust metadata system containing clean data, Prox then needs to translate to the form of metadata used by their partners, the brands and advertisers, and advertising networks. The Tag Translator does this.

Harmonizing metadata is non-trivial, and managing it well is a potential differentiator as this space becomes more competitive.

The Secret of Success

Success for Unacast relies on meeting a number of challenges.

- *Recruiting PSPs*—The value of the network is all about scale. With scale, advertisers can run the kinds of large campaigns that are relevant to a product's success. Most advertisers want to hit all the larger designated market areas (DMAs) with a campaign, not just one city. For PSPs, it's like deciding which party to go to. Do you go to the small party where not many people are showing up, or to the one with lots of action? Unacast's founders experience with building a music streaming service (TIDAL) has parallels with building this kind of ecosystem. It requires confidence.

- *Recruiting brands and advertisers*—These are the companies paying the additional money that makes the opportunity worthwhile for PSPs. This is probably the harder challenge, as PSPs can be recruited based on a vision. Brands and advertisers need the whole system to be working and see real "lift" from their use of the network.

- *Efficiency and effectiveness*—Integrating and organizing the network so that the parties come together efficiently, quickly and with a high quality of metadata integration.

- *Managing the privacy issues*—One person's useful and well-targeted offer is another person's intrusive, spooky irritation. Unacast has taken an ambitious step toward addressing this issue with LocationControl.org, a service where consumers can see the data that PSPs are collecting and either request it to be erased, or correct any mistakes so they get more relevant content.

- *Accelerating development of the ecosystem*—Successful startups appear to be lucky with timing the market. Too early and you can lose momentum and run out of money. Arrive too late, and someone else steals the lead and erects barriers to entry. This is the central challenge of the beacosystem. There are some great opportunities, but it's clear many startups are struggling to manage the balance between revenue and expenses over time. Unacast is impressive because of the scope of its ambition, the number of partnerships it is signing, and the way it seems to be making its own luck.

The Proxbook[16] initiative to make a marketplace where PSPs and brands can find each other through a directory of products and services is one example of the company going beyond the expected in creating a catalyst to speed the market chemistry. Location control is another example of what might be seen as an almost idealistic initiative, but one that also serves Unacast and its stakeholders well.

Bellwether of the Beacosystem

In some ecosystems, there are companies that can still be successful even if their customers fail. Cisco is a classic example. During the Internet bubble, many of Cisco's customers bought millions of dollars of Cisco routers and then failed. Despite that, Cisco still did very well. ADP, the payroll company, is an example of a company whose fortunes are directly tied to the success of the economy. When job numbers go up, ADP does well. Economists can look at how ADP is doing and see an indicator of what to expect for the U.S. economy as a whole.

In Unacast's role as a network of beacon networks, its success is of special interest to those of us vested in the future of the beacosystem. It's hard for Unacast to be successful if there are fundamental issues in the proximity ecosystem. Their success depends on value flowing through the whole beacosystem value chain. If things go well with the industry, they are very well placed. In this way, they are for the beacons what ADP is to the broader economy, a key bellwether to be watched closely.

Summary

We have made the case that beacon networks are of strategic importance to the development of the beacosystem. While vendors tend to use the word "network" to describe any beacons they have deployed, the key from our perspective is that those beacons need to be joined up and made accessible to multiple applications. It's only then that costs are shared and reduced and new ideas can be developed quickly, using existing beacons that are already in place. Likewise, when multiple apps share the same beacons, there is more money flowing through to the beacon and venue owner, and so supply of this key infrastructure increases.

We have seen lots of examples in this chapter of where the spread of networks is starting to happen, be it in our airports, in the streets of New York city, or the shops in the United States or the United Kingdom. As beacon networks grow, the opportunities of joining them up and linking the advertising networks in the digital and physical worlds grows too.

While there are plenty of alternative proximity technologies, very few are being networked in the way beacons are. We are not seeing Wi-Fi proximity networks springing up (except within maps products). There is no reason why this shouldn't happen, but, for now, it's the beacosystem that is driving this network movement. The exciting thing is that beacons that are standalone today can be added to a network fairly quickly. A skeptical retailer may look at others in the mall that are making money by opening up their beacons to other apps and decide to join in. When this happens, they can enable new apps and provide benefits to their customers beyond those that were originally envisaged for the "monogamous" beacons supporting only the retailer's app.

In the next chapter we are going to look at programmatic advertising and OOH advertising businesses with a view to understanding how these amazing economic engines fuel the revenue streams that can grow beacon networks.

---

[16]As has been noted elsewhere, the author has had a role in helping to create Proxbook, producing its predecessor—a simple WordPress database—as a companion to this book and has consulted with and advised Unacast.

CHAPTER 14

■ ■ ■

A Programmatic Advertising Primer

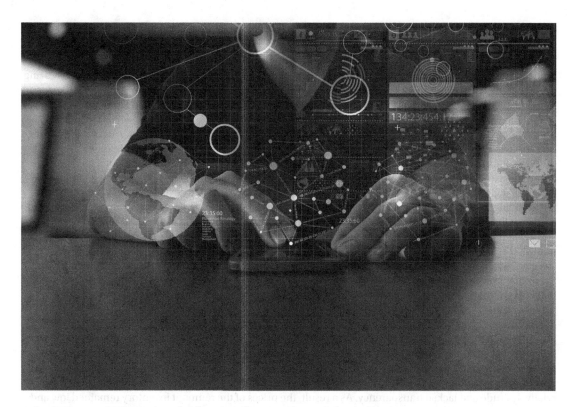

Anke Audenaert, CEO Favrit and Adjunct Professor, Anderson School of Management, UCLA

A frequent question from investors in proximity solution providers is "how do we make money?" Advertising revenue is one of the most frequent answers. Internet advertising is a $49 billion[1] market. It has fueled the development of the search and mapping services we all depend on. We are all Internet advertising experts, in that we are on the receiving end of banner ads, videos, search ads, boosted social media posts,

---

[1]According to PwC and the Interactive Advertising Bureau (IAB)'s July 2015 report.
www.iab.net/media/file/PwC_IAB_Programmatic_Study.pdf

© Stephen Statler 2016
S. Statler, *Beacon Technologies*, DOI 10.1007/978-1-4842-1889-1_14

and sponsored content in our apps and browsers, but in order to design a solution or build a business plan that taps into this revenue, it's necessary to know more. As Internet advertising continues to grow and become more sophisticated, *programmatic advertising* (the automated buying and selling of advertising in real time) is becoming increasingly important component of the Internet advertising market, accounting for 20% of the total and nearly half of the display-advertising segment. Given the sophistication and complexity of the targeting possible with proximity solutions, the programmatic approach is likely to become even more important. While the pilot projects are small in number, proximity advertising can be done using manual processes, but this is surely a transitional approach that will lead to a more automated future.

As a technologist looking at the proximity market, I became conscious of our own ignorance of the world of advertising. When Anke Audenaert invited me to present a lecture on beacon technology to her MBA class, I sat in on her lecture on programmatic advertising. The synergy between our subjects was obvious and so was Anke's experience and clarity. So it's a great pleasure to have her write this chapter to augment our survival guide for the proximity solution provider.

Steve Statler

Some History

Starting with its debut as the Wired.com Banner in 1994[2], display advertising emerged as a powerful way to monetize digital content, powering the growth of native Internet giants like Yahoo! and AOL, and subsidizing the digital presence of traditional media like *The New York Times,* Conde Nast Magazines, and countless others. By 2001, display advertising had grown to a billion dollar industry in the United States alone.

In the early 2000s we saw some seismic shifts in the Internet landscape. On the one hand, content production costs dropped, which in combination with easier content-creation tools made digital publishing accessible to the masses. On the other hand, Google had emerged and made search the default way to access the web's information, allowing anyone's content to be found, whether you published under a recognizable brand name or just on your own blog. A long tail of web sites were started as a result, opening an infinite supply of digital content, and with it, an almost infinite supply of display advertising space.

Leading up to the emergence of the long tail, most digital display advertising had been bought and sold following the same media buying principles used in traditional media, where buyers and sellers connect and agree on where and when a campaign would run. The campaigns would be executed through the publisher's ad server, using an "insertion order," making the ads appear alongside the content the buyer had selected. But, now that the supply of advertising space had exploded, traditional deal-making did not fill all the available advertising space. Smaller publishers had accessible content, but they did not have the sales teams to sell the space directly to advertisers. A vast amount of "remnant inventory" went unsold. That is when *ad networks* emerged. They bought up the remnant space from large and small publishers for cents on the dollar and made it their business to package it in ways that would make the inventory attractive to advertisers. At the core of their packaging approach was the target audience. Ad networks bundle together inventory based on who will typically access the content associated with it. Advertisers can then work with the ad networks to buy advertising space alongside content that is appealing to different demographic groups—women, youth, and so on. The approach these ad networks took to audience targeting was relatively crude and lacked transparency. As a result, the prices of the remnant inventory remained low and the publishing community started to fear that this would also drive down the price of what they considered their "premium advertising space," the inventory they sold directly.

Around 2006, *advertising exchanges* emerged. Ad exchanges bring together the publishers and advertisers to allow the sale of advertising inventory on a one-by-one basis, promising to increase transparency and control for both players. This gave birth to what we now refer to as *programmatic advertising* and the ad tech landscape. While the ad exchanges are at the center of the ecosystem, the landscape now also includes intermediaries that facilitate the sale on both the advertisers' and the publishers' sides.

---

[2]www.wired.com/2010/10/1027hotwired-banner-ads/

Data As the Core Building Block for Programmatic Advertising

Before taking a closer look at the advertising technology landscape, it is important to shed more light on what powers most of the programmatic advertising transactions; user data.

Any advertising professional will tell you that one of the most important factors in a campaign's success is its ability to reach its target audience. It starts with defining that audience as granularly as possible and then getting the campaign in front of these people through the media they use, while minimizing "waste"— ads shown to people outside the target. Traditional media allow for targeting using general demographics like age, gender, and so on. Publishers monitor who their content (such as TV shows) typically appeals to and that information is used in the media buy. However, the traditional descriptive targeting mechanisms are crude and associated with a lot of waste. That is where digital media differs. As people navigate the web or apps, their behavior can be monitored, and the data that results from that help to build up a much more granular profile of the audience consuming the content.

It All Starts with a Cookie

Consider web browsing. Every time a user accesses a web site, a tiny text file gets stored in the user's browser. This text file, referred to as a *cookie*,[3] is unique to the web site and allows the publisher to keep track of users during their visit and to recognize the users on subsequent visits. These cookies were designed to make the browsing experience smooth but they also serve an important purpose in targeting advertising. There are different types of cookies; depending on who controls the cookie, we refer to them as first-party or third-party cookies. First-party cookies are set by the publisher of the web site you visit. The publisher stores the cookies and, through the terms of use, has an implicit contract with the user of the site that determines what the cookies are used for.

Third-party cookies are set by an entity different from the publisher of the web site you are visiting, hence, a third party. There is no direct agreement between the third party and the user, but the web site publisher has agreed to let the third party store a cookie in the browser of its users. Third-party cookies are primarily set for advertising targeting purposes. The companies that set these cookies have agreements with a large number of web sites. This allows them to build a profile of users (cookies) by monitoring the browsing behavior across all these web sites based on the unique text files they store in the users' browsers. They then use this behavioral tracking information to segment users in descriptive categories that could appeal to advertisers for targeting purposes.

These categories are based on the online behavior of a user. For example if a user is browsing around on car review sites and comparing car models, the user may be classified as "an auto intender". Or, if a user is checking out parenting advice sites or buying baby gear online, the user may fit the "new parent" category. The users' personal information is not stored in these categories or segments; instead, a copy of the cookies that were saved in the users' browsers is used as an identifier for users and the different segments they belong to. Next, when users are browsing around online, advertisers will use the cookies in the users' browsers to match them to these segments, allowing them to target the users with meaningful ads.

Data in the form of cookies have become core to the advertising landscape. Advertisers use the cookies as proxies to define their target audience. Cookies stored in users' browsers allow them to find their exact targets. Advertisers can target their campaigns to segments of users that have shown a certain behavior, but they can also advertise to people that have visited their web sites before, in a practice that is called *re-targeting*. Cookies that are set during the user's visit (e.g., when the user is putting products in a shopping cart) can be used to find those users again when they are visiting other web sites. Ads to encourage users to come back (and check out those shoes) are shown to the users.

These granular behavioral targeted campaigns have proven to be effective, and as a result, data has become more valuable than ever to advertisers and publishers alike.

---

[3]en.wikipedia.org/wiki/HTTP_cookie

But Cookies Are Not Enough

While cookies are a powerful way to monitor a user's behavior on the web, they have many shortcomings. Pushed by consumers' increasing concerns around privacy, some browsers are blocking third-party cookies and some users will install tools that limit the storing of cookies in their browsers. An even more important concern for cookie-based advertising is the fact that an increasing proportion of browsing happens on mobile browsers, most of which do not accept cookies and don't allow storage of cookies. Due to these limitations, other means to monitor behavior are emerging. Device IDs and specific mobile advertising IDs have been introduced to allow the connection of online behavior on mobile devices to a unique user. On top of that, companies that work on mapping identification across devices have emerged, in order to allow advertisers to track and target people across different screens.

Complex as the data landscape may seem, it is clear that understanding users and their online behavior is key to executing targeted campaigns. The value of data as a currency will keep increasing, and publishers that can offer the most reliable profile of their users across screens will be in a position to reap the benefits.

The Basic Underlying Principle in Programmatic Advertising

Programmatic advertising[4] refers to all advertising campaigns that are executed without the interference of a human to make the advertising insertion or to optimize the placement.

In order for machines to execute an advertising insertion, the buyers and the sellers agree on the placements they are targeting. Aside from size and format of the placement, sellers describe the ad space in two ways:

- A description based on the context that surrounds the placement (for example, women's fashion, celebrity news, and so on)

- Details about the visitor who will be exposed to the placement (for example, a visitor who is interested in buying a new car; a visitor who just had a baby, and so on)

The way the machines pass this information back and forth is mostly in the form of cookies, the text files that are stored in the users' browsers. On mobile devices, where a lot of the user time is spent on apps rather than in a browser, information about the user is passed on via the advertising ID. This is a built-in feature of the operating systems of the phones (e.g., Android and iOS). App developers can access this advertising ID, which is a unique identifier for a user. They can then link the behavior of a user to that advertising ID, which makes it possible for advertisers to target users with desired behavioral patterns. Cookies and Advertiser IDs all serve as proxies for the user in the targeted advertising transaction.

Another important aspect of programmatic advertising is the fact that the placement of the ad happens in real time and is unique to the combination of the context and the visitor who is on the site at that moment. As such, individual impressions are traded one by one.

---

[4]en.wikipedia.org/wiki/Programmatic_media

Figure 14-1 shows what is going on from the visitor's point of view. He or she browses around online. While visiting different web sites, the sites place first- and third-party cookies on the user's browser. If the user is on a mobile device, additional data is collected by the sites about the visitor's device, its related advertiser ID, and often its location.

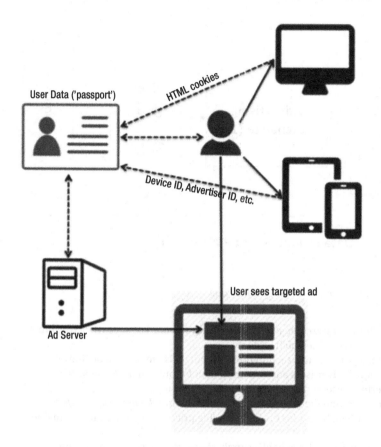

Figure 14-1. *User data-based advertising targeting*

You can basically think of every visitor online as carrying around a passport filled with data that provides details about that user and his/her online behavior. All the first- and third-party cookies are contained in this passport, as is the user's mobile device ID, the mobile advertiser IDs, the Facebook ID, and so on. Then, when the user visits a site, the content of that site loads and simultaneously a call is made to the ad server. The publisher will pass on info about the context for the ad as well as all the info it has about that user—all the info in the user's passport. Advertisers will evaluate that information to see whether they recognize any piece of info associated with that user as an indication that the user falls within their target group. If the advertiser decides that he is interested in the placement, he may buy it and the ad server will send back the ad that specifically targets that user. The user thus sees an ad that is uniquely selected for him/her.

Behind the scenes, there is a lot more going on. When the web site calls the ad server to evaluate what ad to show the user, a whole set of actions happen in real time. It involves different players, who are all part of the *ad tech landscape*.

The Ad Tech Landscape

Figure 14-2 shows a very high-level overview of the different players who are part of the ad tech landscape and whose services are used in programmatic advertising.

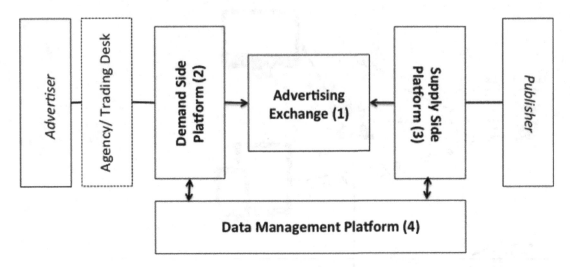

Figure 14-2. *Core participants in the advertising technology landscape*

Central to this landscape is the *advertising exchange*[5]. This is basically the marketplace where the buyers and sellers meet and decide on what ad to serve at which price.

Technology behind the scenes makes a sales transaction possible, but it also makes the buying and selling of ads more complex for traditional advertisers and to some extent for publishers. Because of the technology involved, quite a few intermediaries emerged to lend a helping hand.

The advertisers will typically work through their agencies' trading desks and *demand-side platforms*[6], which will help them buy the right advertising space for the best possible price and that will plug them into the advertising exchanges.

The publishers on the other hand will enlist the help of a *supply-side platform*[7] to ensure that the advertising space they have to offer is filled in with ads that will generate the highest yield. These supply-side platforms will connect to the advertising exchange on the publishers' behalf.

Both advertisers and publishers rely on data management platforms, which help them store, analyze, and connect data to enable the advertising targeting.

Programmatic advertising is relatively young, and the technology is evolving quickly. Different companies focus on different aspects of the technology and different parts of the advertising transaction. The resulting advertising technology landscape is complex and cluttered with many small companies, vying for a piece of the action. A few larger players have emerged over the past few years, and some incumbents have acquired smaller companies to strengthen their technology stack.

---

[5]en.wikipedia.org/wiki/Ad_exchange
[6]en.wikipedia.org/wiki/Demand-side_platform
[7]en.wikipedia.org/wiki/Supply-side_platform

Table 14-1 gives examples of a few players per category. It is by no means an exhaustive list, but it attempts to shed light on some of the important players.

Table 14-1. *Examples of the Main Companies in the Advertising Technology Landscape*

Demand-Side Platforms	Advertising Exchanges	Data Management Platforms	Supply-Side Platforms
Invite Media (Google)	DoubleClick Ad Exchange	Adobe	OpenX
MediaMath	(Google)	Krux	Pubmatic
Turn	Microsoft Advertising	Lotame	Rubicon Project
DataXu	Exchange (Microsoft)	BlueKai (Oracle)	AppNexus
Rocket Fuel	Marketplace by Adtech (AOL)		
	OpenX		
	AppNexus		

The following sections describe the role of each of these players in a bit more detail, starting with the central player, the ad exchange.

The Advertising Exchange

In programmatic advertising, the advertising exchange is where the actual deals happen. While deals in traditional advertising involved a large number of impressions traded at a negotiated price, in the ad exchange, the deals involve individual impressions. Buyers bid for the impressions in an auction format. Most exchanges operate as second-price auctions, meaning that the highest bidder will win the impression and thus the opportunity to show its ad, at a price that is a fraction higher than the second (lower) bid. Exchanges handle millions of impressions, running auctions for each one of them, and they do so in real time. Hence, people often refer to programmatic advertising as RTB (Real-Time Bidding) advertising.

While the transaction is one between an advertiser and a publisher, intermediaries typically manage the execution. The demand-side platforms are the ones that have "seats" on the exchanges, and they bid on behalf of the advertisers or their trading desks. The publishers will work via their supply-side platforms, who will set up the technology inside a publishers' ad server to ensure inventory can be presented for auction in the exchange.

A piece of inventory presented in an auction takes the format of a standardized description of that inventory. It informs potential bidders on the format and size of the ad space and the content surrounding the ad. It also provides info on the person who will be seeing the ad (the person currently visiting the web page where the ad will be shown). All cookies picked up in the users' browser will be attached here. And, if the user is on a mobile device, the device ID, mobile advertising ID, and potentially the location of the user will be passed on as well. The richer the information that can be attached to the piece of inventory, the higher the chances that the inventory is appealing to an advertiser. The publishers will also add a "price floor" to their inventory, which is a minimum price under which the ad space is not sold. Note that prices in the advertising exchanges are typically CPM-based (cost per thousand impressions).

The demand-side platforms know which cookies, types of users, and formats of inventory they are looking for and what they want to pay for them. When the inventory matches their desired targets, they will execute a bid. If they win the bid and the bid exceeds the publisher's floor price, the ad server of their advertiser gets to fill in the ad space with their ad.

The Demand-Side Platform (DSP)

A demand-side platform provides software that enables advertisers to buy inventory in advertising exchanges. DSP's promise to the advertiser is that they will find the inventory the advertiser is looking for at the best available price. DSPs are in theory vendor neutral, so they provide a way for advertisers to buy inventory across different publishers, without having to make individual deals with all of these publishers. Because this allows advertisers to evaluate a very large amount of inventory (billions of impressions daily), they can execute increasingly targeted buys, which require large populations in order to match the target group.

Advertisers provide their DSP with their targeting criteria (the inventory they are interested in) as well as their frequency capping and pricing goals. The DSPs will translate these targeting criteria in inventory descriptions—for example, which cookies, IDs, and so on, align with the advertiser's target. Often, the DSPs will rely on data management platforms to make that translation. In some cases, such as in the case of re-targeting, the advertiser will provide the exact list of cookies they are trying to target (such as the list of cookies for users who have visited the advertiser's site in the past).

DSPs have their own proprietary algorithms that help them execute efficient buys (buying the desired inventory at the lowest price possible). They provide performance reports to the advertisers and they will optimize their campaigns as they progress. DSPs charge a transaction fee for the inventory they trade.

Supply-Side Platforms (SSP)

Publishers use supply-side platforms (SSPs) to sell their inventory programmatically. The SSP provides software that connects the publishers' inventory to different ad exchanges and ad networks where there is demand from advertisers. The software passes on the specifics of the available advertising space, along with the information on the context and the user who will see the ad. The SSP optimizes the way the ad space gets filled for maximum yield. It will work inside the publishers' ad server to route the inventory to where it believes it can garner the highest price. It considers the advertising exchange as one of the options, but it will also consider other ways the ad space may get sold, such as through a pre-negotiated price in a direct sale or by an advertising network. It will put all of the options in the mix and use its proprietary algorithms to send the ad request to where it estimates it will get the highest price.

The SSP software tackles a process that used to be manual, where publishers would work with insertion orders that were scheduled by their advertising operations department. These insertion orders where programmed in bulk, with little option to optimize during the campaign. The SSPs automate this scheduling and yield optimization job, while helping publishers access a much larger demand for their inventory than what they could achieve through direct deals.

Data Management Platforms (DMP)

Data plays a pivotal role in advertising technology, especially data that describes online users. Data management platforms concentrate on storing all that data and categorizing, analyzing, and segmenting the data.

DMPs are used by the advertisers to help them construct the profiles for their targets. The DMPs have their proprietary ways to segment or categorize users based on their online behavior and the cookies associated with that behavior, and the advertisers can tap into those segments. Based on the cookies and IDs saved for the users in a segment or category, the advertisers can then buy advertising targeted at the user associated with those cookies/IDs.

Publishers also use the DMPs, as they like to enhance the data that they have on their site's or app's users. The more information the publisher can offer the advertiser to describe its visitors, the higher the probability that advertisers are interested in that user, and the higher the price the publisher will get for the ad impressions served to that user.

Data storage and management is complex, especially when handling massive data sets and when using the information to connect to real-time technologies. DMPs specialize in exactly that, making the life of the advertisers and publishers easier.

What Is Next?

The advertising technology industry is still young and has seen considerable change while growing up. Some interesting trends that are further shaping programmatic advertising include:

- Increasing inclusion of premium advertising inventory

- A shift to people-based targeting across multiple devices

- An interest in programmatic advertising outside of just the digital screens—especially TV and brick and mortar

- The use of beacons to enhance targeting

Premium Advertising Inventory

While programmatic advertising originally focused on just the "remnant" inventory, it was soon recognized to create efficiencies that could benefit some of the traditional transactions. A more efficient execution and optimization of advertising insertion and its ability to open the inventory to much larger demand makes programmatic advertising appealing to fill advertising space that would previously have been reserved for direct deals between publishers and advertisers. While direct deal making is not going away, the execution of the advertising campaign now often happens automatically, and people will refer to that as "programmatic premium". We also see private marketplaces emerge, where publishers open their premium advertising space to a select group of bidders, using the programmatic buying principles. As publishers keep seeking ways to optimize their yield and advertisers are eager to streamline their media buys, it is believed that soon, all display advertising execution will fall under the programmatic advertising umbrella.

People-Based Targeting Across Multiple Devices

With an ever-increasing amount of media consumed on mobile devices, advertisers are spending an ever-larger part of their budget on advertising in mobile browsers and apps. In order to control who sees the ads, it is important for advertisers to be able to find their targets across devices. While a cookie can be a good proxy to find a user on the desktop, cookies don't translate well to mobile devices. Apps don't work with cookies, and many mobile browsers block the setting of cookies. As a result, many players in the industry are working on alternatives for the cookie. Facebook and Google are both trying to define new standards to identify users across screens with unique user IDs. We will see those IDs gain in importance over time and we will see an increased focus on data that can serve as a better identifier for people than the cookies we rely on today.

Programmatic Advertising Outside of Just the Digital Screens

While digital media offers a vast advertising opportunity, a lot of money is still spent on advertising in other media environments, television being the frontrunner. The TV landscape and its technology are evolving, and many of the programmatic advertising players see the connected TVs as their next frontier. And, although ecommerce is flourishing, many purchases still happen offline. Marketers have always had an interest in opportunities to influence consumers right at the point of purchase.

The Use of Beacons to Enhance Targeting

The emergence of beacon technology allows tracking in-store behavior, which, combined with ubiquitous mobile devices, enables advertisers to put promotions in front of users based on their specific in-store location. Interactions between mobile devices and beacons are personal in nature, and the programmatic advertising model can then be extended to include these new ways to promote products and reach consumers in a brick and mortar environment.

Anke Audenaert

Summary

Now we have a clear picture of programmatic advertising, let's consider how beacons could augment that ecosystem.

Beacons can provide a much more precise level of targeting that supply-side platforms could use to increase the value of the inventory they are managing. For example, ads targeted at people who are in the proximity of a certain category of retail display, such refrigerators. If a user were standing in the white-goods section of Best Buy, ads for refrigerators could appear within their game of Tetris, a mobile web site, or shopping list app.

The targeting could also include factors such as dwell time. If an individual dwells for longer than five minutes in the vicinity of a display of refrigerators, an ad that appeared in the media they were browsing on their phone might be more valuable to a manufacturer of refrigerators. To capture this value, the advertising exchange might work with a supply-side platform to raise the premium for inventory that matches a demand-side platform's targeting of such consumers.

These location triggers would certainly make the inventory that the supply-side platform is managing more valuable, which is to the benefit of the publisher, but the owner of the beacon and the venue that the beacon sits in will want to be adequately compensated too. This will require another party, potentially the data platform, to source the location trigger and broker the compensation to the beacon owner. The beacon owner will then need to compensate the venue owner that permitted the beacon to be put in place. Demand-side platforms need to be able to present these new dimensions of targeting to advertisers. In addition to the examples of location triggers, a valuable set of attributes could be associated with a device ID. If that ID has been seen at high-value locations such as car show rooms, luxury goods merchants, or a high stakes table at a casino, its value becomes enhanced.

There is then the possibility to cross-pollinate the value of the device with the value of yet another location. Establishing premium value to a beacon in a high-stakes location within a casino and enhancing the value of device IDs that visit that location is a fairly obvious move. If there is a correlation between device IDs that visit that part of a casino and ones that frequently visit a late night diner in a low-rent neighborhood, we can start to make less obvious inferences about the value of the beacon in the diner too. In this example, we could automatically infer that the diner has a hidden value as a late night hangout for high-rolling gamblers.

Such changes to the programmatic advertising platforms are unlikely to happen in the early days of the beacosystem. These changes are complex and both the value and volume need to be established before all the players will adopt. Until beacon networks become broadly available across multiple markets, it doesn't make sense for the programmatic advertising platforms to change what they do.

One-stop platforms that incorporate all the elements discussed in this chapter into a single simplified system, such as inMarket and Swirl, are pioneering the use of beacons for advertising. As they establish they can drive lift in the value of their advertising inventory and there is enough volume, the programmatic advertising platforms will change too. When that happens, the market has the potential to grow rapidly.

CHAPTER 15

Understanding the Integration of Mobile, Beacons, and Out-of-Home Media

Dr. Phil Hendrix, Managing Director, immr
Ray Rotolo, SVP, Out Of Home Assets, Gimbal

Out-of-home advertising is one of the first applications for Bluetooth beacons where beacons have been deployed at significant scale. We have seen many hundreds of beacons deployed across major U.S. cities, attached to phone booths and other street furniture. These deployments have been the first instances of the

© Stephen Statler 2016
S. Statler, *Beacon Technologies*, DOI 10.1007/978-1-4842-1889-1_15

beacon network, a set of beacons made available to multiple apps. Beacon networks are likely to be a key part of the development of the beacosystem. They allow beacon-enabled apps to be created and deployed at scale much more economically and rapidly than if beacons had to be purchased and put in place for each new app deployed.

Advertising has provided the life-blood of many forms of media, enabling the production of television, magazines, newspaper, music, video, web sites, and mobile apps that wouldn't otherwise exist. Out-of-home (OOH) advertising is one of the first segments of that larger advertising market where beacons have proven their value.

For these reasons, a closer look at OOH is an important part of this guide to the beacosystem.

This chapter is a revised version of a whitepaper entitled "Watch this Space" published by immr for Gimbal Inc.

Steve Statler

Introduction

Out-of-home (OOH) media are ubiquitous, surrounding us on street corners, roadsides, and in transit, venues, and many other locations. In the United States alone, OOH advertising represents a $7+ billion industry and is projected to grow to more than $8 billion over the next five years (see Figure 15-1). As beacons are deployed across verticals, the environments in which consumers shop, work, and play[1] are becoming "beaconized[2]". The combination of mobile, OOH, and beacons—called *MOHBE*[3]—represents a unique opportunity for advertisers, OOH media, and mobile partners.

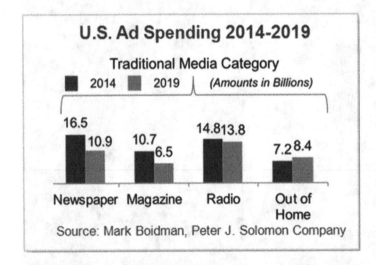

Figure 15-1. United States ad spending

---

[1]www.slashgear.com/super-bowl-weekend-gets-beaconized-courtesy-of-gimbal-31366901/
[2]www.mediapost.com/publications/article/233681/beaconed-or-uberized-let-the-battle-for-our-brain.html
[3]MOHBE is pronounced "moh-bee."

Beacons are already being integrated into a wide range of OOH media, in airports, transit (subway stations, bus shelters, trains, and buses), kiosks, and other "street furniture," and other locations. With MOHBE, businesses are engaging consumers with timely, relevant, and even personalized ads, messages, and offers. In addition to enhancing consumers' experience, MOHBE allows advertisers to target audiences with greater precision, to capture richer data, and to better measure their results.

> *"Over the last twelve months iBeacons/BLE beacons have caught the zeitgeist and emerged as a key anchor technology in the retail space. However, there are many other markets that will generate even bigger volumes of BLE beacon shipments over the next five years, creating a 60 million unit market in 2019."*

> *ABI Research, July 2014*

Outlining the significance of MOHBE for advertisers, mobile app publishers, and OOH media properties, this chapter discusses the following topics:

- Features that distinguish OOH media

- Beacons and platforms

- How mobile, beacons, and OOH are being integrated

- The potential for MOHBE (mobile and OOH, enabled by beacons)

- Recommendations for advertisers, mobile app partners, and OOH media

- Challenges advertisers and the OOH ecosystem must address

OOH Media Overview

National, regional, and local businesses across a wide range of product and service categories rely on OOH to reach consumers. OOH's popularity is due to its reach, visibility, dwell time, and other features shown in Figure 15-2.

Top 10 OOH Advertisers in 2014	Top 10 OOH Categories in Ad Spend
1. McDonald's	1. Misc. Services and Amusements
2. Apple	2. Retail
3. Metro PCS	3. Media and Advertising
4. Verizon	4. Restaurants
5. GEICO	5. Public Transportation, Hotels, and Resorts
6. Warner Bros Pictures	6. Insurance and Real Estate
7. Citi	7. Financial
8. Chase	8. Government, Politics, and Organizations
9. Coca-Cola	9. Communications
10. NBC	10. Schools, Camps, and Seminars
Source: OAAA[4]	

Figure 15-2. *OOH overview*

Seven Features Distinguishing OOH Media

Reach—With hundreds of thousands of displays in malls, airports, bus shelters, billboards, buses, and subways, OOH reaches pedestrians, commuters, and drivers wherever they go[5].

Visibility—Positioned squarely in consumers' line of sight, OOH's visibility delivers frequent exposure. Combined with colorful graphics and clever, creative ads, OOH is likely to get noticed, remembered, and acted upon (see Figure 15-3). Digital OOH (DOOH) enhances visibility even more.

[4]www.oaaa.org/ResourceCenter/MarketingSales/Factsamp;Figures/Revenue/TopOOHSpenders.aspx
[5]www.oaaa.org/OutofHomeAdvertising/OOHMediaFormats/OOHMediaFormats.aspx

Figure 15-3. *An OOH airport display*

Targeting—OOH audiences can be targeted based on their location, interests, demographics, and, with DOOH, time of day. By targeting festivals, business openings, and other areas with concentrated, hyper-local audiences, mobile billboards[6] also bring speed, flexibility, and a high degree of accuracy to OOH.

Dwell Time—On-transit media (e.g., subways, buses, taxis, and airplanes), in doctor's offices, and even at intersections, dwell time can range from a minute to a half hour or more. Since dwell time is often relatively free of distractions, OOH messages and creative that match audience interests and context deliver high recall.

---

[6]www.doitoutdoors.com

Path-to-Purchase—Many OOH media are on or near consumers' path to purchase—for CPG, near grocery stores; for OTC medications, near pharmacies; for autos, near dealers; and so on. Since consumers often decide on purchases at or near the point-of-purchase, OOH ads can significantly influence consumers' consideration and choice of products and brands.

Engaging—In many cases, OOH must capture the consumer's attention and convey a message quickly. To satisfy these requirements, creatives do some of their best work in OOH, using novelty, surprise, humor, and other elements.

Utility—Consumers value OOH ads that contain information they can use, such as new products and services or nearby points-of-interest and activities. Even leading tech companies recognize the value of reaching consumers on the go via OOH. For example, a recent Google Outside campaign took over some 150 DOOH displays in London to showcase the Google Search app for iOS and speech-recognition capabilities.

Beacons and OOH Locations

Beacons are being deployed in many locations where OOH media are present, from shopping malls and airports to transit, attractions, restaurants, bars, and many others.

Shopping Malls—When entering malls with beacons, consumers with shopping apps such as RetailMeNot are receiving push notifications highlighting special offers at participating merchants, specials in the food court, schedules of events, invitations to enroll in the mall's loyalty program, and more. Mobiquity Networks' mall-based ad network is in 236 malls reaching 37,000 storefronts; PlaceWise Media is integrating beacons into its solutions for some 700 shopping destinations.

Airports—In Orlando, London, Hong Kong, and other major airports, beacons are being deployed to guide travelers, show where luggage can be picked up and dropped off, and present offers for food and beverages, travel accessories, and other products and services. Proxama and Eye Airports are deploying 200 beacons across eight London airports, including London Gatwick, delivering targeted content, offers, and rewards to 100 million passengers. MOHBE in airports brings utility for travelers and value to advertisers targeting this high-value segment.

Transit—In subway stations in Boston and other cities, beacons integrated with the transit authority's app or a third-party app are providing directions to the correct platform, showing arrival and departure times, and, in some cases, presenting ads and offers from businesses. In Australia, Adshel is rolling out more than 3,000 beacons across its national OOH network to enhance its targeting and data capabilities in the outdoor advertising space.

Attractions and Events—Museums in Los Angeles, zoos in Italy, SXSW, and many other attractions and events are using beacons to better understand visitors, enhance their experience, and promote sales. Beacon-enabled apps reveal areas visited, dwell time, and other granular aspects, allowing organizers and advertisers to provide visitors with relevant information, services, and offers that match attendees' interests and on-site behavior.

Restaurants and Bars—Restaurants and bars are leveraging beacons to engage and better serve customers. Tillster is integrating beacons into its mobile ordering and payment solution, allowing customers at quick-serve restaurants to order and pay for their food without standing in line or waiting on a server. Touchtunes is introducing beacons into its interactive music and entertainment network in over 60,000 social venues.

Beacon Placement and Purpose

Beacons are a relatively new phenomenon. They can be affixed to surfaces (walls, shelves, etc.) or embedded in objects (such as ATMs, vending machines, fixtures, access points, even products and packaging). In fact, Gimbal recently announced that it is licensing its beacon firmware to enable almost any device with Bluetooth Low Energy (BLE) to act as a beacon.

The primary purpose of a beacon is to send a signal via Bluetooth that can be detected by mobile devices in the vicinity of the beacon. When a mobile app programmed to recognize the beacon's signal comes within a specified distance (e.g., from within inches to up to 50-75 meters), the app "wakes up," detects the beacon's presence, registers the event, and (typically) displays a message, ad, offer or other communication on the user's device.

Beacon Platforms

A beacon platform consists of hardware (beacons themselves), software, and one or more mobile apps capable of recognizing beacons in particular locations.

- *Beacons*—Hardware consists of one or more beacons placed at various locations in and around a location, both indoors and outside. Beacons can also be embedded in fixtures, displays, and kiosks and installed on PCs and other devices via the USB port.

- *Integrated app(s)*—One or more mobile apps capable of recognizing the beacon(s) in a particular location. The apps may include a brand or retailer app; a third-party app, such as RetailMeNot or Shazam; a social media app; or some other app.

- *Beacon management software*—Allows the beacon owner or its partner to configure and monitor the status of beacons. For example, for each beacon specifying unique identifiers and their range; monitoring battery life; and so on.

- *Proximity engagement software*—allows the beacon owner or its agency partner to set up and manage campaigns. Once a beacon's signal has been detected, a campaign simply tells the app what to do, e.g., for first-time visitors, "show a welcome with 25% offer;" for returning guests, present a link to enroll in the loyalty program; as fans exit a venue, present a link to purchase a season pass; etc.

User Requirements

To participate in campaigns in locations enabled by beacons, the user must have a Bluetooth-enabled mobile device; have Bluetooth turned on; have one or more apps on their mobile devices capable of interacting with beacons; and opt-in to receive alerts, messages, and offers from the paired app(s). Google's recently introduced Eddystone platform relaxes the "paired apps" requirement, but introduces trade-offs related to data access and ownership.

How Beacons Multiply the Effectiveness of Mobile and OOH

OOH and mobile are effective channels in their own right. However, the combination of the two is much more effective than either of the channels by themselves. When beacons and BLE (Bluetooth)-enabled devices are introduced into the mix, the effectiveness of mobile as well as OOH is multiplied. Various capabilities enabled by mobile and beacons are being integrated with OOH, as explained next and illustrated in Figure 15-4.

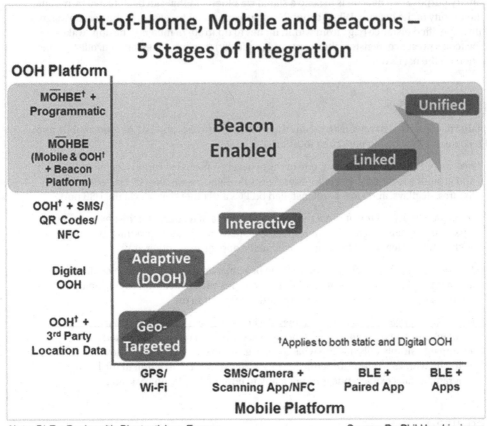

Figure 15-4. *The five stages of MOHBE integration*

Stage 1: Geo-Targeted OOH

By profiling audiences in locations and places, OOH media planners determine the best placements for advertisers and their campaigns. Historically, planners have relied on surveys and other sources of demographic data to profile location-based audiences. Now, third-party mobile data sources such as Placed and PlaceIQ provide richer and more granular data, including demographics as well as user interests, travel history (including stores visited before and after), and even spending patterns. PlaceIQ profiles mobile audiences in a billion 100 x 100 square meter tiles, over 27 unique time periods.

Stage 2: Adaptive DOOH

In the United States, there are more than 110 Digital OOH (DOOH) networks. Like digital media on the Internet, DOOH can display ads dynamically, rotating and displaying ads in 15-60 second intervals. With data from mobile users, Digital OOH (DOOH) advertising shown in, around, and on transit, malls, venues, and other locations can be tailored to audiences based on time of day as well as on location. When a concert, game, or other major event is held at a venue, DOOH can tailor nearby content to fans' profiles and interests. By detecting and adapting dynamically to mobile consumers, DOOH offers an even more flexible and powerful channel for brands, retailers, and locations.

Stage 3: Interactive

Mobile also allows consumers to interact with OOH ads, both static and digital. For instance, consumers can share an ad with others, receive additional information and offers, or respond to a "call to action" (e.g., enroll in a loyalty program; enter a contest; answer a trivia question; and so on). Mobile consumers can interact with OOH ads by sharing an OOH ad or offer on Facebook, Instagram, Twitter, or other social media; responding via SMS to a "text message-enabled" OOH ad; scanning a QR code shown on an OOH ad; or tapping an NFC equipped smartphone on an OOH ad with an embedded NFC sensor. Increasingly, advertisers are including multiple ways for consumers to interact with OOH.

Stage 4: MOHBE (Mobile + OOH Enabled by Beacons)

Integrating beacons into the mobile and OOH mix delivers six important benefits.

- First, while geo-targeting with mobile data improves audience profiling and selection, beacons provide even more precise targeting. For example, consumers who are actually on a particular subway train; in a bus shelter; in a specific department, aisle, or even near a particular display in a store.

- When consumers are exposed to a beacon-enabled OOH ad, the mobile app registers the event along with dwell time (length of exposure) and other useful metrics. By studying traffic patterns, advertisers can determine the best time to engage with visitors. Additional audience insights such as the apps visitors use contribute to better design and content of engagements and even physical signage.

- Beacon-triggered events can also prompt app(s) to engage consumers in *appropriate* ways. For example, present a push notification with a call-to-action or display an ad, reminder, or coupon when the consumer nears a retailer where the advertised product is sold.

- All of this happens *automatically*, without the consumer having to scan or tap an ad, text, or take some other action. Thus, beacons also make it easier for consumers to engage with OOH media.

- A beacon-paired app can also detect when consumers exposed to an OOH ad subsequently enter a store in which beacons are present, enabling the advertiser to attribute behaviors (e.g., store visits) to OOH ad campaigns. These events—uniquely observed with beacon-enabled apps and OOH—provide definitive measures of conversion from digital messaging to physical visits.

- Lastly, these events and others can be recorded as part of an individual consumer's history and used to distinguish first-time, returning, interested, engaged, and other types of consumers based on previous beacon-triggered events.

Stage 5: MOHBE + Programmatic

With programmatic platforms advertisers use real-time bidding to automatically purchase digital inventory (web, in-app, video, and others) that matches and reaches specific, narrowly defined audience profiles. Growing rapidly across channels, programmatic is projected to account for more than half of all digital advertising in the next 18-24 months. OOH is also beginning to integrate inventories with programmatic platforms. Programmatic makes MOHBE even more valuable by simplifying purchasing of ad inventory, which as PJSC's Mark Boidman pointed out is badly needed in OOH and, potentially, by boosting the value of OOH inventory and return on ad spend (ROAS) for both both static and digital OOH.

Industry Leaders' Perspectives on MOHBE

Industry leaders are bullish on the prospects of MOHBE, as reflected in the following comments from immr interviews with industry thought leaders.

"OOH can capture consumers' attention during those 'moments of pause' when they're away from home. Beacons allow us to understand who's passing by and who's pausing, and potentially the next opportunity to engage... they are also cost effective and unobtrusive." David Krupp, CEO, Kinetic U.S.

"Mobile allows consumers to experience the world in connected ways. It's also changing what we know about audiences... 'Did consumers actually see my message? What actions did they take?' Mobile reveals this and more, in real time." Josh Kruter, SVP, Digital, Clear Channel Outdoor

"Beacons engage mobile users and provide a method of attribution to show that OOH works. With other traditional media channels continuing to fall out of favor, OOH should benefit from those trends and grow its share of the market." Mark Boidman, Managing Director, Peter J. Solomon Company

"The movements of people in the real world are incredibly valuable... beacons allow us to present ads and information that are contextual and immediately relevant. But the user experience has to be easy and can't be interruptive." Mike Gamaroff, Managing Director, Kinetic U.S.

"OOH has always been great to target where, but now mobile data allows us to target the when as well. Beacon-enabled campaigns have been off the charts in terms of engagement... With beacons you also get an almost real-time ROI attribution model." Ryan Laul, Director, [d] theory (OMG)

"[With beacons] OOH can engage consumers on their life's journey during the day in a very contextual, relevant way ... delivering the right message at the right time and place to the right person, and then measuring it." Ray Rotolo, SVP, OOH Assets, Gimbal

"Beacons allow brands to understand a user's journey from beginning to end and serve personalized messages—based on location and proximity—that feel less like ads and more like helpful content to consumers." Regis Maher, President and Co-founder, do it outdoors media

Recommendations

The following sections provide some recommendations for advertisers, mobile apps, and OOH media.

Advertisers Should Seize the MOHBE Opportunity

Many large advertisers are well positioned to capitalize on the MOHBE opportunity. Combining beacons with mobile and OOH offers more granular data for targeting; permits advertisers to leverage the consumer's history, location, and context; and allows the brand to engage consumers in personalized and frictionless ways, including retargeting consumers on mobile who have been exposed to an OOH ad. MOHBE is likely to be most valuable for the following types of brands and products:

- Brands with brick and mortar locations

- Brands with their own compelling mobile apps

- Brands introducing new products

- Brands in "high involvement" product categories

- Products with limited availability or supply

- Products for which consumer needs vary by location or season

- Products requiring explanation

Leading national brands, especially those with their own mobile apps and existing advertising on OOH, are uniquely positioned to integrate and reap the benefits of beacons. Customers value the enhanced functionality beacons bring; are more likely to have or download the brand's or a partner's app; and they have locations, content, or other assets that reveal whether consumers visited or took some action. In sum, for these brands, the cost and complexity to "test and learn" with MOHBE are relatively low and the payoff is high.

Mobile Apps Must Partner with Brands and OOH Media

When a mobile app comes within range of a beacon that it recognizes, the app can engage its owner with messages, offers, and ads tailored to the location and individual. Of course, few brands have persuaded more than 10-15% of their customers to download their apps. As a result, brands and retailers are relying on third-party apps—many of them shopping related—to serve as "partner apps" and complete the platform. That's brand + beacons + mobile app. For instance, Lord & Taylor has worked with SnipSnap; Levi Strauss has worked with RetailMeNot; and in Norway, Coca-Cola has partnered with VG, a leading Norwegian newspaper with a popular mobile app.

While Gimbal and other beacon platform providers are facilitating the development of the ecosystem, the playing field is wide open for mobile apps to forge partnerships with OOH media and brands. Since many apps are aimed at consumers within a vertical—for example, health and fitness, travel, entertainment, home and garden, etc.—there are many natural pairings of third-party apps and OOH media for brands and locations.

For mobile apps, MOHBE offers a number of significant benefits, including more personalized user experiences, offers, and content from brand partners tailored to the user's precise location, history, and interests. It also offers additional revenue from in-app ads, push notifications, app downloads, and other sources.

OOH Ecosystem Should Rapidly "Beaconize"

With beacons spreading rapidly, for OOH industry leaders the opportunity is clear—integrate beacons into OOH and work closely with brands and their agency partners (both creative and media buying) to help them recognize, test, and demonstrate the benefits of MOHBE to consumers and advertisers.

Recent developments raise the urgency for the OOH industry. Facebook began giving away beacons to small- and medium-sized businesses (SMBs), part of its plan to become a dominant player in local advertising. The majority of Facebook's 1.4 billion users now access Facebook on their mobile devices. As part of the agreement, SMBs share data from beacon-enabled interactions with Facebook. Through a subsidiary, Google is also investing in OOH companies. With their substantial audiences, assets, and capabilities, Facebook, Google and other digital leaders will continue to be dominant forces in mobile advertising. If OOH incumbents are slow to seize the opportunity and integrate beacons, mobile, and OOH, companies from outside the industry could assume the mantel and disrupt the status quo.

Challenges for the Industry and Its Partners

While mobile and beacon solutions present a unique opportunity for the OOH industry and its partners—OOH agencies, proximity marketing firms, beacon solution providers and app publishers—in order to capitalize on the opportunity, the industry and individual companies must address a number of important challenges.

Consumer Experience—Consistently delivering a positive experience for consumers may well be the single most important challenge. OOH and partners must determine which apps on a consumer's phone are given permission to detect and use a beacon signal; how many beacon-triggered messages can be presented to a consumer during a period of time; how to distinguish and address first-time versus repeat visitors; and others. The OOH industry must work together with leading partners to collectively share best practices and proactively establish standards and certification for participants.

Securing Beacon Networks—Much like a web site, mobile app, or any other digital platform, access to beacon networks must be managed carefully. While technically different, intrusions have the same chilling effect as ad fraud, spam, Wi-Fi sniffing, and other malicious activities. To prevent unauthorized access by apps, advertisers or any other party that has not been given explicit permission, enterprise-grade security is a critical feature in beacon management platforms. OOH media owners must take proactive measures to secure their beacon networks and mitigate these risks.

Managing and Protecting Data—Combined with OOH, beacon-enabled solutions generate an enormous amount of data on "events" as well as consumer responses (or their absence) to campaigns. Examples include data on foot traffic past an OOH site; dwell time by users; and others, all by time of day. In addition to security, additional complexities must be considered—for example, which data to capture; where the data are stored; who has access to the data; how exposure to OOH ads is combined with store visits, spend, and other data from first- and third-party sources; and more. These questions require careful consideration, coordination, and compliance across the MOHBE ecosystem.

Beacons and Privacy—As noted, beacons do not capture or store data; they simply transmit signals that apps can detect and respond to. In addition, consumers must turn on Bluetooth on their mobile devices to receive beacon signals and opt-in to give an app permission to send messages, present offers, etc. Nonetheless, when paired with beacons, mobile apps are in a position to observe new types of user behaviors. To protect consumers' privacy the OOH industry and its app partners must adopt and adhere to best practices like those listed in Table 15-1. The Federal Trade Commission has also issued reports recommending ways that key players in mobile inform consumers about their data and privacy practices.

Table 15-1. Using TACT to Preserve Consumers' Privacy

Goal	Approach
Transparency	Give consumers information about the data being collected, the manner in which it is being collected, and how it will be used.
Added Value	Make consumers aware of the value they are receiving, e.g., how they benefit from providing their personal data.
Control	Give consumers control by informing them who their data is being shared with and allowing them to opt-out of data collection at any time.
Trust	Collect only the data needed and use the data collected to deliver consumer value.

Source: The New Data Values, AIMIA

Summary

Beacons represent an enormous opportunity for the OOH industry and its partners. By integrating beacons, OOH media owners gain a new digital network that complements their physical assets, increasing the value of OOH properties and enhancing the effectiveness of OOH advertising. Advertisers gain a deeper understanding of mobile consumers, the ability to target specific OOH audiences, and measure the impact of their OOH ads. For mobile app partners, beacons provide a bridge between the digital and physical, yielding insights that can be used to improve functionality and the user's experience. These insights translate into more precise targeting, higher eCPMs and, with more relevant, value-added content, more satisfied users. Finally, consumers stand to gain by receiving content (messages, ads, and so on), offers, and services that more closely match their needs and interests, in places and at times when they can use them.

To capitalize on the MOHBE opportunity, key players—including OOH media, agency and tech partners, advertisers, and mobile app publishers—must work closely together to develop, share, and adopt best practices. Provided the consortium integrates these capabilities in a systematic, consumer-centric fashion, the prospects are bright for the OOH industry, advertisers, and consumers.

CHAPTER 16

Alternative Technologies to Bluetooth Beacons

© Stephen Statler 2016
S. Statler, *Beacon Technologies*, DOI 10.1007/978-1-4842-1889-1_16

"The talent is in the choices."

—Robert De Niro

Bluetooth beacons have disrupted and transformed proximity marketing. They have many advantages, but they also have limitations that should be understood and considered when designing a solution. By understanding those limitations and the alternative options, a solution designer can make choices between one technology and another, or choose which ones to blend together in a solution. This chapter, and the other chapters in this section of the guide, look at the main alternatives to Bluetooth beacons to provide location and proximity for mobile apps. This section is designed to give you a good basis for selecting the right tool for the job.

In this chapter, we will discuss:

- Machine vision and camera analytics

- Li-Fi: LEDs and visual light communication (VLC)

- Magnetic resonance

- Ultra wide band

- Wi-Fi

In the other chapters in this section, we will explore:

- Use of GPS, Wi-Fi, and geofencing

- Barcodes, QR codes, RFID, and NFC

- Cellular network technologies

Machine Vision and Camera Analytics

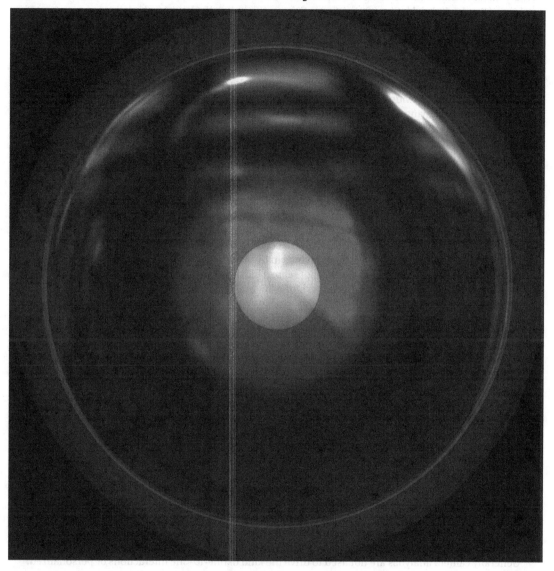

On Dave's return to the ship, after HAL 9000 has killed the rest of the crew]

"Look Dave, I can see you're really upset about this. I honestly think you ought to sit down calmly, take a stress pill, and think things over."

HAL 9000, *2001: A Space Odyssey*

You may have missed the fact that there were some prerequisites for reading this book. Just to refresh your memory, those included the building of a replica of any of the *Star Wars* space vehicles out of Legos and the watching of Stanley Kubrick's film *2001: A Space Odyssey* (including the long psychedelic sequence toward the end). You will need to have completed the second of those prerequisites in order to appreciate this piece of the book on machine vision.

One of the best bits of acting in *2001* was when Dave the astronaut is having a showdown with HAL the psychotic computer. The fact that it's HAL's performance that is so moving (as Dave pulls out his memory cards and he sings "Daisy") just goes to show either how bad the other actors were, or how good Douglas Rain was, the actor who provided the voice for HAL.

The point is, that having a computer able to observe a human, know that the image it's receiving is in fact a human, and even detect the emotions of that human is "flipping" amazing. The even more amazing thing is that exactly that capability is being deployed in retail stores today.

Computer vision algorithms can analyze real-time video feeds and process the imagery, separating moving, overlapping objects, detecting whether they are people and counting the people that have been identified. These "intelligent" camera devices are mounted near potential store locations, to analyze the traffic that might come into a store if it were to be opened there. They are set up by doorways in stores that are open for business, in order to count the potential customers that are passing by and compare that number with total they see coming inside. This yields a passerby to visitor conversion rate, which can be tracked over time of day and by day to measure the effect of window displays and other marketing programs.

For those of us who as children waved our hands in front of the optical sensor at the entrance of the store to make it go "ping" repeatedly, this may not seem a big deal, but the analysis that these devices are doing is a lot more sophisticated than the old-fashioned light sensor.

Capabilities of Camera Analytics

The machine vision of today can detect the gender of customers, their approximate age, what kind of mood they are in, and how engaged they are in any media being presented on displays or billboards.

One vendor, Kairos, claims 94% accuracy in detecting a person, 92% accuracy in detecting gender, and 85% accuracy in detecting mood. Arguably this is better than could be expected from a person doing the same work, given that people are prone to distractions and can be overwhelmed by crowds.

A key point in favor of using this technology is that unlike beacons and other wireless systems, camera-based analytics can count all customers. They don't have to be running a particular app. They don't even need to have a phone.

Like any technology, it's not perfect, so when looking at suppliers, it's important to establish how close to the theoretical 100% coverage they can achieve based on the specifics of the camera positions that are available and the measurements required. One of the challenges is that machine vision can have difficulties distinguishing staff from customers. RetailNext has filed a patent around the use of Bluetooth tags issued to staff to make sure that staff are removed from the results of camera analytics. Radius Networks produces a beacon with a wrist strap made by Swatch, so that staff can wear beacons for just this purpose.

Generally camera analytics are not used to drive the kind of one-to-one interactions or personalized retargeting that beacons can be used for. There are notable exceptions, such as using cameras for virtual changing rooms, where customers pose for the camera and a display presents their image as it would look if they were wearing a variety of different clothes.

Deployment of Camera Analytics

Some systems operate through integration with the video feed from existing security cameras. This can save on capital costs and installation, but may prove to be too restrictive for certain applications where people's faces need to viewed, or a person count is required in a specific part of the store where cameras are not already deployed. In this case specialized camera sensors are used, as depicted in Figure 16-1.

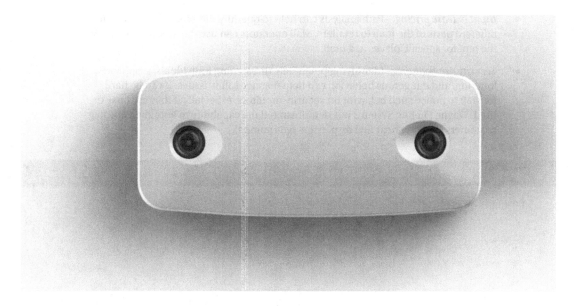

Figure 16-1. *RetailNext's Aurora stereoscopic camera sensor*

Devices can consist of monocular cameras, stereoscopic cameras, and cameras integrated with BLE and Wi-Fi sensors. Wi-Fi sensors can record the network addresses of phones, recording those to compare with future visits and use that to calculate if the customer is a return visitor or not.

The camera hardware typically requires power, which can be delivered over Ethernet cables as an alternative to running a main power line to the device.

Camera devices can cost as much as $1,000 each and so are seen as being quite expensive, especially for larger format stores.

Applications of Camera Analytics

The applications for camera analytics span marketing and operational domains, including:

- *Counting customers and conversion*—Comparing the changing number of visitors across different stores can help identify problems and best practices. Once a count of people entering the store is available, then the conversion ratio between visitors and sales can be calculated using sales receipts.

- *Satisfaction and Service Times*—Time in queues and the time spent waiting to be served correlates with customer satisfaction and likely return visits.

- *Staff scheduling and safety*—Real-time customer traffic numbers provide empirical input to the task of scheduling sufficient sales and security staff for satisfaction and safety, especially in the case of large venues. Counting the number of concertgoers surging into certain areas can be hard to record manually.

- *Merchandising*—Measuring the visits to parts of stores and the dwell time in locations, provides input to the success of product and aisle layouts and the effectiveness of signage and displays. In Figure 16-2 we can see the red areas of the heatmap indicate the busiest parts of the store.

- *Input to lease pricing*—Path analysis can help to quantify the value of store lots in different parts of the mall to retailers. Mall operators can use the numbers to adjust the rent for specific places in a mall.

- *Security applications*—Identifying potentially threatening individuals, suspicious loitering, and dangerous behavior, can help manage safety issues. It can be hard for staff to notice such behavior on security monitors, especially if they are busy or tired. Wayne Fueling Systems has demonstrated the capability to automatically flag customers smoking near fuel dispensers (gas pumps).

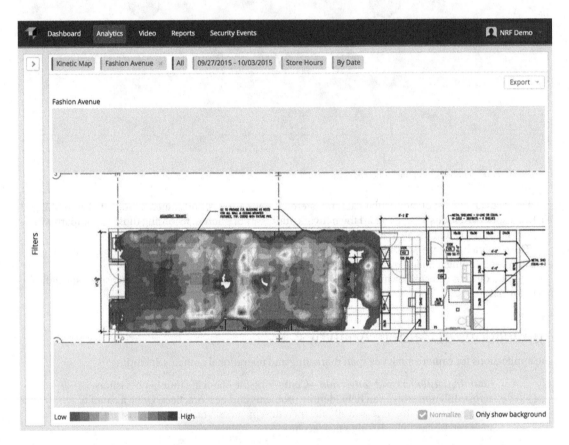

Figure 16-2. RetailNext heatmap showing the busiest parts of the store floor in red

Camera Analytics Summary

The key strength of machine vision/camera technology is the coverage of 100% of the visitors to a venue, with no apps required. It is a passive technology that is good for observation rather than interaction, with the exception of HAL, the psychotic computer from *2001* and a few edge cases where the camera may drive the personalization of content on digital displays. This makes it suited to analytics functions. When alerts and engagement are required, beacons need to be added to the mix. See Table 16-1.

Table 16-1. *Camera Analytics Summary*

Coverage	Up to 100% of customers
Background operation—ability to wake an app that has been terminated	No
Hardware costs:	$500-$1,000 for a stereoscopic sensor
Deployment considerations	Power required, bandwidth for video transmission from multiple cameras required
Accuracy	Aisle level tracking of paths
Vendors	Nomi, RetailNext, Cisco, Axis Communications, Cognimatics

Li-Fi: Visual Light Communication

"A rooster crows only when it sees the light. Put him in the dark and he'll never crow. I have seen the light and I'm crowing."

—*Muhammad Ali*

LED light vendors have been crowing about the capabilities of the latest generation of lighting technology and it's easy to see why (Figure 16-3). Visual light communication (VLC) or Li-Fi is potentially one of the most disruptive of the alternative and complementary technologies to Bluetooth beacons. The location accuracy it yields is extremely precise, as close as four inches in real-world situations. It can also be used to measure the height and orientation of a phone, so that apps can be informed precisely which way the handset is pointing.

Figure 16-3. *The BREEZ series recessed indirect LED light is typical of what might be used to replace fluorescent lights in a retail environment*

For those of us who have struggled to find a specific type of medication at a pharmacy, imagine a product search app that guides you to the correct aisle, the correct shelf, and then the correct place on the shelf.

However, there are limitations. In order to do this, the app performing the computation has to be in the foreground, and a special LED lighting infrastructure needs to be installed.

Vendors are deploying enhanced LED lighting systems with Bluetooth beacons integrated into the fixtures, in order to offer the best of both technologies to venues and the developers of mobile apps. With this mixture, Bluetooth beacons can be used to trigger alerts that encourage the user to open the app and bring it into the foreground, at which point the LEDs can be used and the greater levels of precision can be achieved. The beacons use an optional radio built into the light fixture (the receptacle the bulb screws into) that can perform other functions such as communicating with control systems (see Figure 16-4) and the other lights via a Bluetooth mesh network.

Figure 16-4. *The Distech controller acts as a gateway between the web and Acuity's BLE-network in the store*

In addition to acting as a beacon, the Bluetooth Smart radios can be used to send control signals to dim the lighting and automatically respond as part of cost and energy saving programs. A "demand response system" can reduce the intensity of lights and their power consumption at extreme peak times when the grid is under pressure, or when elevated consumption is in danger of pushing the retailer into a more expensive pricing band for that month's electricity tariff.

Let's look at how the technology works, who the players are, and some of the business and strategic implications of these impressive capabilities.

Calculating Location Using Light

Communication using light isn't new. The Greeks did it, using signal fires on hilltops over a thousand years BC. The ability to turn an LED light on and off at nanosecond speeds creates a lot more data bandwidth than the Greeks had when passing on the warnings about an approaching enemy.

The speeds used for VLC are so fast the human eye can't detect the flickering. Changing the frequency with which an LED bulb is turned on and off is the basis of transmitting data, which could include media streams or much shorter signals. With the right software analyzing the sighting of multiple lights via a phone's front-facing camera, it's possible to work out the location of the phone (a more serious application for the camera than just taking all those "selfies").

The image from a camera that sees the LED lights is used to calculate the angle of arrival of the light signal from a known position in order to deduce the location of the phone. This works in the same way as mariners observing the angle of arrival of light from the stars in order to navigate. Mariners might identity a set of stars, such as the North (Pole) star and the stars in the Orion constellation, that have a predictable position in the sky and work out their own location based on that.

Each light fixture broadcasts an identity code so that the software on the phone can lookup the location of the fixture in the X, Y, and Z axes. This will have been recorded in the cloud based on a site survey. The SDK provided by the LED vendor can then use trigonometry to deduce the location of the phone in X, Y, and Z axes.

Tungsten and fluorescent lights can't easily transmit identity signals that can be used in this way, so this technique is dependent on the adoption of LED lighting infrastructure.

A Wave of Change in Lighting

Venues are moving to LED lighting, but this isn't happening overnight. Replacement cycles for this kind of technology are slow, occurring on average, once a decade. Replacing lighting in a venue is a large, expensive, and disruptive project. As infrastructure changes go, beacons are at the other end of that spectrum of expense and disruption. You can deploy beacons during the day without shutting the store down. It's unlikely that any venue will replace its lighting just to support indoor location in mobile applications. The costs of the new systems are many thousands of dollars for a large venue. However, if a new store is being built, or an old store is being refurbished, then the ROI for LED lighting is significant. In addition to the energy savings, there are savings due to the longer life of the LED lights, which reduce the spending on bulbs and more significantly, the labor costs associated with installing them in hard to reach locations.

On the one hand this switch to LEDs will take a while to happen; on the other hand, the economics are compelling. It's a major wave of change rippling across venues, irrespective of any proximity engagement opportunities. While the pace may be slower, there is a level of inevitability driven by hard cost savings, which we can't claim for the deployment of Bluetooth beacons.

Large Vendors that Are Committed

The other aspect to consider when predicting the future success of Li-Fi is the commitment of the LED vendors to make this work. We have seen opportunistic, tentative support for Bluetooth beacons from companies such as Facebook and PayPal. Facebook are proceeding slowly and PayPal ended up killing their beacon program after a change in leadership and some trials whose results didn't meet the expectations of the new regime.

For the LED lighting vendors such as Acuity, GE, and Philips, multi-billion dollar companies, making Li-Fi a success appears to be a priority. They see what's happening to their current business model. After the initial wave of replacement and adoption of LEDs has happened, a hole in their revenue flow is opening up that needs to be filled. Once all their customers have switched to LED, the annuity revenue stream from replacing failing light bulbs will shrink dramatically. Filling that hole becomes an imperative. They see proximity services revenue as being a way of filling the approaching revenue gap. This threat and the new opportunity are visible at the top levels of their organizations.

Acuity has shown what seems to be the greatest level of commitment to the opportunity, through multiple corporate acquisitions, including ByteLight and Geometri. They are assembling a focused team of staff with new skills, which are not native to the lighting industry, and a complete stack of analytics and Bluetooth beacon technology.

Philips claims to have intellectual property in this area, has been conducting trials with Target, and elevated their trial project with Carrefour, the French hypermarket giant, to being discussed in their Q2 2015 earnings calls.

GE—whose partnership with ByteLight was aborted when their competitor, Acuity, acquired the startup—is promoting its own indoor location service that includes Bluetooth beacons. Like Acuity, GE has licensed technology from Qualcomm to perform indoor positioning with Li-Fi.

A Timing and Coverage Issue

For retail deployments, it's unlikely that every store in a large chain will switch to LED lighting at the same time. The fact that VLC services may not be available at all stores is not a disqualifier for using the services in a subset of stores, but it can impede the marketing of such services. A retail brand doesn't want to promote demand for a product finder and then disappoint large numbers of shoppers when it's not available in their local store.

VLC Li-Fi Summary

The adoption of VLC has a reassuring inevitability about it. The precision is high, the incremental infrastructure is negligible, and the vendors are motivated and capable.

However, the need to have an app running in the foreground imposes major limitations. It's clear that adoption will be slow-paced relative to beacons. This is a prime example of Bluetooth and another location technology being better together in the same solution. See Table 16-2.

Table 16-2. *Visual Light Communication/Li-Fi Summary*

Coverage	Small proportion of customers; requires app to be installed and running in foreground
Background operation—ability to wake an app that has been terminated	No
Hardware costs	Significant
Deployment considerations	Infrastructure replacement on a 10 year cycle or associated with a new venue. Fragmented availability of the service across different stores, some of which may still have legacy lighting
Accuracy	Excellent—sub-meter down to four inches
Vendors	Acuity, GE, Philips

Magnetic fields in liquid form. Photograph of Ferrofluid flowing from one magnet to another. Ferrofluid is a colloidal liquid of nanoscale particles in a carrier fluid that becomes magnetized when approaching a magnet.

"There is a magnet in your heart that will attract true friends. That magnet is unselfishness, thinking of others first; when you learn to live for others, they will live for you."

—Paramahansa Yogananda, Yogi

Magnetic Resonance

Free is a pretty good price. Bluetooth beacons have disrupted other technologies because of the lower costs associated with the hardware and the lower cost of deployment of these battery powered sensors. One of the challengers to Bluetooth beacons has no capital costs and no maintenance costs.

The magnetic resonance location algorithm uses the compass within a smartphone to measure fluctuations in the magnetic fields that emanate from the earth and the steel within the structure of buildings. This is combined with monitoring of the phone's gyroscope, accelerometer, and a floor plan to perform dead reckoning[1] to estimate the current location of a smartphone.

---

[1]Dead reckoning is the process of calculating one's position, […] by estimating the direction and distance traveled […] Oxford Dictionaries web site.

The steel structure of buildings has a magnetic signature that identifies a location within the structure. The building is surveyed using a smartphone to measure the magnetic fluctuations as the person doing the calibrating walks around the building. A map of the building is loaded prior to doing the survey and the surveyor indicates where they are on the map. See Figure 16-5 for an example.

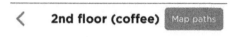

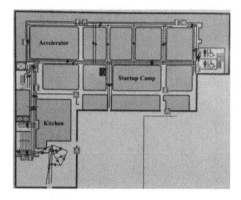

Figure 16-5. *Screenshot of the IndoorAtlas fingerprinting app, used to record the magnetic fields measured during a survey of an office building*

The accuracy of this, for the purpose of performing wayfinding within a big box store, was good 95% of the time (1-3 meters), based on a demonstration this author witnessed. 5% of the time the "blue dot" popped up in the wrong aisle of the Staples store we were in, although the product has improved since then. The experience wasn't perfect, but it was good value for the money.

IndoorAtlas

The leading provider of this technology is IndoorAtlas, a small company that was established in Finland and spun out of the University of Oulu in 2012 (see Figure 16-6). They claim to have a comprehensive patent portfolio on indoor location driven by magnetic resonance. Their survey app now uses Wi-Fi signals to augment the input from magnetic fields and motion.

Figure 16-6. *A wayfinding app powered by IndoorAtlas; the correct floor is identified, the shopper's location, a path to the destination, and a GNC promotion is displayed as the shopper approaches*

All their early wins are in Asia Pacific. Their largest investor and largest customer is Baidu, China's most successful search engine. Other customers include SK Planet in Korea and a chain of shopping malls in Australia.

Like many proximity companies, the product is free when used for modest numbers of users (up to 1000), after which an active user price comes into effect, with pricing per active user less than 20 cents a month.

Given their patent position, there are very few competitors, which works for them at one level but at another level hinders the development of a competitive ecosystem and therefore awareness of the technology. Buyers, and the press, like to have options and competitors to choose from and talk about. One competitor that does exist is a smaller startup called GiPStech. They are based in Italy and use magnetic resonance along with any signals available from existing Wi-Fi and Bluetooth beacons.

Limitations of Magnetic Resonance

Magnetic resonance doesn't work well outside. The technique requires the use of GPS or Wi-Fi to orientate the system so that it knows which building map to use. With that starting point established it also requires the user to be in motion, similar to the way a magnetic stripe on credit card needs to be in motion in order for it to be read.

The other limitations stem from a lack of deep integration by Apple and Google into their operating systems. The app needs to be in the foreground when calculating its location. This is not a technology that can drive an alert to pop up when the app is in the background.

Magnetic Resonance Summary

Where infrastructure deployment and capital costs are at a premium, as it is across hundreds of thousands of venues in China, magnetic resonance deserves serious consideration. It's hard to argue at the price. Given zero cost for the infrastructure, it seems that IndoorAtlas is not getting the mindshare it deserves. Success requires more than just a good idea. IndoorAtlas is seen as a little quirky and "foreign". It will need to overcome this in order to gain broad acceptance in the U.S. market. See Table 16-3.

Table 16-3. *Magnetic Resonance Summary*

Coverage	Small proportion of customers; requires app to be installed and running in foreground
Background operation—ability to wake an app that has been terminated	No
Hardware costs	None
Deployment considerations	No power, data, or devices required in store. Requires a fingerprinting survey, using an app and a floor plan
Accuracy	Requires the handset to be in motion to register the location. Achieves aisle level accuracy with the occasional error
Vendors	Indoor Atlas, GiPStech

Ultra Wide Band

"The wide world is all about you: you can fence yourselves in, but you cannot forever fence it out."

—J. R. R. Tolkien

Ultra Wide Band (UWB) is a radio technology that delivers very impressive accuracy, as fine grain as four inches. It is ahead of many of the competing high-accuracy techniques in the race to market, with production applications operating today. BMW is using Ultra Wide Band technology to help automate its car production line in Regensburg, Germany.

The key dependency on adoption of UWB is an enterprise's willingness to invest in a dedicated UWB infrastructure. UWB beacons are tracked by UWB transceivers. UWB can't track phones, as there's no UWB radio in iOS or Android smartphones. As a result, the application of UWB has been more focused on industrial verticals such as warehouse logistics, manufacturing, and healthcare, where UWB beacons can be attached to forklifts, pallets on the production line, patients, staff, or medical equipment.

Why UWB Is So Much More Accurate

It's interesting to understand why UWB is more accurate than most Bluetooth and Wi-Fi techniques because it's a pretty cool technology and it informs our understanding of Bluetooth and Wi-Fi, as well as UWB.

As its name suggests, Ultra Wide Band uses a very broad range of spectrum (about a thousand TV channels worth) over which to send its signals. This overlaps with the spectrum used by other radio devices. The spectrum used is unlicensed; you don't have to pay to access the airwaves with UWB. The Federal Communications Committee (FCC) permits the overlap with other frequencies because the interference created is so small that the impact is not disruptive to the performance of other wireless signals.

UWB location-tracking solutions use short pulse transmissions across their band of spectrum. This technique is less susceptible to multi-path interference, which is an important advantage. With UWB pulses, it's easier to disregard the pulse signals that arrive via an indirect, reflected path. Multi-path interference is part of what makes proximity measurement with Bluetooth and Wi-Fi signals (which are sustained for longer) less precise for proximity measurement[2].

UWB uses low-power transmissions that provide a range of approximately 50–200 meters. UWB beacons or tags can transmit these pulses very rapidly (up to 200 times a second). This means that very fast movements can be tracked. At their Consumer Electronics Show 2016 keynote presentation, Intel demonstrated the use of UWB sensors on musicians' hands. The musicians moved their hands rapidly through the air to play invisible virtual instruments. Their hand movements were tracked and used to generate sounds that were played in sync with regular, real musical instruments. This required very high fidelity in tracking of movement and a high level of "currency" in order for the instrument to be played in time with the other traditional instruments.[3]

UWB Proximity measurement is performed using time of arrival (ToA) and angle of arrival (AoA) techniques. These measurements are performed using transceiver devices that are placed around a room to perform trilateration of the signals coming from the UWB tags or beacons. As we discuss elsewhere, these techniques are inherently more accurate in fixing a location.

UWB Vendors and Applications

This is not meant to be a comprehensive list of vendors, but we have listed examples of the different types of vendors in the UWB ecosystem.

UWB Chipsets

One of the leading suppliers of UWB chips is decaWave. They claim four-inch accuracy for solutions built with their chipset. They have been active in the standardization efforts since the earliest days and have a long list of value added resellers (VARS) who make development tools, System on Modules (SoMs), devices, applications, and custom solutions based on the decaWave chips. These VARS include Agilion, Bluflux, Ciholas, Idolink, OpenRTLS, Red Point, RTLS, Sewio, Wipelot, and Woxu.

---

[2]The use of signal strength by Wi-Fi and Bluetooth beacons as a proxy for distance is also inherently challenging.
[3]Checkout Grizzly Analytics coverage of the demo and their excellent coverage of RTLS generally at grizzlyanalytics.blogspot.com/2016/01/intels-iot-demos-at-ces-show-importance.html.

Standards Turmoil

The standards history around UWB has been tumultuous. The UWB Forum, which was set up in 2004 to promote the standard, clashed with the rival WiMedia Alliance and disbanded after two of its largest founding members—Freescale and Motorola—left. In 2006 the IEEE committee focused on completing the 802.15.3a standard for UWB disbanded, due to an inability of competing factions within the working group to agree on competing proposals. WiMedia claimed the mantle of developer of UWB standards and produced work focused on use of USB 2.0 over UWB. These were ultimately transferred to the Bluetooth Special Interest Group, Wireless USB Promoter Group. The WiMedia Alliance ceased operations in 2010.

The proposal for Direct Sequence UWB that lost the battle for adoption in what would have been 802.15.3a, later resurfaced and found a home in IEEE Standard 802.15.4-2011. Ultimately the European Telecommunications Standards Institute (ETSI) and the International Standards Organization (ISO) have approved UWB standards. All that maneuvering may have held UWB back from achieving its full potential.

In the chess game that characterizes maneuvering between wireless standards bodies, the UWB queen has been trapped in a corner, much of the market for transmitting large data streams and connecting peripherals in home, office, and industrial locations has been claimed by the Wi-Fi and Bluetooth standards. However, given the strength of UWB for proximity location, this is not checkmate.

Bluetooth wins when a phone needs to be the receiver of the signal from a beacon, but UWB wins when it comes to accurate measurement of distances between beacons and transceiver devices that don't need direct integration with a phone.

UWB Devices

Zebra Technologies is one of the larger solution providers in the UWB space with its Dart product line. We have also referenced them previously as a provider of barcode readers, RFID readers, Wi-Fi access points, and Bluetooth beacons. They provide the following:

- *DartTag*—Powered by 3V batteries that may last up to seven years if the tag is configured to broadcast once a second, IP67 rated, programmable on/off times. 1.57 x 1.57 x 0.78 inches.

- *DartTag badge*—A wearable version of the above; 1.66 x 0.28 x 2.92 inches.

- *Dart sensors*—Receivers of the signals from the UWB tags. These can be daisy chained.

- *Dart hub*—With embedded software, providing power, data, and a synchronized clock for the sensors to which it is connected.

- *DartWand*—Used to inventory and configure the tags.

- *Dart Vision Reader*—An alternative to multiple sensors, for areas that just require presence to be measured, rather than location.

A UWB Integrator and Customer

As solution designers in a cutting edge technology sector you have to be energized and enthused by "the new," while maintaining an appropriate level of skepticism to mitigate the effect of Murphy's Law[4] and the half-truths that are told by those in sales mode.

---

[4]Murphy's Law, which essentially is, "Whatever can go wrong, will go wrong," may have originated from Edward Murphy, an engineer working on research into the human body's tolerance for G-Forces in the 1940s. This R&D project involved crash test dummies, chimpanzees, and a rocket sled mounted on a railroad track. What could possibly go wrong? Read *A History of Murphy's Law* by author Nick T. Spark to find out.

All this is to say that it's a relief, when researching technology, to find credible evidence of actual deployments and a case study that proves the technology delivers what it's supposed to.

Given the claims for UWB's performance, Ubisense's case study of the deployment of their UWB SmartFactory suite at BMW's makes for reassuring reading. Here is a summary drawn from various accounts:

The Situation: UWB at BMW Germany

Ubisense is a British solution provider that focused its application of UWB on the manufacturing sector. It claims to have deployed the technology in over 50 manufacturing facilities, with over 6,000 sensors and 22,000 UWB tags. Its customers include Aston Martin, Audi, Magna, Mini and VW, and BMW.

The BMW installation is at its Regensburg facility in Germany. This factory produces over 1,000 cars a day, with 150 workstations on the 1.9 kilometer production line where 9,000 staff work. Multiple car models are built on the same line, including the BMW 1 Series, BMW 3 Series, BMW M3, BMW Z4, and four-wheel-drive models.

The Problem

With so many interactions and processes occurring simultaneously, errors become inevitable. These resulted in delays and waste, which was proving impossible to monitor and avoid.

The goal was to sustain continuous flow on the production line, optimizing efficiency and reduce the errors, waste, and delays.

The Solution

Over 470 UWB sensors were put in place to monitor the position of the cars and manufacturing equipment such as automated screwdrivers, riveting tools, and inspection devices.

As a vehicle enters a zone, or the equipment approaches a vehicle, the UWB sensors can identify the vehicles and automatically assign and initialize computer assisted process equipment. This eliminates the use of manual barcode scanning, which saves time and avoids mistakes, which can be costly given the products being built.

The UWB sensors were integrated into the existing IT systems at the factory using IBS, a quality management system produced by Siemens.

Results

According to BMW staff, the system completely eliminated costs related to manual tool control, saving hundreds of unproductive hours a day, reducing errors and minimizing the amount of rework that was being done before. Production line stoppages have been reduced and cycle times to produce a car have significantly improved.

Ultra Wide Band Summary

For industrial applications where it's possible to install dedicated sensors and place tags on the objects that need to be tracked, UWB offers high levels of accuracy and set of vertical solutions built on mature technology. See Table 16-4.

Table 16-4. *UWB Summary*

Coverage	Only works when UWB sensors are installed and UWB tags are attached to the assets or people to be tracked
Background operation—ability to wake an app that has been terminated	No
Hardware costs	Situation dependent and high relative to beacons
Deployment considerations	Installation of power for hubs, data lines for sensors. Site survey for location-based applications
Accuracy	Highly accurate and a high level of currency/real time: 10-30 cm
Vendors	decaWave (chips), Zebra Technology (systems), Ubisense (Systems Integrator)

Wi-Fi

"Space is big. You just won't believe how vastly, hugely, mind-bogglingly big it is. I mean, you may think it's a long way down the road to the chemist's, but that's just peanuts to space."

—Douglas Adams, *The Hitchhiker's Guide to the Galaxy*

Given how large the spaces are that we are called upon to help people navigate, it makes sense to leverage a type of infrastructure that is becoming more and more pervasive.

Wi-Fi isn't just about connectivity; it can be used in a number of ways as part of a Real Time Location System (RTLS). In this section, we will look at the use of Wi-Fi access points to track the location of phones. In the next chapter, we will look at the opposite scenario, the phone monitoring the Wi-Fi access points to understand where it is.

The advantage of the access points monitoring the phone is that the phone doesn't need to be running any particular app for this to work. This is a major advantage given that Gartner estimates that "less than 0.01 percent of consumer mobile apps will be considered a financial success by their developers"[5]. Theoretically, every phone with its Wi-Fi radio enabled can be tracked from the access points in a venue. If only it were quite that simple.

In this section, we will look at a variety of the techniques used to enable location tracking via Wi-Fi access points (APs) and discuss some of the key vendors that have commercialized those techniques:

- Cell of origin

- Active versus passive monitoring

- RSSI and angle of arrival

- 802.11mc

- Wi-Fi tags

- Wi-Fi aware

Cell of Origin

While we will look at how vendors have been trying to improve the accuracy of Wi-Fi location systems using some very sophisticated techniques, the simplest level of location tracking can be quite effective, registering the presence of a phone in the range of a given Wi-Fi access point. If that access point is at the entrance to a venue, this may be enough to measure visits to the venue, or at least a representative sample of the visits.

The dwell time of the device, and by extension of that, the person using the device, can be measured. As more devices come within range we can get a sense of how crowded the area becomes over time. These numbers can be used to inform the staffing plans of a venue, to make sure high traffic times have adequate coverage. The duration that customers stay in a store and the correlation of these numbers to sales provides some useful metrics from a relatively crude measure of location.

Every Wi-Fi network device has a unique media access control (MAC) address, which is assigned by the manufacturer. The access point may track these addresses. If the access point sees the same MAC address more than once, this could be used to infer that a visitor has returned. This in turn, could be used as a measure of loyalty. On the other hand, if that MAC address is seen every day, it may not be a loyal customer; it may be that the person who owns the phone is an employee.

As a visitor moves deeper into a venue there will be a handoff to neighboring access points. From this we can get a departmental view of a visitors' movements around the venue. Cisco's CMX platform can be used to pull the data from multiple access points and provide a consolidated view of these numbers within a venue that could have hundreds of access points, even across multiple venues managed as a network.

Active Versus Passive Monitoring

Just because a venue provides Wi-Fi, it doesn't necessarily mean that visitors will use it. Not everyone entering a venue is going to take the time to search for a Wi-Fi network that is available and join it. This reality could make a significant dent in the proportion of phones we can track.

---

[5]Gartner says less than 0.01 percent of consumer mobile apps will be considered a financial success by their developers through 2018; see www.gartner.com/newsroom/id/2648515.

Making sure the Wi-Fi service is fast and easy to join can help increase the number of visitors who use the service. This seems obvious, but you might be excused for thinking that it isn't, given the challenges many of us suffer when trying to use Wi-Fi in some airports and other public places. The reality is that venue owners are generally aware of the frustration caused by slow Wi-Fi, but struggle to justify the costs of the bandwidth and infrastructure to fix the problem. This is a significant challenge if we want to piggyback on such a system for the purposes of using it for real-time location tracking.

Passive monitoring is the monitoring of phones that have Wi-Fi turned on, but haven't joined the network. The prospect of tracking all phones with Wi-Fi turned on, rather than just those that joined a venue's network, is appealing. Unfortunately, there are a few problems with passive monitoring.

Probe Requests

Smartphones, tablets, and laptops will periodically broadcast Probe Request packets to identify the wireless networks that are available. This isn't a constant broadcast. Apple in particular has throttled back how often this is done by iOS. The frequency varies between releases of the same mobile operating system, but iOS 8.1.3 has been measured to broadcast probe requests every 330 seconds, Android L 5.0.1 every 66 seconds.[6]

This means that measuring the location of visitors using probe requests can be limited to measuring their presence in the store, but not their movements within it. A visitor can cover a lot of ground in a minute.

iOS MAC Address Randomization

The other significant issue that was seen as a threat to Wi-Fi analytics companies is that Apple now randomly changes the MAC addresses that iOS devices broadcast in their probe requests. This makes the measure of returning visitors with iPhones a lot harder if the device doesn't associate with the network. It could also inflate the number of visitors reported. One visitor may look like three if their MAC address is rotated three times.

This problem doesn't impact Android devices. Some Wi-Fi analytics vendors assert that Android handsets provide an adequate sample across socioeconomic and demographic segments and iOS handsets can simply be disregarded.

Euclid and the Nordstrom Incident

The other issue is that some people don't think it's appropriate to monitor the presence of phone users passively. When we click through the terms and conditions that are between us and free Wi-Fi, we almost certainly give rights to the venue to track our every movement and maybe even to the life of our first born. However, people who have walked in off the street and have not joined the network have done no such thing.

Nordstrom was sucked into a controversy surrounding its use of Euclid Analytics to monitor customers passively. *Forbes* magazine ran an article with the headline "How Nordstrom Uses Wi-Fi to Spy on Shoppers" in May of 2013. This despite the fact that Nordstrom had posted notices warning customers what they were doing. Shortly after the article was published, Nordstrom stopped using Euclid.

Years have passed since then and Euclid seems to be doing well. Maybe the arms race of oversharing on social media is changing the way new generations think of privacy[7]. Euclid's list of customers has expanded, with over 65 brands using the service. They have succeeded in raising more funding, $20m for expansion. They partner with most of the major Wi-Fi access point providers, so activation of their service doesn't require Wi-Fi upgrades.

---

[6]See "How Talkative Is Your Mobile Device? An Experimental Study of Wi-Fi Probe Requests" by Julien Freudiger PARC (A Xerox Company) at frdgr.ch/wp-content/uploads/2015/06/Freudiger15.pdf.
[7]"The Surprising Benefits of Oversharing," *Harvard Business Review* at hbswk.hbs.edu/item/the-surprising-benefits-of-oversharing.

Euclid started with a vision of bringing Google Analytics capabilities to brick and mortar retailers. As new web savvy marketers join their ranks, retailers are accepting the need to blend their online and offline operations. Having analytics that can measure "bounce rate"[8] and other web style metrics in their stores is increasingly seen as part of that imperative.

Received Signal Strength Indication (RSSI)

By default, the location measurement performed with Wi-Fi analytics is done using RSSI, which is the same method as used with Bluetooth beacons[9]. The accuracy that is yielded is quite poor for the same reasons that impact beacons. The change in signal strength is quite significant when close to the device and much less so the farther the smartphone is from the access point. These differences can be lost in the noise that comes from interference, signal fluctuations, and multi-path effects.

In the case of Wi-Fi, these issues are compounded. The access points are generally placed in the ceiling, because they have to be configured for maximum connectivity and so they don't have the opportunities for flexible configuration and placement that you have with beacons. With beacons, where accuracy is required, the device can be placed close to the point where measurement is required. The signal strength can be dialed down, or the density of beacons can be increased at a lot lower cost than can be done with Wi-Fi access points.

Wi-Fi proximity got a bad reputation for high expense and low accuracy when vendors prescribed increasing the density of the access points, which helped but didn't return great results. One rule of thumb from Cisco is that RSSI will yield accuracy of 8-10 meters.

Trilateration

Wi-Fi analytics software can perform trilateration, which along with AP density, can help increase accuracy. Cisco has a mature Mobility Services Engine product, which is in at least its tenth version and can produce heatmaps and include beacons as a supplement to Wi-Fi.

Angle of Arrival

Similar angle of arrival techniques that we described being used by Quuppa in their Bluetooth product (see Chapter 7 on beacons) are used by a number of Wi-Fi vendors.

Cisco has a Halo, which is a hyperlocation module that can be used to upgrade a regular access point. Halo is a supplementary tubular, 32-part antenna that plugs into the regular access point and surrounds it with a halo. This comes at a cost.

The differences in signal phase coming from a phone are then compared across the 32 antenna elements, in order to compute the angle of arrival, and a much more accurate location estimate can then be delivered through trilateration. Cisco claims Halo can yield one to three meter accuracy. Grumbles from their field organization indicate the accuracy is closer to three meters than to one. Again, the addition of beacons to Halo can help.

---

[8]Bounce rate on a web site is when a visitor to a home page stays briefly and then moves to another site. Euclid calculates bounce rate for retailers as someone leaving a store within five minutes of arriving, based on measuring their presence with Wi-Fi.
[9]See Chapter 5 on standards for a discussion of RSSI.

Ruckus Access points have a multi-part antenna, which according to its sales force is not used to calculate the angle of arrival, but could be used to better isolate the direction of the phone. It appears this isn't done today and the multipart antenna is used in order to optimize connectivity and bandwidth using beamforming[10].

Fine Time Measurement and IEEE 802.11mc

A response to the challenges with using Wi-Fi for precise location and the importance of improving those capabilities is coming in the form of a new Wi-Fi standard, IEEE 802.11mc. This should enable a significant improvement over techniques that use RSSI. Intel claims their chipsets will be able to achieve one to three meters accuracy with IEEE 802.11mc. Chips that support the new standard are available from many of the major chip vendors as of Q1 2106, and it's expected that access points supporting the standard will ship later in that year.

These chipsets are designed to measure the time it takes for the radio packets to be sent between the access point and the mobile device and to estimate the distance that way.

Wi-Fi Tags

Our analysis of Wi-Fi has centered on retail and venues where the goal is to track smartphones, but Wi-Fi infrastructure has much broader applications for tracking objects other than phones.

A small number of companies are manufacturing Wi-Fi tags that are similar to the Bluetooth beacons we see being cranked out by hundreds of companies. Their cost is comparable to a mid- to high-end Bluetooth beacon. The application of these tags is typically for asset and people tracking. Ekahau and Stanley Healthcare (Stanley as in the Stanley knife) are two of the major vendors in this space. Stanley bought Aeroscout and integrated the tags into a broader suite of applications that helps optimize the operations of hospitals and other medical institutions.

The staff and patients can wear the tags to track their respective whereabouts. Babies and mothers can be automatically associated. The tags can maintain a two-way connection with the Wi-Fi access points to return sensor data on temperature, humidity, and motion. They can include buzzers and call buttons.

The tight integration with Stanley's operational systems to monitor everything from staff movements, the finding of valuable medical equipment to hand washing, represents a competitive barrier to entry into the lucrative healthcare market for entrepreneurs considering beacons for similar applications.

Wi-Fi Aware: Neighbor Awareness Networking

Wi-Fi Aware is an emerging standard defined by the Wi-Fi Alliance, the organization behind promoting Wi-Fi standards. Entrepreneurs developing Bluetooth beacons should have some awareness of Wi-Fi Aware. It's starting to be supported in some Wi-Fi chipsets and has been talked of as a potential standard to enable a competing ecosystem of beacons.

The capabilities include proximity ranging and low power operation. Intel, Broadcom, Marvel, Mediatek, and Realtek have all produced chips that have been certified as being complaint with the new standard. It's touted as being OS independent in what it does, but for developers to use it, iOS and Android will need to expose the functionality to developers.

---

[10]With beamforming, rather than broadcasting a Wi-Fi signal in all directions (omnidirectional), an antenna directs the signal narrowly from the AP or beamformer, to the phone or beamformee. This minimizes interference and maximizes signal strength.

Wi-Fi Aware has a lot more functionality than what would be required for beacon support. Another perspective on the standard is that it's more of a competitor to LTE Direct[11], in that it enables a set of peer-to-peer use-cases that enable communication between phones. Use-cases include peer-to-peer gaming and communication between phones in busy environments, where cell network and Wi-Fi networks are congested, bypassing the access points and cell towers, exchanging messages, media (photos at a game or a concert) and voice traffic directly between devices. Apple's support could take the form of integration into Airdrop rather than as an alternative to beacons. It will be interesting to see if Google adds support for the technology in their Nearby API, which already supports audio as well as Bluetooth to implement proximity services.

Wi-Fi Direct may enable the likes of Stanley and Ekahau to enhance their products and may grow the segment they are in with beacons that communicate more efficiently with more hooks into the mobile operating systems.

Don't Panic

It will be hard for Wi-Fi Aware tags to threaten the role of Bluetooth tags unless Apple enables these devices to awaken apps that are in background mode. This seems unlikely. Without this a Wi-Fi tag is not going to have the ability to drive proximity alerts in iOS. This capability underpins a large part of the Bluetooth beacon value in marketing and analytics applications.

Wi-Fi Summary: Wi-Fi versus Bluetooth Beacons

Journalists love a fight, but the relative position of these two radio technologies in the Real Time Location Systems market is more nuanced and complex than the knock down drag-out fight that makes for a good headline.

Bluetooth beacon hooks into iOS and the ability to awaken apps is a cornerstone to beacon usage that will be hard to dislodge. The Bluetooth beacon ecosystem is large and diverse. Beacon costs are low. Features and functions are many. Every major Wi-Fi access provider we looked at is embracing Bluetooth beacons as another node in the networks that they can charge enterprises to manage.

Some, like Cisco, are incorporating beacons into their Wi-Fi positioning systems to increase accuracy at a lower cost and add more flexibility than can be achieved by increasing the density of access points.

Aruba dropped support for Wi-Fi as the basis for their Meridian RTLS system and completely switched to Bluetooth. Apparently this was because of the issues with having to associate with the Wi-Fi network, in order to track location effectively, the passive monitoring of Probe Requests issue and costs, accuracy, flexibility, and a perception that Bluetooth has a better privacy story.

On the other hand, with 802.11mc increasing the accuracy of the tracking of devices that are associated with the network, there is real value in leveraging this communications infrastructure that is already present in Wi-Fi networks.

The Wi-Fi providers have a strong motivation to claim their share of the revenue from beacon fleet management. They have a powerful installed base and a large trusted sales force.

It's likely that Cisco, master of the business of acquisitions, will snatch up some bargains as the Bluetooth beacon startups with value to add run low on cash. So the blurring of the lines between these ecosystems could continue.

---

[11]LTE Direct is a device-to-device technology using (telcos) licensed spectrum, bypassing the need to use cell towers for cell phones to communicate with each other. Information is exchanged using structured packets of data, enabling applications such as social networking, advertising, and gaming.

The best way to ensure harmony between warring nations in centuries past was for the rulers to intermarry. If acquisitions are the business equivalent of that, we may see more love than war as these mergers take place. See Table 16-5.

Table 16-5. *Wi-Fi Summary*

Coverage	Comparable to Bluetooth; all Smartphones have Wi-Fi, but it's not always turned on (of course neither is Bluetooth)
Background operation—ability to wake an app that has been terminated	No
Hardware costs	For low levels of accuracy using existing access points, hardware costs can be lower
Deployment considerations	Wi-Fi infrastructure is already in place; upgrades are needed for higher levels of accuracy
Accuracy	Departmental location accuracy with meter-level accuracy possible
Vendors	Cisco, HP Aruba, Ruckus, Zebra Technology

Summary

We have discussed some impressive technologies with which to build a real-time location solution. Between machine vision, LED lighting, magnetic resonance, Ultra Wide Band, and Wi-Fi, our toolbox seems pretty full.

We don't have time or space to get into the details of another set of proximity and location tools: audio, ultrasound, and infrared, but they have their place. Maybe that place is deeper in the toolbox, but they are there.

Shazam uses audio as a way to bridge the digital and the physical worlds very successfully; Shopkick used ultrasonic beacons to authenticate user's check-in to stores. They then moved to Bluetooth beacons as a lower cost, more secure solution. Infrared beacons are in the field, used as an option for asset tracking in Warren Buffet's furniture warehouse stores.

But wait, there's more. In the following chapters in this alternative technology section of the *Hitchhiker's Guide to the Beacosystem,* we will consider cellular networks, barcodes, QR codes, RFID, NFC, and GPS.

The thing that nearly all of these technologies have in common is that their usage, rather than being mutually exclusive to Bluetooth beacons, is often being blended with beacons to deliver the required user experience.

CHAPTER 17

Geofencing: Everything You Need to Know

Patrick Leddy, Founder and CEO, Pulsate

In the race to become more connected with our customers, a company's ability to build a "customer context stack" will define its overall success.

Hybridizing multiple customer data points from the virtual and physical worlds helps us understand the true expression of who customers are and what they are doing each and every moment. These "mobile moments" provide excellent opportunities to deepen the relationship and create value for both businesses and their customers.

© Stephen Statler 2016
S. Statler, *Beacon Technologies*, DOI 10.1007/978-1-4842-1889-1_17

Inside the context stack, there are many layers, from real-time CRM data to customer location and proximity, which were covered in great detail by my peers in other chapters.

This chapter is about geofencing and its role in the context stack; how it works, how you should implement a best practice solution, and how you can utilize it to influence customer behavior.

Geofences are virtual perimeters that mark locations in the physical world. Unlike their indoor cousins (beacons), geofences do not require the deployment of any physical hardware.

Geofencing comes in many forms and it is nearly as old as the mobile phone itself. In the beginning, mobile operators used cell tower identifiers to approximate the user's physical location.

Early use-cases involved sending SMS marketing campaigns for brands, inventory tracking, and even law enforcement. Many a homicide case has been solved with the release of cell tower data from the operator, helping to place the suspect at the scene of the crime, or to prove their innocence.

This chapter focuses mostly on the marketing applications of geofencing. While mobile operators still offer geo-based SMS broadcasts, this is becoming less scaleable and, dare I say, even spammy.

Enter the App

The next generation of geofencing happens at a mobile app level. It does not involve the mobile operator directly and it combines a range of modern technologies and techniques to engage customers. App-level geofencing should respect the three Ps of mobile: *permission, privacy,* and *preference*.

Permission

Users need to actually download your mobile app. By downloading your app, they are signaling that they want to engage with your company on some level. In addition to downloading your app, in order for the geofencing component to work correctly, they need to give permission for location services to be turned on.

Privacy

Users should not be tracked persistently in the background. The locations visited prior to breaching the geofence are unknown. The mobile device's operating system wakes up the app in the background only when users arrive at the geofence location.

Preference

The engagement should also be strictly on the users own terms. If you spam them with irrelevant communications, or if they feel you are misusing their data, they can easily revoke the location authorization or delete your app entirely.

Setting Up a Geofence

To set up a geofence, follow these steps:

1. Start by defining a physical location using a latitude, longitude, and radius around the location you want to geofence.

2. Next, your mobile app should instruct the OS to monitor for this location. When the user arrives at that location, the OS immediately awakes the app and it can then take some kind of action.

Once you have set up the geofence, you need to consider the use-cases that you want to implement. The three types of action discussed in this chapter are engaging users at the point of entry (push notification), delaying the engagement for a period of time, and tracking the event for analytical purposes.

Before we deep dive into this at an implementation level, let's examine some popular geofence use-cases and compare them with beacon use-cases.

Right Place, Time, and Message

The use-cases described next are by no means an exhaustive list, but rather a few solid ideas to get you started.

Promote, Incentivize, and Reward

Geofences can be an excellent way of reminding customers about a promotion while they are in the area. Previously, you may have sent a push notification earlier in the week with a coupon or some kind of offer, so now is the time to remind them to pay you a visit.

> *"Physically interacting at the right place and time with immediate value builds loyalty and drives sales."*

You can also use a technique known as *random intermittent reinforcement*. The idea is to reward the customers with a treat when they are nearby. Customers perceive this as a random act of kindness and are incentivized to visit your location.

There is no mention in the app of this seemingly random event so it is a surprise for the customer and they don't expect it every time. Of course, it's not random at all, because you base this heavily on segmentation data and rules. For example, one potential segment to target with such a campaign could be, "high-value customers who have not transacted in 30 days and are in the area right now". When you bring personalization and CRM data into this at scale (a calibrated treat for each customer), it can drive significant foot traffic to your location.

Stamp Out Promiscuous Behavior

Geofences are completely virtual; you can place them anywhere in the world. This is where it gets interesting. As part of your geofencing strategy you might want to consider geofencing competitor locations. Knowing when and how often "loyal" customers frequent competitors can add an incredible new dimension to your engagement strategy.

However, sending cheeky push notifications to customers as they arrive at a competitor's location might be crossing the "freaky" line. If you must interject, put a delay on these communications so that it happens later in the day and not while the customer is still at the location. An even better approach is to process this as an analytic event and feed it back into the overall customer view.

Later, you can segment customers who visited competitors versus your own locations and compute an internal loyalty score. The campaigns that you run against different cohorts can be calibrated based on this score; promiscuous customers get different offers and communications to try to modify their previous behavior.

Remind Them the Right Way

When you connect your CRM and loyalty system with the rest of your mobile strategy, don't forget to remind customers how many points they have and when they expire. Do this via a push notification when they arrive at your geofence. Bonus points if you can highlight products the customer is interested in at the same time.

Spike Feelings of Accomplishment

If your app features a check-in function, which is essentially enabling your customers to tell their social media following that they are at XYZ company's location, make sure to remind them of this function with a push notification upon arrival at the location. Don't forget to incentivize this with extra points, unlocking some Easter egg within the app such as social status or some kind of virtual currency. Spiking feelings of accomplishment and helping the customer convey their status are two of the most powerful emotional loyalty switches that you can flip inside a customer's mind.

Ask Them How They Feel

When a customer leaves a geofence around your location, you could delay sending them a communication by an hour and then ask them about their experience of visiting your company on that day. Remember to also provide an incentive for completing the survey. The customer is on a mobile device so keep it short and ask multiple choice questions rather than forcing them to type answers.

Regional Campaigns

Location-based marketing is like a Russian doll. The outer layers, the big dolls, can be defined by geofences. As you peel back the layers and approach the center, beacons come into play.

Large geofence perimeters may be used to segment regional campaigns. If the Superbowl is being played in Miami, a geofence around Florida may be appropriate to encourage local fans to buy tickets for the event. However, such messaging may not be appropriate in other states that have no connection to that year's Superbowl.

Campaigns that are targeted at regions such as the West Coast can be focused simply on the relevant users within a geofence, capturing large portions of the user base that will most likely be far from any beacons that you might use for closer proximity marketing.

Remind Them to Turn On Bluetooth

Even though Bluetooth beacons have given us an incredible ability to target users on an extremely micro level, they become useless when the customer has Bluetooth switched off. The number of customers that have Bluetooth powered on hovers at around the 30% mark for the United States and can be dramatically lower in other counties.

Geofences and beacons are complementary in a range of scenarios, especially when you use a geofence to encourage a user to switch Bluetooth on. If you geofence a location that also contains beacons, it is a good idea after fence entry to check the current Bluetooth status of every device. If it is set to off, you could surface a reminder. "Hi Joe, just a quick reminder to turn on Bluetooth to experience in-store treats and rewards." The most important thing to remember is that you can use geofences to give customer's concrete reasons to switch Bluetooth on.

The Battle of the Location Technologies

When you design location-based use-cases, it is probable that more often than not you will use multiple technologies, beacons, and geofences together in harmony to achieve your goal. Let's begin by comparing the advantages and drawbacks of each technology.

Beacons are a reliable technology once Bluetooth is powered on. They are generally used indoors for understanding very granular proximities. On the other hand, geofences depend on having Wi-Fi turned on (to improve accuracy) and can cover very large areas. We can also geofence competitor locations, which is not possible in most cases with beacons. When it comes to understanding customers inside a building, geofences aren't very helpful because they generally cover large areas of 100 meters and above. Steel and concrete in buildings can also disrupt the radio signals we use to deliver geofence messaging.

Geofences

Pros	Cons
Does not require Bluetooth	Requires Wi-Fi
Can cover massive areas	Does not work well indoors
Can target competitors	Covers large areas: 100 meters and above
No hardware purchase or maintenance	
Instant deployment	

Beacons

Pros	Cons
Works indoors	Requires Bluetooth
Can be very granular	Can only deploy in locations you control
Reliable	Cannot cover very large areas
	Hardware purchase and some maintenance required
	Deployment lead-time

It's clear from this comparison that these two technologies are used for very different reasons and can be used to complement each other.

You should approach the design of location-based use-cases by thinking about customer context and journey. Each customer's journey usually starts long before she walks through your door, and therefore you can divide use-cases into inside the building and outside the building activities. Geofences are excellent for engaging with customers before they reach your location and they can, in fact, be the reason why some customers are visiting your location in the first place.

If geofences are the key driver of foot traffic to a location, beacons are the key enablers of engagement after users enter that location. Where geofences can help identify users within 300 meters of a store and invite them inside, beacons offer greater granularity in terms of what product the customer might be standing beside. Neither geofences nor beacons alone represent a silver bullet for engagement, they are merely the trigger event. Your orchestration layer in conjunction with CRM data needs to be clever enough to start interesting and engaging conversations with customers based on these trigger events.

All Geofences Are Not Created Equal

Whether you build your own geofence solution in-house or use a third-party solution, it is important to note that many providers have different definitions of what geofencing is and how it should work. There are two main types of geofencing solutions that you can build or buy and each comes with its own time, cost, accuracy, and availability implications.

We have provided a checklist at the end of the chapter that outlines what you should aim for when building or buying a geofencing solution. The methods listed next are solutions achievable across both iPhone and Android smartphones.

Active

Only works when the App is open. Implementation difficulty: Medium.

The user has your app open and the app initializes the GPS radio to get high-accuracy latitude and longitude of the user's current location. You then determine if the user's position is inside or outside a list of predetermined locations held either inside the app itself locally or stored remotely on a server.

If you are building an active geofence solution, it is desirable to send location events (when the app is open) to the server to be checked against the database. The benefits of this are two fold. First, it allows you to add new geofences remotely without needing to update your app. Second, it shifts the processing power requirements away from the mobile device to the server, which is usually far more powerful.

You will need to build logic within your server component that takes the location event from the mobile device, with the latitude and longitude, and computes it against the list of geofences (latitude, longitude, and radius) stored in the database to determine if the user is inside or outside of the geofence. While describing this logic in detail is outside the scope of this chapter, one idea might be to base your data store on MongoDB; a popular NoSQL database technology that makes it easier than ever to compute location data in a performant and scalable way.

Once you have implemented your active geofencing solution, you now have the ability to very accurately determine if a user is inside or outside of specific locations. This is an accuracy that passive geofencing cannot compete with. As GPS data is being used here, you can create incredibly small geofences, sometimes as small as 10 meters, and reliably determine if users are inside or outside of these locations and take resulting action based on that.

There is one major caveat with this implementation: users must have the app open on their screens and be "actively" using it for you to determine if they are inside the geofence or not. Depending on your use-case and business goals, this might be a perfectly acceptable tradeoff. However, in our experience most of the companies we have worked with do not like this approach. Their use-cases depended on engaging customers as they pass by, or tracking them when they visit a competitor. We can't rely on users coincidentally having our app open at the exact moment they enter one of our fences. Therefore, active geofencing can be a good way of understanding where customers are after they arrive and if they are likely to use your app as part of a visit to your location but it is not a suitable method to drive foot traffic, track competitors, or to achieve the use-cases described earlier in this chapter.

It is therefore surprising that quite a number of geofencing solutions on the market only allow what is termed as *active geofencing*. If you are implementing this method you should only request one high-accuracy location update (GPS). Do this immediately when the app opens, and then shut down any further location updates to minimize power usage. Requesting high-accuracy location updates makes heavy use of the GPS radio, one of the most battery-intensive tasks on a mobile device.

Passive

Works when app is open, closed, and even terminated. Difficulty level: Hard.

Passive geofencing is a different animal entirely and while it doesn't produce the same accuracy as the "active" method, it does work in the background. This means your app can be closed or terminated out of memory. The phone can be in your pocket and the screen darkened. This presents obvious advantages over the "active" method, as it does not rely on the users having the app open at the point that they enter a geofence.

The only tradeoff is that we cannot be as accurate as with the "active" method. Passive fencing generally won't let you create geofences smaller than 100 meters.

So why the difference in accuracy? Generally speaking, the passive method uses very little or no GPS data (a very different approach to active) and instead relies on a combination of cellular and Wi-Fi data.

As we cannot rely on our app being open (it may even have been terminated by the user), we must enlist the support of some native operating system APIs to help us out. iOS comes with an API as part of CoreLocation called *RegionMonitoring* (the same API we use to monitor for beacons). Before beacons were even invented, developers could ask the RegionMonitoring API to monitor for a geofence by providing it with a latitude, longitude, and radius.

The app can then go to sleep without fear of being terminated, comfortable in the knowledge that the iOS will wake the app back up (in the background) and tell it if any of the geofences that you are monitoring for have been breached. The app can then take a resulting action such as surfacing a local notification or a piece of content because it knows that the fence has been breached. More advanced mobile marketing SDKs could take the geofence entry event from the OS and then network out to an API. From there, a web-based platform could ingest the geofence event, check who the users are, determine their segments and frequency caps, and then decide whether to send a campaign.

As part of iOS and Android's normal operation, they constantly connect to cell towers and scan for available Wi-Fi networks. The native geofencing APIs mentioned previously leverage existing device services, meaning that they do not cause any additional battery drain. The OS manufacturers have a database of where each cell tower is physically located. When your phone is connecting to a cell tower to maintain network, it is very easy for the phone to become location-aware. The cell tower data will give a location in terms of several hundred meters of accuracy, but when Wi-Fi data is brought into the mix, things get a lot more accurate.

iPhone and Android devices actually crowdsource the plotting of Wi-Fi networks or specific SSIDs to very accurate latitudes and longitudes. When an iPhone or Android device sees an SSID not previously known to Apple or Google, the operating system will fire up GPS in the background and tag the location of that SSID and then send it back to the Google or Apple database.

When we enlist the help of the native geofence APIs on the device, it is combining the cell towers that it sees along with what Wi-Fi networks it encounters. Note that you don't have to be connected to these Wi-Fi networks; this is ambient scanning of available Wi-Fi in the vicinity of the user's device. As practically all Wi-Fi SSIDs have previously been location tagged, it's very easy for the OS to know where it is located and determine if any geofences have been breached.

As Wi-Fi data is heavily employed for passive geofencing, we generally advise that geofencing does not work accurately if Wi-Fi is turned off on the device (which will be a portion of your user base). In nearly all cases, you will not see a geofence event callback from OS when Wi-Fi is turned off. In rare situations, the user might open another app that uses GPS data. In these cases, the OS will take the more accurate GPS data used by that other app and could use that to determine that the user is inside a geofence.

At first glance, the passive method seems like an attractive option. With the built-in native APIs you tell the OS where you want to geofence, it wakes up your app at the right time and place with all the heavy lifting taken care of. Simple, right?

Unfortunately, it is not that straightforward. While you might get some encouraging results in proof of concept mode, you will run into problems as you scale. There are some underlying peculiarities or bugs with the way these native geofencing APIs perform.

Working with iOS

If you are implementing geofencing on iOS, you need to be aware of certain issues and limitations of the native APIs.

Bursting

iOS has an issue that happens when monitoring for multiple geofences. The effect is that intermittently you will get callbacks for every geofence you are monitoring for, even though of course you cannot be in 20 places at once. If you want to test this for yourself, launch the native Reminders app on iOS (it uses the same API), add a bunch of tasks, and then tag them against locations. Usually you will get reminded of each task as you approach the correct location. Every so often, however, you will get notifications for all of the tasks at the same moment.

False Alarms

On occasion, the operating system will report you as being at a geofence that could be several miles away. Your phone can connect to cell towers over great distances, and occasionally, it might make a momentary connection to a tower that is far away. In the absence of the ambient Wi-Fi data to verify your location, this seems to trick Region Monitoring into thinking you are in the wrong location.

Circles Only

The native geofencing APIs allow you to define only circular geofences so you cannot create a polygonal boundary around a rectangular area.

20 Geofences Limit

You are limited to monitoring for 20 geofences at the same time with the native geofencing APIs and this is a big constraint if you have a lot of locations. This frustrated us for some time until we came up with a better way of doing it. The solution is pretty straightforward, so we will detail it here.

Solving the 20 Fence Limit

The trick is to pull down a list of geofence locations you want to monitor for, ideally from a remote server. Then, pass the latitude, longitude, and radius of the nearest 1,000 fences (for example) to that user. One thousands fences is quite a lot, so it could be all of the fences for that state or country. You should then store the 1,000 locations locally, putting 20 of the nearest locations into Region Monitoring memory slots.

At that point you should instrument another native iOS API called SignificantChange Location. This wakes up the app (in the background) with every cell tower change as the user moves through a location. The OS gives us the nearest approximate location (latitude and longitude). The app is now awake in the background following the cell tower change. You should use the user's new location and the Haversine formula (Google it) to calculate the nearest 20 geofence locations to the user's current location.

At that point, swap the nearest 20 fences into Region Monitoring's memory and repeat the process for every cell tower change. This means that you will be constantly monitoring for the nearest 20 geofences. Using SignificantChange Location will not cause additional battery drain because the OS has to handle cell tower change events as part of its normal operation.

Working with Android

If you are implementing geofencing on Android, you need to be aware of certain issues and limitations of the native APIs.

Limits and Power Use

Android supports 100 geofences per app (the more geofences the greater the power usage, so it's smart to load less than 100 geofences and update the geofence list every 1km).

Sensor Usage

For Android geofencing, you should use the Fused Location API and Geofencing API. The Fused Location API uses GPS, Wi-Fi, cell towers, and phone sensors. Data from sensors can help reduce power consumption because we do not need to request location updates while the user is not moving.

Accuracy and Intervals

Priority:

- PRIORITY_HIGH_ACCURACY—Use this setting to request the most precise location possible. With this setting, the location services are more likely to use GPS (Global Positioning System) to determine the location.

- PRIORITY_BALANCED_POWER_ACCURACY—Use this setting to request location precision to within a city block, which is an accuracy of approximately 100 meters. This is considered a coarse level of accuracy and is likely to consume less power. With this setting, the location services are likely to use Wi-Fi and cell tower positioning. Note, however, that the choice of location provider depends on many other factors such as what sources are available.

- PRIORITY_LOW_POWER—Use this setting to request city-level precision, which is an accuracy of approximately 10 kilometers. This is considered a coarse level of accuracy and is likely to consume less power.

- PRIORITY_NO_POWER—Use this setting if you require negligible impact on power consumption and still want to receive location updates when available. With this setting, your app does not trigger any location updates, but receives locations triggered by other apps.

The Interval method sets the rate in milliseconds at which your app prefers to receive location updates. Note that the location updates may be faster than this rate if another app is receiving updates at a faster rate, or slower than this rate, or there may be no updates at all (if the device has no connectivity, for example).

Geofence Vendor Checklist

Whether you are thinking of building or buying, the following checklist should serve as a shopping list to create a reliable, accurate, and scalable solution:

	Should not require the deployment of hardware
	Should work passively, when the screen is off, and when the app is closed and even terminated
	Should not use GPS in background modes
	Should not create excessive battery drain
	Can be managed and updated remotely
	Should provide for better accuracy and reliability above and beyond default operating system APIs
	Should overcome known issues with default system APIs

Summary

Geofencing is an incredible way to target customers. When blended with CRM data and real-time data segmentation, we can begin to understand customer context in the exact moment. Geofences placed nicely with beacons allow us to drive foot traffic to the location, then allow the beacons to do their job of delivering more granular context. You need to think about what use-cases are important for your business.

Finally, in building your geofencing solution, you need to decide what your business objectives are and what trade-offs active versus passive (accuracy versus availability) you are willing to make. Do you need high accuracy when the users have the app open, or do you need to wake the app up when users are broadly in your area? Only you can decide, based on your own unique use-cases.

CHAPTER 18

∎ ∎ ∎

Barcodes, QR Codes, NFC, and RFID

Theresa Mary Gordon and Steve Statler

In this chapter we will review several proximity technologies that enable automated identification of physical objects and provide alternatives to Bluetooth beacons:

- Barcode and QR (Quick Response) code technologies, which enable interactions with tags that are "in sight"

- Radio Frequency Identification (RFID) and Near Field Communication (NFC), which enable interactions with radios that are generally "in reach" but may be out of sight

© Stephen Statler 2016

S. Statler, *Beacon Technologies*, DOI 10.1007/978-1-4842-1889-1_18

We will outline and compare their various functions with regard to consumer marketing and business applications.

Each technology provides a different trigger for communication, object identification, data collection, and dissemination or experience customization.

Criteria for Comparison: One of These Things Is Not Like the Other...

The key criteria we will use to compare these technologies are:

- Distance—How far or close does an object need to be to work

- Device or application—What do you need to have or can you use to collect and decipher the information

- Visibility—Does the object need to be in sight or in reach of the device

Based on these straightforward factors, we will analyze the traits and values of RFID, NFC, barcodes, and QR codes. We will see how these impact deployment and adoption of each, and will then outline, in more detail, the amount and types of data they can each hold. Finally, we will look at costs associated with each and some specific business use-cases.

A Quick Overview

Barcodes (Figure 18-1) were the first commercially distributed system created to automate the decoding of a number from an image in order to identify a product. Dedicated scanners were originally required to read the codes. These projected a light (sometimes a laser) onto the barcode and read the reflected light with a photosensor that was "scrubbed" over the image.

Figure 18-1. A barcode encoding the text "Hitchhikers Guide" created with www.morovia.com/free-online-barcode-generator

RFID radios are embedded in devices and tags and can often resemble a paper sticker. Under the surface, they have a metallic layer that is a radio antenna and a tiny integrated circuit (IC) (see Figure 18-2). The IC stores and processes the data to be transmitted, collects the electrical power over the air (from the RFID reader signal, which provides enough energy to transmit the code back to the reader), and creates the radio frequency (RF) signal for the transmission.

Figure 18-2. *The under side of an RFID tag exposing the metallic antenna*

Both barcodes and RFID tags are applied to objects so they can quickly be scanned, identified, and tracked so that the information can be shared digitally.

However, barcodes are a "line of sight" technology. They may provide a similar function as RFID tags, but they need to be seen by a reader to provide data. RFID only needs to be in reach to engage a reader.

Both barcodes and RFID tags have evolved offspring with enhanced and specialized functionality. They have "begat" the QR code (Figure 18-3) and NFC tag, respectively.

Figure 18-3. *QR code encoding* www.hitchhikersguidetothebeacosystem.com *created using* www.morovia. com/free-online-barcode-generator/qrcode-maker.php

QR codes are also a line of sight technology. They need to be seen by a reader to provide data. You can read the QR code in Figure 18-3 with Scan (www.scan.me[1]), one of the many apps available on Apple's App Store and Google Play that reads QR codes. QR codes are basically two-dimensional barcodes. They were initially deployed in Japanese car manufacturing and gained wider adoption due to their increased capacity to store information and the speed with which they can be read compared to one-dimensional codes.

NFC (Figure 18-4) is based on RFID technology, with a restricted range of up to 10 centimeters. Its applications have been standardized around a set of use-cases that are simple and easy to execute. Unlike RFID, NFC is supported by most smartphones, although Apple has restricted NFC on the iPhone to only work with Apple Pay. NFC's sweet spot is use for payments, setting up other wireless connections, identification and access tokens, social networking, smartphone task automation, and smart poster manual check-in (see Figure 18-5).

Figure 18-4. *Two NFC tags next to a one-cent coin[2]*

---

[1]When Snapchat, the social media platform used by young people who want their posts to be temporary, bought the Scan.me company, they instantly made QR codes a lot cooler. A unique Snapchat Snapcode is associated with each user's profile. Snapchat users can follow each other by scanning these icons, which can be printed on posters and T-shirts and added to web pages.

[2]The one cent Euro coin is comparable in size to a U.S. one cent. Image courtesy of Holgerjakobs under license creativecommons.org/licenses/by-sa/4.0/legalcode

Figure 18-5. *"Intel flushes away lengthy process for toilet paper requests"[3] with near field communication and QR code, barcode, NFC, QR code, RFID technology comparison*

[3]"Deep in the bowels of Intel headquarters in Santa Clara, Calif., the restrooms have been plumbed with technology." "There is [generally] a 15- to 30-second time period from when a person sees something to when they will report it—if you make it really easy," said Maestas. "Outside that 30-second window, the opportunity is lost." www.intelfreepress. com/news/intel-takes-toilet/7787/

	Barcodes	QR Code	RFID	NFC
Technology	Digital image	Digital image	RF (Radio Frequency)	RF (Radio Frequency)
Operating frequency	Varies by system	Varies by system	125 or 134kHz	13.56MHz
Range	Up to a few meters (as codes are scaled up in size)	scanning distances vary by image size	With a handheld UHF reader ~10 feet for passive tags/active tags can be read from 100-1,500 feet (many variables)	Up to 8 inches
Data exchange rate	Varies by system	Up to 177 × 177 modules	Up to 640Kbps	424Kbps
Active/passive	N/A	N/A	Passive/active/ semi-passive	Passive/active/ semi-passive
Read rate	One at a time	One at a time	Up to 1000s simultaneously	One at a time
Communication modes	Read	Read	Read/write	Read/Write, Peer to Peer, Card Emulation
Line of sight	Required	Required	Not required	Not Required
Interference	Environmental obstructions	Environmental obstructions	Possible metal/liquid interference	Possible metal interference
Data storage	14 numeric digits for the GS1 standard	Depends on complexity of image	Generally 2KB	Varies by tag; on average: 64, 128 or 512 bytes and 1024 bytes, can go upward of 8KB
Common applications	Data exchange, ID, inventory, ticketing	Advertising, authentication, information delivery, packaging, ticketing	Asset tracking, data exchange, ID, inventory, labeling, loss prevention, ticketing	Access, advertising, authentication, connectivity, data exchange, information delivery, packaging, payment, ticketing
Technology Native to Mobile Devices	No, read using barcode scanner	No, requires an app	No, requires an RFID reader	Yes
Automation	Requires user	Requires user	Can be automated	Requires user
Global Uniform Standard	GS1, UPC/EAN	ISO/IEC 18004-2006	ECPglobal Gen2 (ISO 18000-6C)	NFC Data Exchange Format (NDEF)
Consumer Focused Applications	No	Yes	Yes	Yes
Communication	One-way	One-way	Usually one-way, but can be two-way	Two-way

Barcodes

Barcodes were developed to solve a problem in the grocery industry. Stores were in need of a way to speed up the checkout process, and the solution sought was a way to tag items to enable them to be scanned and processed quickly. A faster checkout allows for lower levels of staffing while maintaining shorter lines, which leads to higher customer satisfaction and retention.

As with most new technologies, the path to the market was not linear and involved years of development, experimenting with circular codes, different inks, printing technologies, and scanner systems. Insights were also gleaned from a similar solution called KarTrak ACI that was deployed in the railroad industry to label train cars. It is said that the first true deployment of barcodes in retail began with the scanning of a pack of Wrigley's gum in a supermarket in Ohio in June of 1974.

Since then, a variety of different techniques that govern the way characters are encoded using changes in the relative size and spacing of the lines within barcodes have been developed. These are known as *symbologies*, and each is designed for a specific use-case and business vertical.

Barcode Symbologies

For example, Universal Product Code (UPC) barcodes are the barcodes we see in the grocery store and on retail products that are used for checkout and inventory. A UPC contains 12 numeric digits. There are also postnet barcodes, which the U.S. Postal Service uses for ZIP codes; maxicodes, which the United Parcel Service (UPS) uses and are both vertical and horizontal and contain up to 93 alphanumeric characters; Optical Character Recognition (OCR-A and OCR-B) barcodes, which are human-readable versions of codes; and Magnetic Ink Character Recognition (MICR), which is a special font for bank checks.

Barcode Scanners

As there are different symbologies, there are also a variety of types of scanners. One that should be familiar to all of us is the barcode reader, also called a point-of-sale (PoS) scanner, which can be a handheld or stationary input device.

The stationary versions—the laser scanners embedded in the flow desk of checkout systems—use lasers that are optimized for reading barcodes that may be positioned at odd angles or difficult to read with other systems, such as if the printing has become smudged or damaged.

The handheld scanners found more commonly at convenience stores and in some other retail categories are being switched to optical scanners that don't require the code to be scrubbed past. This is being driven because the laser scanner cannot read barcodes or QR codes displayed on phones, a need that is becoming increasingly more common.

When enterprises develop coupon, membership, or payment systems that rely on the entry of a code at the points-of-sale, they need to be aware of whether the PoS has laser scanners or optical scanners. Trying to read barcodes of any kind on phone screens with a laser scanner will not work.

UPC Codes

When creating a product that needs to be scanned at PoS systems across multiple retailers, it will be necessary to purchase Universal Product Code (UPC) codes. Not all products require UPC codes. Consider your local fast food store, where the product range is limited and PoS are configured with a button per product. Your coffee and croissant don't need to be scanned. Purchasing and maintaining a UPC prefix, a barcode from the GS-1, can be quite expensive. GS-1 is a neutral, not-for-profit, international organization that oversees, develops, and maintains standards for barcodes for use in supply chains across multiple industries. The cost can range from $250 up to $10,000+ for unique barcodes depending on how many you need. There is also an annual renewal fee for participation in the GS1 that can range from $50 to $2,100.

These, and hardware costs for readers, are key operational costs in the consumer, health, and retail industries.

Quick Response Codes

For the many companies who had successfully deployed one-dimensional barcodes as part of their inventory and point-of-sale process, moving to two-dimensional QR codes for messaging or marketing did not take a particularly big leap of faith. Barcodes were already being scanned at checkout to collect product information and speed up the process, so maybe with QR codes this same approach could be used to work for other purposes as well, as we will see later.

The patterns of square dots arranged in a grid used for QR codes, in addition to having advantages of speed and capacity over one-dimensional codes, incorporate redundancy and error correction. This helps to deal with the wear and tear of codes that are damaged in people's purse, wallet, or warehouse. The additional dimension also permits more creative presentation with other embedded images being added to the QR code and the presentation of the codes in different colors.

For our purposes, QR codes are similar to beacons in that a consumer or end user must have an app to interact with them. With a beacon, Bluetooth must be on and a beacon-enabled app must be downloaded. With QR codes, the user must have the QR-enabled app downloaded on their phone to collect and decipher the data from the image.

Cost Effective

QR codes are a cost-effective technique because they are easily created and printed on a surface for distribution, often being incorporated into existing print materials. Additionally, QR code creation tools are often free.

All QR Codes Are Not Equal

The more data that needs to be encoded in the QR code, the more complex the image and the finer the resolution of the dots in the grid. This makes for a less robust QR code, one that can be harder to read and has less resilience to scratches and other distortion. So despite the greater capacity in the QR code, solution designers tend to try to reduce the amount of information that has to be encoded.

All QR Code Apps Are Not Equal Either

Image recognition is a complicated process that relies on both the app's coding and the device's software and hardware. These variables can make it difficult to optimize the recognition and scanning process across the board, so some apps may work better than others based on which device you use. For example, a QR scanning app that takes advantage of a camera phone's autofocus feature may not work as well on an older, cheaper phone that lacks an autofocus. The capabilities and limitations of both devices and apps are worth considering when designing solutions.

The Human Dependency

Encouraging consumers to download a third-party app to read a QR code is easier said than done. Knowing which app to use and when to use them can be confusing for customers.

Any time a system relies on staff or customers to do something, we are creating an obstacle to success. With all the advantages of low cost and the ubiquity of camera phones, that extra step required to read QR codes may seem trivial, but it is actually quite significant. For the QR code to trigger properly, a consumer must have or get the appropriate QR app, scan the QR code by aligning the device, scanner, or mobile phone directly in the line of sight of the image and then the reader must see the QR code image. Unless the consumer is given reason to believe the content will be of particular interest, it is likely that they won't be bothered.

Compatibility

Not all QR codes are readable by all apps. There are over 100 different QR apps, and QR codes are not the only type of 2D barcode formats. There are also formats like DataMatrix, ScanLife Ezcode, and Microsoft Tag (Tag). Some formats are open source and widely recognized, while others have their own proprietary reader.

Looks Matter

While the technologists among us may see beauty in a barcode or QR code, marketing professionals don't always agree. The perception that QR Codes are ugly has proved a barrier to their deployment in merchandising materials.

Fortunately, since QR codes are so robust and can be decoded even when elements are lost or distorted, this has opened up artistic possibilities. Imaginative artistic renditions of QR codes have turned the "ugly" problem into an opportunity. QR codes can be rendered in color, have logos embedded in them, and have the pixels generally messed with, all to artistic effect. This has yielded a blood red QR code, rotated by 45 degrees with blood dripping from it, to advertise the True Blood TV series. Other examples include jigsaw pieces being embedded in the code to promote an Autism charity, and changes to the shape of the pixels in the code so that the image looks more like an impressionist painting.

Microsoft Tag is another format that allows for customized and artistic codes. Their custom tool allows users to generate codes that can incorporate a wide variety of artistic designs.

Examples

Companies like Walmart, Heinz, Home Depot, Sephora, and McDonald's are some of the brands that have deployed and continue to use QR codes to provide relevant product information and marketing campaigns. Walmart has used them to run back-to-school clothing offers, while Sephora has used them to promote lipstick. QR codes have even been used on Heinz ketchup bottles to support cause marketing, and Home Depot deployed them to convey instructions on how to care for greenhouse plants.

McDonald's uses QR codes in its packaging at 14,000 U.S. restaurants. A QR code links you to a product's nutritional information with a simple click.

Challenges

While QR codes have arguably brought beauty, speed, and robustness to barcode scanning, we shouldn't ignore the challenges inherent in the approach.

How often have we heard the complaint, "It's not scanning!"? There are numerous possible reasons for this. Maybe the user doesn't have the right app. If you are scanning a QR code on a phone, maybe the screen isn't bright enough. Are you using a laser scanner to read a QR code on a phone? Is there enough light in the room? Did the image get wet or smeared? Or maybe an incoming message blocked the display of the QR code on the screen.

These are some of the issues to consider with the use of QR codes. So with that in mind, let's look at another technology that can address a number of these potential problems: RFID.

RFID

RFID can be seen as the "evolved" form of barcode technology; the wireless version. RFID was one of the first forms of contactless technology and is currently in widespread use and is still growing. It is similar to a barcode in that an RFID tag is attached to an object and then has to be scanned and read so the contents of the tag can be known. It is dissimilar in that it does not have to be seen or aligned with the reader to work.

The RFID system consists of small radios embedded in devices and tags that provide information to the RFID reader. RFID tags can be embedded or stored in, not just applied to, the objects being tracked. The viability of these storing methods will be influenced by the read range of RFID tags, which will vary based on many factors. In some systems, tags can be read from 100 feet, in others it can be as little as ten centimeters.

Tagging is the RFID process where a small microchip is attached to an antenna to create a unique "tag" or label. The antenna enables the chip that stores the unique ID and information on it to be read from a long distance. An RFID tag or label produces a signal that "sends" information to a digital receiver without needing to come into contact or be seen by that receiver, thus creating a contactless way to provide individual IDs for physical objects. Every tag/label becomes an entry point for engagement and distributing information, while the receiver becomes the solitary collection point.

RFID communication is often one-way only, meaning that the reader can only read from the tag and can't modify its electronic content. However, it can be two-way with the right setup. RFID tags create a many-to-one system, where information from many "tagged" objects is read by one reader or endpoint and converted to digital data. For example, E-ZPass and other toll systems use RFID. The E-ZPass readers are the single collection point that reads the individual identification information stored on the many E-ZPasses located in the many individual vehicles that drive by.

RFID Radios: Active, Passive, or Semi-Passive

RFID systems are based on three primary radio wave frequencies: low frequency (LF), high frequency (HF), and ultra-high frequency (UHF). These operating frequencies are 135KHz, 13.56MHz, 2.45GHz, 5.8GHz, 860 to 960MHz, and 433MHz. NFC (Near Field Communication) operates at 13.56MHz.

RFID tags can be active, passive, or semi-passive based on power. Each has unique standards governing them and, as of now, passive UHF RFID is the only type regulated by a single global standard, UHF Gen 2. Standards promote growth and help ensure consistency in development and deployment across industries.

Active RFID tags have a transmitter and power source, usually a battery. Passive tags do not have their own power source and are read one-way from the tag to the reader. The reader powers the chip and antenna (electronics) in the tag through the electromagnetic signal it transmits. Semi-passive tags use a battery to run the tag's electronics that may include sensors such as a temperature monitor. The transmitter itself works the same way as a passive tag and is powered by the reader signal. Both passive and semi-passive tags have a shorter range and slower transmission speed as compared to the active tag (of the order of 10 feet versus 100 feet for an active tag).

Active RFID tags can be powered on when they receive a radio signal from a reader and respond by signaling back. This allows them to conserve power since they do not necessarily radiate radio transmissions until they receive a reader signal.

RFID needs a reader and does not communicate directly with mobile devices. However, a great example of complementary crossover development with RFID is a Bluetooth UHF RFID reader by Technology Solutions UK Ltd (TSL). It uses Bluetooth to allow mobile devices to communicate with a variety of UHF RFID host devices.

RFID Storage Capacity

RFID tags have more capacity than barcode labels in regard to the amount of data they can hold. The amount an RFID tag can hold varies by type of tag and tag vendor, with a typical RFID tag being capable of holding 2KB of data. RFID tags can also be programmed and reprogrammed, which gives them an edge over barcodes and QR codes that must be reprinted to accommodate changes.

RFID Applications

The RFID wireless tag and reader process is very efficient for cataloging and monitoring inventory across the supply chain, and for tracking multiple, high-volume items and activities quickly. This provides a cost-effective way to collect and manage information (IDs and data) from many assets and activities to one central collection point for analysis, insights, and actionable data.

RFID is used across industries for everything from inventory accuracy, shrinkage reduction, and loss prevention to authenticating people with their ID badges, improving processes, and even ensuring patient safety. For example, the University of Vermont Medical Center in Burlington, Vermont, used RFID to reliably track five million medications from ordering through dispensing.

RFID Tag Placement

The fact that RFID does not require line of sight for engagement to work and can operate with standalone readers, without human intervention, is a major differentiator. RFID systems can read hundreds of tags in seconds, and with RFID you can assess the number of tagged items whether they are on the highway, in the bag or box, or even on a conveyor belt. What's more, this can be done from over 100 feet away, regardless of the direction of the tag relative to the reader.

RFID tags—because they do not need to be oriented toward a reading device and can be read through most packaging materials—can be embedded into items at the point of manufacture or enclosed and attached to items and labels as they are packaged. RFID tags will continue to work when covered, and generally even when their appearance is damaged, or if they get wet or dirty during transit.

RFID Costs

Costs of implementing a system varies on volume of tags, equipment choices, and extent of automation. Small, passive RFID tags for basic paper and non-metal distribution use can begin around 7 to 15 cents per tag, and climb to well over a dollar for larger ones and those used on metal, auto parts, and equipment. This cost is a key barrier to RFID mass adoption in retail. For higher-value items (electronics or higher value items of apparel), the return on investment (ROI) is there, but for lower-cost retail items, the mostly negligible cost of printing barcodes has a significant advantage.

Active powered RFID tags, on the other hand, start at around $20.

Reader costs are often tied to application and software, with geozone and active assets readers on the low end starting in the $100 range and manual handheld readers starting at about $2,000.

Both RFID and barcodes are useful auto-ID technologies. Barcodes are more ubiquitous than RFID, but as cost barriers are coming down, we see increased RFID penetration and adoption.

NFC

Near Field Communication (NFC) is a subcategory of RFID, with the same "out of sight" capability, but designed to work within a shorter communication range.

NFC operates in the 13.56MHz frequency range, requiring NFC enabled items and devices to be in close proximity of each other, usually 3-4 centimeters, to exchange information. With RFID, we saw how a tag could be read from far away.

NFC tags, like RFID tags, vary in the amount of data they can hold and where and how they can be used.

When choosing a tag, the application, use-case, and environment are key considerations. Memory capacity is just one of several features to understand. Other features to consider are scan distance, type of tag, reliability, and format, as different integrators provide different products.

NFC operates on a higher data transfer rate than RFID, allowing for data transfer of up to 424Kbps. This means quicker engagement and allows for larger amounts of data to be read without sacrificing speed.

Where RFID was many-to-one, NFC is more secure, providing a one-to-one data exchange of one-way and two-way communication. Additionally, NFC systems boast automatic connection to more advanced communication systems, such as Bluetooth and Wi-Fi. NFC can also be compatible with one-way readable RFID tags operating at the same frequency.

Using NFC

Using NFC is simple. You place an NFC enabled device, usually a smartphone or tablet, close to an NFC tag or other NFC enabled device, and they connect. This connection initiates an activity or shares information with a device. For example, sending a URL from a poster to a phone, payment credentials to a PoS, or an electronic key to open a door.

This simple connection is because NFC technology relies on a uniform standard of interoperability globally. This means all data exchange, simple transactions, and wireless connections use the same NFC specifications around the world. The uniformity is promoted by the NFC Forum, which specifies tag types so as to be operable with NFC devices. This is the backbone of interoperability between different NFC tag providers and NFC device manufacturers that ensures a consistent user experience. This global, uniform source of engagement is what energizes the proponents and advocates of NFC.

One of the strengths of NFC is that it requires minimal setup to start using its basic functions. Most smartphones and many tablets, cameras, and other consumer devices are now NFC enabled off-the-shelf and out of the box. As a solutions designer, the big appeal of this is that integrating new and additional devices into an already running system is simple. Because most devices come with all of the necessary components, there should be no additional costs or complications.

Forbidden Fruit

Apple's introduction of NFC support with the iPhone 6 was a huge boost in the arm for NFC payments. However, it's important to understand that Apple has yet to open up developer access to NFC, so its only use is to enable Apple Wallet. The lack of iOS support for NFC applications is a significant barrier to broader adoption, especially in the United States, where iOS has its largest market share.

NFC's Lower Barrier to Entry

A strength of NFC is that there is a low barrier to entry. While QR codes require the correct app and conditions, and barcodes and RFID tags need specific, often costly, readers, NFC is readily available to pretty much everyone.

This even includes applications for the visually impaired. For instance, there is an installation in Bulgaria that uses NFC tags to enable the blind to read travel information at bus stops. The tags help visually impaired travelers determine where they are and how to select the proper route to get to their destination.

With accessibility and ubiquity comes convenience. Consumers can deliver payment options, coupons, loyalty programs, and brand apps, as well as links to join in interactive games, product information, and social media connections. They can make a payment, hail a cab, enter a hotel room, or get a seat on a bus. They can also use their smartphones to read a smart poster, tag, label, or other tap point to quickly and easily get more information on products and services.

NFC's Three Modes: Discovery, Peer-to-Peer, Card Emulation

NFC relies on creating tags and labels, both passive and active, which contain chips and antennae just like those for RFID. NFC has three modes of operation, or ways in which it interacts with and exchanges information.

These three basic modes of operation are discovery mode (often referred to as "read-and-write"), peer-to-peer mode, and card emulation mode.

- *Discovery mode* is the basic one-way read/write connection like RFID, where passive tags are written, encoded with information, and then read by an active NFC enabled device. In discovery mode, NFC is used as a "pointer" at tap, which means it uses a URL and "points" to, or sends the user to, a specific site. Wristbands, convention, and exhibition passes and numerous other forms of printed and distributable marketing materials and media assets (like posters, coasters and business cards) are embedded with NFC tags that allow consumers to tap on them and engage a URL, which will redirect them to branded information.

- *Peer-to-peer mode* enables two-way NFC communication and data exchange between the two points, enabling a device to act or be seen as both a reader and a tag. This allows two NFC enabled devices to share data, like contact information and pictures, or pair with Bluetooth or Wi-Fi. NFC has been incorporated into the Bluetooth specification because it offers a fast and simple way to pair Bluetooth devices.

  This bi-directional communication capability allows for another consumer use-case: geo-targeted and geofenced message delivery. One of the benefits that NFC offers is no more need to "pair" devices. This makes them simpler to use and improves security by not maintaining connections.

- In *card emulation mode,* NFC mobile devices act as a smart card, like your credit card. Rather than you having to swipe a magnetic strip or insert into a reader, it works in a contactless manner with an NFC reader. In this mode, the mobile phone acts as the card and the NFC reader creates an active RFID field to read it. This is generally used for payment, access, and ticketing systems where consumers use their smartphones in place of credit, debit, transit, and access cards.

NFC in transportation provides a more efficient mobile or smart card consumer experience with cashless ticketing and cashless payments. This streamlining can improve operational costs and enhance the customer experience by reducing wait and access times. Potentially, this could even simplify the exchange of different currencies and improve international travel.

NFC Adoption

NFC-enabled payment systems and mobile wallets are starting to gain traction across all retail sectors. With Clipper in San Francisco Bay, Orca in Seattle, Octopus in Hong Kong, and the FareBot app from Android for NFC devices, as well as mobile payment apps with NFC options, including Apple Wallet, Samsung Pay, and Android Pay, contactless "smart" cards and NFC technology are changing the way we shop, pay, and travel.

Push versus Pull

With RFID, NFC, barcodes, and QR codes, users are actively seeking information, choosing to engage the technology. This is called pull communication, when you want to know something and reach out to extract that information from the environment and "pull" it to you.

iBeacon and Eddystone UID enable push communication. In push communication, information is broadcast or pushed to a receiver. Like QR codes, the receiver must download an app to receive these communications. But once that app is downloaded and enabled, the recipients will passively receive information, even if they don't always actively want to receive or engage with the information being distributed.

When applied to marketing, push and pull refer to how consumers are approached and how you advertise to them. Both techniques can be effective, and skillful marketing will take advantage of both. Successfully doing so creates interactive communication.

Interactive communication relies on a back-and-forth exchange, the dynamic, two-way flow of information, give and take, where both parties are engaged, albeit in different ways at different times. This is how beacons and these "automated identification technologies" work together. Sometimes you call someone (pull), sometimes you are called (push) in order to update, alert, share, and so on. You connect, share, assess, and reconnect. As connected consumers living "smart" lives; these seamless, multichannel "informed" communications are what drive our decisions.

How Does This Play Out?

Mobile marketing using proximity allows brands to connect consumers through their phones and other mobile devices with technology like NFC, Bluetooth beacons, and QR codes. Our smartphones and mobile devices, including wearable technology, have become extensions of us, and the central point of connectivity between us and our world, communities, and activities. We use our phones for traveling, shopping, ticketing, access, payments, and more, and now expect the information and data gathered and stored on them to be remembered, analyzed, and utilized to make future engagements easier and faster.

Technologies like NFC, paired with beacons, can support this cycle and be deployed for advertising, in-store marketing, couponing, and loyalty.

Consider a scenario where use of NFC and beacons are integrated. Consumers enter a store or restaurant where they are able to tap their phone on an NFC-enabled item and get information or a coupon and join a loyalty program or download the Bluetooth beacon app. This connects them to the brand or environment for future engagement, allowing them to be notified and receive additional offers and promotions when in range of the beacons on their next visit. The brand or advertiser can distribute NFC tags in marketing materials to new audiences as a cost-effective way to promote and support beacon app adoption and use.

Mobile wallets are prime examples of where these systems unite to bring the most value to the business and the consumer. Beacons can be used to ping the consumer's mobile phone, welcoming loyal customers as they enter the store and providing them with a VIP product offering or discount, or updating them on their favorite brand. Apple Wallet can use Bluetooth beacons in the store to trigger a Wallet Pass with a promotion displayed on the home screen. Finally, the customized, streamlined experience is completed when NFC is used to pass the payment credentials to the PoS when an item is purchased.

For marketing, this scenario can be played out in endless variations in stadiums, movie theatres, and other venues where you can use technology as a call to action on posters and other media, inspiring consumers to download the beacon app and engage with the environment. From that point on, you can use beacons to provide alerts, promotions, offers, check-ins, photo opportunities, and much more.

Summary

Each of these technologies comes with its own strengths and weaknesses, applications, and limitations.

These implementations can have a tremendous impact beyond the customer experience through to manufacturing and supply-chain management across industries. Real-time data spanning, purchase, and distribution can improve decisions about where products are made and how and when they are delivered. Businesses can direct and redirect shipments on demand. They can close the gap between what they produce and what they sell. This can impact just-in-time inventory and can help retailers make more sales.

The best technology for the job will rely on a variety of factors: specific needs, scale of project, which industry you're in, budget, existing resources, deployment challenges, and integration with smart systems, to name just a few. Ultimately, each solution is going to be different, and decisions will need to be made on a case-by-case basis.

These decisions don't have to be an either-or discussion. The development and implementation of these technologies is an ongoing, ever evolving, "What works best when," "What is most cost-effective," "What else can we try," discussion. It is about what actually works and what provides a seamless user experience. About what will make the technology disappear behind the activity and what will refine the process, enhance engagement, and improve the next experience.

■ ■ ■

CHAPTER 19

Augmenting Beacons with Cellular Network Technologies

Mario Proietti, Founder and CEO, LocationSmart

Some Limitations of Beacons

Some of the key attributes that make beacons powerful in identifying that a target user's device is present at a specific location also lead to some limitations. Some of these attributes and limitations include:

- Short range (a target user must be in close proximity to a beacon to be detected)

- Deployment is venue-by-venue (proliferation will take time)

- Disparity of solutions across venues (capabilities of systems deployed in different places may vary)

- Differences in functionality across device types (each manufacturer may standardize on different technologies or feature sets, making consistent user experiences more difficult)

- Data management for non-centrally administered deployments (data discrepancies and degradation may be introduced over time as beacons are moved, replaced, or fail, or due to variations in individual venue administrative practices)

- Cost to deploy and upgrade (labor-intensive to proliferate quickly and/or vastly)

- A significant proportion of phone users turn off Bluetooth and Wi-Fi, while keeping their cellular connection on, in order to save power

Beacons enable precise detection of presence and positioning because of their relatively short communication range. As a result, to effectively locate users, their devices must be in very close proximity to a beacon (typically within 50 meters). To detect a user's presence anytime, anywhere would require an impractically large number of beacons. Even detecting presence anytime or anywhere that is important or desirable using only beacons is likely an unachievable challenge as well. Achieving a broader degree of ubiquitous presence detection beyond the communication range of even a vast number of deployed beacons requires use of other means of detection or location determination.

While GPS is great at locating a device outdoors or in relatively open environments, even GPS has limitations in many indoor or other situations obstructed from satellite visibility. Something more is needed for greater indoor presence detection that relies less heavily on venue-specific implementations.

According to a 2012 survey conducted by *TIME* magazine, 84% of people worldwide said they couldn't go a single day without their cell phone. *Deseret News* reported in 2014 that a Mobile Mindset Study by Lookout found that 58% of smartphone users don't go more than one hour without checking their device. With this proliferation of cell phone use bordering on addiction finding its way into nearly every aspect of people's lives, cellular networks offer one of the broadest and most accessible means of device location[1].

An example of cellular network location is visible to most smartphone users when they first open their mapping or navigation applications and see the large blue circle around their location that progressively becomes smaller. These applications often use information from the cellular network to quickly present the initial location estimate represented by the large circle. That initial location estimate is then used to help initialize and validate the more accurate location derived from other technology available on the device, such as Wi-Fi or GPS. This same capability can provide benefits when used in conjunction with beacons as well.

---

[1]Sources: www.nydailynews.com/life-style/addicted-phones-84-worldwide-couldn-single-day-mobile-device-hand-article-1.1137811 and www.deseretnews.com/article/865596120/58-percent-of-smartphone-users-dont-go-1-hour-without-checking-it-2-are-you-one-of-them.html?pg=all

How Cellular Network Location Works

First, what is it about a cellular network that enables cellular devices to be located?

Cellular networks consist of an array of strategically located wireless base stations (commonly referred to as *cell sites*) that are interconnected via a backhaul network to the Internet and public telephone networks through mobile switching centers. Each mobile switching center may interconnect hundreds or thousands of cell sites. A simplistic analogy is to envision the area surrounding each cell site as an individual cell of a honeycomb and the cellular network as an entire beehive comprised of one or more honeycombs.

The coverage area of a single cell site ranges from very small, such as one floor or suite of rooms in a building, to very large, such as a few miles along an interstate highway, and any place in between. In addition to coverage limitations, each cell site has a limit to the number of users (i.e., simultaneous calls, text messages, or data traffic) it can adequately support. Cell site deployments are engineered to provide the coverage and capacity necessary to serve their subscriber base. Areas with greater population densities therefore tend to have more cell sites than those areas with less population density. A typical metropolitan area might have a vast array of several thousand cell sites to serve its dense population of users. An interstate highway between population centers might only be served by a handful of cell sites strung miles apart along the highway.

The term "cellular" stems from the arrangement of cell sites and the patchwork of communication coverage that their carefully planned deployment provides. Cellular network engineers strive to install cell site equipment and their antennae in an optimized fashion so that the coverage areas of adjacent sites overlap just enough to allow a device to move from one cell to another without ever losing contact completely. Yet, engineers also strive to ensure that the coverage is not overlapping so much that the cell sites interfere with each other or provide wasted coverage and capacity in one place.

To add capacity at a single cell site while avoiding too much overlapping coverage, engineers typically segment the coverage of most larger cell sites (known as *macrocells*) into segments called sectors. A typical macrocell might have three sectors (envision a pie cut into three slices, each representing a sector of the cell). In some cases, engineers intentionally deploy cell site equipment to have overlapping coverage in order to serve greater network capacity in a particular area with large numbers of users or heavy network usage. Thereby network usage in that area can be distributed across all the sites covering it.

Engineers may also deploy cell sites with small coverage areas in the midst of larger cells and sectors to improve both coverage and capacity. These smaller cells—known as microcells, picocells, and femtocells—may be deployed to fill small holes in coverage or increase capacity in areas of concentrated usage (e.g., a microcell at an airport terminal, mall, or conference center; a picocell in an elevator shaft, one floor of a large building, or a tunnel; or a femtocell in a home or small office).

As the proliferation of smartphones and other connected devices has skyrocketed, the tools used by cellular network engineers have come to include other even more sophisticated and creative means of delivering surgically precise and economical coverage and capacity. These include so-called leaky coax, fiber-fed antenna systems, distributed antenna systems, and on and on. However, that's a topic for yet another book.

With this broader deployment of microcells, picocells, femtocells, and more creative solutions to beef up indoor coverage, increase capacity, or fill in coverage gaps, cellular networks have become an ideal means of determining a device's location as well as serving its communication needs. The ability to locate devices present in these more concentrated cells can approach the proximity detection and location determination accuracy of Wi-Fi networks and beacons themselves (such areas of high population density— and cell site density—will tend to be areas where beacons are likely to be deployed as well).

At its most basic, cellular location determination or proximity detection is based on the knowledge within the cellular network of the identity of the cell site that is providing service to a mobile device and the known location of that particular cell site. By inference, if a device is connected to a particular cell site, and that cell site's location is known, then the approximate location of the user may also be known. As the area covered by a cell site becomes smaller, the uncertainty in where the user is located also becomes smaller, and thus a more accurate user location can be inferred. In this sense, cellular location determination is very similar to identifying the proximity of a device to a beacon where the cell site is essentially the "beacon". Two means of location determination using cellular network capabilities are commonly referred to as network-based location and cell ID look-up.

Cell ID Look-Up versus Network-Based Location

There are two broad means of location determination possible via cellular networks depending on the device and network capabilities. (Note this excludes use of GPS, Wi-Fi, and other means of location that might use the cellular network to communicate or augment the resulting location capability. These are covered in Chapter 17.)

Cell ID Look-Up

The protocols used to communicate between cellular base stations (at cell sites) and mobile devices include data fields containing the identity of the base station (the "cell ID"). This method of location uses the cell ID that a mobile device detects in its regular communication with the cellular base stations. Large databases of cell IDs and their corresponding latitude and longitude coordinates are aggregated either by crowdsourcing or obtained directly from network operators. Some providers of cell ID location services include LocationSmart, Google, and RX Networks. Such services make use of databases containing cell ID coordinates of more than forty million cell sites deployed around the world.

These cell ID coordinate databases must be continually refreshed to stay up to date as cell sites are moved, added, or modified by network operators as they maintain, expand, and optimize their networks. In addition to obtaining periodic database updates directly from network operators, cell ID service providers also use crowdsourced data from providers of smartphone applications, embedded vehicle-tracking devices and wireless modules embedded in a host of other equipment. To enable this crowdsourcing, cooperative application publishers and mobile service providers that locate devices using GPS or other means program those devices to also report observed cell site IDs when communicating with application servers. In this way, millions of devices serve as database contributors through their normal day-to-day use.

Cell ID location service providers enable application providers to locate cellular devices by querying their databases for the location of cell IDs reported by their device software or mobile applications. Devices that are not locatable using GPS or other means are thereby made locatable. Any device on the cellular network is capable of observing the cell ID through normal cellular network communications. However, a device must have some special programming or application installed that can report the information to an application server for it to be looked up in a cell ID database. Figure 19-1 illustrates the data flow for this cell ID look-up method of cellular network location.

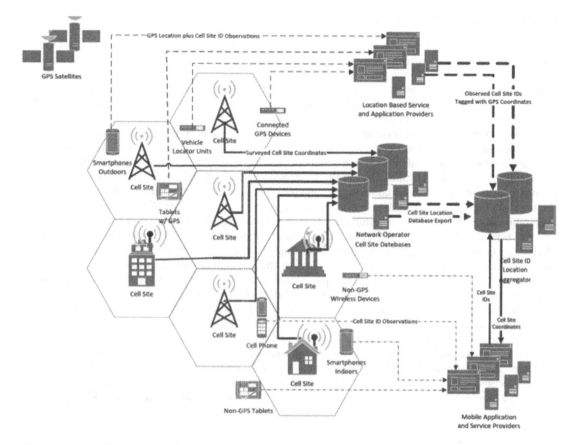

Figure 19-1. *Architecture and data flow diagram for a typical cell id look-up implementation*

The cell ID look-up method is an active process from the standpoint of the device to be located. That is to say, the device must actively execute specific processing so that the look-up can be conducted by the application or service provider interested in its location. The device must have specialized software running on it (an application, embedded program or built in operating system functionality) to perform the collection and reporting of its cell ID observations to the operator of the intended service or application. If the software is in an application, the user must download the application if it is not already pre-installed on the device. For certain devices, such as those used for commercial vehicle tracking, remote equipment monitoring, or automotive telematics services, the cell ID reporting capability may be built into their core functionality. The cell ID parameters used by such software are typically part of the information output from the wireless communications chipsets within cellular devices to facilitate communication management and diagnostic functions.

The cell ID look-up method is typically used by embedded communications modules or devices that are not equipped with GPS or other location capabilities or that require a backup to such capabilities. These are generally very low power and small devices that might be installed for remote monitoring, environmental sensing, motion detection, etc. In many cases, they have a need for low power consumption, very low cost, or use in areas that lack visibility to GPS satellites. Devices with GPS and other location capabilities may also use cell ID look-up as a backup when the device is in an area or environment that prevents GPS operation (e.g., underground, indoors, inside an enclosure, electromagnetic interference, low battery, etc.).

Network-Based Location

Some wireless network operators allow application providers or trusted parties to query their network for the location of a device via network API gateways or service delivery platforms. These services are available from most operators in the United States, Canada, and the United Kingdom as well as the larger operators in India, Spain, and Brazil such as Vodafone, Airtel, and Telefonica. Some of the companies authorized to offer services using cellular network location include LocationSmart and Location Labs in the United States and OpenMarket in the United Kingdom.

This method uses the near real-time knowledge within the network about which cell site(s) are communicating, or have recently communicated, with the device to be located. This is typically a passive process from the standpoint of the device in that it does not require any application-specific action or processing to be performed by the device itself. The device simply needs to be turned on and connected to the network with normal network communications enabling the device's location to be determined. Since this is an inherent capability that networks use to manage communications with all devices on the network, the location of any device can be determined as long as it is connected to the network at the time.

This is frequently dramatized in television and cinema when the good guys urgently map the location of a bad guy or missing good guy by "pinging" or "tracing" their device on the spur of the moment. In these circumstances, the users and device are clearly passive participants in the location process. In real-world applications, the user's consent is generally required in advance of such "pinging" for any commercial use. These user privacy considerations will be covered a bit later in this chapter.

In addition to the consent of the user, the network-based location method also requires authorization from the network operator to gain access to their networks for location purposes. To make this method accessible for application developers and enterprises, location aggregators such as LocationSmart implement the necessary privacy controls and trusted connections with the various cellular network operators. They are then able to offer access across all the available networks to application providers and enterprises via a single relationship, contract, and interface (e.g., secure RESTful web services APIs). Figure 19-2 illustrates the data flow for this network-based location method of cellular network location.

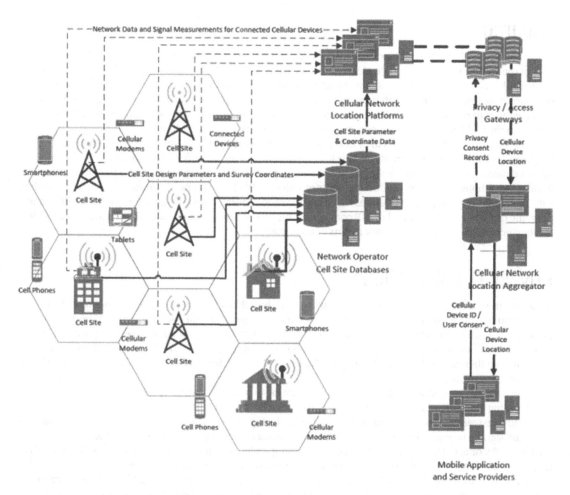

Figure 19-2. *Architecture diagram of a typical network-based location implementation*

Network-based location varies in sophistication and capability depending on the technology implemented by each cellular network operator. This can range from a database look-up of the coordinates for the cell site to which a device is currently connected to more sophisticated location determination processes using information about all cell sites a device's signal may be able to reach, as well as the respective signal strengths, timing measurements, angles of arrival, and other information available within the network. These more sophisticated methods may utilize technology built into the cellular infrastructure equipment itself or specialized equipment installed in the network specifically for location determination purposes.

Network-based location offers a more secure location source than location derived from GPS and other sensors resident on the mobile device itself which can be spoofed or manipulated with downloadable applications for this purpose or by other means implemented on the device. Since network-based location comes from data and equipment within the network operator's infrastructure, it is not susceptible to such manipulation.

Network-based location determination can be as ubiquitous as the network's coverage footprint, but generally provides a less accurate location than other forms of location determination, including beacon detection. On the other hand, no special software, downloaded application, or user action is required to take advantage of this method of location. This method of location often takes advantage of location technology similar to that deployed for cellular emergency call routing and caller location (e.g., wireless Phase I E911 location in the United States and Canada).

Accuracy

The accuracy of cellular network location methods is generally proportional to the spacing of the cell sites in the vicinity of the device being located or the coverage area of the specific cell site(s) to which it is connected. Given typical network deployments, location determination in urban and heavy traffic areas is more accurate than the accuracy in rural and sparsely populated areas. For instance, for cell sites deployed to deliver indoor coverage (e.g., microcells, picocells, or femtocells), their coverage range is frequently limited to the building itself or even only specific rooms or sections of a building.

Therefore, a device connected to or in range of such a cell site can be located almost as accurately as a beacon or Wi-Fi detection method. This location accuracy may range from tens of meters to a few hundred meters. Typical accuracy for cell sites covering outdoor urban areas might be in the range of several hundred to a thousand meters (i.e., on the order of a block, ZIP+4 area, or neighborhood). Cell sites covering suburban areas provide progressively less accurate location generally in the range of one to three kilometers or on the order of a neighborhood or ZIP code area. Cell sites covering less populated or rural areas provide location accuracies ranging from a few to tens of kilometers.

Privacy Considerations

Since obtaining a mobile device's location using network-based location capabilities does not rely on an application downloaded onto the device by the user, there are some specific privacy implications that must be addressed before access to a device's location may be granted to an application or service provider. For a service or application to take advantage of network-based location, the user must first be given notice that location from their network operator is going to be used for the service/application and the user must give their consent to do so.

The user may be notified about the use of network location when signing up for the service, downloading an application, or upon first use of the service. Consent is obtained from the user by requesting a reply to a text message, soliciting an affirmative reply during a call to or from the device, or completing an online sign up process that authenticates that the cellular device is in the possession of the user (e.g., by sending a PIN or activation code to the device and asking for it to be entered online). Access to the device's location is then enabled for the service or application once the user has granted consent.

If the user denies or later revokes that consent, location is no longer made available to that service or application. Like the on-screen icons showing applications with location access on smartphones, periodic reminders are sent to the device via text messaging, in-app messages, or automated phone calls indicating that the service they've chosen may be accessing the location of their device. The user may be given an opportunity to reply to these notices to update or revoke their consent or given instructions on how to do so online or by calling their service provider. A set of industry-developed best practices and uniform guidelines for the privacy considerations associated with network-based location are documented in the "CTIA Best Practices and Guidelines for Location Based Services," available on the CTIA web site.

Cost Considerations

Network-based location and cell ID look-up are both transactional in nature, whereby a service or application provider makes a request to the provider of the location services when a location update is desired. This query for location typically has a cost associated with it that varies based on the volume of location activity used by the application or service offered. In general, the higher the volume of location activity, the lower the incremental transaction cost for the location updates. Figure 19-3 illustrates an approximate relationship between location update cost and location transaction volume for both methods of location. While not exact, the graph is intended to portray the general economies of scale that accrue as usage volumes for an application or service increase.

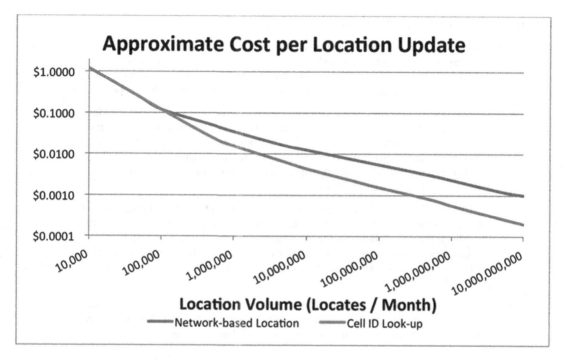

Figure 19-3. *Approximate cost per location update*

A cost advantage of cellular network-based location comes from the user not being required to download and use an application resident on the mobile device. Network-based location is certainly used quite regularly in conjunction with a downloaded mobile application, but use of a mobile application is optional. Users may access services or applications that use network-based location simply by subscribing to them on a web site, by signing up with a provider in person, or responding to an online or offline offer via almost any communication means. Once the user signs up for a service or application and provides consent to be located by responding to a text, in-app message, or call, the service may then be used without having to download anything onto the device. This provides lifecycle cost savings to the application or service provider by not having to design, develop, test, and maintain a downloadable mobile application across various device platforms and operating system versions.

Any development can be exclusively focused on server-side functionality which reduces development, deployment, and operational complexities and cost. Any service upgrades may be deployed through purely server-side upgrades. Avoiding a downloadable application also helps streamline the user adoption process by eliminating the hurdles of user application discovery, download, retention, and competition for device home screen real estate. These can sometimes be restricting issues to user adoption and continued use for many mobile application providers.

Representative Use-Cases

Cell ID look-up and network-based location are used across a variety of industry verticals and use-cases. The range of applications is as diverse as the range of uses for mobile devices. Some specific examples are described in the following sections.

Contact Center Automation

Contact centers use network-based location to provide streamlined services to callers whose location is relevant at the time of their call. The location may be used to route the call to the appropriate contact center to receive the call, to prioritize the caller's standing in a queue, or to present a contact center application or agent with the location information to aid in selecting content for a response to the user's inquiry. Some specific examples:

- *Roadside assistance.* The caller's location is used to route the call to the appropriate answering center that serves the area the caller is calling from and then the location is presented to a live agent assigned to help the caller once the call is connected. This information is also used to confirm verbally provided caller location details and avoid potentially large errors due to misinterpretation or confusion on the part of a caller, who may be in a stressful situation.

- *National retailer call routing.* The caller's location is used to route calls to a national toll-free number to an agent or brick and mortar location in the service area in which the caller is located. This allows the call to be routed most quickly and efficiently to an agent who is authorized to work with the caller. This eliminates the need for the caller to enter the ZIP code or annunciate the city and state, both of which can be prone to high error rates.

- *Travel assistance services.* Callers located in areas where travel is adversely affected by severe weather conditions or flight cancellations are routed to dedicated agents or prioritized in call queues to address the urgency of their requests.

Proximity Marketing

Here are some specific examples:

- *Loyalty program offers.* Members of resort and membership club loyalty programs who are enrolled to receive promotional offers and special event notifications are located via network-based location so that events and notifications most relevant to their location are selected for them and sent via text messages or e-mails without them having to download an application.

- *Nearby deals.* Some radio stations announce advertiser offers accessible through text messaging short codes whereby a user may text a specific keyword to the radio station's or advertiser's short code and receive a coupon or promotional offer for the related product or services. For programs using network-based location, the user's phone is located when they text their response to the call to action and more relevant offer near them is sent compared to users whose phones are not located.

Workforce Management/Transportation and Logistics

Here are some specific examples:

- *Contract worker monitoring.* Businesses that rely on workers who bring their own devices and vehicles use work force management applications that use network-based location to monitor the location of the worker's devices during job assignments. The business integrates this insight along with information from full-time employee data obtained through a downloadable application. This saves the complexity and difficulty of enforcing specific device types or providing application training to contract workers only assigned on a temporary basis.

- *Third-party logistics brokerage.* Millions of shipments per year are put out for bid and assigned through a network of third-party logistics brokers and services to facilitate the match-making activity between shippers and transporters. These shipments are frequently arranged through third-party logistics brokers that use online load-matching services. Many of these assignments are between parties that do not have a longstanding or on-going business relationship and therefore it is impractical to have a pre-arranged set of tools and technology to help manage and gain insight into the status of shipments once assigned and in transit. Network-based location allows the brokers and shippers to gain this important insight by simply having the truck drivers carrying the shipments opt their phone into a tracking application. The application begins monitoring the location of the phone upon job assignment and periodically thereafter until the shipment has been delivered. The driver's phone is then opted out and no further location monitoring takes place. This simplicity has allowed independent owner operators and individual truck drivers to win new business and brokers to deliver a higher level of service when assigning shipments to them. Shippers and recipients of goods are also able to gain greater insight into the status of their goods in transit and to plan operations at source and destination more effectively.

Mobile Gaming/Lottery/Daily Fantasy Sports

A number of states allow online and mobile wagering, sport book, and lottery ticket purchases as long as a user's location can be verified to be within state boundaries or on the premises of authorized wagering venues. Network-based location is utilized to securely verify the location of participants' devices without reliance only on device-based location capabilities that may be manipulated without detection. The network-based location is correlated with other location and device attributes to achieve the most reliable location verification possible.

While daily fantasy sports are not deemed to be gambling, certain jurisdictions may impose rules on their activity to administer local regulations more effectively. Being able to ascertain the location of a daily fantasy sports participant allows providers of such services to comply with these local regulatory differences.

Fraud Prevention/Transaction Verification

Network-based location is used to verify travel activity of cardholders when debit or credit card transactions are detected outside of their usual home areas. Cellular network-based location is being used for travel within the cardholder's home country as well as internationally to help improve customer service by reducing the number of inadvertent declined transactions as well as to identify potentially fraudulent ones more effectively.

Asset Tracking

Devices installed in packaging of sensitive materials and cargo containers are located using cell ID look-up when devices are inside containers or buildings that prevent location via GPS. They are also periodically located using cell ID look-up to minimize battery drain from frequent or unnecessary GPS location updates.

Systems monitoring aircraft engines equipped with embedded cellular telemetry modules use cell ID look-up to tag engine diagnostic updates with location information to ascertain travel patterns and confirm the location of engines requiring maintenance actions.

Oil field operations management systems monitoring fluid levels use cell ID look-up to confirm the location of movable tanks requiring service as they approach high or low capacity limits.

Future Developments

More accurate location determination by cellular network operators is being driven by United States Federal Communications Commission (FCC) rulemaking to address needs expressed by the public safety community for more useful location information during emergency calls originating from indoors. The rulemaking is driving industry efforts to meet implementation milestones beginning in 2020 and beyond. The technical standards and operational considerations are being formulated through industry organizations such as the Emergency Services Interconnection Forum (ESIF) within the Alliance for Telecommunications Industry Solutions (ATIS) and the Communications Security, Reliability and Interoperability Council (CSRIC), an FCC advisory committee. These organizations are undertaking collaborative initiatives among carriers, Internet and broadband service providers, public safety community stakeholders, technology supplies, and emergency service providers. The objective of the enhancements being pursued is to allow first responders to achieve indoor location knowledge accurately enough to get to a person in need of assistance with as little ambiguity as possible—to the exact floor, room, and corner of a building.

New technologies to meeting this objective are in developmental and testing stages to meet the timeline for implementation under consideration over the next five years. Some of the technologies under consideration include coordinated Wi-Fi access point and beacon database management, enhanced Wi-Fi positioning techniques, enhanced beacon detection and positioning, overlay terrestrial trilateration positioning systems, and LTE trilateration systems.

Summary

Beacons can provide targeted information about where people are with their devices or inform them about what's nearby. Being able to provide similar insights to and about people when they are not close to beacons depends on leveraging alternative technologies. With the vast proliferation of cellular networks and people's dependence on their cellular devices, cellular network location capabilities provide a broad and accessible solution. Two methods of cellular network location available to developers include cell ID look-up and network-based location.

Cell ID look-up allows an application server to query a database of cell site locations for any mobile device capable of reporting the identity of the cell site providing cellular service to it. To accomplish this, the device requires software to report the cell site identities it observes on the air embedded in normal cellular network communications. This allows devices that are not equipped with GPS or other location capabilities or that are in situations where those solutions can't operate (e.g., indoors) to be located anywhere there is cellular service available.

Network-based location allows application servers to obtain the location of a device by querying the cellular network in real-time for the location of the cell site serving the device. This method does not require any specialized software on the device. It simply requires the user to opt-in to a service and for the device to be connected to the cellular network. Thereby an application server may obtain location information without installation of a mobile application on the device.

Both methods enable location determination useful in a variety of applications ranging from contact center automation, field services, mobile workforce management, proximity marketing, asset tracking, mobile gaming and lottery regulatory compliance, financial transaction verification, and transportation and logistics. As cellular network operators continue to enhance their networks to meet the needs of first responders for better indoor location, those and other technologies will provide new solutions applicable to these and other commercial services as well.

Thanks to the following subject matter experts for their contributions to this chapter:

- Brenda Schafer, vice president of product management and marketing at LocationSmart

- Dr. Khaled Dessouky, founder/president at ComVerity

- Justin McNew, founder/president at JMC Rota

- Nick Weidmann, marketing manager at LocationSmart

CHAPTER 20

■ ■ ■

Where Beacons Are Making a Difference

Dr. Phil Hendrix, Managing Director, immr

As with any new technology, beacons are the subject of considerable speculation and even hype. Still in the early stages, beacon deployments have met with success as well as disappointment,[1] prompting some to question whether beacons will ever fulfill their promise. This chapter shows how beacons, properly integrated with mobile solutions, are transforming customer experience, improving operations, and boosting the bottom line for brand, retailers, and other businesses.

The discussion highlights applications across five key verticals where beacons are making a difference, proving valuable and even indispensable to end users as well as the organizations deploying them. The verticals include airports, attractions, restaurants, retail, and enterprises, while the applications include location-specific alerts and notification, indoor navigation with "points of interest," timely and relevant content and offers that consumers value and respond to, and more. Each section identifies customer needs and problems that beacons are solving. In our experience, this step is critical and often distinguishes between deployments that succeed and those that fall short or fail altogether.

---

[1]Boden, Rian. 2014. "Melbourne Beacon Trial Disappoints • NFC World+." *NFC World+*. www.nfcworld.com/2014/11/17/332684/melbourne-ibeacon-trial-disappoints/

In addition to the verticals and applications presented here, beacons are making a difference in many other instances. The summary includes a list of 30 use-cases and a matrix highlighting the most compelling applications across the five key verticals. A full list highlighting the most significant applications across more than 20 verticals, including events, healthcare, movie theatres, transit, and others, is available from the author.

The use-cases presented in the following sections are a snapshot of current efforts— innovative businesses and imaginative developers are finding new ways to integrate beacons into mobile solutions. Given the benefits and growing momentum, companies in many verticals will soon be asked and forced to answer, "why aren't our apps beacon-enabled?"

Airports Are Taking Some of the Stress Out of Travel

From Miami[2] to Hong Kong[3], the millions who travel each day through the world's airports can look forward to easier and more enjoyable experiences thanks to beacons. For even the most seasoned frequent flyers, circumnavigating through airports can be a hectic, nerve-wracking, and even costly experience. Travelers must contend with a number of challenges, including:

- Last-minute gate changes and flight delays

- Connecting flights in distant concourses and terminals

- Choosing where to eat given schedule, budget, and lines

- Finding baggage claim and luggage

- Locating and choosing transportation from the airport to a hotel or venue

- Finding the car, especially after a lengthy trip

- Locating family members who have gotten lost or separated from the group

- Retrieving commonly lost items, such as luggage, electronics, passports, and wallets

- Flight delays and cancellations due to weather or mechanical problems, especially when rebooking or overnight accommodations are required

- On international trips, passport, visa, customs, and related issues

While booking and in-flight experience have received considerable attention, airports and airlines have begun to focus more attention on travelers' needs in the airport, from arrival to departure and all points in between. To assist travelers, airports and airline partners have historically relied on signage, printed materials, and personnel. Going beyond these traditional solutions, airports like Miami International[4] and Schiphol in Amsterdam[5] are developing and deploying innovative, beacon-powered mobile apps that enable travelers and enhance their experience.

---

[2]Tran, David. 2016. "Miami Launches Mobile App With Retail Shopping Features | DFNI". Duty Free News International - Travel Retail News. www.dfnionline.com/latest-news/retail/miami-launches-mobile-app-retail-shopping-features-10-02-2016/

[3]"SITA Supports Beacon Technology Trials At Hong Kong International Airport". 2016. Airport Technology. www.airport-technology.com/news/newssita-supports-beacon-technology-trials-at-hong-kong-international-airport-4603028

[4]"Miami International Airport Launches App To Provide Passengers Personalised Updates." 2016. Airport Technology. www.airport-technology.com/news/newsmiami-international-airport-launches-app-to-provide-passengers-personalised-updates-4808152

[5]"Amsterdam Airport Schiphol First Airport In Europe With Full Beacon Coverage." 2016. Schiphol.Com. www.schiphol.com/SchipholGroup/NewsMedia/PressreleaseItem/AmsterdamAirportSchipholFirstAirportInEuropeWithFullBeaconCoverage.htm

Airports in countries around the world are turning mobile devices into digital concierge, guiding and assisting travelers with timely, personalized directions, information, alerts, and notifications.

- Beacons allow airports' and partners' mobile apps to recognize travelers who have opted-in as they approach, enter, and move within the airport as well as in adjacent areas such as ground transportation and parking.

- Much like a personal navigation device (PND), beacon-powered apps provide "blue dot" navigation and step-by-step directions indoors, where GPS doesn't work, guiding travelers from parking and check-in to gates, concessions, baggage claim, and customs.

- With access to airport operations data, mobile apps notify travelers of gate changes, flight delays and other disruptions and, with beacons pinpointing their location, redirect them in real-time to the proper gate or nearest support center.

- Useful for travelers as well as airport concessions, apps display on a map nearby stores, restaurants and other points-of-interest as well as information and access to ground transportation, parking, and other amenities.

- With proximity revealed by beacons and (potentially) audience characteristics such as destination, time available, and others, brands and airport businesses can present timely, relevant mobile ads and offers that travelers value and respond to.

Beacon-powered apps can also ease the burden on airport personnel, offloading many of the questions they must currently answer. JFK and other airports are also using beacons to identify lines that are getting too long and creating choke points,[6] thereby reducing wait times, one of the most frustrating parts of air travel. By streamlining customer experience and connecting consumers to shopping, restaurants, entertainment, and other products and services, beacon-powered apps also boost on- and off-airport businesses, providing additional revenue for airports and their partners.

With the number growing by the day, the list of beacon deployments includes airports in every part of the world, including N. America (Austin, Burbank,[7] Dallas – Ft. Worth,[8] Miami International, Orlando[9] and others); Europe (Bologna[10], Nice,[11] eight UK airports,[12] and others); and Asia (Hong Kong,[13] Tokyo,[14] and others).

---

[6]Gan, Vicky. 2015. "How JFK Is Making Wait Estimates More Accurate Than Ever." Citylab. www.citylab.com/navigator/2015/08/your-phone-could-help-make-airport-lines-shorter/401942/

[7]"Thanks Again® Airport Loyalty Program Launches Beacon-Enabled Smartphone App for Burbank Bob Hope Airport | Virtual-Strategy Magazine." 2016. Virtual-Strategy.Com. www.virtual-strategy.com/2016/02/05/thanks-again%C2%AE-airport-loyalty-program-launches-beacon-enabled-smartphone-app-burbank-bob-#axzz40YD7Wozs

[8]"Dallas Fort Worth International Airport Unveils New Mobile App with Enhanced Customer Focus, New Turn-By-Turn Navigation Nov 20, 2015." 2016. Dfwairport.Mediaroom.Com. dfwairport.mediaroom.com/2015-11-20-Dallas-Fort-Worth-International-Airport-Unveils-New-Mobile-App-with-Enhanced-Customer-Focus-New-Turn-by-Turn-Navigation

[9]Berthene, April. 2015. "Beacons Guide the Way at Orlando International Airport." Mobile Strategies 360. www.mobilestrategies360.com/2015/11/25/beacons-guide-way-orlando-international-airport

[10]"Bologna Airport to Leverage Beacons, NFC Tags, and QR Codes." 2016. *Future Travel Experience.* www.futuretravelexperience.com/2016/01/bologna-airport-to-leverage-beacons-nfc-tags-and-qr-codes/

[11]"Nice Airport Leveraging Beacon Technology Through New App." 2016. *Airport Business.* www.airport-business.com/2016/02/nice-airport-leveraging-beacon-technology-through-new-app/

[12]"Proxama and Eye Airports Bring Beacons to UK Airports - Eye Airports." 2015. Eye Airports. eyeairports.com/archives/2118

[13]"How Beacons Are Making Passengers Stress-Free At Hong Kong Airport." 2016. Indiatoday.Intoday.In. indiatoday.intoday.in/story/hong-kong-airport-sita-beacon-technology-stress-free-passengers/1/445153.html

[14]"Jul 14, 2014 JAL And NRI Start Demonstration Test of iBeacon and Smartwatch for Advancing Airport Passenger Service." 2016. Press.Jal.Co.Jp. press.jal.co.jp/en/release/201407/003000.html

Much like digital signage, mobile apps powered by beacons will soon be a fixture in airports. SITA,[15] the airport industry's largest provider of technology services, expects most major airports will have beacons fully deployed by 2020. Integrating beacons with partners' systems and apps (airlines, car rental, concessions and other companies) adds to the complexity and requires more time. However, integrated solutions reach many more travelers and offer deeper functionality.

As these examples show, by deploying and integrating beacons, airports and their partners are transforming travelers' pre- and post-flight experiences and reducing stress for travelers and personnel. Beacon-powered solutions are also lowering the cost of delivering services and support and providing a powerful new channel for brands and airport businesses to engage receptive customers.

Attractions Are Engaging Guests with Content

Every major city in the world has a variety of attractions, including museums, zoos, aquariums, gardens, theme parks, and many others. Attractions differ in a number of ways, including their focus, size, and audiences. Smaller attractions, such as the Petersen Automotive Museum[16] in L.A., may attract fewer visitors but they are no less fervent than guests who visit larger attractions such as the Metropolitan Museum of Art[17]. While visitors may spend a couple of hours at the World of Coca-Cola[18] in Atlanta, they can spend days taking in and absorbing the 19 museums that make up the Smithsonian[19]. While attractions such as the National Wrestling Hall of Fame[20] tend to attract predominantly adult audiences, zoos and theme parks appeal to families with kids of all ages. Finally, guests may include occasional and even first-time visitors as well as "regulars," some of whom have joined as members.

Despite their variety, attractions and their guests share a number of common characteristics:

- Attractions offer immersive experiences where guests can learn, appreciate, reflect upon, be entertained, and possibly even inspired.

- While attractions offer lectures, demonstrations, and interactive experiences, most curate and display artifacts and exhibits of every imaginable sort, from art to animals, automobiles, airplanes, and even space ships. The items displayed are often rare, even one-of-a-kind, exposing guests to experiences that are not available elsewhere.

- Most attractions consist of a combination of permanent and temporary exhibits, with the latter changing periodically over the course of the year.

- The majority of attractions appeal to families, exposing adults and kids to new experiences, stimulating their creativity and expanding their appreciation for the world around them.

- Quite often selected exhibits within an attraction are much more popular than others, resulting in queues and crowds in some areas and light traffic in other areas.

---

[15]"Airports | SITA." 2016. www.sita.aero/solutions-and-services/sectors/airports

[16]"How Technology Transformed a 21-Year-Old Car Museum." 2016. Eweek.Com. www.eweek.com/mobile/how-technology-transformed-a-21-year-old-car-museum.html

[17]"Beacons: Exploring Location-Based Technology In Museums." 2016. The Metropolitan Museum Of Art, i.e. The Met Museum. www.metmuseum.org/about-the-museum/museum-departments/office-of-the-director/digital-media-department/digital-underground/2015/beacons

[18]"Explorer Mobile App | World Of Coca-Cola." 2016. World Of Coca-Cola. www.worldofcoca-cola.com/plan-your-visit/world-coca-cola-explorer-mobile-app/

[19]"Smart Phone Services for Smithsonian Visitors." 2010. www.si.edu/content/opanda/docs/Rpts2010/10.07.SmartPhoneServices.Final.pdf

[20]"National Wrestling Hall of Fame." 2016. nwhof.org

Regardless of size or audience, attractions face a number of challenges:

- Satisfying guests' curiosity—Guests are curious and often want to know more about exhibits. While signage and staff can answer some questions, providing additional content that satisfies guests' curiosity is a never-ending challenge.

- Promoting exhibits—Making guests aware of and encouraging them to visit less familiar and possibly less popular exhibits.

- Engaging guests—Providing experiences that engage guests, regardless of their age or familiarity with the exhibits.

- Stimulating patronage—Enticing guests to visit more often and support the attraction by patronizing the gift shop, making a donation, or even becoming a member.

To achieve these objectives attractions historically relies on a mix of maps, guidebooks, and other printed materials, as well as audio guides, tours, and interactive sessions led by paid and volunteer staff. Staff members are trained to answer a myriad of questions, from hours and amenities to "why are giraffes' tongues so long?"

From museums to wineries and zoos, attractions are rapidly integrating beacons with mobile apps to enhance guest experiences using some variation of the approach outlined here:

- For each exhibit, content is produced that explains in more detail what the exhibit is all about. The content is accessible via the web or within the app.

- As a guest approaches an exhibit, the beacon-powered app recognizes the guest's location and the app (or web site) displays the content for that exhibit.

- As with social media, visitors can "like" attractions and post comments. User-generated comments, photos, and ratings can be displayed as part of the exhibit's content.

- The app can also recommend and provide directions to other exhibits that are likely to be of interest.

- Trivia, passbooks, and other elements of gamification can be incorporated, challenging kids and adults alike.

In the hands of imaginative designers, beacons transform mobile apps and devices into docent, concierge, and tour guide, all in one. For example:

- In Istanbul[21] and other countries, museums are providing self-guided tours, triggered by beacons. More sophisticated solutions can tailor tours to a visitor's schedule (e.g., one to four hours), interests (modern versus 19th century artists), and more.

- Zoos in Italy[22] and elsewhere are providing additional information on animals, including origin, habitats, risk of extinction, eating habits, offspring, and much, much more.

---

[21]"Smart Technologies Continue To Arouse Curiosity." 2016. Dailysabah. www.dailysabah.com/life/2016/02/06/smart-technologies-continue-to-arouse-curiosity

[22]Boden, Rian. 2015. "Italian Zoo Visitors Walk on the Wilder Side with iBeacon Network • NFC World+." *NFC World+*. www.nfcworld.com/2015/05/15/335252/italian-zoo-visitors-walk-on-the-wilder-side-with-ibeacon-network/

- The Kew Royal Botanic Gardens[23] in London and others are providing information on exotic species. Some gardens even offer tips for related plants suitable in guests' own gardens.

- Many attractions, including The World of Coca-Cola[24], provide links that make it easy to shop for and purchase prints, stuffed animals, apparel, and other memorabilia that extend the guest experience and support the attraction.

By making engaging content for each exhibit automatically accessible, beacon-powered apps are providing highly personalized, immersive experiences. The content and forms of engagement are limited only by the imagination of designers and budget. While museums are leading the way, attractions of all sorts are rapidly integrating beacons and mobile solutions to transform[25] the guest experience.

Restaurants Are Making Diners Happy

There is a good chance that diners will be seeing more beacons with their meals—that is, in the restaurants that serve their meals. Actually, they won't be seeing them because beacons work in the background.

At breakfast, lunch, and dinner, a majority of the meals consumed by Americans are prepared by restaurants. Long dominated by McDonald's, Taco Bell, and other QSRs (quick-serve restaurants), the restaurant industry's growth has been propelled by Chipotle, Panera, and other so-called fast casual restaurants. In addition to national and regional chains, the industry includes a large number of independent restaurants.

At QSR and fast casual restaurants, millions of consumers daily take part in a now familiar drill. They drive up or walk in, wait in line, look at the menu behind the register, place an order, pay, step aside, wait for the order, request or pick up condiments, and, if dining in, find a table and enjoy their meal. While the ritual is familiar, several aspects detract from the customer's experience and interfere with the restaurant's objectives:

- Consumers don't like to wait in line.

- Despite new and improved digital signage, consumers have a limited opportunity to view the menu, much less learn of and consider new items.

- Requesting a variation (for example, "hold the pickles") can complicate and delay the process.

- Whether an order is placed at the counter or drive-thru, as many as 2-3% of customers' orders have errors, with the number higher during busy times.

- While enjoying or completing their meal, if diners want to order dessert or additional items they must repeat the drill.

- When a dining experience is exceptionally good or bad, short of asking to speak with the manager (which few do), customers cannot easily provide feedback or resolve the issue.

---

[23]"A Visual Guide to the DISCOVER KEW iBeacon Mobile App." 2015. Jon-Paul Little. jonpaullittle.wordpress.com/2015/12/23/a-visual-guide-to-the-discover-kew-ibeacon-mobile-app/

[24]"Coca-Cola Signals Beacon's Hyper-Targeting Promise with Interactive Attraction Guide - Content - Mobile Mark." 2016. Mobilemarketer.Com. www.mobilemarketer.com/cms/news/content/17821.html

[25]Doug Thompson. 2014. "From Disney To Tulips: iBeacon and the Future of Attractions - Beekn." Beekn. beekn.net/2014/01/disney-tulips-ibeacon-future-attractions/

Recognizing these and other challenges, QSRs and fast casual restaurants are racing to incorporate digital and mobile solutions into the dining experience. Taco Bell's CEO heralded their new mobile app, which enables ordering and customization as, "the biggest breakthrough since the drive-thru." Along with mobile apps, beacons are helping to streamline and enhance the entire guest experience, especially ordering and payment. For example:

- Using Taco Bell's mobile app, customers can order ahead and, as they approach and come within range of the restaurant's beacons, a team member can deliver the food at curbside, eliminating the need to wait in the drive-thru line.

- Using a mobile app like Downtown[26], restaurant customers can view the menu on their device, place their orders, and have their food delivered to their table, bypassing the usual lines. During the meal, customers can order additional items and have them delivered to their table. Finally, without ever leaving the table, customers can pay their tab, eliminating the need to wait, all enabled by beacons.

- With a number of third-party apps, customers can enroll in a restaurant's loyalty program. Beacons in the restaurant allow customers to automatically check in and receive points for visits and purchases. Beacon-powered loyalty apps are being used by a growing number of restaurants.

By integrating beacons and proximity into mobile solutions, leading restaurants are streamlining and improving order accuracy, saving customers' precious time and enhancing diners' experience. These customer-centric innovations are also boosting orders and average ticket size, which improves margins and profitability. Loyal customers also appreciate the seamless recognition and rewards that beacons automatically enable, strengthening customer loyalty, persistence, and advocacy.

Retailers Are Combining Digital and Physical Shopping

With beacons integrated into their platforms, retailers from Europe's Carrefour[27] to CVS[28], Barney's[29] are providing timely, relevant offers that customers value and respond to. In the early days of location-based advertising, one of the oft-mentioned scenarios depicted consumers walking past Starbucks and receiving an offer to purchase a coffee or latte. Fortunately, the wisdom of bombarding consumers with unsolicited, untargeted offers has been roundly critiqued and the scenario debunked. In virtually every category, brick and mortar retailers face two critical challenges—how to attract more shoppers to their stores more often, and how to generate more sales from customers who visit their stores. Since malls and shopping centers are dependent on their stores success, these questions are equally if not more important for Westfield, Simon, and other properties.

---

[26]"Better, Faster Ordering Experience with Downtown and Estimote." 2016. Estimote Community Portal. community. estimote.com/hc/en-us/articles/203307786-Better-faster-ordering-experience-with-Downtown-and-Estimote

[27]Journal, RFID. 2016. "Carrefour Puts Beacons In Its Romanian Hypermarkets - RFID Journal." Rfidjournal.Com. www.rfidjournal.com/articles/view?13361

[28]Gagliordi, Natalie. 2016. "How the Quiet Rise of Beacons Has Reshaped Retail Marketing | Zdnet." Zdnet. www.zdnet.com/article/how-the-quite-rise-of-beacons-has-reshaped-retail-marketing/

[29]Moin, David. 2016. "Barney's Homecoming Brings Modernity to Chelsea." WWD. wwd.com/retail-news/specialty-stores/barneys-homecoming-brings-modernity-chelsea-10343352/

While mobile and beacons are critical parts of the solution, determining the most appropriate use-case(s) and strategy for a particular retailer is complicated by a number of factors.

- "Retail" encompasses a broad category of very different types of stores. While there are similarities, the differences between a Macy's and a 7-Eleven, not to mention Home Depot, Costco, Walgreens, and other types of stores, require different approaches.

- In addition to differences across store types, shoppers' needs and interests vary across segments (teens vs. adults), time (hour, day of week, and season), and occasion (e.g., a fill-in trip to the grocery store versus shopping for a party prior to the big game).

- Shopper needs even vary in the same store. For example, in a department store such as Macy's, consumers shopping for a product such as mattresses have requirements and expectations that are very different from shoppers, say, in the cosmetics department.

- Even within the same store type and same category, customers may be browsing to see what's new, researching products and brands, searching for specific item (or set of items), or simply comparing prices on a product and brand they've already decided to purchase.

While the intensity of competition also varies, brick and mortar retailers are under intense pressure Amazon and other online competitors to improve shoppers' experience. Consumers view shopping online much more favorably than shopping in stores—in fact, Amazon enjoys a 2:1 "favorability margin[30]" over the average brick and mortar retailer. Sales from the recent holiday season showed the power of Amazon's appeal, in particular—the online leader accounted for nearly 43%[31] of e-commerce sales.

Amazon has built its formidable franchise by removing sources of friction and personalizing and enriching shoppers' experience. While pioneering one-click shopping, Amazon continues to make shopping easier with services such as subscriptions for reordering regularly purchased products, Prime subscriptions for next day ordering, same day delivery and others. Amazon is also the undisputed leader in personalization, presenting on its opening page no less than eight different personalized options to entice consumers to shop.

In contrast, with the typical brick and mortar retailer, a shopper may have received an e-mail in their inbox, picked up at entrance to the store one of the ubiquitous circulars showing items on sale, and scanned a directory or signage pointing to specific departments. Retailers offer little if any personalization that makes in-store shopping easier, more enjoyable, and productive. In terms of integrating digital and mobile solutions into the shopping experience, brick and mortar retailers to date have barely scratched the surface.

Integrated with mobile apps, beacons play a vital role in removing frictions and personalizing shoppers' experience. Consider the following examples, all enabled by beacons and a retailer's own or third-party mobile app:

- Like Amazon, beacons can show and direct consumers to the best deals throughout the store and in specific departments.

- Like Kmart's BLUE LIGHT specials, beacons can direct shoppers to items that are available in limited quantities or on sale for a limited time.

---

[30]Hendrix, Phil. 2014. "If Shopping Is Broken, Can Mobile Fix It?" www.immr.org/if-shopping-is-broken-can-mobile-fix-it.pdf
[31]Kapner, Suzanne. 2016. "Holiday Sales Rise, But Not All Retailers Are Cheery." *WSJ*. www.wsj.com/articles/retailers-sales-results-ease-some-concerns-about-holiday-season-1452195398

- In combination with beacons, a shopping list prepared online or based on previous purchases, can guide a shopper through the store. As the customer navigates down an aisle, the app can display items on the list as well as related, complementary, or alternative items.

- With beacons pinpointing a shopper's location down to the aisle, the app can display trending items in the department, reviews from previous buyers, as well as online items not available in the store.

- A customer's purchases can be held for pickup or delivered to their home. As customers approach merchandise pickup, a beacon signal can prompt the staff to retrieve their order, streamlining fulfillment and reducing wait times.

- While viewing a product in the store, shoppers can use the app to request assistance from a salesperson or remote support team.

Imagine the power of beacon-powered shopping apps when combined on an opt-in basis with a customer's preferences and past purchases. In essence, the combination provides Amazon-like personalization to deliver frictionless, rewarding shopping experiences in stores. Retailers are also utilizing beacons to help customers navigate to specific departments or find specific items and reward customers for visiting the store and specific departments.

In virtually every category, leading retailers as well as malls in North America, Europe, and Asia[32] are deploying and experimenting with ways to integrate beacons into their mobile solutions, enhancing the shopping experience. Leading retailers deploying beacons include CVS, Rite Aid[33], Macy's[34] and Target. Clearly, careful thought and planning[35] are required to avoid spamming customers with irrelevant and unsolicited offers and instead provide timely, relevant content, offers, and services that customers welcome.

Enterprise: Automating and Verifying Field Inspections

Most discussions related to beacons center around consumer applications. A number of significant applications are emerging within enterprises as well, particularly in industries that have equipment in the field that require periodic inspections. Consider for a moment the vast number of fire extinguishers. They are on every floor of every office and commercial building, in elevators, stores, warehouses and factories, and in many other places the average person is unaware of.

With equipment in the field, regular inspections and maintenance can be critical. For example, in the event of a fire, a single, non-working extinguisher can mean the difference between a small, contained fire that is quickly extinguished with minimal damage and a three-alarm blaze that results in significant property damage and puts building occupants at risk. While inspections may seem to be routine, they can have serious, even life and death consequences. As a result, there are strict industry regulations governing compliance and vendors and customers must carefully monitor the status and working condition of extinguishers in the field.

[32]Boden, Rian. 2015. "Cyber Group And Sensoro Roll Out Beacons Across Greater China • NFC World+." NFC World+. www.nfcworld.com/2015/08/27/337322/cyber-group-and-sensoro-roll-out-beacons-across-greater-china/
[33]"Rite Aid Preps One Of The Largest Beacon Activations Across All 4,600 Stores |". 2016. Geomarketing. www.geomarketing.com/rite-aid-preps-one-of-the-largest-beacon-activations-across-all-4600-stores
[34]Petro, Greg. 2016. "2015: The Year Of The Mobile Beacon (Part One)". Forbes.Com. www.forbes.com/sites/gregpetro/2015/03/06/2015-the-year-of-the-mobile-beacon-part-one/
[35]Kaplan, David. 2016. "Retailers Resist Consumers' Demand For Real-Time Smartphone Promos". Geomarketing. www.geomarketing.com/retailers-resist-consumers-demand-for-real-time-smartphone-promos

Despite advances in technology, inspections and maintenance in many fields are still performed manually, in much the same way they've always been. While the process varies across vendors and owners, the process for inspecting extinguishers typically consists of the following:

- On a regularly scheduled basis, inspectors travel to locations and physically inspect the devices.

- At the beginning of a shift, inspectors are given a list, generally on paper, with the location, age, and other information specific to each extinguisher scheduled for inspection that day.

- In each location, the inspector examines the extinguishers, the cases in which they are housed, user instructions, and any other materials to confirm that extinguishers are visible, accessible, and in proper working condition.

- If there is an issue that needs to be addressed, the inspector either corrects the problem or initiates a work order to fix or replace the unit.

- The inspector then notes the time and disposition of the inspection, again, generally on paper.

Enterprises and their vendors are rapidly equipping field inspectors with mobile devices and solutions, shifting from paper-based tasks to digital systems.

As it turns out, beacons are a perfect complement to mobile field inspections. From fire extinguishers to railway equipment, enterprises are streamlining and improving the process of inspections, as the following case, complements of SAP, illustrates:

- A large industrial enterprise can have hundreds of fire extinguishers in a single facility, and many thousands across facilities spread around the globe. Given the associated risks, inspecting and keeping extinguishers in working order is a mission-critical safety process.

- Installed in each unit, beacons can be integrated into a mobile inspection app, allowing the app to "recognize" each extinguisher in close proximity.

- By pinpointing the exact location of each unit, the beacon-powered app reduces the amount of time inspectors spend searching and ensures that units are not overlooked.

- As an inspector approaches a particular extinguisher, its beacon triggers the app to recognize the unit and pull up a pre-populated template with information specific to that unit. This "automatic detection" reduces time as well as errors that can arise as inspectors check and verify the serial number, compare it to specs on their worksheet, etc.

- Beacons also provide independent verification that each extinguisher was indeed inspected by confirming that the inspector was in its presence for a designated amount of time on a particular date.

- Finally, any issues that require follow up can be communicated instantly to a dispatcher, along with specifics describing the problem. When a maintenance person is dispatched, the beacon in the extinguisher allows the unit to be located and repaired more quickly and easily.

For a short demo of this application, see the "Proximity Aware SAP Work Manager" video[36] on YouTube, courtesy of SAP. Another example illustrating the compelling application and benefits for a UK railway company is provided by Mubaloo[37].

Extinguishers represent just one of many examples of equipment in the field. Across commercial, transit and industrial applications, the number of pieces of equipment in the field requiring regular inspection and maintenance is staggering. Fail-safe compliance is often critical and mistakes can be costly, even deadly, thus exposing the manufacturer, building owners, and companies to huge liabilities. Integrating mobile and beacon technologies bring much needed automation and consistency to field inspections.

Summary

The examples in this chapter provide convincing evidence that beacons, properly integrated with mobile solutions, are transforming customer experience and improving marketing, operations, and customer service across verticals. The examples represent a sample of a larger set of use-cases, all illustrating the value of beacons.

Despite these successes, beacon deployments and integration are not without challenges and risks. While many companies are treading ahead deliberately and experimenting, others have forged ahead without adequately developing a strategy to solve significant problems and deliver compelling use-cases.

Figure 20-1 shows a matrix highlighting the most compelling applications, from a list of 30, across the five verticals. A full list of applications across some 20+ verticals is available on request from the author[38]. While specific use-cases vary across verticals, in general successful applications are delivering compelling solutions on one or more of the following dimensions of the PEER framework[39]:

- *Personalize*—As illustrated by applications in retail and attractions, beacons allow apps to deliver personalized, highly relevant content, messages, offers, and services that consumers appreciate, value, and respond to.

- *Enable*—By removing frictions and making apps "smarter," beacon-powered mobile solutions are helping consumers accomplish tasks more easily and effortlessly, from shopping and browsing to ordering, paying, and more. Navigating through a busy airport to catch a flight is a classic and compelling example, but there are many other "frictions" waiting to be removed.

- *Enhance*—By extracting insights from anonymized patterns of behavior over time, innovative beacon-powered apps can surprise and delight consumers. For example, displaying comments from previous users "in the moment" are making the experience in an attraction even more memorable. Businesses and consumers are just beginning to appreciate the power of fusing the digital and physical. However, once experienced, neither will want to revert to the status quo.

- *Reward*—By recognizing loyal customers, beacon-powered apps can automate and deliver privileges, recognition, rewards, and other incentives valued by customers. This capability gives brands and companies a powerful new set of tools to compete for consumers' attention and affection.

---

[36]"Proximity Aware SAP Work Manager." 2016. YouTube. youtu.be/3lz5QQzWfN4.

[37]"Beacons In Enterprise: The Opportunities - Mubaloo." 2015. Mubaloo. mubaloo.com/beacons-enterprise-opportunities/

[38]immr.org/Contact/contact.html

[39]Hendrix, Dr. Phil. 2013. "Raising the Bar – How Leading Companies Are Using Mobile and PEER[SM] Strategies to Boost Customer Loyalty." immr. www.immr.org/raising-the-bar-mobile-and-loyalty.pdf

Applications of Beacons across Selected Verticals					
	Airports	Attractions	Restaurants	Retail	Enterprise
1 Advertising		Useful	Useful	Useful	
2 Alerts	Indispensable	Useful			
3 Asset tracking					Indispensable
4 Authentication					Indispensable
5 Automation					Indispensable
6 Check-in	Indispensable		Useful		
7 Clienteling				Useful	
8 Content		Indispensable		Useful	
9 Customer service	Valuable			Useful	
10 Detection/Presence	Indispensable	Indispensable	Indispensable	Indispensable	Indispensable
12 Games		Valuable			
13 Greeting/Thanks					
14 History/Log		Useful			
15 Market research					
16 Navigation	Indispensable	Indispensable		Indispensable	Indispensable
17 Offers/Coupons	Valuable	Valuable	Valuable	Indispensable	
18 Ordering			Indispensable		
19 Parking	Valuable	Useful			
20 Payment	Valuable	Valuable	Indispensable	Valuable	
21 Points-of-interest	Valuable	Indispensable		Valuable	
22 Price comparisons				Valuable	
23 Product information				Valuable	
24 Product pick-up	Valuable			Useful	
25 Rewards			Useful		
26 Social				Useful	
27 Ticketing	Valuable	Valuable			
28 Tracking/counting	Indispensable	Indispensable	Indispensable	Indispensable	Indispensable
29 Vending					
30 Wait list	Useful	Valuable	Useful		

Key

● Indispensable
◑ Valuable
◔ Useful

Figure 20-1. *Matrix highlighting the most compelling beacon applications*

Of course, the prospects and ultimate value of these solutions are in the hands of brands, retailers, developers, and technology partners. Based on the use-cases and momentum, the future for beacons and proximity-enabled apps is bright.

CHAPTER 21

Using Beacons in Payments

Steve Statler and Kris Kolodziej, President of IndoorLBS

"Money often costs too much."
—Ralph Waldo Emerson

Afghanistan

Mobile payments are a battleground, not unlike ... Afghanistan. It's an area of strategic importance, where the conflict seems unending, and the battle involves both super powers and smaller actors using guerilla tactics. Some of the most powerful have failed to conquer this domain, and yet they continue to try. What are they fighting for and why is it so hard?

© Stephen Statler 2016
S. Statler, *Beacon Technologies*, DOI 10.1007/978-1-4842-1889-1_21

The Afghan terrain frustrated the British, the Russians, and the Americans. Mobile payments frustrated the multi-billion-dollar behemoth that is Google. Despite its massive resources and the IQ of its employees, Google Wallet was defeated, not by another technology super power, but by the hostility of the locals—the retailers—who didn't trust them and saw only an organization trying to encroach, uninvited, into their territory.

In 2010, three of the largest U.S. mobile carriers—AT&T, T-Mobile USA, and Verizon—formed an alliance called Isis (you couldn't make this up) and were repelled for many reasons, including a struggle to work with the locals while trying to apply their own rules to this unfamiliar area. Even a coalition of retailers (MCX), native to the region, has struggled. A number of their leaders have been terminated, and they have found the terrain very challenging.

Like Afghanistan, payments are Balkanized regionally. Each country's payments industry is different, with its own laws and customs. Sure, there are players that work across regions, but conquering one doesn't mean you can retain control of them all. When you look at the dynamics within the regions, there are a multitude of networks, with strange names and customs.

Beacons and Mobile Payments

So what's all this got to do with beacons? Beacons and retail are synonymous, and payments are the strategic heart of retail. After all, what is retail if it's not about the acceptance of payment for goods? The global payments industry is a 1.7 trillion dollar business[1] and is growing rapidly. If you control payments, you have extraordinary insights into who is buying what. This "attribution" that can provide proof of the value of marketing spending enables a string of businesses where beacons are key. The prize is big. Beacons can help target shoppers. They can help to engage them, and, if the right integration with payments is there, they can help prove that the money spent on the first steps resulted in a sale.

Many solutions developers have used beacons as a differentiator for their attacks on the payments space. We will look at a number of examples of those.

A payments system is built on many things—security, regulation, technology—but one of the most entrancing and elusive aspects is the user experience.

A Change Ready to Happen

The United States has been stuck in the dark ages of payments, being one of the last countries to move away from magnetic stripe cards. This is problematic because of the significant levels of fraud that comes with it, which is almost three times that of the European Union[2], where mag stripe has long been made obsolete by more secure EMV[3] chip technology. One of the reasons for this resistance to change is that the mag stripe experience is pretty good. So the challenge for mobile payments is, can we do better? Beacons may hold an answer to that.

We have seen beacon-enabled mobile payment experiences that are exceptional. While progress in the United States is slow, there are projects in Turkey and Denmark where beacons are being used at scale. This is important to understand when deciding if paying by beacon is worthwhile. Even though Apple Pay has a lot of momentum, there are still actors that have plans in play. We could still see beacons earn a significant place as part of mobile payments systems around the world.

---

[1]McKinzey & Company. "Global Payments 2015: A Healthy Industry Confronts Disruption."
[2]Payments Cards and Mobile Card Fraud Report 2015: www.paymentscardsandmobile.com/wp-content/uploads/2015/03/PCM_Alaric_Fraud-Report_2015.pdf
[3]EMV stands for Europay, MasterCard and Visa, the three payment networks that defined the standard for what is referred to as "chip and PIN".

Why Mobile Payments?

It's easy to understand why Google, a business founded on advertising, would find mobile wallets interesting. A mobile wallet can provide a valuable place to present more advertising and to measure the effect of the advertising that has been presented elsewhere. The carriers' motivation is clear; they are central to mobility and so have a claim on a share of the revenues coming from this new territory. Why have the retailers fought for control so fiercely? Is it just a lack of trust in Google and the phone companies? That might be part of it, but there is more to it than that.

The introduction of mobile payments is seen as a once in a generation disruptive event, a transition in power. There is the opportunity to break the hold of a system that merchants see as unfair and replace it with something that is just.

The Curse of Interchange[4]

Imagine a service that you have to use where you don't even get to agree on the price, where your supplier has full control of the price you pay. That's how retailers see the credit card business. Retailers have to accept credit cards, otherwise customers will stay away. When they sign up to accept payments via a card network, merchants have to agree to pay swipe fees that vary in ways they can't control.

The banks that issue the cards to shoppers offer air miles and money back rewards as an incentive to grow their base of cardholders. Yet, it's not the card issuers that fund those rewards. That money comes out of the pockets of the retailer who is obliged to pay the interchange or swipe fees. Gas stations can pay as much as three dollars on a tank of gas for the privilege of accepting your American Express card. It's their largest expense, along with labor.[5]

Few retailers can refuse to accept credit cards, but, with the advent of mobile wallets, if those wallets were to link our bank accounts with their back accounts without a credit card involved, those retailers could save billions.

One of the main technologies at the heart of mobile wallets is NFC. Beyond the RFID radio that is part of NFC is a card emulation protocol that makes the phone behave like a credit card, as far as the point of sale is concerned. This may sound like a sensible way of maintaining continuity with the current systems: a smooth migration from payment with cards to payment with phones. To a retailer, this looks like a continuation of the system of oppression they are trying to escape.

Will Mobile Break the Curse?

Retailers have become interested in mobile payment apps that use means other than the credit card networks to transfer funds.

Starbucks mobile app has been one of the most successful examples of what is possible. With 7 million transactions a week, it accounts for 16 percent of all of Starbucks purchase transactions. The experience is a differentiator. Rather than NFC, the Starbucks app uses a QR code displayed on the phone (or Apple Watch), which is read by the point of sale optical scanner, to trigger a cloud payment. The payment for a coffee comes from a stored value account that has been pre-paid by the customer with a credit card. This experience not only helps to build loyalty, it also significantly reduces the credit card interchange costs. The credit card fee is only incurred once when the sorted value account is credited. Then whenever the app is used for individual payments, spending down from that lump sum, the credit card networks are not involved and the transaction costs become negligible.

---

[4]If you are one of the odd folks who find the topic of payments to be fascinating and you want to learn more, check out "Payments Systems in the U.S.," by Carol Coye Benson et al.
[5]The card networks such as MasterCard, Visa, and American Express, have a different perspective on the value they bring to retailers. They would point out that credit cards reduce friction in the sales process and encourage customers to spend more at a retailer, that there is a "cost of cash" (counting, secure transfers, risk of theft) and that card networks insulate merchants from card fraud.

Isis Versus Starbucks

When Isis did their trials with Jamba Juice, their experience didn't go so well. The telcos behind Isis required users of their wallet to jump through hoops before they could even start to use their payment system. Hoops like visiting a carrier store to have a special version of their SIM card installed, a confusing process for both customers and staff. Visiting these stores, waiting to be served, and explaining what you are trying to do to someone who may not have been well trained is not high on anyone's list of favorite ways to spend time. It's down there with a trip to the dentist.

After running the gauntlet at their local carrier store, the number of people who were in a position to then use the Isis wallet was many orders of magnitude smaller than those willing to use Starbucks' wallet/app. To compound this, the average customer's frequency of visits to buy juice is lower than visits to buy coffee. The result was that so few people used the service that the staff working at Jamba Juice did not become familiar with accepting the new payment method and confusion reigned.

To change habits, you have to focus on a something that happens frequently. Payments are a habit; we do it without thinking. When we have to think, things happen more slowly, and that impacts the user experience and increases wait times at the cash register.

Proximity Has its Perks

Starbucks proved that a mobile purchase experience based on QR codes can be phenomenally successful. Could we do better with Bluetooth beacons? The experience using Qualcomm's Perks app tells us that the answer is a resounding "Yes!"

Within one month of launching a Bluetooth beacon-enabled payment app, 20% of all the transactions at the café where it was deployed were being conducted using "beacon payments." In a fraction of the time, more people were using beacons to pay than Starbucks achieved over a period of several years.

The experience was magical. While beacons unlocked the magic, and users received loyalty points that earned them a free drink, the real joy came from the purchase experience. The experience resembled what it might have been like as a local at a small town store, being treated like a regular, being served faster, and having to do next to nothing to pay.

Perks is a café in the massive Qualcomm headquarters lobby. It's busy, with two point of sale (PoS) terminals and a steady stream of Qualcommers and visitors buying Pete's Coffee, snacks, and meals. Users of the app registered their credit card details on the web and downloaded an app that gave them three ways to pay. They could scan a QR code at the point of sale, tap an NFC tag, or leave their phone in their pocket and ask to "pay by beacon."

As you approach the PoS, your name and photo appeared on an iPad sitting next to the PoS, courtesy of the beacon. This enabled the barista to greet you by name. If several people paying by beacon were in front of the PoS, their pictures were ordered based on the signal strength being measured. The name of the person in front of the queue appeared first on the tablet. The beacons allowed the system to scale over two point of sale terminals. The customers lining up in front of one terminal were not visible on the tablet that was associated with the other terminal. This ability to scale over multiple PoS devices with beacons is key to deployments in larger retail environments[6].

---

[6]Pulling this off isn't a given. One of the issues with the PayPal beacon experience (as tested at Toys-R-Us) was that the system had problems distinguishing which PoS customers were paying at. The reasons for that issue are a matter for speculation, but could be due to the beacon design, beacon placement, the transmission strength, and the way their orchestration layer applied (or failed to apply) heuristics to manage any ambiguity.

For many customers who had been visiting Perks for years, using the Perks app was the first time they had been greeted by name. Guess what they did when that happened? They smiled. Guess what the barista did? They smiled back. You could have finished the trial there and it would already have been considered a success in terms of building loyalty and improving service.

But it got better. Once the greeting was taken care of, the customer ordered their drink, the barista entered the amount the drink cost on the iPad, this deducted the value from the customer's card, and then the barista entered the transaction a second time on the legacy point of sale terminal[7]. The customer picked up the drink and continued their conversation with their colleague or guest. Just to recap, the barista is having to double the data entry they would normally perform, by entering the amount into the iPad and the PoS. However, the customers are doing a lot less; well, nothing, really, other than ordering, agreeing to pay, and collecting their drinks.

There was a fear that this double entry would slow things down, that the baristas might not like having to do more work. But the reverse was true: lines moved faster, because it's the customer that slows things down. The baristas loved it. They liked being smiled at and having less stress with long lines, and they quickly got used to the simple system.

You may wonder how many people used the NFC tap or the QR code versus "pay by beacon". Almost everyone used the beacon. Tapping and scanning may not seem like a lot of work, but compared to "doing nothing" and keeping your phone in your pocket with the beacon, it wasn't even close.

Beacon Cloud Payment Flow

It's helpful to understand an example of the steps to making beacon-triggered cloud payments happen.[8] Let's walk through the nine steps illustrated in Figure 21-1.

1. The customer downloads the payment app and enters their payment card details via a secure web form[9]. The card details are stored in a vault that is PCI DSS compliant[10].

2. The customer's phone (with the payment app installed) sees the beacon situated next to the point of sale.

3. The app sends the UUID of the beacon[11] up to the cloud service to indicate which point of sale terminal the customer is standing in front of.

4. The cloud service understands that beacon 1234 is associated with PoS #2 at the Perks Café, at a given address, and sends the photo and name associated with the customer's account to the point of sale.

---

[7]Since this was a pilot project the beacon function wasn't integrated with the legacy PoS, which continued to operate as if the beacon system didn't exist. A PoS integration would have taken too long to organize. Pay-by-beacon transactions were rung up as if they were being paid via a coupon on the legacy PoS so they could be tracked. Entering the transaction a second time on the iPad initiated the transfer of funds from the customer's credit card to a holding account. The funds from the beacon system were then periodically transferred to the café, so the operator could take receipt of those funds and balance their books. If the system had gone into production, the cloud payments system would have been integrated into the legacy PoS so that double entry was no longer necessary.

[8]This is not exactly how the Perks system was implemented—that's confidential—but it provides a simplified sense of how a beacon-triggered, cloud-based wallet can work.

[9]This includes the payment card number. The first six digits of this are the Bank Identification Number (BIN), which indicates the type of card and the bank that issued it. The rest of the payment card number is the Primary Account Number (PAN), which identifies the cardholder's account at the bank.

[10]PCI DSS is the Payment Card Industry Data Security Standard defined by the card issuers and used to regulate the security of all the systems used to store, transmit, and process payments.

[11]The actual UUID may be obfuscated via access control.

5.   The barista verifies that the customer is the person whose name and photo are showing on the point of sale, or the tablet next to it, and enters the amount they agreed to pay. This is sent back to the cloud service.

6.   The cardholder ID is used to retrieve the payment card details.

7.   These card details, or a token that corresponds to the card details, are sent to the acquiring bank or payments processor that the merchant uses. That processor uses the appropriate payments network, e.g. Visa, to verify that the customer can pay and sends the transaction through the payment network so funds from the customer's account will be deposited into the merchant's account.

8.   The acquiring bank or processor confirms back to the application cloud service that the payment request was successful.

9.   The cloud service signals to the point of sale that the payment was successful and the barista hands over the drink to the customer.

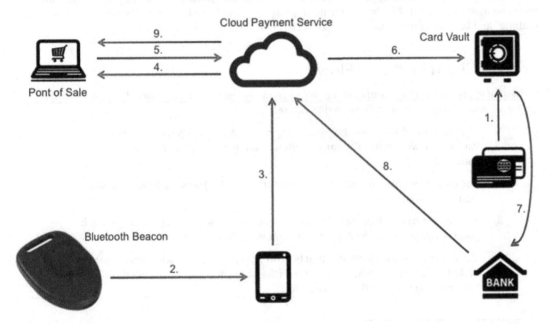

Figure 21-1. *A model for beacon cloud payments*

No More Perks

Alas, the Perks pilot is no more. The adoption numbers speak for themselves, but you had to be there to appreciate the magic of the experience. It's hard to point to a good reason as to why the pilot didn't go into production, other than that Qualcomm is in the beacon business, not the point of sale business. Square had a similar service, but without Bluetooth beacons, their location fix wasn't accurate enough for the system to scale in a multi-checkout environment, or in urban areas where their GPS location didn't function well.

Google has been conducting their own pilot of "hands-free payments" in San Francisco with McDonald's and Papa John's[12]. Hopefully, this will be a better time and place to see the hands-free approach take off.

Card Not Present Impacts Cloud Payments

The riskiest scenario for use of cards in payments is what is called "Card Not Present". There is significantly more fraud if a merchant accepts payment with a card number from a customer over the phone or online, where the card is not present at the merchant's site. As a result, the payment networks increase the interchange costs. The amount varies based on a set of arcane criteria, driven by the kind of retailer[13] that is receiving the payment. The increase in interchange is significant relative to the razor-thin margin most retailers live on.

For payment by beacon, this is an important issue to consider. If the card being used has been registered online for use in a beacon-based payment use-case such as Perks, that transaction is classified as Card Not Present, even though the customer is present.

The net of this is that a cloud-based wallet can significantly push up the interchange costs for a retailer. At least, that would be the case if a credit card transaction occurs every time a payment is made. If you take the Starbucks approach and debit a lump sum as a top-up into a pre-paid or stored value system, the fact that the card fee for the top-up is charged at Card Not Present rates is less material, so long as the pre-payment can be amortized over several transactions. For example, if a Card Not Present transaction to top up a Starbucks account with $100 costs two dollars, but that $100 lasts for 20 purchases of coffee paid from the prepaid account, which might cost five cents a transaction to use, then the net transaction cost per coffee is just 15 cents per transaction, which is a lot less than Starbucks would pay if a customer paid for each drink with their credit card. As a result, Starbucks reduces the overhead of conventional card payments by using a cloud-based wallet.

Of course, if a bank is operating the cloud payment system, they may get to change the rules to eliminate the Card Not Present charge.

Fragmentation and the Point of Sale

One of the challenges with developing wireless payments systems is that, for the deepest level of functionality and control of the user experience, you need to integrate with the point of sale. However, the way we pay in different kinds of stores varies significantly, making this difficult. Depending on the kind of store, the point of sale vendors vary and the flow of control between the payment network, bank, and merchant changes. The systems used are different for vending machines, big box stores, grocery, gas pumps, self-service cafes, mass transit, and restaurants.

Think about what has to happen if, at a gas station, you "put $30 on pump seven," compared with the purchase of groceries at a market. The first requires a pre-authorization of funds to make sure the customer has $30 to spend, and then an actual payment amount that is posted based on signals from the fuel dispenser. The grocery transaction is a lot more straightforward. The cost of the groceries is totaled and a payment request is sent over the card network.

---

[12]time.com/3900986/google-hands-free-payments/
[13]Visa USA's interchange fee schedule usa.visa.com/dam/VCOM/download/merchants/visa-usa-interchange-reimbursement-fees.pdf

There are dozens of different PoS vendors across these sub-verticals within retail. These PoS vendors are gatekeepers for aspiring beacon payments providers. Think of them as trolls guarding a bridge to a castle. Only, these trolls are busy, with a backlog of features, and will need to be convinced that working with a new payments player is worth delaying the implementation of other features for their customers. Solution designers need to have a plausible case for how they are going to help the PoS vendors make money. If you want to integrate beacons into vending machines, the PoS hardware may be from Crane or USA Technologies. For gas pumps and C-Stores, it's Gilbarco, VeriFone, and Wayne. Food service is very fragmented, but Micros are the dominant player. For specialty retail, speak to Epicor, and for grocery, speak to NCR.

The other issue is that there can be fragmentation of different PoS systems used across even a single merchant's stores. This is more common than you might think, with the exception of some of the very largest merchants who own the PoS software they use (McDonald's or 7-Eleven, for instance). Many chains have a potpourri of different systems they use. This is especially true for franchise businesses like fast food or gas stations, where the PoS is owned by the franchisee rather than by the retailer brand.

You can see that having a vertical focus is important if you are going to make progress in the payments market. Either that, or deep pockets and powerful friends. Otherwise, you could have a wonderful payment app that can't actually work with the systems that are operating in retail stores.

Despite all these challenges, there are examples of real progress with Bluetooth beacons helping to improve the way we pay.

MobilePay: Danske Bank in Denmark

In the United States, "banks have been backward in coming forward" with mobile payments systems. This is a shame because they have strength in two things that are essential for conquering this new frontier: trust and relationships. That trust and credibility puts them in a great position to bring customers, retailers, and payment infrastructure providers together.

As an example, Danske Bank has achieved more in mobile payments than most. They are the largest bank in Denmark, with a 28% market share in a country of 5.7 million people. They also have a significant presence in a number of other markets. Their MobilePay app (shown in Figure 21-2) is deployed in Norway, Finland, and Denmark. Danske Bank has put their full force behind the app and the numbers speak for themselves. MobilePay transactions more than doubled from 7 billion Kroner ($980m) in 2014, to 18B Kr or ($2.5B) in 2015. There were over 10 million MobilePay transactions in the month of December 2015 alone.

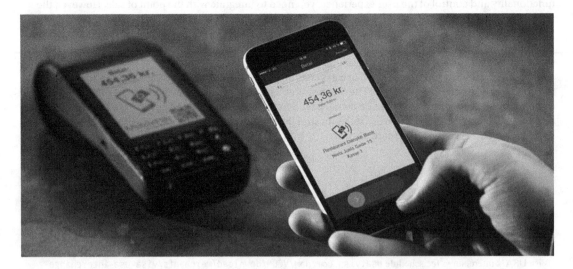

Figure 21-2. The MobilePay app being used with a MobilePay beacon at a Bilka store

MobilePay is accepted across a range of retail segments (Figure 21-3), including vending machines (tanning booths), big box electronics, groceries, transportation systems, and quick serve restaurants (QSR, or fast food to you and me), including McDonald's, Starbucks, Burger King, and convenience stores such as 7-Eleven.

Figure 21-3. *A MobilePay beacon paired with a point-of-sale terminal*

Danske Bank is using MobilePay as a way of engaging younger customers who have a greater affinity with paying by phone, where "oldsters" may argue that cards are just as convenient, assuming you own a wallet or purse to hold the cards in.

This convenience aspect is key. In many parts of the world, contactless payments using NFC-enabled cards are becoming commonplace. This allows someone who has remembered to bring their card to tap it on an NFC-enabled PoS terminal and pay for small ticket items (~$50 or less) without needing to use a PIN or having to slot the card into the EMV card readers that U.S. citizens are just starting to get used to.

That's a tough bar to compete with, as far as convenience goes, but MobilePay supports payments that go beyond small ticket. The payment flow has been key to the success of MobilePay in grocery stores.

At a grocery store, a MobilePay customer can tap their phone on a MobilePay beacon and enter their PIN in advance of all their groceries being scanned. When it comes time to agree on the total price, a single swipe on their phone authorizes the payment. This has the potential to speed up the payment process and shorten lines compared to a card payment process that requires a PIN to be entered for larger transactions and is backloaded to the end of the checkout process, just when the patience of the people behind you is shortest and you want to get away.

Net Clearance is the San Diego-based company that produces the wireless hardware and middleware that enables MobilePay. They manufacture all the hardware used for MobilePay and their other customers locally in San Diego. Their CEO estimates that, in the grocery store payment scenario, using their app can reduce payment times by 30 seconds per customer, and that, in some locations, in particular some grocery stores, their transaction share is up to two thirds of all payments because of this.

On the technical side, MobilePay offers the same "trifecta" of technologies that Perks used: QR-codes, NFC, and Bluetooth, plus Wi-Fi. Android and Microsoft Windows phones can be tapped on the NFC tag, which kickstarts the app. iOS phones use Bluetooth to make the association between phone and PoS. The payment credentials are sent either via NFC or Bluetooth in the case of iOS. The final authorization is done using a cloud connection, which could be via Wi-Fi or a cellular connection.

Over 200 PoS system brands are integrated with MobilePay, which is a major achievement. This enables over 30,000 retailers to use the system. One of the reasons for this level of adoption is that the system bypasses the credit card networks that are the cause of so much discontent in the retailer community. Transactions are brokered between the merchants and the individual customer's accounts, avoiding the large interchange fees that fuel the credit card system.

The issue with banks offering payment apps is that this can potentially be a source of market fragmentation. No merchant wants to support a payment system that only works for a subset of its customers who use a specific bank. In the United States, there are tens of thousands of banks and credit unions. To work around this, Danske Bank offers its service not just to its own customers, but to those of its competitors too, a smart move which helps it build its brand and acceptance of the app across the entire market of users in its regions.

Other benefits of using the app are the ability to track receipts without collecting scraps of paper, and significant money back on transactions at some stores. The collection of receipts is a non-trivial feature. A feature you don't get from Google or Apple Pay. In the United States, merchants are reluctant to share what is called Level Three transaction item data. This requires deeper middleware integrations with the point of sale, as well as willingness from merchants to share the data. In return, the retailer receives more information from MobilePay about the customer who is making the purchase in their store, something they wouldn't get from a credit card transaction.

fastPay in Turkey

DenizBank is a Russian owned bank that provides retail banking services in Turkey. Headquartered in Istanbul, they are ahead of U.S. banks in offering a proximity-enabled mobile wallet to their customers. fastPay enables peer-to-peer payments between individuals. The app also allows customers to make ATM withdrawals without the use of a card.

The bank works with Blesh, the Turkish beacon manufacturer, which was one of the first beacon vendors to support Google's Physical Web URI beacons. Blesh iBeacons in DenizBank branches enable customers to automatically claim their place in the line for personal service (shown in Figure 21-4).

Figure 21-4. *On entry to the DenizBank branch, the fastPay app automatically generates the customer's ticket number so they can be served*

Blesh claims over 10,000 beacons deployed around Turkey, with their top venues being malls and supermarkets (28%), cafes and restaurants (17%), and banks (11%). They report the most beacon triggers from malls (27%), airports (15%), and cafes (12%). The highest conversion rates for notifications to clicks come from cafes (25%), malls (22%), and subways (21%).

The fastPay beacons are placed in self-service cafes across Turkey to enable the push of promotions such as a free dessert to passersby (see Figures 21-5 and 21-6).

Figure 21-5. *The fastPay app pushes the notification of an offer from a café, triggered by a beacon outside a cafe*

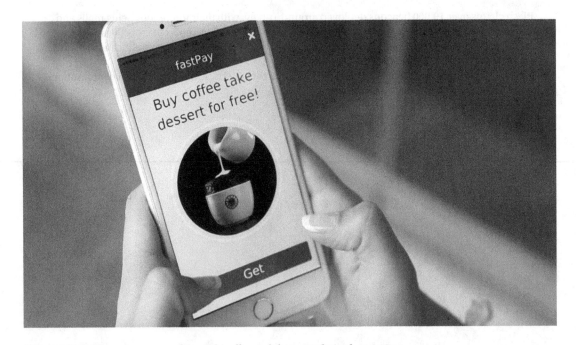

Figure 21-6. *The customer can accept the offer and then put their phone away*

Once lured into the establishment by the alerts, payments for meals can be made from the table without having to wait for service (this is achieved through the direct sending of funds using the app; no beacons are involved). Alternatively, the customer can pay "hands-free" without ever having to touch their phone[14] (see Figure 21-7).

Figure 21-7. *Customers enter the café with their phones in their purse and the phone detects the Blesh beacon and sends the customer's details to the iPad on the counter of the café without any intervention by the customers*

Merchants use a tablet that DenizBank provides (shown in Figure 21-8), which communicates directly with the fastPay app on the customer's phone to authenticate their presence close to the tablet. Customers can then verify their identity and willingness to pay verbally.

---

[14]Check out the videos of the fastPay and Google hands-free user experience at www.blesh.com/hands-free-payment-google-makes-its-move/

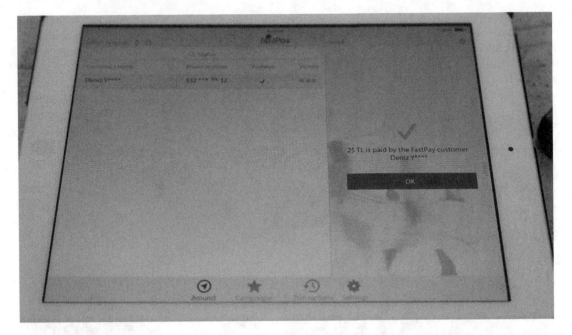

Figure 21-8. *The PoS app on the tablet used by the café displays the identity of the customer and allows the server to enter the amount to be charged, authorizing the charge based on verbal agreement with the customer*

The app, like MobilePay, is available to non-DenizBank customers. The wallet can be linked directly to the user's bank account, or associated with a credit card. The wallet is pre-populated with funds, which helps mitigate insufficient funds issues and interchange costs of card transactions.

Initial uptake for fastPay has primarily been for self-service cafés where the hands-free component is very appealing. The push into other sub-verticals such as grocery is ongoing.

Digicash in Luxembourg

At the heart of the European Union, nestled between Germany, France, and Belgium, is Luxembourg. The country is 998 square miles with a population of less than half a million. Luxembourg is the site of the European Court of Justice, has a national dish called Bouneschlupp (a soup made with green beans, potatoes, bacon, and onions), and a bank-sponsored payment app called Digicash (shown in Figure 21-9).

Figure 21-9. *The Digicash beacon in use at the Auchan hypermarket*

The app was launched in 2012 and is promoted by the four main banks in Luxembourg (BCEE, POST Luxembourg, BIL, and BGL BNP Paribas). This gives it coverage of 80% of the country's primary bank accounts. It uses SEPA, the Single Euro Payments Area, interbank payment system to send funds, supporting both person-to-person and person-to-retailer. A full 8% of the population is estimated to have downloaded the app, and 10% of the nation's point of sales are said to be integrated.

The system supports QR codes, NFC, and Bluetooth beacons using a Digicash device that plugs into the PoS. Payment is made using PIN code authentication. The app collects digital receipts and can accumulate loyalty points at certain retailers such as the Auchan hypermarket.

The solution being offered by Digicash is very similar in architecture and functionality to MobilePay in Denmark. The difference is that it is owned by a solution provider that has apparently been very successful in recruiting the four major banks in that geography to adopt the same solution. MobilePay, on the other hand, is owned by a single bank and is being used by that bank to compete with the other banks in its region.

Digicash has yet to achieve the level of consumer adoption that the Danish solution has, despite the fact that it is offered by four banks rather than one. It seems that a solution that has direct ownership from one bank, that is using it to acquire its competitor's customers, will be driven harder and enjoy more success than a solution that may enhance the service offered by all the country's banks but isn't being driven by a competitive motive.

Bluetooth in Apple Wallet

Apple Pay is famous for rescuing NFC payments from a near-death experience. The white light had appeared, and NFC was wandering toward it, away from the pain, suffering, and neglect it had experienced during a difficult childhood spent with Isis and Google Wallet. Then Apple Pay arrived and, in the tender hands of CEO Tim Cook, NFC was reborn as a quick and convenient way to pay.

Anyone counting on the idea of Apple using Bluetooth as the mechanism for cloud payments was disappointed, but Bluetooth wasn't banished from Apple Pay. It lives on thanks to Passbook, a preloaded iOS app that presented location-triggered passes (see Figure 21-10), which could be coupons and tickets, that pop up as alerts on the home screen. Passbook was folded into Apple Wallet, right next to the debit and credit cards used for payments. As a result, Bluetooth beacons or GPS coordinates can be used as triggers to push the passes onto the lock screen.

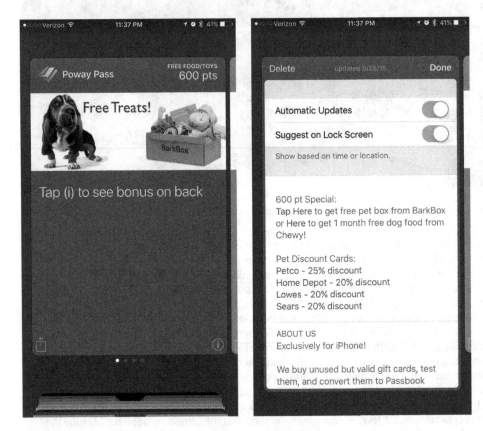

Figure 21-10. *An Apple Wallet Pass, front and back—the pass can be updated with new images and text from a remote server*

These passes have a life of their own within the Wallet. They can be downloaded from web pages, from Facebook ads, or from text and e-mail messages. Once the user has added them to the Wallet, they stay there until they have been deleted. Until that happens, they can be updated remotely with content controlled from a retailer or a brand's content management system (CMS). PassJoy is one of the vendors that produces such systems. Figure 21-11 shows a screenshot from that CMS.

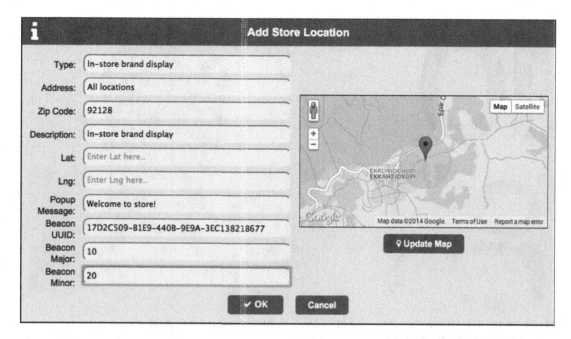

Figure 21-11. *PassJoy allows beacon triggers to be set for Apple Wallet passes, as well as creating and scheduling changes to the content displayed on the passes*

Apple Wallet Passes address the perennial issue of how to get a beacon-enabled app installed on your customer's phone. If they have an iPhone, Apple Wallet is already there, and it's staying there; they can't delete it. All that is needed is an ad that is compelling enough that they click and add a pass to the Wallet. Passes consist of a few images and some HTML, so they are relatively cheap and easy to create.

Brands such as Neiman Marcus have built campaigns around this digital Trojan horse. One of the prebuilt options for a pass is to link to a full-blown app that can be directly downloaded from the App Store.

Given its low cost and simplicity, this half step toward an app download is an underused tactic.

Brixton Pound

Brixton is a district of London famous for its music scene. Major venues include The Brixton Academy and The Fridge. David Jones (Bowie) lived his first seven years at 40 Stansfield Road, Brixton. This ethnically diverse town has seen more than its fair share of social problems and families living on low incomes.

In response to those issues, in 2009 a local community group developed the Brixton Pound, a currency that can only be spent at local stores (see Figure 21-12). Approximately 250 local businesses accept the currency. 200 of them accept pay-by-text transactions.

Figure 21-12. *The Brixton Pound issued a B£10 Bowie in 2015, the year before his death*
Image courtesy of The Brixton Pound

Having a currency that can only be spent locally helps support local merchants. These funds have been measured to stay three times longer in the local community than British Pounds Sterling spent with national retail chains.

In 2014, a Brixton Pound iOS app was launched. Carrying two currencies was considered cumbersome, so the app allowed users to dispense with the Brixton bank notes and use a pre-paid account already setup for pay-by-text as a funding source for a Bluetooth beacon application.

Users could step inside an initial set of 30 pilot stores that accepted Brixton Pounds and also had Kontakt.io Bluetooth beacons. This would trigger a Brixton Pound shortcut to appear on the lock-screen of the phone, so that it was easy to access the payment facilities in the app.

The app used a pay-by-text SMS service, which predated the arrival of the beacons. Having the beacons in store made it easier to send money than using the basic SMS service. All customers had to do was enter the amount they wanted to pay the store. The merchant ID, which would otherwise have to be discovered and entered manually in a text message, was automatically selected thanks to the address being broadcast to the app from the beacons.

The app could also be used by customers to top up their prepaid account while on the go. For merchants, it enabled them to create promotional content relevant to their store, that would be displayed within the app when the customer entered the store.

Alas, the Brixton Pound app is no more, although it is rumored to be returning. The concept was clearly cutting edge, and the cause was worthy. Given the cost of app development and the size of the Brixton area, it's understandable that such an effort was not sustainable. Success in payments is all about achieving volume.

Many Others

There are other payments players who have announced support for Bluetooth beacons. They include:

- iMobile3—PassMarket digital wallet

- Mozido—P2P proximity payment pilot

- PayPal—Piloted, but never launched after reported issues with support across multiple PoS devices in close proximity

- Paydiant—Acquired by PayPal. Produces white label mobile wallets, works with Subway and CurrentC, operated by the MCX consortium

- Pey—Works with Bitcoin transactions; signed up 50 merchants in Germany

- TruBeacon—Produces white label payment apps; focuses on U.S. Credit Unions

- SnapScan—South African-based; introduced SnapBeacons to work with its payment app, used by approximately 40 Johannesburg and Cape Town retailers

CurrentC or Not CurrentC

The biggest wildcard of these is Paydiant and its client, the Merchant Customer Exchange (MCX), with the CurrentC wallet. MCX's members include 7-Eleven, Alon Brands, Best Buy, CVS Health, Darden Restaurants, HMSHost, Hy-Vee, Lowe's, Michaels, Publix, Sears Holdings, Shell Oil Products US, Sunoco, Target Corporation, and Walmart.

Satisfying all of those stakeholders is an incredibly difficult task, given the differences in the requirements they have from almost every sector of retail. The organization has been working since 2012 on its payments solution. It has been running pilots, most recently in Columbus, Ohio, but has yet to perform large-scale deployments.

The CurrentC app is available on the app store and provides payment, offers, and loyalty functions. It supports multiple funding sources: checking accounts, gift cards, and the Target credit and debit cards.

There has been an organized campaign of one-star reviews that include some emotional and misleading comments from people that appear to object to the idea of retailers working together on a payment system and the blocking of Apple Pay by some MCX members.

Originally, all of MCX's members were required to pledge to wait for CurrentC and not support competing solutions, but as of early 2016, its largest members, including Walmart, have started to deploy their own solutions, as well as Apple Pay and Android Pay.

The power of the retailers that belong to MCX is awesome, in the non-Millennial sense of the word. It's tempting to write off the effort because of the scale and the failures of Isis and Google Wallet that have preceded it. However, the MCX investors have a "right to win," and they have the expertise, deep pockets, and motivation needed to exercise that right.

Summary

For those of us that love a challenge, the lure of mobile payments is hard to resist. There are huge rewards for winning, both in terms of the fees that can be charged and the intelligence that can be gained by seeing who is buying what and why.

The move to mobile payments represents a potential disruption, an opportunity to change who controls the reigns of power and lift the interchange "tax" on the retailers. Will the credit card networks keep their hold and retain their place, or will the new systems linking banks and merchants more directly prevail? In some countries it looks as though the coup will succeed. Here in the United States, it seems like the card networks will prevail.

The opportunity for change goes beyond monetary and strategic value, though. There is a chance to change the way millions of people pay for goods and services every day and to make their experience better. This seems to be a battle worth fighting. Bluetooth, combined with other wireless technologies, has an exciting role to play as part of that revolution.

■ ■ ■

CHAPTER 22

The Future, Standards, and IP: Please Stop Killing Us

An open letter to Tim Cook, CEO, Apple and Larry Page, CEO, Alphabet

—Dear Larry and Tim,

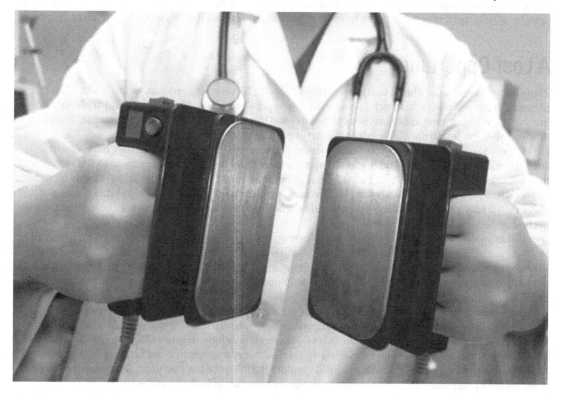

Executive Summary

Apple and Google are pursuing a course that could cost lives, and one that risks the future of the Bluetooth beacon ecosystem. The remedy, which is within your companies' control, is inexpensive, good for your businesses, and will save the lives of thousands of people.

S. Statler, *Beacon Technologies*, DOI 10.1007/978-1-4842-1889-1_22

Bluetooth beacons are set to drastically improve the accuracy of the cell phone 911 system. Unfortunately, the way your companies have approached developing competing proprietary standards for Bluetooth beacons is defeating that initiative and also putting the breaks on the development of this key part of the Internet of Things.

The root of the problem is that, despite popular belief to the contrary, there is no Bluetooth standard for beacons. Instead, your companies' proprietary standards have influenced an ecosystem that, while it seems to be healthy, is flawed and fractured. Given the strategic importance of the mobile OS, your companies are the only ones that can solve the issue.

Please encourage your teams to do the right thing and cooperate on open Bluetooth beacon standards. If they do, chances are that some major issues in the e911 system can be resolved quite rapidly, which will allow the Bluetooth beacon ecosystem to be resuscitated from its current lethargic state. This would also boost mobile advertising revenues and make smartphones even more useful than they already are, which should, in turn, should drive up your sales.

There are over 146 million wireless 911 calls per year in the United States. If you are outdoors when disaster strikes, the e911 system does a pretty good job of sending your location to first responders. Those systems stop working well indoors, which is where we seem to spend a lot of our time these days. In addition to the well known issues with GPS indoors (it doesn't work at all), the current system has no way of knowing what floor an emergency caller is on in a multi-story building. You, like me, are probably at the age where your friends are starting to worry about their health, and all the things that can suddenly, dramatically change it. As the doctor of a friend of mine who almost died of a stroke said, "Time equals brain." Even a few minutes of delay getting patients to the hospital can drastically impact their chances of recovering.

A Lost Opportunity

These issues have caused a bit of an uproar, so the FCC and CTIA have agreed that, by 2017, 40% of all cell phone 911 calls will have a "dispatchable address" (as opposed to a latitude and longitude), including a floor number. An improvement to be sure, but still not so good if you are in the other 60%. So you may want to cut down on your salt intake until 2021, when the target goes up to 80%.

So how are the phone companies going to meet these targets? The good news is they have already started working together on it. They are building a National Emergency Address Database (NEAD), which they will use to track every Wi-Fi access point and Bluetooth beacon in the country. This is strictly for public safety use only. So when you, or a bystander that sees you collapsed on the floor, dial 911, the phone will check the ID of any local Wi-Fi access points and beacons against that database and use the information to get first responders to the right place.

Unfortunately, as many of us with data plan overages can testify, Wi-Fi isn't everywhere. Commercial Wi-Fi access points can be expensive ($1,300 or more), which somewhat limits their ubiquity. Fortunately, Bluetooth beacons run pretty cheap, $5-$40, and are being deployed in the millions, with ABI predicting over 400 million to be shipped by 2020. Lighting companies are even building them into the next generation of LED lighting.

Public safety could be a driver that accelerates the deployment of more beacons. Low-cost beacon modules could be deployed as a part of fire extinguishers, smoke alarms, and exit signs. Insurance companies may give building owners a break on their rates if they have beacons that are registered with NEAD. Meeting an obligation to do everything that is reasonably possible to avoid fatalities would reduce legal liability for emergencies occurring in inside buildings. Given the low cost of adding beacons to existing powered safety equipment, it's not a stretch to imagine a mandate in building codes.

Standards Gap Prevents Beacon Use for e911

The team building the NEAD database was working on adding Bluetooth beacons to the database, and then reality struck. The standards for beacons are such a mess that it's not practical to use the majority of the beacons being deployed commercially for e911.

Not only are the iBeacon and Eddystone UID standards different, the bigger issue is that most beacons don't use those standards. Companies investing in large-scale deployments want to control who gets to see their beacons. In order to do that, they are using proprietary, non-standard techniques to implement conditional access to their beacons. Apple's (confidential!) iBeacon 1.0 specification, for example, which is over two years old, didn't address this requirement, so almost every one of the hundreds of beacon OEMs claiming iBeacon compliance has created, in essence, its own "standard". Google has launched Ephemeral IDs, but there will still be many competing proprietary standards and businesses that refuse to adopt a standard that registers the location of every beacon with Google.

As a member of the NEAD team says:

> *The NEAD development team has not abandoned the concept of using BT beacons for E911 location. Reality did strike—in that it became apparent that not all Bluetooth beacons can be relied upon for consistent ID/location use—but the plan is still to utilize those that can be relied upon (along with Wi-Fi Aps). Identifying a way for emergency services to access Bluetooth IDs would go a long way to resolving this issue.*

What About the Bluetooth Beacon Standard?

Again, contrary to first glance and popular opinion, there is no Bluetooth beacon standard; that Bluetooth Profile doesn't exist (yet?!). Sure, there is a standard for the transport that beacons use for the broadcast of the advertising packets, but nothing in the standard actually mentions beacons. The high level addressing, configuration, and conditional access are all left to the manufacturer to make up as they see fit.

So who could help reconcile these hundreds of incompatible implementations? The Bluetooth SIG is ideally placed. Google and Apple are already fully paid up members, and Apple is even one of the seven top-level "Promoter" members, with keys to the executive washroom. Apple and Google together could make this happen.

Risk of Litigation

The patent attorneys have been busy. As the startup community has created solutions to fill the gaps, they have been diligently applying for patents to cover these "innovations". HP, Connect Quest, and Gimbal are three companies that have a lead in this area. Good for them. There isn't a lot of money being made in the beacosystem today, but, once there is, expect a call. While this doesn't appear to have stopped people so far, the threat of litigation is there, and is going to have a cooling effect on this beacon ecosystem that Apple and Google have curated.

What could be done to address this issue? If there were a Bluetooth beacon standard that covered these essential aspects, all the holders of IP would have to refrain from suing their fellow Bluetooth Special Interest Group (SIG) members over aspects that are covered by the Bluetooth Standard, as they promised when they joined. If you use the standard, you have to join the SIG. This should give some comfort to large companies contemplating making big investments in deployments.

Don't Standards Kill Profits?

Is the beacosystem really well served by having a hundred different ways of controlling who sees a beacon or how to set up its parameters? No!

Granted, this will increase the commoditization of the lower parts of the beacon stack, but that's happening anyway. Very few companies make money from beacon hardware. And, frankly, our ecosystem could do with fewer choices in terms of generic beacon hardware. The last thing we want is for companies thinking of deploying beacons to need to hire consultants like me to help them weed through the 200+ vendors of beacon hardware. Of course, I'm grateful for the business, but most sensible beacon vendors are focusing higher in the stack to add value and make profits.

Having 20, rather than 200, great beacon hardware vendors competing on quality, battery life, and cost would help everyone else thinking of deploying this technology. The lower the cost and the better the quality, the more deployments are going to be made.

It's the Network

e911 is not the only network that would benefit from real standards for "ephemeral IDs"—commercial networks would too. And the sooner those networks get joined up and take off, the better for almost everyone in the beacosystem. Having one app per beacon is like having an expensive boat anchor wrapped around the neck of your project. It slows everything down and adds capital and operational expense to deployments.

Deploying a beacon-enabled app should be as simple as going online, selecting the beacons you are interested in using, and clicking a button. Yet, while every beacon manufacturer has a different set of standards, it fragments the size of potential networks.

A "Lost" Opportunity for Maps

Both Apple and Google Maps are now using beacons as a way of improving the accuracy of indoor navigation. Given most beacons are broadcasting ever-changing, proprietary UUID formats, these will be invisible to the maps apps. This is a "lost opportunity," as those proprietary signals will just be seen as noise. A Bluetooth standard for conditional access beacon packets could support access being granted for maps, for e911, and any for other application that was deemed to be for the public's benefit.

The Way Forward

If Apple and Google decided to unify the identification of beacons in a Bluetooth standard, would the beacon ecosystem adopt that standard? Yes, I think so. There would be a stampede.

Beacons would get better, the cost would come down further, e911 would get a lot more accurate a lot faster, and the pace of innovation, which admittedly isn't slow, would reach another level—it would go ballistic. We all need these things.

Is it really worth delaying ambulances and hobbling this beautiful thing your companies have created by having conflicting standards with big gaps that open up the possibility of lawsuits?

As our NEAD insider says:

The NEAD development effort is generating a ground swell of support from the FCC, wireless carriers, a great many public safety organizations, and other stakeholders. It does seem to present a golden opportunity to add a key and potentially life-saving use-case for Bluetooth beacons.

We want smartphone experiences that are context sensitive, that blend the digital with the physical. Let's merge click-stream analytics with foot-stream analytics. Context-sensitive apps can become widespread with standards, and beacon networks can be built on those standards.

Bluetooth beacons are the tendons that join the muscle of the digital world with the bones of our physical world. Please heal the divisions with a standard we can all use to build better solutions.

Yours respectfully,

Steve Statler

Index

▧ C

Get the eBook for only $5!

Why limit yourself?

Now you can take the weightless companion with you wherever you go and access your content on your PC, phone, tablet, or reader.

Since you've purchased this print book, we're happy to offer you the eBook in all 3 formats for just $5.

Convenient and fully searchable, the PDF version enables you to easily find and copy code—or perform examples by quickly toggling between instructions and applications. The MOBI format is ideal for your Kindle, while the ePUB can be utilized on a variety of mobile devices.

To learn more, go to www.apress.com/companion or contact support@apress.com.

Printed in the United States
By Bookmasters